Olivia PD 701

MW00466007

SIGNIFICANT CASES IN JUVENILE JUSTICE

SIGNIFICANT CASES IN
JUVENILE JUSTICE

SECOND EDITION

Craig Hemmens
Missouri State University

Benjamin Steiner
University of Nebraska-Omaha

David Mueller
Boise State University

OXFORD
UNIVERSITY PRESS

Oxford University Press is a department of the University of Oxford. It furthers the University's objective of excellence in research, scholarship, and education by publishing worldwide.

Oxford   New York
Auckland   Cape Town   Dar es Salaam   Hong Kong   Karachi
Kuala Lumpur   Madrid   Melbourne   Mexico City   Nairobi
New Delhi   Shanghai   Taipei   Toronto

With offices in
Argentina   Austria   Brazil   Chile   Czech Republic   France   Greece
Guatemala   Hungary   Italy   Japan   Poland   Portugal   Singapore
South Korea   Switzerland   Thailand   Turkey   Ukraine   Vietnam

Copyright © 2004, 2013 by Oxford University Press.

For titles covered by Section 112 of the US Higher Education Opportunity Act, please visit www.oup.com/us/he for the latest information about pricing and alternate formats.

Published by Oxford University Press.
198 Madison Avenue, New York, NY 10016
www.oup.com

Oxford is a registered trademark of Oxford University Press

All rights reserved. No part of this publication may be reproduced, stored in a retrieval system, or transmitted, in any form or by any means, electronic, mechanical, photocopying, recording, or otherwise, without the prior permission of Oxford University Press.

Library of Congress Cataloging-in-Publication Data

Hemmens, Craig.
Significant cases in juvenile justice/Craig Hemmens,
Missouri State University; Benjamin Steiner,
University of Nebraska-Omaha; David Mueller, Boise State University.
pages cm.—(Criminal justice case briefs)
Includes bibliographical references and index.
ISBN 978-0-19-995841-2 (paperback)
1. Juvenile justice, Administration of—United States—Cases.
I. Steiner, Benjamin.   II. Mueller, David.   III. Title.
KF9780.H46 2013
345.73'08—dc23   2012045207

1 3 5 7 9 8 6 4 2

Printed in the United States of America
on acid-free paper

CONTENTS

ACKNOWLEDGMENTS

Craig Hemmens would like to thank Mary, Emily, and Amber for their love and support.

Benjamin Steiner would like to thank his wife, Emily, for her support during the completion of this edition.

David Mueller passed away unexpectdly while the second edition of this book was in production. Craig and Ben will forever cherish the opportunity we had to work with and get to know Dave, who was a kind man, wonderful father, and outstanding teacher.

The authors would also like to thank the reviewers who helped shape this book:

First edition: George Burruss, Georgia Southern University; Mayling Chu, California State University–Stanislaus; William Kelly, Auburn University; Peter Kratcoski, Kent State University; Leona Lee, John Jay College of Criminal Justice; Barbara Sims, Pennsylvania State University; and Becky Tatum, Georgia State University.

Second edition: Earl Ballou, Jr., Palo Alto College; Valerie R. Bell, Loras College; Lisa Kara, Blue Ridge Community College; Sara Ellen Kitchen, Chestnut Hill College.

PREFACE

This book is intended to serve as a supplement to an undergraduate criminal justice textbook on juvenile justice or juvenile law. It may also be used by a graduate student in criminal justice or a law school student struggling to understand the law while wading through the myriad (and often contradictory) opinions contained in the typical law school casebook.

While nothing substitutes for reading the original case opinion, the reality is that only those with a passion for the subject and plenty of time can afford to always go first to the source. This book is intended to assist those who are trying to read the original opinion, and to provide more detail than can be contained in a typical textbook.

The book is divided into sections that mirror the typical criminal justice textbook and law school casebook approach to the subject, so that students and instructors can easily refer to related cases. All the significant United States Supreme Court cases are included, through the 2011–2012 term.

Each case brief follows the same basic format: Facts, Issue, Holding, Rationale, Case Excerpt, and Case Significance. The *Facts* section includes the relevant facts of the case that led to the eventual Supreme Court (or lower court) decision, as well as a brief explanation of the decisions in the lower courts. The *Issue* is the question presented to the court for its ruling. The *Holding* is the result, the decision by the court. The *Rationale* section contains the explanation of the court for its decision. The *Case Excerpt* section provides students with some of the language used by the court. The *Case Significance* section contains a discussion of why the case matters to criminal justice.

Juvenile law differs from corrections law and criminal procedure (the other two volumes in this series) in that most of the leading cases in juvenile justice do not come from the Supreme Court. The Supreme Court has decided relatively few cases dealing with juvenile justice; consequently, lawyers and students of the law are forced to look elsewhere to learn the status of juvenile law in the United States.

We hope that this book is of use to instructors and students seeking to understand the often arcane world of juvenile justice and juvenile law. We welcome any comments or suggestions that readers have.

TABLE OF CASES

CASE HOLDINGS

CHAPTER ONE JUVENILE CURFEW

BYKOFSKY v. BOROUGH OF MIDDLETOWN, **410 F. Supp. 1242 (M.D. Pa. 1975):** Curfew ordinances that include a wide range of exceptions are nonetheless constitutional.

ILLINOIS v. CHAMBERS, **360 N.E.2d 55 (Ill. 1976):** The enactment of well-crafted statewide juvenile curfews is constitutional.

JOHNSON v. CITY OF OPELOUSAS, **658 F.2d 1065 (5th Cir. 1981):** Curfew ordinances that restrict all movement of juveniles during specified hours are unconstitutional.

WATERS v. BARRY, **711 F.Supp. 1121 (D.D.C. 1989):** Overly restrictive curfew ordinances that violate the fundamental rights of juveniles are unconstitutional. However, a properly crafted ordinance should not impede the government's right to search and seize juveniles who violate such curfews.

PANORA v. SIMMONS, **445 N.W.2d 363 (Iowa 1989):** Curfew ordinances that are designed to keep juveniles off the street at night do not necessarily infringe on the autonomy of parental rights. People in the Interest of J.M., 768 P.2d 219 (Colo. 1989) Curfew ordinances enacted to discourage loitering and other order maintenance problems are constitutional so long as they do not unduly infringe on juvenile liberty interests.

BROWN v. ASHTON, **611 A.2d 599 (Md. App. 1992):** It is unconstitutional to enforce curfew ordinances for reasons other than their specified intent. However, officials who enforce unchallenged ordinances may be shielded from civil liability.

CITY OF MAQUOKETA v. RUSSELL, **484 N.W.2d 179 (Iowa 1992):** Curfew ordinances that attempt to restrict all movement of juveniles without consideration to legitimate exceptions are too broad and thus unconstitutional.

QUTB v. STRAUSS, **11 F.3d 488 (5th Cir. 1993):** Carefully crafted curfew ordinances that incorporate a range of legitimate exceptions do not unconstitutionally infringe upon parental privacy rights, nor do they violate the equal protection clause.

STATE v. BEAN, **869 P.2d 984 (Utah App. 1994):** Police officers who have reasonable suspicion that a juvenile has consumed alcohol and is violating a curfew ordinance may briefly detain that juvenile for the purposes of identification and a warrants check.

MATTER OF APPEAL IN MARICOPA COUNTY, **887 P.2D 599 (ARIZ. APP. 1994):** Innocuous behavior such as a juvenile walking in a park in violation of a curfew ordinance is not an activity protected by the First Amendment.

CHAPTER TWO JUVENILES AND THE POLICE

HALEY v. OHIO, **332 U.S. 596 (1948):** The due process clause of the Fourteenth Amendment applies to the police in obtaining juvenile admissions or confessions.

HARLING v. UNITED STATES, **295 F.2d 161 (D.D.C. 1961):** Injurious statements by a juvenile while in police custody cannot be used as evidence in criminal court proceedings if the juvenile is subsequently transferred to criminal court.

GALLEGOS v. COLORADO, **370 U.S. 49 (1962):** Prolonged periods of isolation of a juvenile by the police may result in confessions that are deemed involuntarily obtained and in violation of the juvenile's due process rights.

UNITED STATES v. MILLER, **453 F.2d 634 (4th Cir. 1972):** If, after having been informed of his constitutional rights and intelligently waiving them, a juvenile submits fingerprints and handwriting samples, they may be used in delinquency proceedings in juvenile court.

IN RE J.B., **328 A.2d 46 (N.J. Juv. & Dom. Rel. Ct. 1974):** A warrantless arrest of a juvenile for a misdemeanor not committed in an officer's presence is unlawful. However, a juvenile can be taken into custody for engaging in conduct defined as juvenile delinquency.

UNITED STATES v. BARFIELD, **507 F.2d 53 (5th Cir. 1975):** Advice given by federal agents to tell the truth does not amount to coercion, and any consequent confessions are admissible. In the Interest of Dino, 359 So.2d 586 (La. 1978) The state must affirmatively show that the juvenile engaged in a meaningful consultation with an attorney or an informed parent, guardian, or other adult interested in his welfare before he waives his right to counsel or privilege against self-incrimination.

FARE v. MICHAEL C., **442 U.S. 707 (1979):** The request by a juvenile probationer during police questioning to see his or her probation officer after having received the Miranda warnings by the police is not equivalent to asking for a lawyer and therefore is not considered an assertion of the right to remain silent.

UNITED STATES v. SECHRIST, **640 F.2d 81 (7th Cir. 1981):** Probable cause is not needed to take a juvenile's fingerprints if the juvenile is already in lawful custody at the time of the magistrate's order.

NEW JERSEY v. T.L.O., **468 U.S. 1214 (1984):** For a search to be valid, public school officials need only reasonable grounds to suspect that the search will produce evidence that the student has violated either the law or school regulations.

UNITED STATES v. BERNARD S., **795 F.2d 749 (9th Cir. 1986):** If a juvenile states that he or she understood his or her rights and spoke primarily in English during questioning by government agents, a language barrier is not a defense to a voluntary waiver.

LANES v. STATE, **767 S.W.2d 789 (Tex. Crim. App. 1989):** Police officers must have probable cause or a warrant to make an arrest in juvenile proceedings.

SMITH v. STATE, **623 So.2d 369 (Ala. Cr. App. 1992):** A juvenile who requests to see his or her grandmother has invoked the right to remain silent, and subsequent statements regarding a crime are illegally obtained.

IN RE J.M., **619 A.2d 497 (D.C. Ct. App. 1992):** The nature of consent must be determined by the totality of the circumstances in which it occurred.

IN THE INTEREST OF J.L., A CHILD, **623 So.2d 860 (Fla. App. 1993):** A minor's presence in an area in which a crime had recently been reported, without other circumstances, does not warrant an investigatory stop and pat-down search of the minor by the police. In the Interest of S.A.W., 499 N.W.2d 739 (Iowa App. 1993) If police officers have reasonable suspicion that criminal activity may be afoot, they have reasonable cause to stop a juvenile.

IN RE STARVON J., **29 Cal.Rptr.2d 471 (Cal. App. 1994):** If a minor's statements were made voluntarily, there is nothing illegal about the circumstances and length of the minor's detention.

IN RE TYRELL J., **876 P.2d 519 (Cal. 1994):** If a minor is subject to a valid condition of probation that requires him or her to submit to warrantless searches by any law enforcement officer, he or she has no reasonable expectation of privacy.

STATE v. SUGG, **456 S.E.2d 469 (W. Va. 1995):** A juvenile may waive his or her Miranda rights even in the absence of parents, as long as the juvenile knowingly, voluntarily, and intelligently waives such rights, viewed in the totality of the circumstances.

VERNONIA SCHOOL DISTRICT 47J v. ACTON, **515 U.S. 646 (1995):** A school district drug testing policy that applies to student athletes is reasonable under the Fourth Amendment.

BOARD OF EDUCATION POTTAWATOMIE COUNTY v. EARLS, **545 U.S. 1015 (2002):** A school district's drug testing policy for its students involved in extracurricular activities is a reasonable means of furthering the school district's important interest in preventing and deterring drug use among schoolchildren, and does not violate the Fourth Amendment.

YARBOROUGH v. ALVARADO, **541 U.S. 652 (2004):** Determinations about when a suspect is in custody should be driven by objective criteria like restrictions on freedom of movement, and not by subjective criteria such as age and past contact with the police.

SAFFORD UNIFIED SCHOOL DISTRICT #1 v. REDDING, **557 U.S.—(2009):** School officials may not conduct strip searches of students who are suspected of bringing forbidden prescription and over-the-counter drugs to school.

CAMRETA v. GREENE, **563 U.S.—(2011):** The Supreme Court may review a lower court's ruling at the behest of government officials who won final judgment on qualified immunity grounds but could not for this case due to details specific to it. J.D.B. v. North Carolina, 564 U.S.___(2011) A child's age properly informs the Miranda custody analysis, so long as the child's age was known to the officer at the time of police questioning, or would have been objectively apparent to a reasonable officer.

CHAPTER THREE ENTRY INTO THE COURT SYSTEM

IN RE FRANK H., **337 N.Y.S.2d 118 (1972):** The intake conference is not a critical stage in the juvenile justice proceeding; therefore, a juvenile does not enjoy the constitutional right to counsel during intake.

WANSLEY v. SLAYTON, **487 F.2d 90 (4th Cir. 1973):** The juvenile court may find a child incorrigible. In the Welfare of Snyder, 532 P.2d 278 (Wash. 1975) A minor's spontaneous admissions to a mother in the presence of a juvenile probation officer, while subject to the jurisdiction of the juvenile court, are admissible.

IN RE WAYNE H., **596 P.2d 1 (Cal. 1979):** An incriminating statement that a minor makes to a probation officer at intake cannot be admitted as evidence of guilt.

IN THE INTEREST OF E.B., **287 N.W.2d 462 (N.D. 1980):** The state is not required to prove a juvenile's absences from school were voluntary, willful, or without justification.

WASHINGTON v. CHATHAM, **624 P.2d 1180 (Wash. App. 1981):** Although a juvenile has a right to be considered for diversion, he or she does not have the constitutional right to be guaranteed admission into a diversion program.

STATE v. MCDOWELL, **685 P.2d 595 (Wash. 1984):** If a juvenile is offered diversion for a misdemeanor and refuses, the prosecutor can file the case as a felony.

UNITED STATES v. NASH, **620 F.Supp. 1439 (S.D.N.Y. 1985):** Any postarrest statements made prior to presentment to a magistrate must be suppressed.

CHRISTOPHER P. V. NEW MEXICO, **816 P.2d 485 (N.M. 1991):** A juvenile's Fifth Amendment privilege is violated by a court's order compelling him or her to discuss alleged offenses with a psychologist, without advice of counsel, during a psychological evaluation ordered by the court for the purpose of determining whether he or she would benefit from treatment in the juvenile justice system.

UNITED STATES v. A.R., **38 F.3d 699 (3d Cir. 1994):** Psychiatric evaluations for the purpose of determining adult transfer status are not critical stages of the proceedings and thus are not subject to the protections of the Fifth and Sixth Amendments of the United States Constitution.

R.R. v. PORTSEY, **629 So.2d 1059 (Fla. App. 1994):** Absent rule or statute that allows such proceedings, the court does not have the authority to hold a detention hearing with the juvenile's presence secured only by videophone.

STATE v. K.K.H., **878 P.2d 1255 (Wash. App. 1994):** Procedures for determining probable cause may vary by jurisdiction as long as they can withstand constitutional scrutiny.

STATE v. LOWRY, **230 A.2d 907 (N.J. 1997):** The rights of privacy, security, and liberty against unreasonable searches and seizures are applicable to juveniles in accordance with reason and due process of law.

CHAPTER FOUR DETENTION

BALDWIN v. LEWIS, **300 F.Supp. 1220 (Wisc. 1969):** A juvenile cannot be denied due process of law in violation of the Fourteenth Amendment during his or her detention hearing.

MARTARELLA v. KELLEY, **349 F.Supp. 575 (S.D.N.Y. 1972):** A program at a detention center that does not furnish adequate treatment for children who are not true temporary detainees violates their right to due process, but their joint custody with juvenile delinquents is not unconstitutional.

COX v. TURLEY, **506 F.2d 1347 (6th Cir. 1974):** Failure to notify a juvenile's parents of his or her detention and to hold a probable cause hearing after confinement constitute cruel and unusual punishment.

MOSS v. WEAVER, **535 F.2d 1258 (5th Cir. 1976):** Pretrial detention without a determination of probable cause violates the Fourth Amendment requirements of due process.

MARTIN v. STRASBURG, **689 F.2d 363 (2d Cir. 1982):** The provision of the Family Court Act for preventative detention violates the due process clause of the Fourteenth Amendment.

D.B. v. TEWKSBURY, **545 F.Supp. 896 (D. Or. 1982):** Detaining juvenile pretrial detainees in jail under certain circumstances constitutes punishment and thus violates the due process clause. Confinement of runaway children or children out of parental control in jails constitutes punishment and violates their due process rights. Lodging juveniles in a modern adult jail pending adjudication of criminal charges would be fundamentally unfair so as to violate their due process rights.

IN THE INTEREST OF DARLENE C., **301 S.E.2d 136 (S.C. 1983):** Family courts may exercise their contempt power in such a manner that a status offender will be incarcerated in a secure facility.

SCHALL v. MARTIN, **104 U.S. 2403 (1984):** The section of the Family Court Act allowing preventative detention is valid under the due process clause of the Fourteenth Amendment.

RENO v. FLORES, **507 U.S. 292 (1993):** Juveniles who are supected of being illegal aliens and subject to deportation do not have a fundamental right to freedom from physical restraint?

HORN BY PARKS v. MADISON COUNTY FISCAL COURT, **22 F.3d 653 (6th Cir. 1994):** The failure of jail officials to take more than ordinary precautions to protect a juvenile defendant from suicide does not constitute deliberate indifference to his or her medical needs.

CHAPTER FIVE WAIVER TO CRIMINAL COURT

KENT v. UNITED STATES, **383 U.S. 541 (1966):** The transfer of jurisdiction in a juvenile hearing is a critically important stage in the judicial process.

UNITED STATES v. HOWARD, **449 F.2d 1086 (D.C. Cir. 1971):** As long as the court conducts a full hearing and exercises all relevant options, proper consideration is deemed to have been given before transfer to a criminal court.

PEOPLE v. FIELDS, **199 N.W.2d 217 (Mich. 1972):** A statute regarding transfer is unconstitutional if it lacks standards.

FAIN v. DUFF, **488 F.2d 218 (5th Cir. 1973):** A juvenile is placed in double jeopardy if, after adjudication in a juvenile court, he or she is again tried in criminal court.

UNITED STATES EX REL. BOMBACINO V. BENSINGER, **498 F.2d 875 (7th Cir. 1974):** If nothing in the procedure of a transfer is fundamentally unfair, transfer of jurisdiction is valid.

BREED v. JONES, **421 U.S. 519 (1975):** A juvenile who has undergone adjudication proceedings in a juvenile court cannot be tried on the same charge as an adult in a criminal court because to do so would constitute double jeopardy.

IN RE MATHIS, **537 P.2D 148 (OR. APP. 1975):** The decision to transfer a juvenile to criminal court is constitutional if based on the strength of the evidence, the juvenile's age, and the need for long-term care.

RUSSELL v. PARRATT, **543 F.2d 1214 (8th Cir. 1976):** A prosecuting attorney's unreviewable decision to charge a juvenile as an adult does not violate the juvenile's due process rights.

UNITED STATES v. J.D., **517 F.Supp. 69 (S.D.N.Y. 1981):** The statute as applied in this case was unconstitutional because it violated the juveniles' Fifth Amendment privilege against self-incrimination.

MATTER OF SEVEN MINORS, **664 P.2d 947 (NEV. 1983):** The appropriate criteria for transfer of juveniles from juvenile to criminal court are threefold: (1) the nature and seriousness of the charges; (2) the persistence and seriousness of past adjudications of criminal behavior; and (3) subjective factors such as age, level of maturity, and family relationships.

STATE v. MUHAMMAD, **703 P.2d 835 (Kan. 1985):** When a juvenile is notified of a hearing, given the right to be present, and represented by counsel, due process and fair treatment requirements are met even if the juvenile does not appear.

R.H. v. STATE, **777 P.2d 204 (Alaska App. 1989):** A juvenile's privilege against self-incrimination is violated by a court-ordered psychiatric evaluation.

PEOPLE v. P.H., **582 N.E.2d 700 (Ill. 1991):** A gang transfer provision of a statute is constitutional.

C.M. v. STATE, **884 S.W.2d 562 (Tex. App. 1994):** There is sufficient evidence in a case for a trial court to make the decision to transfer a juvenile to the criminal court.

LASWELL v. FREY, **45 F.3d 1011 (6th Cir. 1995):** Admitting to charges in a preliminary hearing does not automatically transform a detention hearing into an adjudication; therefore, there was no double jeopardy in the criminal proceeding.

STATE v. VERHAGEN, **542 N.W.2d 189 (Wis. App. 1995):** A juvenile defendant has the burden of proof in a reverse waiver proceeding.

O'BRIEN v. JOHN MARSHALL, **Superintendent, 453 F.3d 13 (U.S. App. 2006):** The Fifth Amendment does not preclude considering a defendant's attitude, whether or not characterized as silence, in determining that he was not likely to be rehabilitated and should be tried as an adult.

STATE v. DIXON, **967 A.2d 1114 (VT. 2008):** A trial court abuses its discretion in a transfer proceeding when it fails to consider all the appropriate criteria in determining when to transfer a juvenile; furthermore, the *Kent* factors are not the only criteria a court should consider.

CHAPTER SIX ADJUDICATION IN JUVENILE COURT

IN RE GAULT, **387 U.S. 1 (1967):** Juveniles must be afforded basic due process rights during adjudication proceedings if such proceedings can result in the deprivation of liberty (e.g., confinement in a locked facility).

IN RE WINSHIP, **397 U.S. 358 (1970):** Proof beyond a reasonable doubt, not simply a preponderance of the evidence, is required in adjudication hearings in which the act charged would have been a crime had it been committed by an adult.

MCKEIVER v. PENNSYLVANIA, **403 U.S. 528 (1971):** Juveniles do not have a constitutional right to trial by jury, even in delinquency proceedings.

IVAN v. CITY OF NEW YORK, **407 U.S. 203 (1972):** The *Winship* ruling—that juveniles are entitled to proof beyond a reasonable doubt in adjudication hearings—shall be retroactively applied to all cases in the appellate process.

UNITED STATES v. TORRES, **500 F.2d 944 (2d Cir. 1974):** The Federal Juvenile Delinquency Act, which holds that a juvenile who consents to an adjudication hearing in federal court gives up the right to trial by jury, does not violate a juvenile's rights.

GOSS v. LOPEZ, **419 U.S. 565 (1975):** Juveniles who face the possibility of even short-term suspension from school must be afforded due process protections.

IN RE JESSE McM., **164 Cal.Rptr. 199 (Cal. App. 1980):** Juveniles do not have the right to a public trial.

IN THE INTEREST OF C.T.F., **316 N.W.2d 865 (Iowa 1982):** Juveniles have a constitutional, but not a statutory, right to a speedy trial.

IN RE MONTRAIL M., **601 A.2d 1102 (Md. 1992):** The merger doctrine (the process by which a lesser offense is merged into a greater offense) applies to all juvenile cases and does not constitute double jeopardy.

BOYD v. STATE, **853 S.W.2d 263 (Ark. 1993):** When a juvenile is tried as an adult, the rules of adult criminal trials apply.

IN RE MARVEN C., **39 Cal.Rptr.2d 354 (Cal. App. 1995):** The state carries the burden to prove that a juvenile under the age of 14 clearly has the capacity to appreciate the wrongfulness of his or her conduct.

IN RE CAREY, **615 N.W.2D 742 (MICH. APP. 2000):** When questions arise as to a defendant's competency to stand trial, due process requires that he or she is entitled to a competency evaluation.

CHAPTER SEVEN DISPOSITION

BOARD OF MANAGERS OF ARKANSAS TRAINING SCHOOL FOR BOYS v. GEORGE, **377 F.2d 228 (8th Cir. 1967):** Disposition placements made solely on the basis of race are unconstitutional.

UNITED STATES EX REL. MURRAY V. OWENS, **465 F.2d 289 (2d Cir. 1972):** The New York statute that permitted a 15-year-old juvenile who had committed an act equivalent to a serious crime to be tried without a jury and sent to an adult correctional institution did not violate due process protections.

BAKER v. HAMILTON, **345 F.Supp. 345 (W.D. Ky. 1972):** Placement of a juvenile in an adult jail without total separation from adult inmates is unconstitutional.

STATE IN THE INTEREST OF D.G.W., **361 A.2d 513 (N.J. 1976):** The juvenile court is authorized to impose restitution upon youthful offenders as long as due process is observed.

THOMPSON v. CARLSON, **624 F.2d 415 (3d Cir. 1980):** Punishment imposed for an adult conviction supersedes any provisions imposed as a result of earlier adjudication as a juvenile.

STATE v. QUIROZ, **733 P.2d 963 (Wash. 1987):** A juvenile court judge may take into account prior diverted offenses when sentencing a juvenile.

IN RE MARCELLUS L., **278 Cal.Rptr. 901 (Cal. App. 1991):** Evidence obtained from an otherwise illegal search may be introduced in cases where the minor was subject to a valid search clause.

IN RE BIHN L., **6 Cal.Rptr.2d 678 (Cal. App. 1992):** Unjustified searches can be valid if a juvenile is subject to a search as a condition of probation.

MATTER OF SHAWN V., **600 N.Y.S.2d 393 (A.D. 1993):** A balance must be struck between the needs of the juvenile and the need for public safety when determining appropriate disposition under the "least restrictive" confinement standard.

P.W. v. STATE, **625 So.2d 1207 (Ala. Cr. App. 1993):** Reasonable court costs and fines can be levied against juvenile offenders as long as issues of indigency, when relevant, are addressed.

IN RE JAMONT C., **17 Cal.Rptr.2d 336 (Cal. App. 1993):** Probation conditions that permit searches without individualized suspicion do not violate a juvenile's Fourth Amendment right to privacy.

G.A.D. v. STATE, **865 P.2d 100 (Alaska App. 1993):** The need for public protection prevails over a juvenile's right to "least restrictive" placement.

A.S. v. STATE, **627 So.2d 1265 (Fla. App. 1993):** Parents of an adjudicated delinquent are not responsible for restitution to the victim unless the court finds a lack of good faith effort on the part of the parents to raise the juvenile.

UNITED STATES v. JUVENILE NO. 1, **38 F.3d 470 (9th Cir. 1994):** A probation condition prohibiting a juvenile from carrying a firearm is valid under the First Amendment.

STATE IN THE INTEREST OF T.L.V., **643 So.2d 290 (La. App. 1994):** Juvenile courts are not bound by a state's mandatory adult sentencing guidelines.

EDDINGS v. OKLAHOMA, **445 U.S. 104 (1982):** Total exclusion of mitigating factors during the sentencing phase of juvenile capital cases is improper.

THOMPSON v. OKLAHOMA, **487 U.S. 815 (1988):** The Eighth and Fourteenth Amendments prohibit the execution of juveniles whose crimes took place when the juvenile was 15 years old.

STANFORD v. KENTUCKY, **492 U.S. 361 (1989):** The Constitution does not prohibit states from imposing a death sentence on a juvenile who was 16 years old at the time his or her crime was committed.

ROPER v. SIMMONS, **543 U.S. 551 (2005):** Imposition of a death sentence on a person who commits murder at age 17 or younger is cruel and unusual, and thus prohibited by the Eighth and Fourteenth Amendments.

GRAHAM v. FLORIDA, **560 U.S.—(2010):** The Eight Amendment's cruel and unusual punishments clause does not permit a juvenile offender to be sentenced to life in prison without parole for a nonhomicide crime.

of juveniles in cold, dark isolation cells containing only a mattress and a toilet constitute cruel and unusual punishment. Confinement of juveniles in a former women's reformatory are antirehabilitative and in violation of due process and equal protection.

MORALES v. TURMAN, **383 F.Supp. 53 (E.D. Tex. 1974):** Confined juveniles have a right to proper treatment. Some of the practices and procedures of the Texas Youth Council constituted cruel and unusual punishment.

NELSON v. HEYNE, **491 F.2d 352 (7th Cir. 1974):** Practices in the Indiana Boys' School constituted conditions that violated the Eighth and Fourteenth Amendments.

CRUZ v. COLLAZO, **450 F.Supp. 235 (D.P.R. 1978):** A juvenile does not have a liberty expectation under the law to remain in one juvenile institution, so the transfer without a judicial hearing did not violate due process or equal protection rights.

C.J.W. BY AND THROUGH L.W. V. STATE, **853 P.2d 4 (Kan. 1993):** The state owed a duty to the 12-year-old juvenile who was sexually assaulted while in a juvenile detention facility by a 17-year-old fellow inmate, to warn the juvenile detention authorities of the 17-year-old inmate's propensity for violence and sexually deviant conduct and to take reasonable steps to protect the juvenile from such an inmate when such information was known by both the juvenile caseworker and the Social and Rehabilitation Services Department.

STATE EX REL. SOUTHER V. STUCKEY, **867 S.W.2d 579 (Mo. App. 1993):** A residential youth facility administrator's regulatory duty to report a runaway to police is a duty owed to the state, not to the victims.

HORN by Parks v. MADISON COUNTY FISCAL COURT, **22 F.3d 653 (6th Cir. 1994):** The failure of jail officials to take more than ordinary precautions to protect a juvenile defendant from suicide does not constitute deliberate indifference to his or her medical needs.

TUNSTALL EX REL. TUNSTALL V. BERGESON, **5 P.3d 691 (Wash. 2000):** The state is constitutionally required to provide educational services to children incarcerated in Department of Corrections facilities up to age eighteen.

CHAPTER EIGHT **CONDITIONS OF CONFINEMENT**

INMATES OF THE BOYS TRAINING SCHOOL v. AFFLECK, **346 F.Supp. 1354 (D.R.I. 1972):** Isolation

CHAPTER NINE **THE RELEASE DECISION**

REED v. DUTER, **416 F.2d 733 (7th Cir. 1969):** The equal protection clause of the Fourteenth Amendment requires that juveniles be afforded the same rights and privileges as adults in the appointment of counsel for indigency appeals.

P.R. ET AL. v. STATE, **210 S.E.2d 839 (Ga. App. 1974):** If a juvenile is found guilty of a crime that deprived another of property, the Court can order the juvenile to pay restitution for the amount of the stolen item.

M.J.W. v. STATE, **210 S.E.2d 842 (Ga. App. 1974):** The juvenile court may impose community service if its intent is partly rehabilitative in nature.

STATE EX REL. J.R. v. MACQUEEN, **259 S.E.2d 420 (W. Va. 1979):** A juvenile must be afforded all of the constitutional protections afforded an adult in parole revocation proceedings. Parole can be revoked upon finding of clear and convincing proof of substantial violation of parole conditions; a conviction of formal charges is not a prerequisite to parole revocation.

IN THE MATTER OF RODRIGUEZ, **687 S.W.2D 421 (TEX. APP. 1985):** A probation condition that specifies a child's curfew is reasonable.

WATTS v. HADDEN, **627 F.Supp. 727 (D. Colo. 1986):** The responsibility of the Bureau of Prisons and the United States Parole Commission to determine appropriate treatment for inmates sentenced under the Youth Rehabilitation Act does not decrease as the affected population dwindles, and remains until no Youth Corrections Act offenders remain in the system.

IN THE INTEREST OF DAVIS, **546 A.2D 1149 (PA. SUPER. 1988):** Due process rights to confront and cross-examine an accuser must extend to juvenile probation revocation hearings.

IN RE CURTIS T., **263 Cal.Rptr. 296 (Cal. Ct. App. 1989):** The access condition of a home supervision agreement allows officers access to the bedroom of a minor if they are there to arrest him for a violation of the agreement.

J.K.A. v. STATE, **855 S.W.2d 58 (Tex. App. 1993):** The court is not required to conduct a full due process adjudication hearing to find that a juvenile has violated a rule of probation.

IN THE MATTER OF LUCIO F.T., **888 P.2d 958 (N.M. App. 1994):** Juvenile court proceedings to revoke prior juvenile probation due to adult offenses for which the appellant has been convicted in criminal court do not amount to new or separate punishment, and therefore do not constitute double jeopardy.

MATTER OF TAPLEY, **865 P.2D 12 (WASH. APP. 1994):** Release policies based on a juvenile's behavior do not violate the right to due process as long as administrative regulations and policies do not create an expectation that a juvenile's release date will be the latest date possible.

J.R.W. v. STATE, **879 S.W.2d 254 (Tex. App. 1994):** The decision to transfer a delinquent juvenile to adult prison on his eighteenth birthday, as authorized by state law, was supported by the evidence presented. In the Interest of D.S. and J.V., Minor Children, 652 So. 2d 892 (Fla. App. 1995) The condition that juvenile delinquents not associate with gang members was proper.

IN RE KACY S., **80 Cal.Rptr.2d 432 (Cal. Ct. App. 1998):** It is reasonable and constitutional to require a juvenile to submit to a urine test for the purpose of detecting illegal drugs or alcohol as a condition of his or her probation.

IN RE J.W., **787 N.E.2d 727 (Ill. S.C. 2003):** An act requiring a juvenile sexual offender to register as a sexual offender for the rest of his life is constitutional. A condition that a juvenile not reside in or enter an entire town during the term of his probation is too broad, and thus violates his constitutional rights.

INTRODUCTION: THE HISTORY OF THE JUVENILE COURT

For nearly a century, the American juvenile justice system has operated under the assumption that juvenile offenders should be handled both separately and differently from adult offenders. The creation of a separate juvenile justice system represented an acceptance of the Progressive-era notion that the law should distinguish between the offender and the offense, and could prevent future delinquency with proper individualized response and treatment. In this sense the juvenile court's creation and propagation supported a belief that social problems could and should be dealt with on an individual level, rather than by treating juvenile crime as a symptom of social structural flaws. The primary justification for creating a separate juvenile justice system was to distinguish between punishment and treatment. The criminal justice system at the turn of the century emphasized the classical school's belief in punishment and deterrence as proper goals. Separating juvenile offenders from adult criminals allowed juveniles to be treated rather than punished.

The idea that juveniles should be treated differently from adults represented a radical shift from earlier attitudes toward juvenile offenders. At common law only children under the age of seven were considered incapable of felonious intent, which became known as the "infancy defense." Children between the ages of seven and 14 were considered similarly incapable, unless it could be established that the child was able to understand the consequences of his or her actions. Those over the age of 14 were considered fully responsible for their actions. At common law juvenile offenders received the same punishment as adult offenders and were usually housed in the same facilities. Before the establishment of New York's House of Refuge in 1825,

no state bothered to separate children from adults in prison. By 1899 there were 65 facilities for juveniles in the United States, but juvenile offenders still received the same punishment as adults.

Several events contributed to the creation of a separate juvenile justice system. The Industrial Revolution of the late nineteenth century transformed America from a rural country to an urban nation. As more and more people moved to the cities, the number of children in urban areas increased dramatically. Many of these children were left unsupervised while both parents worked, and juvenile delinquency became a problem in many cities. At the same time immigration from Europe rose dramatically, and many immigrants chose to live in urban areas. These immigrants brought with them values that differed from those of the white, Protestant middle class that dominated America at the time. Reformers such as Jane Addams became concerned about the welfare of these urban children, while others feared that the influx of new, different cultures and values created confusion and social disorganization. The Progressive movement combined these concerns to produce wide-ranging social reforms. The plight of the urban poor received a great deal of attention. Social welfare societies and similar organizations sprung up across the country. A popular topic of both Progressive reformers and criminal justice professionals was the care and control of children.

Progressive-era reformers called for a separate system of juvenile courts that would focus primarily on helping wayward children, as opposed to the strictly adversarial, punishment-oriented adult criminal courts. This became known as the "child-saving movement." Proponents of a separate juvenile justice system believed that juveniles lacked the maturity and level of culpability that traditional criminal sanctions presupposed, and that juvenile offenders should therefore not only be treated as less blameworthy but also as more amenable to treatment and rehabilitation than hardened adult criminals.

A major justification for creating juvenile courts was the parens patriae doctrine, which derived from English common law. This doctrine grew out of the belief that the king was the symbolic father of the country, and as such assumed absolute responsibility for the nation's children. Thus the king's chancellors adjudicated all juvenile questions separately from the criminal courts. Adoption of the parens patriae doctrine in the United States allowed the state to intervene and act in the best interest of the child whenever it was deemed necessary.

Progressive reformers believed that a system of individualized justice could right the social wrongs that led to the downfall of so many children. They believed that through science, the causes of juvenile delinquency could be discovered and the problem cured, just as doctors diagnosed and treated sick patients. Individualized treatment was essential. All that was necessary to solve the juvenile delinquency problem, they believed, was to create an institution that had the means to accomplish this goal. The juvenile court was intended not to punish, but to treat. Each juvenile was unique, and therefore each case required different treatment. Each child's situation would be explained to the court, which would then decide not how to punish the child, but how to help him or her. Help could take many forms, from a stern lecture to assignment to a training school to permanent removal of a child from his or her home.

State intervention was not limited to juveniles who had committed crimes. The parens patriae doctrine compelled the state to intervene in the lives of children who strayed from the path of righteousness. Any delinquent act or status offense could result in intervention. Some have seen the creation of the juvenile court as little more than a method of controlling the masses of children born to recent immigrants. Others have claimed that the idea was embraced by the state because it was cheaper and easier to implement than extending full due process rights to children or incarcerating them along with adults. Others are more reluctant to attribute such dark motives to the Progressive reformers, arguing instead that they were motivated largely by their concern for the well-being of the urban poor and by their fear that the social structure was disintegrating. Whatever the motives, the result was an entirely new method of dealing with juvenile offenders.

In 1899 the first juvenile court was established in Illinois, marking the formal beginning of a separate juvenile justice system. Other states quickly followed Illinois' lead. Within 12 years, 22 states had adopted some form of juvenile court system. By 1920 all but three states had juvenile courts, and by 1932 all but two states had enacted juvenile codes. By 1945 every state had a juvenile court system. The juvenile court systems in most states were organized as entities entirely distinct from the adult systems. Juvenile proceedings were held in their own courtrooms, with judges who heard only juvenile cases. Some states even went so far as to erect separate physical facilities for adult and juvenile courts.

Juvenile court procedure was markedly different from that of the general jurisdiction court. Hearings were private and informal in nature. Due process requirements such as the right to a trial by jury and the right to have a lawyer present were discarded as unnecessary to achieve the purpose of the juvenile court, which was not to assess blame, but to determine the best method of treatment. The juvenile court was intended to help children, to assist in discovering the causes of their delinquency, and to provide the counseling and treatment necessary to set them on the path to upstanding adulthood. Juvenile court judges enjoyed enormous discretionary power. Juvenile court jurisdiction was classified as civil rather than criminal. A whole new vocabulary sought to differentiate juvenile court activities from adult criminal court activities. Juveniles were not arrested; they were "taken into custody." Instead of indicting a juvenile, prosecutors "petitioned the juvenile court." Juveniles were not convicted; they were "adjudicated delinquent." Juvenile court sanctions were not referred to as sentences, but as "dispositions." Juveniles were not sent to prisons; they were sent to "training schools," or some other euphemistically named institution.

By the 1970s and '80s, however, support for rehabilitation had begun to wane. The disenchantment with rehabilitation was replaced by a fervor for retribution. The rise in juvenile crime that began in the 1960s became a rallying cry for advocates of holding children responsible for their actions. Between 1960 and 1975 juvenile arrests increased over 140 percent, while adult arrests during the same period went up less than

13 percent. The belief that the juvenile court's primary purpose was to act in the best interests of the child had been a cornerstone of the American juvenile justice system for decades. However, instead of protecting children because of their age, society would now hold them accountable despite their age. Some began to blame the juvenile justice system's emphasis on rehabilitation for its failure to prevent crime. Conservative critics began to call for a shift from rehabilitation to a focus on the more limited goals of retribution and deterrence. The result was a shift in the attitudes of many juvenile courts, as well as state legislatures.

In this book we provide a summary of leading cases in a variety of areas in juvenile justice, arranged chronologically so that the reader can trace the shift in legal thinking over time.

CHAPTER ONE

JUVENILE CURFEW

BYKOFSKY v. BOROUGH OF MIDDLETOWN, *410 F.SUPP. 1242 (M.D. PA. 1975)*

ILLINOIS v. CHAMBERS, *360 N.E.2D 55 (ILL. 1976)*

JOHNSON v. CITY OF OPELOUSAS, *658 F.2D 1065 (5TH CIR. 1981)*

WATERS v. BARRY, *711 F.SUPP. 1121 (D.D.C. 1989)*

PANORA v. SIMMONS, *445 N.W.2D 363 (IOWA 1989)*

PEOPLE IN THE INTEREST OF J.M., *768 P.2D 219 (COLO. 1989)*

BROWN v. ASHTON, *611 A.2D 599 (MD. APP. 1992)*

CITY OF MAQUOKETA v. RUSSELL, *484 N.W.2D 179 (IOWA 1992)*

QUTB v. STRAUSS, *11 F.3D 488 (5TH CIR. 1993)*

STATE v. BEAN, *869 P.2D 984 (UTAH APP. 1994)*

MATTER OF APPEAL IN MARICOPA COUNTY, *887 P.2D 599 (ARIZ. APP. 1994)*

INTRODUCTION

Since the early 1990s, juvenile curfews have become an increasingly popular method for attempting to control juvenile crime and victimization (Crowell 1996). To date, however, few empirical studies have been able to conclusively demonstrate that curfews actually "work" (Howell 2003). Part of the challenge for social scientists is that curfews are just one in a myriad of juvenile crime suppression and prevention programs currently in existence. In addition, curfews tend to be implemented across wide geographic areas—entire cities or states—making it difficult for researchers to construct comparable control groups in order to isolate a curfew's positive effects. In light of these challenges, much of the research on curfews has focused on issues such as program descriptions, enforcement patterns, and questions of constitutionality (see Fritsch, Caeti, and Taylor 1999; Hemmens and Bennett 1999; Ruefle and Reynolds 1995). Nevertheless, there has been interesting work conducted on the topic.

In a national study of local police departments, Ruefle and Reynolds (1995) found that juvenile curfew ordinances existed in 77 percent of major American cities with a population base of over 200,000. Nearly one-half of the cities in this study had either revised an existing curfew ordinance or had passed new curfew-related legislation since 1990. According to Crowell (1996), juvenile curfews enjoy considerable political support among parents, law enforcement personnel, and government officials that appears to cut across both racial and gender lines. Despite their popularity, however, curfews also appear to have serious drawbacks. One problem is the potential for crime displacement. Research by Hunt and Weiner (1977) found that although a late-night curfew in Detroit, Michigan, did help to suppress some crime during its routine hours of enforcement, this suppression effect was offset by an observable displacement. That is, criminal activity *increased* during noncurfew hours (e.g., between 2 p.m. and 4 p.m.). More recent research also indicates that the intuitive appeal of juvenile curfews may be unwarranted. For example, in a study of 57 cities nationwide, McDowall, Loftin, and Wiersema (2000) found that the introduction of curfew laws had little positive effect on juvenile arrests in any serious crime category. Males and Macallair

(1998), as well as Adams (1997), have noted similar outcomes.

In light of the many findings of "no effect," Howell (2003:136) argues, "[c]urfew laws cannot reasonably be expected to reduce violent juvenile crimes significantly because, ironically, most of them are imposed at a time—late at night—when few juvenile violent offenses occur." In support of this argument, Snyder, Sickmund, and Poe-Yamagata (1996) found that most violent juvenile crime actually takes place between the hours of 3 p.m. and 4 p.m., and less than 20 percent of all violent juvenile crime takes place during normal curfew hours. Similarly, Fox and Newman (1997) report that less than 8 percent of all violent juvenile crime occurs between the hours of 11 p.m. and 1 a.m., a time at which many curfews are slated to take effect. These findings suggest that more aggressive after-school programs, rather than late-night curfews, might be a more promising approach to controlling juvenile crime (see Gottfredson, Gottfredson, and Weisman 2001).

Beyond the question of effectiveness, scholars have also raised serious questions about the constitutionality of curfew ordinances. These objections stem in large part from the vast discretionary power afforded to police in the enforcement of curfews and the potential for arbitrary and discriminatory enforcement, particularly against minority youth. Various courts have found that curfews occasionally violate the constitutional rights of both juveniles and their parents with respect to freedom of movement, free association, due process, and family privacy issues in regard to child rearing practices (Hemmens and Bennett 1999). Given these findings and concerns, curfew statutes appear to represent an uncertain, if not constitutionally questionable, means of crime control.

REFERENCES

Adams, K. (1997, November). "Juvenile Curfew as Crime Prevention." Paper presented at the annual meeting of the American Society of Criminology, San Diego, CA.

Crowell, A. (1996). "Minor Restrictions: The Challenge of Juvenile Curfews." *Public Management,* August: 4–12.

Fox, J., and S. Newman. (1997). "Juvenile Crime Rate Spikes When School Lets Out, Study Indicates." *Criminal Justice Newsletter* 28: 5–6.

Fritsch, E., T. Caeti, and R. Taylor. (1999). "Gang Suppression Through Saturation Patrol, Aggressive Curfew, and Truancy Enforcement: A Quasi-Experimental Test of the Dallas Anti-Gang Initiative." *Crime & Delinquency* 45: 122–140.

Gottfredson, D., G. Gottfredson, and S. Weisman. (2001). "The Timing of Delinquent Behavior and Its Implications for After-School Programs." *Criminology & Public Policy* 1: 61–86.

Hemmens, C., and K. Bennett. (1999). "Juvenile Curfews and the Courts: Judicial Response to a Not-So-New Crime Control Strategy." *Crime & Delinquency* 45: 99–121.

Howell, J. (2003). *Preventing and Reducing Juvenile Delinquency: A Comprehensive Framework.* Thousand Oaks, CA: Sage.

Hunt, A. L., and K. Weiner. (1977). "The Impact of a Juvenile Curfew: Suppression and Displacement Patterns of Juvenile Offenses." *Journal of Police Science and Administration* 5: 407–412.

Males, M., and D. Macallair. (1998). *The Impact of Juvenile Curfew Laws in California.* San Francisco: Justice Policy Institute, Center on Juvenile and Criminal Justice.

McDowall, D., C. Loftin, and B. Wiersema. (2000). "The Impact of Youth Curfew Laws on Juvenile Crime Rates." *Crime & Delinquency* 46: 76–91.

Ruefle, W., and K. Reynolds. (1995). "Curfews and Delinquency in Major American Cities." *Crime & Delinquency* 41: 347–363.

Snyder, H., M. Sickmund, and E. Poe-Yamagata. (1996). *Juvenile Offenders and Victims: 1996 Update on Violence.* Washington, DC: Department of Justice.

BYKOFSKY v. BOROUGH OF MIDDLETOWN

410 F.Supp. 1242 (M.D. Pa. 1975)

FACTS

On behalf of her 12-year-old son, plaintiff Bykofsky brought suit against the Borough of Middleton in Pennsylvania seeking declaratory, preliminary, and permanent injunctions for violating her son's rights by enacting an unconstitutional juvenile curfew ordinance. The ordinance, which set graduated curfew times for minors of varying age groups, basically prohibited minors from being on the streets of the Borough of Middleton during late-night hours. However, the ordinance also contained various exceptions, including (1) minors in the company of a parent; (2) minors in the company of another responsible adult who is authorized to take the parent's place; (3) minors exercising their First Amendment rights; (4) cases of reasonable necessity, but only after the minors' parents inform the Middleton Police Department; (5) minors who remain on the sidewalk of their own, or a consenting neighbor's, residence; (6) minors returning home by direct route from and within 30 minutes of the termination of a school, religious, or other voluntary association meeting; (7) minors in possession of a special permit obtained from the mayor; (8) minors who are, as a result of mayoral approval, part of an exempted group from the curfew; (9) minors in possession of a valid work permit going to or from work during curfew hours; (10) minors traveling in a motor vehicle with parental consent for normal intra- and interstate travel; and (11) minors 17 years of age who are exempted from the curfew by the mayor based on their level of maturity. According to Bykofsky, the curfew ordinance was unconstitutionally vague; it violated juveniles' due process rights (e.g., freedom of movement and the use of public streets) and the First Amendment (e.g., freedom of speech, freedom of association, and freedom of assembly). Moreover, she argued, the curfew violated the right of inter- and intrastate travel; it encroached on family autonomy and the rights of parents to raise their children; and finally, it violated the equal protection clause of the Fourteenth Amendment. The trial court denied Bykofsky's motion for a preliminary injunction and she appealed to the US District Court.

ISSUE

Was the curfew ordinance unconstitutional?

HOLDING

No. The court held the curfew ordinance to be valid and not impermissibly vague. In doing so, the court argued that the Constitution allows minors to be more closely supervised and regulated than adults. It also argued that the curfew ordinance is a reasonable exercise of government power.

RATIONALE

The main question the court wrestled with in this case was whether or not the Middleton curfew ordinance was reasonable. The court opined that reasonableness is best determined by weighing the legitimate interests of the state against the competing interests of the minor. To do this, the court examined why the ordinance was established in the first place. It found that the ordinance was enacted (1) to protect young children in Middleton from each other and from other persons on the street during nighttime hours; (2) to aid in the enforcement of parental controls and parental responsibility for their children; (3) to protect the public from nocturnal mischief by minors; and (4) to reduce the incidence of juvenile criminal activity. The court went on to argue that the ordinance did in fact further these interests. Moreover, these interests outweigh the interests of juveniles to move freely upon the streets during the nighttime curfew hours. The court also took notice of the fact that the ordinance was narrowly constructed, as evidenced by the many exceptions. Hence, the ordinance was upheld as a reasonable and constitutionally permissible exercise of government power to "advance and protect the safety and welfare of the general community and the minors who reside therein."

CASE EXCERPT

"The court holds that the legislative determination in the instant case that the age of eighteen provides the dividing line between minors and adults with respect to a nighttime curfew is not unreasonable, does not create an arbitrary classification, and hence is not violative of equal protection. In addition, since the ordinance applies alike to all persons under the age of eighteen there clearly is no equal protection violation within the class subject to the curfew."

CASE SIGNIFICANCE

As an extension of the parens patriae philosophy, the *Bykofsky* ruling is significant insofar as it found that juveniles could indeed be treated differently from adults. This precedent-setting decision, however, was based on the argument that states have a legitimate interest in advancing public safety and community welfare even when such interests come into conflict with the freedom of movement of juveniles. Given its many exceptions, the ordinance was upheld and later became a model for other local governments to follow.

ILLINOIS v. CHAMBERS
360 N.E.2d 55 (Ill. 1976)

FACTS

In 1973 Illinois legislators enacted a statewide juvenile curfew statute making it unlawful for persons under 18 years of age to be out in public unaccompanied and

ILLINOIS v. CHAMBERS *(cont.)*

unsupervised by a parent or legal guardian between the hours of 12:01 a.m. and 6:00 a.m. on weekends and 11:00 p.m. and 6:00 a.m. Sunday through Thursday. Exceptions to the ordinance included only those situations where youth were engaged in legitimate business or occupation sanctioned by the state. In the early-morning hours of March 25, 1973, Chambers, her sister, and a friend were parked in a vehicle on a one-lane bridge with the vehicle lights turned off. While on routine patrol, an Ogle County sheriff's deputy spotted the vehicle and approached to investigate. During questioning, the deputy determined that all of the vehicle's occupants were within curfew age, and subsequently arrested the youth for violating the curfew ordinance. Both Chambers and her sister were subsequently found guilty, and each was assessed a fine of ten dollars plus court costs. At her appeal, Chambers argued that the curfew statute unconstitutionally restricted her freedom of movement and her First Amendment rights of free speech, assembly, and association. Moreover, she claimed that the statute was invalid because no governmental interest justified the broad prohibitions contained in the statute. In addition, the statute itself contained "an inherent potential for arbitrary enforcement." Chambers appealed her original conviction, and the appeals court reversed. The Illinois Supreme Court then took the case.

ISSUE

Did the curfew statute violate the constitutional rights of minors with regard to freedom of movement and other First Amendment rights?

HOLDINGZ

No. The court held that the curfew statute was a constitutional exercise of the state's rights and responsibilities to protect and promote the welfare of underage youth. As such, the court reasoned that the state must not presume that children have an unlimited right to association, or to decide the time or place of assembly. The court further argued that since the statute's coverage extended to all parts of the state, and was not confined to a particular geographic area, it was neither arbitrary nor discriminatory.

RATIONALE

As in the *Bykofsky* case, the court argued that the state has a legitimate interest in protecting the safety and well-being of juveniles. One of the defining features of juvenile curfew statutes is that children who are at home (preferably supervised by a responsible adult) during the late-night and early-morning hours are protected from physical as well as moral dangers. Though the court recognized that this assumption is not always true, it felt satisfied that the state was justified in proceeding from such an assumption. More important, the court argued that because juveniles are perceived as more easily influenced into making poor and irrevocable life choices, their actions can be more closely regulated than those of adults: "In legislating for the welfare of children, the state is not required, in our opinion, to proceed upon the assumption that minor children have an absolutely unlimited right not only to choose their own associates, but also to decide when and where they will associate with them. Recognition of such a right would require wholesale revision of the large body of law that relates to guardian and ward, parent and child, and minors generally." For example, such a radical rethinking of public policy could potentially result in doing away with compulsory school attendance laws, as well as those that regulate underage drinking: "A child is carefully safeguarded against errors of choice and judgment in most of the ordinary affairs of life, and we see no constitutional impairment in the limited restriction upon the child's judgment that is involved in this statute. It is only during the very late-night and early-morning hours that the State has interfered, and then only by requiring that the child be accompanied by an adult."

CASE EXCERPT

"The statute is concerned with the conduct of children under the age of 18, and it affects their conduct only between the specified hours, and then only if they are not accompanied by an adult. The exception for minors engaged in a business or occupation necessarily includes getting to and from the job. The statute is not aimed at any of the fundamental values of speech, association or expression protected by the first amendment, and indeed the suggestion that those values are impaired by the restriction here involved seems to trivialize them."

CASE SIGNIFICANCE

Like the earlier ruling in *Bykofsky,* the court in this case upheld the constitutionality of the curfew ordinances on the grounds that it advanced the welfare of children. In addition, the court noted that state-wide curfew ordinances, like the one in question here, might actually be preferable to curfews enacted at the local level because statewide curfews impose their restrictions across a broad geographic area and are less likely to result in discriminatory enforcement. In short, the significance of this case is that it extended the constitutionality of well-crafted curfew ordinances from the local to the state level.

JOHNSON v. CITY OF OPELOUSAS
658 F.2d 1065 (5th Cir. 1981)

FACTS
At 2:05 a.m. on August 16, 1978, Johnson, then 14 years old, was arrested by an Opelousas, Louisiana police officer for violating the city's nocturnal juvenile curfew ordinance. Upon being found guilty of the curfew violation, Johnson was first placed on probation, then placed in a private juvenile facility, then released to the custody of his mother. The curfew ordinance enacted in this case made it unlawful for unemancipated minors under the age of 17 to be upon the streets of Opelousas between the hours of 11:00 p.m. and 4:00 a.m. Sunday through Thursday, and 1:00 a.m. to 4:00 a.m. on Friday and Saturday nights unless accompanied by a parent or other responsible adult, or unless the minor was upon an emergency errand. Minors found violating these provisions were considered neglected children. At the time of his appeal, Johnson (then 17 years old) challenged the constitutionality of the curfew ordinance claiming it (1) was both unconstitutionally vague and overbroad; and (2) violated his First (e.g., freedom of speech, association, assembly) and Fourteenth Amendment rights (e.g., freedom of movement and use of public streets).

ISSUE
Does this curfew ordinance violate the constitutional rights of juveniles?

HOLDING
Yes. The Opelousas curfew ordinance violated the First and Fourteenth Amendment rights of juveniles.

RATIONALE
The court recognized in this case that juvenile curfew ordinances are fairly common measures to prevent juvenile crime. However, it also noted that the federal courts had not yet adequately addressed the constitutionality of such ordinances. Moreover, those cases that had been previously taken up by the federal courts had not yet encountered an ordinance that encompassed the breadth of the ordinance in question. In its ruling, the court took notice of the fact that the Opelousas ordinance provides very few exceptions, and thus prohibited juveniles from engaging in legal, prosocial activities such as religious or school meetings, organized dances, and theater and sporting events. For instance, the ordinance made no exceptions for youth standing on the sidewalk in front of their own houses, engaged in legitimate employment, or traveling through the City of Opelousas on an interstate trip. Thus, the court argued that the ordinance might actually have the effect of inhibiting parents from urging their children to engage in prosocial activities during nighttime hours. According to the court, the ordinance, as it was originally constructed, "sweeps within its ambit a number of innocent activities which are constitutionally protected [and] the stifling effect upon these legitimate activities is overt and is both real and substantial." Given the fact that less drastic measures were available to control the activities of juveniles during the late-night hours, coupled with absence of reasonable exceptions, the court ruled that the Opelousas ordinance was unconstitutionally overbroad.

CASE EXCERPT
"While Opelousas may have legitimate concern over minors being on the streets at night in general, a point on which we express no opinion here, its interest in whether juveniles engage in these specific nighttime activities is not sufficient to justify the removal of the decision as to these activities from the childrens' parents."

CASE SIGNIFICANCE
This curfew ordinance was struck down as unconstitutionally overbroad due to its lack of legitimate exceptions. Rather than helping parents control the late-night activities of their children, the court found that this ordinance actually usurped parental authority and thus placed an undue burden on both parents and children. In effect, the court argued, this particular curfew ordinance created a police state that relieved parents of their rights to control their own children, and placed that control in the hands of government officials.

WATERS v. BARRY

711 F.Supp. 1121 (D.D.C. 1989)

FACTS

Plaintiffs in this case were granted a temporary restraining order barring the District of Columbia from enforcing a blanket juvenile curfew law. While the law was being challenged in court, the District adopted a new curfew ordinance that provided for various and significant exemptions to the old curfew restrictions. At the time of this hearing, the new law had not yet gone into effect. Thus, the court allowed the new ordinance to be substituted in place of the old one for review purposes. The court also granted the plaintiffs the ability to claim class status so the issue would not be rendered moot. The ordinance imposed a blanket curfew on all individuals below the age of 18, in effect making it a crime for minors to be on the streets of the District of Columbia between the hours of 11:00 p.m. and 6:00 a.m. on weekdays and 11:59 p.m. and 6:00 a.m. on weekends. Exceptions to the ordinance included (1) minors traveling in a motor vehicle as well as those accompanied by a parent; (2) minors returning by way of direct route from certain specified events (e.g., those approved in advance by the mayor's office) within 60 minutes of the activity's termination; (3) minors carrying proof that they were engaged in legitimate employment activity during curfew hours; and (4) minors moving by reasonable necessity to carry out emergency errands. The court reviewed the new curfew ordinance based on plaintiffs' claims that the ordinance unduly violated First, Fourth, and Fifth Amendment rights.

ISSUES

Does the new curfew ordinance infringe upon First (freedom of association) and Fifth (due process and equal protection) Amendment rights? Does the ordinance violate juveniles' Fourth Amendment right against unreasonable search and seizure as a result of a curfew stop?

HOLDING

Yes and no. The curfew ordinance adopted by the District of Columbia did violate equal protection and due process by making impermissible distinctions between juveniles and nonjuveniles. However, the ordinance did not violate a juvenile's Fourth Amendment protections against unreasonable search and seizure.

RATIONALE

In spite of the various exceptions outlined above, the court found that the District of Columbia's ordinance had the potential to trample upon the association and liberty interests of the plaintiffs. The court noted that high school social activities, political activities, scientific discoveries, and religious pursuits often require otherwise law-abiding youth to be on the District's streets during the curfew period; but in order to do so, juveniles (or their parents) would first have to register for an application with the mayor's office. In the eyes of the court, this hurdle, however small, would have a substantial chilling effect on the legitimate activities of District youth. The court went on to list other activities that were taken for granted elsewhere in the country, such as the right to attend late-night sporting events, to sit outside on a humid summer night, or to walk home at one's leisure from religious or recreational events. Thus, the court referred to the District's ordinance as "a bull in a china shop of constitutional rights," because it effectively "subject[ed] the District's juveniles to virtual house arrest each night without differentiating either among those juveniles likely to embroil themselves in mischief, or among those activities most likely to produce them." With this said, the court went on to reject the plaintiffs' contention that the ordinance unduly violated juvenile's Fourth Amendment rights against unreasonable search and seizure. Instead, it argued the right to be free from unreasonable search and seizure "exists only so long as there is not probable cause to believe that an offense had been committed." In this case, the ordinance made it a crime for juveniles to be in public places during certain hours. Had the ordinance been found constitutional, its proscriptions would have provided valid substantive references for determining the presence or absence of probable cause. In other words, assuming the ordinance had been found constitutional, if a police officer were to reasonably conclude that an individual out on the streets during the curfew period looked "young," that officer would have probable cause to believe that the individual was engaged in an illegal act. Moreover, if the individual in question could not provide evidence that he or she was over the age of 18, or that he or she fell within one of the act's other exceptions, search, seizure, and arrest of that individual would not violate the Fourth Amendment.

CASE EXCERPT

"While similarities between the New Law and the ordinance upheld in *Bykofsky* do exist, it is important to note the respects in which the two diverge. First, unlike the *Bykofsky* ordinance, the New Law makes no exception for minors accompanied by adults generally, but exempts only minors accompanied by their parents. Second, unlike the *Bykofsky* ordinance, the New Law makes no exception for minors occupying the sidewalk in front of their own homes. Third, while the District contends that the New Law's 'reasonable necessity' exception mirrors that in the *Bykofsky* ordinance, it is apparent that the latter's 'reasonable necessity' exception is considerably more flexible, and grants greater leeway to account for the emergencies that arise in the course of daily existence. Fourth, unlike the *Bykofsky* statute, the New Law does not allow a minor whose legitimate nighttime activities are not otherwise accommodated by the ordinance to obtain a permit authorizing such activities…Sixth, the New Law does not contain a blanket exception for any minor exercising First Amendment rights protected by the United States Constitution, such as the free exercise of religion, freedom of speech and the right of assembly."

CASE SIGNIFICANCE

As in the *Opelousas* ruling, the court reiterated its concerns about the reach of this particular ordinance. The court's major concern was that the ordinance effectively barred all types of juvenile activities after dark without making crucial distinctions between positive, prosocial juvenile activities and those that are likely to result in criminal activity. Such restrictive ordinances, the court ruled, not only result in virtual house arrest for all juveniles regardless of their intent, but the lack of legitimate exceptions also helps to undermine the purpose of the curfew ordinance as it was originally conceived. In short, for a juvenile curfew ordinance to pass constitutional muster, it must be narrowly construed and cannot be used indiscriminately against juveniles based solely on their status as minors.

PANORA v. SIMMONS

445 N.W.2d 363 (Iowa 1989)

FACTS

Simmons, then 15, and a friend were skateboarding in the parking lot of a Panora, Iowa shopping center. At 10:35 p.m. both boys were cited by a Panora police officer for violating the city's curfew ordinance. The ordinance prohibited juveniles under the age of 18 from being in public places between the hours of 10:00 p.m. and 5:00 a.m. At trial, Simmons was found guilty and subsequently fined one dollar plus a surcharge and costs; however, criminal sanctions were not applied. In addition to prohibiting movement between the hours of 10:00 p.m. and 5:00 a.m., the Panora ordinance (1) warned parents to closely supervise their children's activities during curfew hours; (2) warned business owners to refrain from catering to minors during curfew hours; and (3) instructed police officers to arrest curfew violators and return them to the custody of their parent, guardian, or other caregiver. Simmons appealed his conviction arguing that the Panora ordinance was unconstitutionally vague; it unconstitutionally interfered with parenting rights; and it unconstitutionally interfered with gathering, walking, and loitering.

ISSUE

Was this curfew ordinance unconstitutionally vague?

HOLDING

No. The ordinance in question allowed for several legitimate exceptions to the rule and provided a means by which juveniles were returned to the custody of their parents. Though the ordinance did hinder a juvenile's right to intracity travel during certain times, this right must be balanced against the city's coequal interest in providing a reasonable response to perceived problems such as juvenile vandalism, crime, and drug use. Likewise, the ordinance did not unduly interfere with childrearing practices, nor did it intrude upon family autonomy. In fact, the ordinance may actually help to promote family ties by encouraging youth to stay home after hours.

RATIONALE

The court couched its ruling in language set out by the Supreme Court that said in part that the activities and conduct of minors may be regulated to a greater extent than that of adults. Although the court recognized that minors have a right to engage in intracity travel, it reasoned that this is not necessarily a fundamental right for due process purposes. In other words, the ordinance in question need not meet a strict scrutiny test. Instead, a more appropriate test would be one that can determine whether there is a rational relationship between the goals of the ordinance and the means used to achieve those goals: "In weighing the minor's interest in intracity travel against the city's interest in providing a prophylactic solution to the perceived problems inherent in unrestricted minor travel, we believe that

PANORA v. SIMMONS (cont.)

the ordinance is a reasonable exercise of the city's power to legislate for the good of its citizens." The court also recognized that "the city has a strong interest in protecting minors from the national epidemic of drugs, and the curfew ordinance is a minimal infringement upon a parent's right to bring up his or her child." In effect, the court said that the Panora curfew ordinance helped to strengthen the hand of parents in their role as the primary agents of social control. Moreover, the court noted, the ordinance actually helped to "promote family life by encouraging children to stay at home."

CASE EXCERPT

"We agree with these authorities that a minor's right of intracity travel is not a fundamental right for due process purposes, and the ordinance need not meet a strict scrutiny test. Rather, we need to determine only whether there is a rational relationship between the goals of the ordinance and the means chosen. We believe there is. In weighing the minor's interest in intracity travel against the City's interest in providing a prophylactic solution to the perceived problems inherent in unrestricted minor travel, we believe that the ordinance is a reasonable exercise of the City's power to legislate for the good of its citizens."

CASE SIGNIFICANCE

This curfew ordinance was clearly designed to promote family life by encouraging juveniles to stay at home rather than remaining on the streets during the late-night hours. What distinguished it from other curfew ordinances nationwide was the exception that allowed juveniles to independently travel to and from parentally approved public functions. This distinction, the court argued, allowed parents to retain primary responsibility over their children's movement. In addition, the ordinance provided no sanctions for parents who failed to properly supervise their children, thus avoiding the possibility of penalizing parents for their inattentiveness, an issue that could raise questions of constitutionality.

PEOPLE IN THE INTEREST OF J.M.
768 P.2d 219 (Colo. 1989)

FACTS

At 11:45 p.m. on August 16, 1985, an officer from the Pueblo, Colorado police department was dispatched to Vinewood Park to investigate a report of vandalism. After searching the park on foot, the officer found J.M. and a female companion—both juveniles—hiding in some bushes near where the offense took place. Though the officer was able to establish that J.M. was not responsible for the vandalism, he was nevertheless arrested for being in possession of an alcoholic beverage and for violating the city's juvenile curfew ordinance. J.M. was tried in a delinquency proceeding and convicted of violating the curfew statute; however, he was acquitted of the possession charge. Upon adjudication as a delinquent, J.M. was fined twenty-five dollars. Later, he appealed the adjudication on the grounds that the Pueblo curfew ordinance was unconstitutional. At the time of his arrest, the Pueblo curfew statute made it unlawful for an individual under the age of 18 to loiter on or about any street, sidewalk, gutter, parking lot, alley, vacant lot, park, playground, or yard, whether public or private, between the hours of 10:00 p.m. and 6:00 a.m. unless accompanied by a parent, guardian, or other responsible adult over the age of 21.

ISSUE

Did the curfew statute in question infringe upon a minor's rights under the state or federal constitutions?

HOLDING

No. The court ruled that the Pueblo ordinance prohibiting loitering by juveniles after curfew did not infringe upon J.M.'s rights under the Colorado Constitution or the US Constitution. Moreover, it noted that the ordinance was carefully crafted to promote legitimate state interests without unduly infringing upon First Amendment freedoms.

RATIONALE

In upholding the constitutionality of the Pueblo ordinance, the Colorado court revisited the ruling in *Bykofsky*. In that case the US District Court held that the establishment of juvenile curfew ordinances can be justified on four grounds: (1) the protection of children from each other and from other persons on the street during nighttime hours; (2) the protection of the public from nocturnal mischief by minors; (3) the reduction of juvenile criminal activity; and (4) the enforcement of parental control of and responsibility for their children. The Colorado court argued that each of these interests qualifies as a "legitimate state interest." Furthermore, the court noted that the Pueblo ordinance is narrowly constructed so as to achieve its stated goals without unduly infringing upon the freedoms and liberty interests of minors. The court went on to state that although many curfew statutes look alike, most fall into one of two broad categories: those proscribing "presence" and those proscribing "loitering." Curfews that are designed to prohibit the mere presence of minors on the streets after a certain hour are often deemed unconstitutional primarily because they are seen as an overly broad restriction on minors' liberty interests and First Amendment activities. However, curfews that are designed to prohibit wandering or other aimless activity of minors during the curfew hours, but which allow juveniles to participate fully in employment, religious, civic, and societal activities, have generally been upheld. The Pueblo ordinance, the court reasoned, tends to favor the latter. That is, it restricts the activities of minors for only a limited period of time in certain public places, and it is drawn as narrowly as practicable. Despite obvious restrictions, the court ruled that minors are still free to participate in any activity, social, religious, or civic, so long as their travels take them directly to or from that activity: "The ordinance simply prevents youths from aimlessly roaming the streets during the nighttime hours. In light of the state's legitimate interests, and the state's special role in the control and supervision of minors, we do not believe that this ordinance unconstitutionally infringes upon J.M.'s liberty interest."

CASE EXCERPT

"There may be unusual cases in which a minor's first amendment activities will be curtailed through enforcement of the ordinance, but we cannot say that the asserted overbreadth of this statute is substantial in relation to its plainly legitimate sweep. It is up to the party invoking the doctrine to demonstrate a realistic danger that the [ordinance] itself will significantly compromise recognized First Amendment protections of parties not before the Court. J.M. has not established a realistic danger that the ordinance will abridge the protected rights of other minors. Thus, he lacks standing to pursue this claim."

CASE SIGNIFICANCE

The court upheld the constitutionality of the ordinance arguing that its creators had struck a clear and reasonable balance between the freedom of movement of juveniles and the best interests of the general public. More important, the court ruled that the consequences of the ordinance were reasonably related to legitimate state interests, including the protection of juveniles from others on the street at night, the protection of the public from juvenile mischief at night, the reduction of juvenile crime, and the enforcement of parental responsibility and control over their children.

BROWN v. ASHTON

611 A.2d 599 (Md. App. 1992)

FACTS

During the summer months of 1990, citizens of Frederick, Maryland, began complaining to city officials that the noise level and harassment of pedestrians by youth around downtown Frederick were becoming unbearable. The source of the problem, according to local residents, was a Chinese restaurant, the Rainbow, that doubled as a dance club catering to youth in the evening hours. To assuage public concerns, the mayor directed police to aggressively enforce a juvenile curfew ordinance previously enacted in 1978. The ordinance made it illegal for persons under age 18 to remain in public places or business establishments between the hours of 11:00 p.m. and 6:00 a.m. Sunday through Friday, and 11:59 p.m. and 6:00 a.m. on Saturday. Exemptions included (1) children accompanied by a parent or guardian; (2) children engaged in an errand directed by a parent; (3) children engaged in a cultural, scholastic, athletic, or recreational activity supervised by a bona fide organization; and (4) children engaged in lawful employment during curfew hours. On Saturday, October 20, 1990, police set up curfew checkpoints at 11:59 p.m. around the Rainbow restaurant and began checking identification of individuals who appeared to be under age eighteen. Among the detainees was Vanessa Brown, an 18-year-old who claimed she had left her identification at home. Brown, who was six months pregnant at the time, protested and struggled with police. Brown was subsequently handcuffed and put onto a bus used by police as a makeshift holding area until her true age could be determined. Brown's mother was contacted and she brought her daughter's identification to police. According to police records, some 15 to 20 minutes elapsed from the time Brown was approached until she was eventually released. Brown and her mother subsequently sued the Frederick Police Department alleging negligence, assault and battery, false imprisonment, invasion of privacy, and intentional infliction of emotional distress. They also claimed that the curfew ordinance violated the due

BROWN v. ASHTON *(cont.)*

process clause, the equal protection clause, and the First Amendment of the US Constitution.

ISSUES

Did the juvenile curfew ordinance violate Brown's rights to due process and equal protection, as well as her First Amendment rights? Should the police be held civilly liable for enforcing the curfew ordinance, which later was determined to be unconstitutional?

HOLDING

Yes and no. On the question of constitutionality, the court held that it could find no compelling government interest in severely restricting the nighttime activities of persons under age 18 in Frederick. On the question of civil liability, the court held that city officials who originally enacted the curfew, as well as the police who later enforced it, were acting within the proper scope of their authority to do so. Thus, they could not be held civilly liable for any reasonable action taken.

RATIONALE

In rendering its decision, the Maryland Appellate Court appeared to diverge significantly from previous rulings regarding the constitutionality of juvenile curfew ordinances. That is, the court rightly pointed out that juvenile curfew statutes "unconstitutionally burden fundamental constitutional rights of adults." But the court went on to suggest that because minors do not lose constitutional rights because of their age, "as a matter of logic the Frederick ordinance and all similar juvenile curfew ordinances are unconstitutional." At this point the court backs up to examine this so-called logic and recognizes that the Supreme Court has previously said that activities and conduct of individuals under the age of 21 may be regulated to a far greater extent than those of adults. Specifically, the Supreme Court ruled in *Bellotti v. Baird,* 443 U.S. 622, 634 (1979) that three factors justify this differential treatment of juveniles: (1) the peculiar vulnerability of children; (2) their inability to make critical decisions in an informed, mature manner; and (3) the importance of the parental role in child rearing. Nevertheless, after examining the complaints waged by local residents, the court concluded that the Frederick ordinance "burdens the fundamental rights of minors and is not justified by any compelling government interest." As to the issue of civil liability, the court found that the

police had acted in good faith in their enforcement of what was later determined to be an unconstitutional statute. In granting immunity to the police, the court ruled, "if a police officer has probable cause to arrest a person...there is no basis upon which a person can assert that a search and seizure pursuant to that lawful arrest is unconstitutional." Because the police acted within the scope of their law enforcement function, the officers in question were protected by a qualified immunity against civil liability for nonmalicious acts performed in the normal course of their duties. Since no malice could be found in the FACTS of this case, the officers—as well as the city—were shielded from civil litigation.

CASE EXCERPT

"In light of these now established principles, *i.e.,* (1) curfew statutes like that at issue here unconstitutionally burden fundamental constitutional rights of adults; and (2) minors do not lose constitutional rights because of their age, it would seem to follow as a matter of logic that the Frederick ordinance and all similar juvenile curfew ordinances are unconstitutional. This logic, however, ignores a critical factor...the activities and conduct of those under twenty-one may be regulated and restricted to a far greater extent than those of adults."

CASE SIGNIFICANCE

This case dealt with a curfew ordinance that was enacted in 1978 for emergency circumstances and was rarely enforced between 1978 and 1990. In 1990, however, city officials resurrected the ordinance as a way to combat loitering, noise, and harassment problems in an area frequented by young people. The court ruled that the problems experienced in Frederick were "non-emergency" circumstances and enforcement of the curfew ordinance in this particular case was unconstitutional. However, the court went on to note that enforcement of the ordinance was well within the scope of police authority, and the officers in question could not be sued for monetary damages so long as their actions were supported by probable cause. This case is significant because it pointed up the fact that curfew ordinances enacted for a specific purpose (e.g., emergency circumstances) may not be enforced as a matter of convenience to alleviate other, unrelated social problems, particularly when enforcement may result in the deprivation of basic juvenile rights. In short, this was not a compelling state interest. In addition, this case also pointed up the fact that government officials (in this case police officers) cannot be held liable for their actions if those actions are based on a law that is later found to be unconstitutional.

CITY OF MAQUOKETA v. RUSSELL
484 N.W.2d 179 (Iowa 1992)

FACTS
In the evening hours of August 26, 1990, Russell and Campbell (both minors at the time) attended a teen dance in Maquoketa, Iowa. After the dance, the two girls wandered the streets talking with friends, and eventually accepted a ride from a third party. While cruising around, the driver was stopped by a Maquoketa police officer and the trio was arrested for violating the city's juvenile curfew ordinance. Both girls were found guilty and each was fined a total of thirty-two dollars. The Maquoketa ordinance made it unlawful for minors to be on any streets, sidewalks, or public places between the hours of 11:00 p.m. and 6:00 a.m. unless accompanied by a parent, guardian, or other responsible adult, except if traveling a direct route between home and bona fide employment or between home and a "parentally approved supervised activity." On appeal, Russell and Campbell claimed that the curfew ordinance was unconstitutionally overbroad and thus a violation of the due process clause of the Fourteenth Amendment. The case was appealed to the Iowa Supreme Court.

ISSUE
Was this juvenile curfew ordinance constitutional? •

HOLDING
No. This ordinance was deemed unconstitutionally overbroad because it imposed a total restriction on the movement of juveniles without providing legitimate exceptions for emancipated juveniles or in cases of emergency.

RATIONALE
The Maquoketa ordinance was deemed overbroad for two primary reasons. First, the court argued that the language contained in the ordinance was vague and thus raised troubling questions: What is a parentally approved supervised activity? Which parents need to approve? Who must supervise the activity? What is an acceptable activity? Because the ordinance provided no direction on these questions, "opportunity arises

for selective enforcement." Second, the ordinance provided very few exceptions for minors engaged in legitimate, law-abiding activities. For instance, the court noted that juveniles traveling alone to and from church services (e.g., midnight mass) were theoretically in violation of the ordinance. The lack of exceptions, in particular, implicated fundamental rights such as freedom of religion, speech, assembly, and association. In short, the imprecise language of the ordinance, in addition to the paucity of legitimate exceptions, made it unconstitutionally overbroad.

CASE EXCERPT
"We recognize that an ordinance which restricts minors' rights to an extent greater than it restricts adults' rights may be sustained if the State or municipality demonstrates that it protects minors' peculiar vulnerability, accounts for their lesser ability to make sound judgments, and reflects society's deference to the guiding role of parents. Though minors possess fundamental constitutional rights, their rights are not automatically coextensive with the rights of adults. But as the foregoing examples demonstrate, the ordinance here is not drawn narrowly to provide exceptions for emancipated minors and fundamental rights under the First Amendment. For these reasons we think the ordinance is unconstitutionally overbroad."

CASE SIGNIFICANCE
The ordinance in this case was highly restrictive and broadly constructed. Though the ordinance did provide several exceptions (e.g., travel accompanied by an adult, direct travel to or from work, or participation in a parentally approved activity), no exceptions were made for other legitimate circumstances such as emergency errands, proximity to home, and a juvenile's maturity level. The court found that such a narrow definition of legitimate nighttime activities violated juveniles' First Amendment rights to freedom of religion, speech, assembly, and association because it hindered their ability to participate in such activities unless accompanied by an adult.

QUTB v. STRAUSS
11 F.3d 488 (5th Cir. 1993)

FACTS
On June 12, 1991, the Dallas City Council enacted a juvenile curfew ordinance in response to public

QUTB v. STRAUSS *(cont.)*

demands for more legislation to protect the city's youth. The Dallas ordinance made it a misdemeanor for persons under the age of 17 to remain in public places or establishments between the hours of 11:00 p.m. and 6:00 a.m. on weekdays and 12:00 midnight and 6:00 a.m. on weekends. Yet city officials also devised a litany of exceptions, such as (1) if the minor was accompanied by a parent or guardian, or on an errand for a parent or guardian; (2) if the minor was traveling to or from work or an employment-related activity; (3) if the minor was attending a school, religious, or civic function, or generally exercising his or her First Amendment speech or associational rights; (4) if the minor was engaged in interstate travel; (5) if the minor remained on a sidewalk in front of his or her own home, or the home of a neighbor; or (6) in cases of emergency. The ordinance also required police to ask the age of suspected curfew violators and to inquire into the reasons for their being in a public place during curfew hours before taking any enforcement action. If convicted, the offender was subject to a fine of $500 for each separate offense. Furthermore, parents or business owners who knowingly allowed juveniles to violate the curfew ordinance could also be fined $500 for each separate offense. Two weeks after the Dallas ordinance was enacted, Qutb and three other parents filed suit against the city of Dallas seeking a temporary restraining order and a permanent injunction against its enforcement. In part, the plaintiffs alleged that the ordinance (1) was overly broad; (2) violated juveniles' First, Fourth, and Fifth Amendment rights; (3) violated the equal protection clause; and (4) violated the rights of parents to raise their children in the manner in which they see fit.

ISSUES

Did the Dallas curfew ordinance violate the equal protection clause? Did the curfew ordinance violate parental rights to determine how their children should be raised?

HOLDING

No and no. The Dallas ordinance did not violate fundamental rights of juveniles. To the contrary, the ordinance actually furthered compelling state interests in keeping juveniles safe insofar as it protected them from crime on the streets. Given the many broad exemptions listed, the ordinance did not violate parents' rights, nor did it significantly impinge

on their role regarding proper family management practices. In short, the impositions on parents were minor.

RATIONALE

To justify its decision, the court argued that states have a compelling interest in increasing the safety of juveniles and preventing crime. While it recognized that some juveniles (and by default, their parents) might be inconvenienced by the restrictions placed on freedom of movement, the court reasoned that the ordinance was narrowly constructed with an eye toward respecting the rights of the affected minors. The court took great pains to point out the various exemptions constructed by city officials and argued that free movement of juveniles is possible even during curfew hours: "It is true, of course, that the curfew ordinance would restrict some late-night activities of juveniles; if it did not, then there would be no purpose in enacting it. But when balanced with the compelling interest sought to be addressed—protecting juveniles and preventing juvenile crime—the impositions are minor." As to the question of whether or not the ordinance impinges on parental rights, the court argued that the only aspect of parenting this ordinance bears upon is the parents' right to allow the minor to remain in public places, unaccompanied by a parent or guardian or other authorized person, during the hours restricted: "Because of the broad exemptions included in the curfew ordinance, the parent retains the right to make decisions regarding his or her child in all other cases."

CASE EXCERPT

"It is true, of course, that the curfew ordinance would restrict some late-night activities of juveniles; if indeed it did not, then there would be no purpose in enacting it. But when balanced with the compelling interest sought to be addressed— protecting juveniles and preventing juvenile crime—the impositions are minor. The district court failed to observe that none of the activities it listed are restricted if the juvenile is accompanied by a parent or a guardian."

CASE SIGNIFICANCE

The court ruled in this case that the Dallas juvenile curfew ordinance was specifically tailored and narrowly constructed to address the city's articulated and compelling interests of protecting juveniles from harm and reducing juvenile crime and violence.

Despite the protests from both juveniles and their parents, the court reasoned that the Dallas ordinance did not violate the equal protection clause because it allowed juveniles to remain in public places even during curfew hours for a variety of legitimate reasons. In addition, the court noted that although the curfew ordinance might intrude upon parents' right to privacy, such intrusions apply only to parents who would allow their children to engage in no productive activity during the late-night hours. This case is significant insofar as the ordinance in question has served as a model for other city and state legislators contemplating the enactment of similar juvenile curfew ordinances. In fact, other laws modeled after the Dallas ordinance have, in most cases, withstood judicial scrutiny. Finally, it should be noted that the federal court of appeals decided this case and its ruling may carry more weight than similar cases decided by the federal district court.

STATE v. BEAN
869 P.2d 984 (Utah App. 1994)

FACTS
While on routine patrol around 2:50 a.m. on January 26, 1991, a Salt Lake sheriff's deputy noticed two young males walking in front of a strip mall. Minutes earlier, the deputy had received a radio transmission from area police who were looking for a male suspect in the general vicinity. Noticing that one of the boys looked very young, the officer pulled his vehicle alongside to investigate if either was in violation of the local curfew ordinance. During questioning, the officer claimed that both boys smelled of alcohol, so he asked them to produce identification. The officer ran a warrants check and discovered that one of the boys was wanted on an outstanding warrant. The deputy subsequently arrested the boy on the outstanding warrant and for consumption of alcohol by a minor. A later search at the jail resulted in additional charges for unlawful possession of a controlled substance and possession of drug paraphernalia. The defendant appealed his conviction claiming that the evidence used to convict him should have been suppressed because (1) the initial stop was more than a "level one" encounter (discussed below) and was not supported by reasonable suspicion; (2) his subsequent detention for questioning violated his Fourth Amendment rights; and (3) the stop and subsequent detention violated his right against unreasonable searches and seizures guaranteed by Article I, Section 14 of the Utah Constitution.

ISSUES
At the time of the initial encounter, did the officer have reasonable suspicion to believe that the defendant was violating the local curfew ordinance? If so, did this reasonable suspicion justify the detention of the juvenile for the purposes of identification and a warrants check?

HOLDING
Yes and yes. At the time of this case, the state of Utah classified police-citizen encounters in one of three ways: (1) a "level one" stop allowed an officer to approach a citizen at any time and ask questions, as long as the citizen was not detained against his or her will; (2) a "level two" stop allowed an officer to seize a person if the officer had "articulable suspicion" that the person had committed or was about to commit a crime, but the detention must be temporary and last no longer than is necessary to effectuate the purpose of the stop; and (3) a "level three" stop allowed an officer to arrest a suspect if the officer had probable cause to believe an offense had been committed or was being committed. FACTS in this case suggested that the defendant willingly cooperated with the officer under the guidelines of a level one stop. However, once the officer detected the odor of alcohol, the encounter escalated to a level two stop, which provided the officer with articulable suspicion to conduct the warrants check.

RATIONALE
The court reasoned that the initial encounter between the officer and the defendant clearly qualified as a level one stop. The deputy pulled alongside the defendant and then stopped approximately 10 feet in front of him. He did not use the cruiser's lights or siren; he did not order the suspect to stop. In fact, he never touched, restrained, or threatened the suspect at any time prior to arrest. He merely asked for identification after smelling the odor of alcohol. Consequently, the initial encounter between the officer and the defendant was a level one stop and the Fourth Amendment was not implicated. Only after detecting the smell of alcohol on the defendant's breath did the officer develop articulable suspicion to ask for identification. Once the warrants check indicated that the defendant was wanted, the officer then developed probable cause to make the

STATE v. BEAN (cont.)

arrest. Thus, the defendant's Fourth Amendment rights were not violated.

CASE EXCERPT

"In response to an attempt to locate suspects, Deputy Schroeder pulled up alongside defendant and then stopped approximately ten feet in front of him. At the outset, Deputy Schroeder was the only officer present. He used no lights or sirens, and did not call out to defendant or tell him he must stay. Deputy Schroeder did not display his weapon, nor did he touch, restrain, or threaten defendant. He merely asked for defendant's identification. Consequently, we conclude that Deputy Schroeder's initial encounter with defendant was a level one stop and the Fourth Amendment was not implicated."

CASE SIGNIFICANCE

This case is significant insofar as it helps to shed light on police powers in the enforcement of juvenile curfews. Note that the juvenile in question was not stopped for violating the curfew ordinance; rather, he was confronted for the purpose of identifying a suspect in an unrelated call. The court ruled that questioning a juvenile who might be in violation of a curfew ordinance for identification purposes is a legitimate use of field interrogation techniques. If, as a result of that questioning, an officer developed probable cause for arrest, any evidence gathered would be legally admissible in court. Given the fact that the officer in this case did not employ coercive or threatening techniques, and coupled with the brevity of the initial encounter, the court ruled that the juvenile's constitutional rights were not violated even though police had in fact questioned him. In short, police procedure regarding the proper handling of juveniles is similar to the handling of adults under similar circumstances.

MATTER OF APPEAL IN MARICOPA COUNTY

887 P.2d 599 (Ariz. App. 1994)

FACTS

On Saturday evening, May 1, 1993, a 15-year-old girl obtained her father's permission to go out with a group of friends. At approximately 11:00 p.m., she went to a friend's house in Phoenix, Arizona to watch television.

According to the juvenile, the friend's parents were asleep and in order not to wake them, she and her friend walked to a nearby park across the street from her friend's house. At 11:22 p.m. a Phoenix police officer responded to an anonymous report of a juvenile disturbance in that same park. Upon arriving, the officer heard loud laughing and found the juvenile along with two male companions, ages 16 and 17, in the park. The officer asked the juvenile her name and age. When she responded that she was 15 years old, the officer took her into custody for violating Phoenix's 10:00 p.m. curfew for juveniles under the age of 16. At her trial, the juvenile's father testified that he gave his daughter permission to go to her friend Richard's house and to be in the park across from Richard's house. On cross-examination, however, the father recanted, claiming that he did not actually have specific knowledge that his daughter would be in that park. On redirect, he stated that if he had known his daughter was going to the park he would not have forbidden her from doing so. The juvenile court ruled that the girl had in fact violated the curfew ordinance and imposed a fifty-six dollar penalty. The case was appealed to the Arizona Court of Appeals.

ISSUES

Did the Phoenix curfew ordinance unduly restrict the rights of juveniles and parents? Was the ordinance so unconstitutionally broad or vague as to be impossible to equitably enforce?

HOLDING

No and no. The juvenile's decision to go to the park in violation of the curfew ordinance was not an activity protected by the First Amendment. The curfew ordinance did not violate the fundamental rights of juveniles nor was it impossible to enforce equitably.

RATIONALE

The court recognized in this case that a walk in the park is a simple amenity of life often taken for granted: "The right to walk the streets, or to meet publicly with one's friends for a noble purpose or for no purpose at all—and to do so whenever one pleases—is an integral component of life in a free and ordered society." However, the court went on to note that, in this case, the juvenile's decision to walk when and where she did was not an activity protected by the First Amendment. In defending its reasoning, the court again pointed to the "particular vulnerability" of children as well as the state's interest in keeping kids safe from the corrupting influences of crime and drugs. It went on to note that juvenile crime as well as drug use appeared to be on the rise nationwide. These problems, "while not peculiar to minors, [are] more damaging to them because they are more vulnerable." Furthermore, this vulnerability tends to increase during curfew hours and could result in serious consequences for minors. Beyond the argument that curfews protect juveniles from crime and drugs, the court also lamented the apparent demise of the traditional family unit (e.g., the two-parent household). The implicit argument made by the court was that single-parent households have less direct control over their children's activities, and thus curfews can help to keep these children safe by shunting them indoors during peak crime periods.

CASE EXCERPT

"There is sufficient evidence in the record to support a finding that the juvenile lacked her parents' specific permission to be in the park. Her father admitted that he did not know in advance that she was going to the park. Thus, it was impossible for him to have given his specific permission for her to go the park. Rather than being in the park *with her parents' permission,* the juvenile was in the park *without her parents' objection.* The juvenile did not meet her burden of proving that the parental permission exception exempted her from the curfew."

CASE SIGNIFICANCE

The court found that the Phoenix curfew ordinance was constitutional in part because of its various exceptions, including parentally approved late-night activities. However, in this case, the juvenile had exceeded the limits of her parent's approval, even though the father later claimed that he had no objections to his daughter's conduct. Though the court acknowledged that the ordinance could result in the violation of some juvenile's constitutional rights, it reasoned that the protection of society and the minor intrusion on parental authority clearly outweighed the juvenile's freedom of movement.

DISCUSSION QUESTIONS

1. Research indicates that juvenile violence is more prevalent directly after school than during late-night hours, so why are most juvenile curfew ordinances slated to take effect late at night?
2. In the *Bykofsky* case, the court upheld a juvenile curfew ordinance on the grounds that it was designed to "protect young people...and to reduce the incidence of juvenile criminal activity." If most juvenile violence occurs between 3:00 and 4:00 p.m., would it be constitutional for a city to enact a daytime curfew for juveniles? Justify your answer.
3. In *Panora v. Simmons,* the court argued that the juvenile curfew ordinance helped to "promote family life by encouraging children to stay at home" during the late-night hours. Is promoting family life really a legitimate state interest?
4. In *Qutb v. Strauss,* a juvenile convicted of violating the Dallas (Texas) curfew ordinance was subject to a fine of $500 for each separate offense. If the child is indigent (e.g., has no job and no means of income), should his or her parents be held civilly liable for the fine?
5. Assume you were the police officer in *State v. Bean.* What would you have done if the juvenile suspect had stood silent and refused to answer your questions?
6. Review the case of *Matter of Appeal in Maricopa County.* In your opinion, did the court overstep its authority by imposing a fifty-six dollar fine on the juvenile for taking a late-night walk in the park? Recall that the child's father said that if he had known his daughter was going to the park he would not have forbidden her from doing so.
7. What elements of a juvenile curfew seem to cause courts the greatest problem and lead to the curfew being declared unconstitutional?
8. What elements of a juvenile curfew are typically determined by a court to be constitutional?
9. What evidence, according to the courts, exists to suggest juvenile curfews are effective?
10. What evidence, according to the courts, exists to suggest juvenile curfews are ineffective?

CHAPTER TWO

JUVENILES AND THE POLICE

HALEY v. OHIO, *332 U.S. 596 (1948)*

HARLING v. UNITED STATES, *295 F.2D 161 (D.D.C. 1961)*

GALLEGOS v. COLORADO, *370 U.S. 49 (1962)*

UNITED STATES v. MILLER, *453 F.2D 634 (4TH CIR. 1972)*

IN RE J.B., *328 A.2D 46 (N.J. JUV. & DOM. REL. CT. 1974)*

UNITED STATES v. BARFIELD, *507 F.2D 53 (5TH CIR. 1975)*

IN THE INTEREST OF DINO, *359 SO.2D 586 (LA. 1978)*

FARE v. MICHAEL C., *442 U.S. 707 (1979)*

UNITED STATES v. SECHRIST, *640 F.2D 81 (7TH CIR. 1981)*

NEW JERSEY v. T.L.O., *468 U.S. 1214 (1985)*

UNITED STATES v. BERNARD S., *795 F.2D 749 (9TH CIR. 1986)*

LANES v. STATE, *767 S.W.2D 789 (TEX. CRIM. APP. 1989)*

SMITH v. STATE, *623 SO.2D 369 (ALA. CR. APP. 1992)*

IN RE J.M., *619 A.2D 497 (D.C. CT. APP. 1992)*

IN THE INTEREST OF J.L., *A CHILD, 623 SO.2D 860 (FLA. APP. 1993)*

IN THE INTEREST OF S.A.W., *499 N.W.2D 739 (IOWA APP. 1993)*

IN RE STARVON J., *29 CAL.RPTR.2D 471 (CAL. APP. 1994)*

IN RE TYRELL J., *876 P.2D 519 (CAL. 1994)*

STATE v. SUGG, *456 S.E.2D 469 (W. VA. 1995)*

VERNONIA SCHOOL DISTRICT 47J v. ACTON, *515 U.S. 646 (1995)*

BOARD OF EDUCATION POTTAWATOMIE COUNTY v. EARLS, *545 U.S. 1015 (2002)*

YARBOROUGH v. ALVARADO, *541 U.S. 652 (2004)*

SAFFORD UNIFIED SCHOOL DISTRICT #1 v. REDDING *557 U.S.—(2009)*

CAMRETA v. GREENE, *563 U.S.—(2011)*

J.D.B. v. NORTH CAROLINA, *564 U.S.—(2011)*

INTRODUCTION

Traditionally, the role of police officers has been threefold: order maintenance, law enforcement, and service. Throughout the 1900s the police typically focused on the first two components of their duties. However, in the past couple of decades the concept of community policing has emanated from the mouths of practitioners and scholars alike. Police departments have attempted to become more service friendly in an effort to solve problems and move away from the "Band-Aid" approach of just making arrests.

This does not mean that the police have become soft on crime; more appropriately, the police have expanded their duties. Instead of just patrolling an area, police officers, in departments that employ a community policing approach, often interact with citizens and work with them to strengthen informal controls within neighborhoods in an effort to reduce crime.

One area where this new style of policing has become especially prevalent is in the law enforcement approach to juvenile delinquency. In the past, the police typically responded to juvenile issues with threats and warnings that eventually led up to arrest. However, the contemporary police officer is often found interacting with youth in an effort to discover the root of the problems that may be causing juveniles to create disturbances. In addition, police are often found organizing athletic leagues, neighborhood projects, and youth advisory groups, all in an effort to improve relations with juveniles in their communities. Police agencies have also developed juvenile units within their departments. These units attempt to intervene, either with preventative measures or by arrest, in the lives of troubled or at-risk youth. Today, police are also commonly found in all levels of schools. Whether they are teaching classes such as Drug Abuse Resistance Education (DARE) and law related education, or working as school resource officers (SROs), the police work with youth more directly than ever before.

In view of the increased contact with juveniles, a substantial amount of case law related to police procedure for dealing with juveniles has emerged. As in the court process, procedures for dealing with juvenile suspects are somewhat different than those for dealing with adults. In the early part of the 1900s, juveniles were not afforded many of the rights guaranteed to adults in the Constitution. The state operated under the doctrine of parens patriae and did whatever it determined was in the best interest of each child. This carried over to police procedure, as there was little protection for juvenile suspects' rights. However, in the late 1940s and early 1950s juveniles' civil liberties began to receive some attention. The courts began to hear appeals from the juvenile court on constitutional issues dealing with juvenile delinquency procedure. The courts have reviewed the procedures in which the police interrogate, search, and seize juvenile suspects. In the wake of the court holdings, some changes began to occur. Similar to adults in the criminal system, juveniles are now protected by the due process clause of the Fourteenth Amendment and additionally afforded most of the protections of the Fourth, Fifth, and Sixth Amendments.

In reviewing these cases and individual situations the courts have taken a totality of the circumstances approach to determining whether a juvenile's rights have been violated. Some of the factors that the courts have considered are a juvenile's age, prior record, maturity, and education, as well as whether a parent or guardian was present. Some states, as well as several courts, have mandated that a parent or guardian be present during any questioning of a juvenile suspect, whereas others operate on a case-by-case basis.

Despite the protections the courts have afforded juveniles, some of the old laws that operate under the parens patriae philosophy are still prevalent in the state statutes. Juveniles can still be arrested and occasionally taken into custody for status offenses, such as breaking curfew and running away. The police and courts will also act in loco parentis and take juveniles into custody for being incorrigible or beyond their parents' control. In addition, the juvenile courts have recently entered the public school arena by defining what school officials can do in an effort to maintain school order and student safety. Given the emerging police presence in the schools, these decisions have had some impact on law enforcement's approach to school safety. These court decisions have affected the way in which the police approach juvenile delinquency and handle juvenile suspects. In this chapter we review some of the leading cases dealing with juveniles and the police.

HALEY v. OHIO

332 U.S. 596 (1948)

FACTS

A confectionery store was robbed near midnight on October 14, 1945, and Karam, its owner, was shot. It was the prosecutor's theory, supported by some evidence (which it is unnecessary to relate) that Haley and two others, Lowder and Parks, committed the crime, with Haley acting as a lookout. Five days later, around midnight October 19, 1945, Haley was arrested at his home and taken to police headquarters. There is some contrariety in the testimony as to what then transpired. There is evidence that Haley was beaten. He took the stand and so testified. His mother testified that the clothes he wore when arrested, which were exchanged two days later for clean ones she brought to the jail, were torn and bloodstained. She also testified that when she first saw him five days after his arrest he was bruised and skinned. The police testified to the contrary on the entire line of testimony. Beginning shortly after midnight Haley was questioned by the police for about five hours. Five or six of the officers questioned him in relays of one or two each. During this time no friend or counsel of the boy was present. Around 5:00 a.m., after being shown the alleged confessions of Lowder and Parks, Haley confessed. A confession was typed in question and answer

HALEY v. OHIO *(cont.)*

form by the police. At no time was Haley advised of his right to counsel, but the written confession started off with the following statement: "We want to inform you of your constitutional rights, the law gives you the right to make this statement or not as you see fit. It is made with the understanding that it may be used at a trial in court either for or against you or anyone else involved in this crime with you, of your own free will and accord, you are under no force or duress or compulsion and no promises are being made to you at this time whatsoever." Haley was put in jail about 6:00 or 6:30 a.m. on Saturday October 20, shortly after the confession was signed. Between then and Tuesday October 23, he was held incommunicado. A lawyer retained by his mother tried to see him twice but was refused admission by the police. His mother was not allowed to see him until Thursday October 25, but a newspaper photographer was allowed to see him and take his picture in the early morning hours of October 20, right after he had confessed. He was not taken before a magistrate and formally charged with a crime until October 23, three days after the confession was signed. Haley appealed to the Ohio Supreme Court, but it dismissed the appeal. The US Supreme Court then granted certiorari.

ISSUE

Does the due process clause of the Fourteenth Amendment prohibit the use of coerced confessions against a juvenile?

HOLDING

Yes. The Fourteenth Amendment prohibits police from violating the due process clause in obtaining admissions or confessions from adults and juveniles. Coerced confessions cannot be used in court.

RATIONALE

The Court contended the methods used in obtaining this confession could not be squared with due process of law, which the Fourteenth Amendment commands. According to the Court, age 15 is a tender and difficult age for a boy of any race. He cannot be judged by the more exacting standards of maturity. A 15-year-old questioned through the dead of night by relays of police is a ready victim of the inquisition. He needs someone on whom to lean lest the overpowering presence of the law, as he knows it, may crush him. But not even a gesture toward getting a lawyer for him was

ever made. This disregard of the standards of decency was underlined by the fact that he was kept incommunicado for over three days during which the lawyer retained to represent him twice tried to see him and twice was refused admission. A photographer was admitted at once, but his closest friend, his mother, was not allowed to see him for more than five days after his arrest. It was said that these events were not germane to the present problem because they happened after the confession was made. But they show such a callous attitude of the police toward the safeguards, with respect for ordinary standards of human relationships, that they compelled the Court to take with a grain of salt their present apologia that the five-hour interrogation of this boy was conducted in a fair and dispassionate manner. The age of petitioner, the hours when he was questioned, the duration of his quizzing, the fact that he had no friend or counsel to advise him, and the callous attitude of the police toward his rights combined to convince the Court that this was a confession extracted from a child by means that the law should not allow. Neither man nor child can be allowed to stand condemned by methods that flout constitutional requirements of due process of law. That assumes, however, that a boy of 15, without aid of counsel, would have a full appreciation of that advice and that on the FACTS of this record he had a freedom of choice. The Court chose not to indulge those assumptions. The Fourteenth Amendment prohibits the police from using the private, secret custody of either man or child as a device for wringing confessions from them.

CASE EXCERPT

"The age of the petitioner, the hours when he was grilled, the duration of his quizzing, the fact that he had no friend or counsel to advise him, the callous attitudes of the police towards his rights combine to convince us that this was a confession that was wrung from a child by means which the law should not sanction."

CASE SIGNIFICANCE

This case is important for several reasons. First, it was the first time the Supreme Court entered the juvenile arena and afforded juveniles rights analogous to those bestowed upon adults by the Constitution and Bill of Rights. The Court determined that juveniles must be afforded due process. Although the Court did not specify which rights are guaranteed to juveniles, the holding laid the framework for future decisions that did specify those rights. Second, in holding as they did, the Court forced lower courts to examine juvenile cases and specifically police treatment of juveniles with a closer eye. Many lower courts began, through case law, to establish some procedures the police must follow when dealing with juveniles.

HARLING v. UNITED STATES

295 F.2d 161 (D.D.C. 1961)

FACTS

The police took Harling, aged 17, into custody on February 21, 1960, and placed him in a lineup where he was identified by a store clerk as one of two persons who had robbed the store and as the one who had stabbed him. Harling was taken to the Receiving Home for Children, where he spent the night. The following morning he was taken to the Robbery Squad for questioning. At 3:00 p.m. that afternoon the store owner identified Harling as one of the robbers and the assailant of the clerk. Harling was subsequently returned to the Receiving Home to await a hearing in juvenile court. Two weeks later that court waived its jurisdiction and ordered Harling held for trial under the regular procedure for adults in United States District Court. At the trial, the storeowner testified that when she identified Harling at the robbery squad he admitted he had taken part in the robbery, but denied stabbing the store clerk. A police detective testified that Harling had made similar statements to him during questioning earlier that day. Harling's lawyer objected on the ground that a statement taken from a witness who had been under arrest and not taken to an arraigning magistrate during the interval from 10:30 that night until 10:30 the following morning, at which time Harling made the admissions to the detective, was inadmissible.

ISSUE

Are statements made by a juvenile to the police while in the jurisdiction of the juvenile court, and prior to any waiver proceedings, admissible in criminal court proceedings?

HOLDING

No. Injurious statements by a juvenile while in police custody cannot be used as evidence in criminal court proceedings if the juvenile is subsequently transferred to criminal court.

RATIONALE

The court relied on *Pee v. United States* (274 F.WD 556 (1959)), which made clear that from the moment a child commits an offense, he or she is exempt from the criminal law unless or until the juvenile court waives its jurisdiction. During that period the juvenile rules apply. The juvenile rules require a hearing within five days of a detention. The Federal Rules of Criminal Procedure require a preliminary hearing without unnecessary delay; however, those rules do not apply in juvenile proceedings. It is because juveniles are typically exempt from criminal penalties that the safeguards of the criminal law have no application in juvenile proceedings. Aside from the requirements of the applicable statutes, the principles of fundamental fairness govern in fashioning procedures to serve the best interests of the child. The court contended that it would offend these principles to allow admissions made by the child in the noncriminal setting of juvenile proceedings to be used later for the purpose of securing a criminal conviction. In addition, if admissions obtained in juvenile proceedings before waiver of jurisdiction may be introduced in criminal proceedings after waiver, the juvenile proceedings would serve as a part of the criminal process. This would destroy the juvenile court's parens patriae relation to the child. The court relied on a prior case, where it was strongly intimated that any departure in practice from that philosophy would require the application of procedural safeguards observed in criminal proceedings. To avoid impairment of the function of the juvenile court it must be insulated from the criminal proceeding. This requires that the admissions by a juvenile in connection with the noncriminal proceeding be excluded from evidence in the criminal proceeding.

CASE EXCERPT

"It would offend these principles [of fundamental fairness] to allow admissions made by the child in the non-criminal and non-punitive setting of juvenile proceedings to be used later for the purpose of securing his criminal conviction and punishment."

CASE SIGNIFICANCE

The court, in this case, maintained the proposed division between the juvenile and adult criminal court that is intended in the statutes. The juvenile court was designed to keep youth away from the harshness of the criminal court. In this case, the

HARLING v. UNITED STATES *(cont.)*

court did not allow further questioning of a juvenile by the police after juvenile court proceedings have begun to be used in the juvenile's hearing to determine if he or she should be transferred to criminal court. In doing this, the court provided the juvenile rights that are afforded adults once they have been charged in criminal court. This is of interest because the court, although intending to keep the juvenile court distinct from the adult criminal court, formalized its procedures, making it more like the adult criminal court.

GALLEGOS v. COLORADO
370 U.S. 49 (1962)

FACTS
Gallegos, a 14-year-old boy, and another juvenile followed an elderly man to a hotel, gained entrance to his room on a ruse, assaulted and overpowered him, stole thirteen dollars from his pockets, and fled. Picked up 12 days later by police, Gallegos immediately admitted the assault and robbery. Over two weeks later, he was convicted in a juvenile court of assault to injure, and was committed to the State Industrial School for an indeterminate period of time. Subsequently the victim died, and Gallegos was charged with first-degree murder. At his trial in a state court, a jury found him guilty. The crucial evidence introduced at the trial was a formal confession, which Gallegos had signed before his victim died, before he had been brought before a judge, and after he had been held for five days without seeing a lawyer, parent, or other friendly adult, although his mother had attempted to see him. The Colorado Supreme Court upheld his conviction, and he sought a writ of certiorari from the US Supreme Court.

ISSUE
May police isolation of a juvenile for prolonged periods result in confessions that are considered involuntary?

HOLDING
Yes. The isolation of a juvenile for prolonged periods by the police may result in confessions that are deemed involuntarily obtained and in violation of the juvenile's due process rights.

RATIONALE
After Gallegos's arrest on January 1, his mother tried to see him on Friday, January 2, but permission was denied. The Court pointed out the length of the questioning, the use of fear to break a suspect, and the age of the accused are illustrative of the circumstances on which cases of this kind turn. In addition, the fact that Gallegos was only 14 years old was significant. There was no evidence of prolonged questioning. But the five-day detention, during which time Gallegos's mother unsuccessfully tried to see him and he was cut off from contact with any lawyer or adult advisor was problematic. The prosecution said that Gallegos was advised of his right to counsel, but that he did not ask either for a lawyer or for his parents. The Court emphasized that it was dealing with a person who was not equal to the police in knowledge and understanding of the consequences of the questions and answers being recorded and who was unable to know how to protect his own interests or how to get the benefits of his constitutional rights. Gallegos cannot be compared to an adult in full possession of his senses and knowledgeable of the consequences of his admissions. He would have no way of knowing what the consequences of his confession were, without advice as to his rights from someone concerned with securing him those rights, and without the aid of more mature judgment as to the steps he should take in the predicament in which he found himself. The age of the petitioner, the long detention, the failure to send for his parents, the failure immediately to bring him before the judge of the juvenile court, and the failure to see to it that he had the advice of lawyer or a friend combined to make the Court conclude that the formal confession on which this conviction may have rested was obtained in violation of due process.

CASE EXCERPT
"It is inconceivable that any court of justice in the land, conducted as our courts are, open to the public, would permit prosecutors serving in relays to keep a defendant witness under continuous cross examination for thirty-six hours without rest or sleep in an effort to extract a 'voluntary' confession."

CASE SIGNIFICANCE
The Court, in this case, extended the rights the Supreme Court had initiated to juveniles in *Haley*. This Court again drew a clear distinction between treatment of juvenile and adult suspects. They pointed to long detentions

and the denial of access to a parent or guardian, as well as the juvenile's age as factors they considered when applying the totality of the circumstances test. Many states do not allow juveniles under a certain age to be questioned without a parent or counsel. Essentially, the Court indicated that a suspect who is 14 years of age is not capable of protecting his own interests as an adult could. The Court contended that a youth of that age does not have the maturity to appreciate the consequences of waiving his or her rights. Therefore, they did not allow the questioning, which they considered to be coercive, to be used in a subsequent trial.

UNITED STATES v. MILLER
453 F.2d 634 (4th Cir. 1972)

FACTS
Miller was charged with juvenile delinquency in an information alleging violations relative to possession of stolen mail and the forgery and uttering of United States Treasury checks. Miller, who was 14 years old at the time of the offense, was tried in district court and found to be a juvenile delinquent. He was committed to the attorney general for a period of four years. Miller, upon appeal, challenged the introduction into evidence of certain written and oral statements given by him to a postal inspector, and in addition contended that fingerprints and handwriting samples taken from him by said inspector were also improperly used in obtaining his conviction. The thrust of his argument was that a 14-year-old boy is conclusively presumed to be incapable of waiving his rights to counsel as well as his other constitutional protections, even though the record clearly shows that the Miranda warnings were given. In this case Miller went voluntarily, but alone, to the postal inspector's office, waived and signed a form waiving his rights, and then provided the handwriting sample and fingerprints.

ISSUE
Is the use of handwriting samples and fingerprints obtained after a waiver of rights without adult guidance or legal advice valid in the prosecution of a 14-year-old charged with delinquency?

HOLDING
Yes. If, after having been informed of his or her constitutional rights and intelligently waiving them, a juvenile submits fingerprints and handwriting samples, they may be used in delinquency proceedings in juvenile court because they were obtained without coercion.

RATIONALE
The court contended that when determining whether any individual has intelligently waived his constitutional rights, it is necessary to examine the totality of the circumstances. In other words, each case must be looked at individually. The court contended that additional clarification must be made by the officer in an effort to make sure the juvenile understands the rights he is waiving. In absence of such clarification the juvenile's answer shall not be given much weight. The atmosphere of an investigator's office can be overpowering to the juvenile, especially if he is unaccompanied by an adult. The court contended the state had met its burden in the present case. The court is not prepared to hold that a 14-year-old boy is never capable of making an intelligent waiver of his rights. The court did not find anything in the record to indicate that Miller did not fully understand what he was doing when he waived his rights. Consequently, the waiver and subsequent handwriting samples and fingerprints were admissible.

CASE EXCERPT
The District Judge, who had an opportunity to observe the appellant, explicitly noted that the youthful defendant understood his rights and indeed had a better comprehension of them than many adults who appear before the court.

CASE SIGNIFICANCE
The importance of this case lies in the court's decision to rely on a totality-of-the-circumstances approach in determining the admissibility of the juvenile's statements, handwriting samples, and fingerprints. In taking this approach, the court allowed a 14-year-old to voluntarily waive his rights absent a parent or counsel. In doing so the court contended that a 14-year-old may be mature enough to understand his or her rights guaranteed under *Miranda*. The court substantiated its ruling by pointing to the lack of coercion on the part of the government, as well as the fact that the juvenile's rights were fully explained to him by the officer. Furthermore, the court reminded that the juvenile appeared at the government office

UNITED STATES v. MILLER *(cont.)*

voluntarily by himself. Consequently, in looking at the whole situation, or totality of the circumstances, the court did not feel the juvenile was under any undue duress to make the statements and provide the samples.

IN RE J.B.

328 A.2d 46 (N.J. Juv. & Dom. Rel. Ct. 1974)

FACTS

Two officers on patrol received a dispatch from head-quarters followed by a call from an officer at the scene of an accident. The information in the dispatches was that a car had struck a parked car; that witnesses had seen a white, long-haired male flee the car; and that the ignition key was missing from the car. As the officers drove toward where the fleeing suspect was supposed to have gone they observed a 15-year-old white male with long hair walking on the sidewalk several blocks from the accident. His lip was bleeding, his arm appeared to be hurt, and his clothes were wet. The officers stopped him and asked him to account for himself. He provided several inconsistent stories. One of the officers conducted a search of the juvenile, and later testified that he was looking for the ignition key. Instead, he uncovered two bags of marijuana in the juvenile's pocket. The officer placed the juvenile under arrest. The officers transported the juvenile to the hospital, where a more thorough search uncovered a third bag of marijuana. The officers were later informed the car from the accident was stolen. Both officers testified that at the time of the search, they only believed the juvenile to be guilty of the hit-and-run.

ISSUE

Are warrantless arrests of juveniles lawful when the alleged offense is not committed in the presence of the officer?

HOLDING

No. A warrantless arrest of a juvenile for a misdemeanor not committed in an officer's presence is unlawful. However, a juvenile can be taken into custody for engaging in conduct defined as juvenile delinquency.

RATIONALE

New Jersey law does not allow for a warrantless arrest for a misdemeanor unless the offense was committed in the officer's presence. The exception to this rule occurs when the suspect admits to the officer that he has committed the misdemeanor. These rules apply to both adults and juveniles. The offense that warranted the stop and subsequent search in this case was leaving the scene of an accident. The state contended the juvenile was doing so in the officers' presence when they stopped him. However, the court maintained that the driver of a vehicle must either be witnessed driving the car or leave personal identification behind indicating that he was driving the car. Neither occurred in this case. The test for the search of a person is whether or not probable cause can be established that the suspect committed a felony offense. The court contended the officers had probable cause to believe the juvenile drove the car, pointing to the juvenile's age, appearance, and location. However, the court pointed out that the officers did not have reason to believe the car was stolen. The state contended that the juvenile admitted to fighting when he accounted for his whereabouts, which warranted taking him into custody. The court denied this contention, pointing to the officers' testimony that they did not believe the juvenile. However, the court pointed to New Jersey law, which allows for an officer to take into custody a juvenile who is believed to be delinquent. Within that law, idly roaming the street at night is deemed delinquent. Therefore, the court contended that the officers had probable cause to believe the juvenile was engaging in conduct defined as juvenile delinquency. Therefore, the initial search was lawful and the subsequent search was a fruit of that search.

CASE EXCERPT

"I have no difficulty finding that the arresting officers had probable cause to believe that the juvenile was at the time of the search engaging in conduct then defined by law as juvenile delinquency."

CASE SIGNIFICANCE

In this case, the New Jersey court first bestowed some protections on juvenile defendants by prohibiting the police from taking a juvenile into custody for a misdemeanor offense unless it is committed in the officer's presence. This is analogous to case law in adult criminal court. However, the court did allow the search in this case, by holding that police can take a juvenile into custody for "juvenile delinquency," which in this case was idly roaming the streets and breaking the curfew ordinance. This is important because the officer did not even make this claim in defending his actions.

However, the court still allowed the detention and subsequent search. The New Jersey court interpreted the statute to act in loco parentis, which is consistent with other states that fashioned their juvenile code based on the parens patriae philosophy.

UNITED STATES v. BARFIELD
507 F.2d 53 (5th Cir. 1975)

FACTS
Barfield, 14, and two others were found guilty of burglarizing a bank and were committed to the custody of the attorney general for the duration of their minority. The defendants appealed on the ground that the district judge admitted into evidence statements obtained in violation of their Fifth Amendment privilege against self-incrimination. One of the defendants, Rybka, was questioned in his home in the presence of his mother. He was advised of his rights and signed a form that waived them. Rybka first denied any knowledge of the burglary, but later admitted to his participation. However, the admission came after an agent told Rybka that it would be in his best interests to tell the real story and that telling a lie might result in his being left "holding the bag." Barfield was questioned in the home in which he was living and in the presence of an adult who owned the home. Barfield was advised of his rights and signed the customary waiver. Barfield initially denied involvement in the burglary, but after 45 minutes made a full disclosure as to his part in the crime. The testimony concerning Barfield's questioning was in conflict; however, on cross-examination Barfield said that he told the truth because Mrs. Tripp, the owner of the home, advised him to do so.

ISSUE
Did the advice of federal agents create a climate of coercion such that statements made by juveniles could be deemed involuntary?

HOLDING
No. The advice given by federal agents to tell the truth did not amount to coercion; consequently, the confessions were admissible.

RATIONALE
The court contended that there may be circumstances where an admonition to the accused to tell the truth may render a subsequent statement inadmissible but

it was now clearly the law that ordinarily such an admonition does not furnish sufficient enticement to render objectionable a confession thereby obtained unless threats or promises were brought into play. The court relied on a previous case in which a government agent advised a suspect of the penalties for making a false statement. In that case, the court held there was no Fifth Amendment indisposition in this warning to tell the truth. The court contended that the same reasoning applied here. In addition, the interviews were conducted in the presence of an adult in the defendant's home. Further, the defendants waived their rights voluntarily before any questioning was begun. Consequently, the admissions were admitted.

CASE EXCERPT
"Undoubtedly, there may be circumstances when an admonition to the accused to tell the truth may render a subsequent statement inadmissible but it is now clearly the law that ordinarily such an admonition does not furnish sufficient inducement to render objectionable a confession thereby obtained unless threats or promises are brought into play."

CASE SIGNIFICANCE
In this case, the court clearly took a totality-of-the-circumstances approach in determining the admissibility of the juveniles' statements. The court drew a comparison between the officer's advice to tell the truth and the advice of officers of the penalties for a crime, given in a previous case, which was decided in favor of the state. In addition, the court pointed out that the juveniles were questioned in their homes in front of a parent or guardian. Further, the juveniles and their guardians were advised of the juveniles' rights. These two FACTS were given substantial weight by the court in making its decision. As such, the court demonstrated how factors are weighed in the totality-of-the-circumstances test. Consequently, the court determined there was not a significant amount of coercion that resulted from the officer's advice.

IN THE INTEREST OF DINO
359 So.2d 586 (La. 1978)

FACTS
After the parents of Cynthia Tew discovered her missing from home, several neighbors including Dino began searching for her. Dino, who was 13 years old,

IN THE INTEREST OF DINO *(cont.)*

indicated he had found Cynthia, critically injured with severe head wounds, behind the Tew and Dino homes. Tew subsequently died at the hospital. The police asked Dino to give a witness information statement. On this occasion, according to police, Dino was not a suspect. Dino did not implicate himself in the crime and his parents were not in the room when the statement was taken. Due to discrepancies between Dino's statement and other sources, it was agreed Dino would take a polygraph test to clear his name. Two attempts at this test were cancelled. In addition, Dino's father gave a statement that contradicted his son's. An officer testified Dino became a suspect at this time. The day after Dino's father gave a statement Dino awoke after a bad dream about himself and the victim. Dino's mother called the investigating officer and provided the information. She requested they speak with Dino after her husband returned from work. The officer insisted she bring Dino in for questioning. She left a message with her husband's work and unsuccessfully attempted to call a lawyer. Upon their arrival, an officer took Dino into a room and his mother was kept in a separate room. The officers did not ask if she wanted to be present. She was not told that her son was a suspect or informed of his rights. According to the testimony, Dino was neither told he was free to leave nor required to remain for the four to eight minutes he was in the room with the officers. He was read his rights and had them explained to him. According to the officers, he waived them verbally and in writing. He then gave an oral inculpatory statement. Dino later testified that he did not receive an explanation of his rights and did not understand the paper he signed. In addition, a psychologist testified that Dino could not have understood his rights in the language in which they were written, but could have comprehended them in simpler terms. After the confession, the officer informed Dino's mother of what had transpired and informed her that she was required to sign the waiver her son had signed. She signed it without reading it.

ISSUE

Was the defendant's waiver of his rights voluntarily, knowingly, and intelligently made?

HOLDING

No. In order for the state to meet its heavy burden of demonstrating that a waiver is made knowingly and intelligently, it must affirmatively show that a juvenile engaged in a meaningful consultation with an attorney or an informed parent, guardian, or other adult interested in his or her welfare before waiving the rights to counsel or privilege against self-incrimination.

RATIONALE

The state contended that the Miranda warnings did not come into play in this case because the youth was brought in for questioning voluntarily by his mother. However, the defendant was the primary suspect. In addition, he did not act voluntarily when he was brought in by his mother. Further, he was placed in a room with two policemen, without counsel, parent, or friends. These factors, taken with the fact that he had no prior involvement with the justice system, created an aura that would lead a reasonable person to conclude he was not free to leave. As for the waiver of Miranda rights, the court took a totality-of-the-circumstances approach. In this case, it was clear Dino had no more knowledge than any other 13-year-old of his rights. In addition, he was questioned without an adult, before the filing of charges, without being told he was a suspect at the police station. Therefore, the court concluded that the state had not met its burden of proving the waiver of rights was knowingly and intelligently made. In addition, the court illustrated this could have been different had the juvenile been allowed to consult with his mother or an attorney. The court pointed to Pennsylvania, Indiana, and Georgia, where adult consultation is mandated.

CASE EXCERPT

"Because most juveniles are not mature enough to understand their rights and are not competent to exercise them, the concepts of fundamental fairness embodied in the Declaration of Independence of our constitution require that juveniles not be permitted to waive constitutional rights on their own."

CASE SIGNIFICANCE

The Louisiana court applied the totality-of-the-circumstances test in determining whether the juvenile made a voluntary waiver of his rights. However, the importance of this case lies in the court's decision that the protections of *Miranda* were applicable. Normally a suspect who comes to the police department voluntarily and makes a statement is not in custody; therefore, *Miranda* does not apply. However, the court pointed out that the juvenile was brought in by his mother, who was subsequently barred from the room.

In addition, the 13-year-old juvenile was placed in a room alone with several officers and asked to understand a Miranda rights form. In examining all of the factors in this case, the court pointed to the juvenile's age, the absence of his mother or counsel, the lack of explanation of his rights, and multiple officers in a closed room to illustrate that no juvenile would feel free to leave, and therefore he should be afforded the protections of the court.

FARE v. MICHAEL C.
442 U.S. 707 (1979)

FACTS
Michael C. was implicated in the murder of Robert Yeager. The murder occurred during a robbery of the victim's home on January 19, 1976. A small truck registered in the name of the respondent's mother was identified as having been near the Yeager home at the time of the killing, and a young man matching the respondent's description was seen by witnesses near the truck and near the home shortly before Yeager was murdered. On the basis of this information, police took the respondent into custody at approximately 6:30 p.m. on February 4. The respondent was 16 and a half years old at that time, and on probation to the juvenile court. He had been on probation since the age of twelve. Approximately one year earlier he had served a term in a youth corrections camp under the supervision of the juvenile court. He had a record of several previous offenses. Upon his arrival at the station house two police officers began to interrogate him. The officers and the respondent were the only people in the room during the interrogation. The conversation was tape-recorded. One of the officers initiated the interview by informing the respondent that he had been brought in for questioning in relation to a murder. The officer fully advised him of his Miranda rights. An exchange then occurred during which the officers made sure the respondent knew his rights and the crime he was being questioned about. The respondent indicated he would talk without a lawyer, but requested to see his probation officer. The officers told the respondent they would not get his probation officer, but that he had a right to an attorney. The respondent indicated he would speak to the officers without an attorney and proceeded to answer questions put to him by the officers. He made statements and drew sketches that incriminated him in the Yeager murder. Largely on the basis of the respondent's

incriminating statements, probation authorities filed a petition in juvenile court alleging that the respondent had murdered Robert Yeager, and that he should therefore be adjudged a ward of the juvenile court. The respondent thereupon moved to suppress the statements and sketches he gave the police during the interrogation. He alleged that the statements had been obtained in violation of *Miranda* in that his request to see his probation officer at the outset of the questioning constituted an invocation of his Fifth Amendment right to remain silent, just as if he had requested the assistance of an attorney. Accordingly, the respondent argued that since the interrogation did not cease until he had a chance to confer with his probation officer, the statements and sketches could not be admitted against him in juvenile court proceedings. In support of his suppression motion, the respondent called his probation officer, Charles P. Christiansen, as a witness. Christiansen testified that he had instructed the respondent that if at any time he had a concern with his family, or ever had police contact, he should get in touch with his probation officer immediately. The witness stated that on a previous occasion, when respondent had police contact and subsequently failed to communicate with Christiansen, he had reprimanded him. This testimony, the respondent argued, indicated that when he asked for his probation officer, he was in fact asserting his right to remain silent in the face of further questioning.

ISSUE
Is the request by a juvenile probationer to see his or her probation officer during questioning the same as a request for the assistance of an attorney, thus invoking the Fifth Amendment right to remain silent?

HOLDING
No. The request by a juvenile probationer during police questioning to see his or her probation officer after having received the Miranda warnings by the police is not equivalent to asking for a lawyer, and therefore is not considered an assertion of the right to remain silent.

RATIONALE
"The rule established by the Court in *Miranda* is clear. In order to use statements obtained during custodial interrogation of the accused, the State must warn the accused prior to such questioning of his right to remain silent and of his right to have counsel, retained or appointed, present during interrogation. The California

FARE v. MICHAEL C. *(cont.)*

court in this case, however, has significantly extended this rule by providing that a request by a juvenile for his probation officer has the same effect as a request for an attorney. Based on that court's belief that the probation officer occupies a position as a trusted guardian figure in the minor's life that would make it normal for the minor to turn to the officer when apprehended by the police, and based as well on the state-law requirement that the officer represents the interest of the juvenile, the California court found that consultation with a probation officer fulfilled the role for the juvenile that consultation with an attorney does in general, acting as a protective to dispel the compulsion inherent in custodial surroundings."

The per se aspect of *Miranda* was, however, based on the unique role the lawyer plays in the adversary system of criminal justice in this country. The Court contended that a probation officer is not in the same posture with regard to either the accused or the system of justice as a whole. In this case, the probation officer had the responsibility for filing the petition alleging wrongdoing by the juvenile and seeking to have him taken into the custody of the juvenile court. It was the probation officer who filed the petition, and it was the acting chief of probation for the state of California, a probation officer, who was the petitioner in the US Supreme Court. The fact that a relationship of trust and cooperation between a probation officer and a juvenile might exist, however, does not indicate that the probation officer is capable of rendering effective legal advice sufficient to protect the juvenile's rights during interrogation by the police, or of providing the other services rendered by a lawyer.

If it were otherwise, a juvenile's request for almost anyone he considered trustworthy enough to give him reliable advice would trigger the rigid rule of *Miranda*. Since a probation officer does not fulfill the important role in protecting the rights of the accused juvenile that an attorney plays, the Court declines to find that the request for the probation officer is tantamount to the request for an attorney. This totality-of-the-circumstances approach is adequate to determine whether there has been a waiver even where interrogation of juveniles is involved. Further, no special factors indicated that the respondent was unable to understand the nature of his actions. He was a 16-and-a-half-year-old juvenile with considerable experience with the police. He had a record of several arrests. He had served time in a youth camp, and he had been on probation for several years. He was under the full-time supervision of probation authorities. There was no indication that he was of insufficient intelligence to understand the rights he was waiving, or what the consequences of that waiver would be. He was not worn down by improper interrogation tactics or lengthy questioning or by trickery or deceit. The Court concluded, rather, that whether the statements, obtained during an interrogation of a juvenile who has asked to see his probation officer, but who has not asked to consult an attorney or expressly asserted his right to remain silent, are admissible on the basis of waiver, remains a question to be resolved on the totality of the circumstances surrounding the interrogation.

CASE EXCERPT

"Where a conflict between the minor and the law arises, the probation officer can be neither neutral nor in the minor's corner."

CASE SIGNIFICANCE

The importance of this case is that the Supreme Court overturned the California court's decision that a probation officer is analogous to a parent or an attorney. Previous court decisions have equated a juvenile's request to see his or her parent or guardian as equivalent to that of a request to see an attorney. The courts have justified this on the basis of the juvenile's age and sophistication. However, in this case the Court clearly distinguished between asking for the assistance of a trusted person and asking for an attorney. The ramifications of this decision have caused some states to allow questioning of a juvenile without a parent and in some cases denying a juvenile's request for a parent. In this case, the Court did not rule on that issue, but did allude to it in its rationale. In addition, in this case the Court clearly defined a juvenile probation officer as a peace officer, not an advocate for the juveniles under his or her supervision. Furthermore, the Court again reaffirmed early decisions to utilize the totality-of-the-circumstances approach in determining the voluntariness of a confession.

UNITED STATES v. SECHRIST

640 F.2d 81 (7th Cir. 1981)

FACTS

Employees of the Menominee Tribal Court on the Menominee Indian Reservation in northeastern

Wisconsin discovered that a break-in had occurred the previous evening at the Tribal Court Clerk's Office. During the course of the investigation the police interviewed Sechrist, a juvenile, who had previously worked at the courthouse. Sechrist denied any knowledge of the burglary and any knowledge of where money was kept. He also told the agents his fingerprints would not be found on items from inside a file cabinet that had been pried open and vandalized. Sechrist's fingerprints were taken and compared with those found on items lying on the floor in the clerk's office the morning following the break-in. It was determined that eight of the latent prints were those of the defendant. An information was filed charging Sechrist with the burglary and a warrant was issued for his arrest. In addition, the government filed a certification that no state jurisdiction existed. On that day, Sechrist was a resident of a facility operated by the state of Wisconsin for delinquent children, where he had been committed for another matter. A detainer was forwarded to the facility and Sechrist signed it the following day requesting a speedy trial. A few days later, deputy marshals took custody of Sechrist. Motions to dismiss the information and suppress the fingerprints were filed at the initial hearing. The court denied these motions and Sechrist was found delinquent.

ISSUE

Can a juvenile's fingerprints be taken based on less than probable cause if the juvenile is legally detained?

HOLDING

Yes. Probable cause was not required to take fingerprints because the juvenile was already in lawful custody at the time of the magistrate's order.

RATIONALE

The government conceded that there was not sufficient evidence before the magistrate to constitute probable cause. Any analysis of a Fourth Amendment claim involves a potential violation at two different levels: the seizure of the person necessary to bring him or her into contact with the government agents and the subsequent search for and seizure of the evidence. When the agent took Sechrist's fingerprints, he was incarcerated awaiting trial for another matter. Because he was in custody, there could be no Fourth Amendment violation with respect to the first level, the seizure of the person. As for the second claim, the Fourth Amendment tests a search or seizure under a standard of reasonableness,

in which the need to search or seize is balanced against the invasion into one's privacy that the search or seizure entails. The government did have grounds to suspect Sechrist was the thief, although probable cause could not be established. A person's reasonable expectation of privacy and the process of the search and seizure measure the degree of invasion of one's privacy. The taking of fingerprints does not entail a significant invasion of one's privacy. Consequently, the minimal burden imposed on Sechrist did not infringe his Fourth Amendment rights. Although the Federal Juvenile Delinquency Act invests greater rights in a juvenile than in an adult it does not require probable cause with respect to photographs and fingerprints.

CASE EXCERPT

"The taking of a person's fingerprints simply does not entail a significant invasion of one's privacy."

CASE SIGNIFICANCE

The importance of this case is twofold. The court first distinguished between juveniles in custody and those who are not, in terms of the expectation of privacy the juvenile has. The court determined that juveniles in custody for another matter have no reasonable expectation of privacy with regard to their fingerprints or photographs, which they have already had to produce for that other matter. In addition, the court also held that the invasion of privacy required to obtain a juvenile's fingerprints was not significant. Therefore, the court allowed the taking of a juvenile's fingerprints without first establishing probable cause.

NEW JERSEY v. T.L.O.

468 U.S. 1214 (1984)

FACTS

Upon discovering the respondent, then a 14-year-old freshman, and her companion smoking cigarettes in a school lavatory in violation of a school rule, a teacher at a New Jersey high school took them to the principal's office, where they met with the assistant vice principal. When the respondent, in response to the assistant vice principal's questioning, denied that she had been smoking and claimed that she did not smoke at all, the assistant vice principal demanded to see her purse. Upon opening the purse, he found a pack of cigarettes and also noticed a package of cigarette rolling papers that are commonly associated with the use of marijuana.

NEW JERSEY v. T.L.O. *(cont.)*

He then proceeded to search the purse thoroughly and found some marijuana, a pipe, plastic bags, a fairly substantial amount of money, an index card containing a list of students who owed the respondent money, and two letters that implicated her in marijuana dealing. Thereafter, the state brought delinquency charges against the respondent in juvenile court. After denying the respondent's motion to suppress the evidence found in her purse, the juvenile court held that the Fourth Amendment applied to searches by school officials but that the search in question was a reasonable one, and adjudged the respondent to be delinquent.

ISSUE

Do public school officials need probable cause or a warrant in order to search juveniles?

HOLDING

No. Public school officials do not need a warrant or probable cause before conducting a search. For a search to be valid, all they need are reasonable grounds to suspect that the search will produce evidence that the student has violated either the law or the rules of the school.

RATIONALE

In determining whether the search at issue in this case violated the Fourth Amendment, the Court was faced initially with the question whether that amendment's prohibition of unreasonable searches and seizures applies to searches conducted by public school officials. The propositions that the Fourth Amendment applies to the states through the Fourteenth Amendment and that the actions of public school officials are subject to the limits placed on state action by the Fourteenth Amendment might appear sufficient to answer the suggestion that the Fourth Amendment does not proscribe unreasonable searches by school officials. The Court contended that today's public school officials do not merely exercise authority voluntarily conferred on them by individual parents; rather, they act in furtherance of publicly mandated educational and disciplinary policies. In carrying out searches and other disciplinary functions pursuant to such policies, school officials act as representatives of the state, not merely as surrogates for the parents, and they cannot claim the parents' immunity from the strictures of the Fourth Amendment. To hold that the Fourth Amendment applied to searches conducted by school authorities was

only to begin the inquiry into the standards governing such searches. Although the underlying command of the Fourth Amendment was always that searches and seizures be reasonable, what is reasonable depends on the context within which a search takes place. The determination of the standard of reasonableness governing any specific class of searches requires balancing the need to search against the invasion that the search entails. To receive the protection of the Fourth Amendment, an expectation of privacy must be one that society is prepared to recognize as legitimate: "The Court contends maintaining order in the classroom has never been easy, but in recent years, school disorder has often taken particularly ugly forms: drug use and violent crime in the schools have become major social problems. It is evident that the school setting requires some easing of the restrictions to which searches by public authorities are ordinarily subject. The warrant requirement, in particular, is unsuited to the school environment: Requiring a teacher to obtain a warrant before searching a child suspected of an infraction of school rules or of the criminal law would unduly interfere with the maintenance of the swift and informal disciplinary procedures needed in the schools."

Consequently, the Court held school officials need not obtain a warrant before searching a student who is under their authority. Rather, the legality of a search of a student should depend simply on the reasonableness, under all the circumstances, of the search. Determining the reasonableness of any search involves a twofold inquiry: First, one must consider whether the action was justified at its inception; second, one must determine whether the search as actually conducted was reasonably related in scope to the circumstances which justified the interference in the first place. Under ordinary circumstances, a search of a student by a teacher or other school official will be justified at its inception when there are reasonable grounds for suspecting that the search will turn up evidence that the student has violated or is violating either the law or the rules of the school. Such a search will be permissible in its scope when the measures adopted are reasonably related to the objectives of the search and not excessively intrusive in light of the age and sex of the student and the nature of the infraction. The conclusion that the decision to open T.L.O.'s purse was reasonable brought the Court to the question of the further search for marijuana once the pack of cigarettes was located. The suspicion upon which the search for marijuana was founded was provided when the vice principal observed a package of rolling papers in the purse as he removed the pack of cigarettes. Although T.L.O. did not dispute the reasonableness of the vice principal's belief that the rolling papers indicated the presence of marijuana, she did contend that the scope of the search conducted exceeded permissible bounds when he seized and read certain letters that implicated T.L.O. in drug dealing. This argument, too, was unpersuasive. The discovery of the rolling papers concededly gave rise to a reasonable suspicion that T.L.O. was carrying marijuana as well as cigarettes in her purse. This suspicion justified further exploration of T.L.O.'s purse, which turned up more evidence of drug-related activities: a pipe, a number of plastic bags of the type commonly used to store marijuana, a small quantity of marijuana, and a fairly substantial amount of money. Under these circumstances, it was not unreasonable to extend the search to a separate zippered compartment of the purse, and a search of that compartment revealed evidence inferring that T.L.O. was involved in marijuana trafficking was substantial enough to justify examining the letters to determine whether they contained any further evidence. In short, the Court could not conclude that the search for marijuana was unreasonable in any respect.

CASE EXCERPT

"Under ordinary circumstances, a search of a student by a teacher or other school official will be justified at its inception when there are reasonable grounds for suspecting that the search will turn up evidence that the student has violated or is violating either the law or the rules of the school."

CASE SIGNIFICANCE

With this case the Court significantly enhanced the power of school officials, and subsequently law enforcement, in lowering the burden school officials must meet prior to searching a student's belongings. School officials can now search a student's belongings if they have reason to believe the student is engaged in behavior which is in violation of the law or school rules. As in the past, the Court utilized the parens patriae philosophy to justify its decision by indicating that school officials are entrusted with their students' safety and well-being while they are at school. In addition, the Court maintained that some constitutional requirements would interfere with the need for swift and informal discipline in the school setting. However, this case also has implications for law enforcement, as

they are allowed to utilize evidence seized by the school officials in their own criminal investigations. It is now common to find police officers assigned to schools for the purposes of protecting the students and improving police and youth relations. Consequently, the police often will have evidence of a crime, seized in a search by school officials, turned over to them even though their own burden of probable cause was not met.

UNITED STATES v. BERNARD S.
795 F.2d 749 (9th Cir. 1986)

FACTS

On May 3, 1985, an altercation occurred between Bernard and Goode in a house on the San Carlos Apache Indian reservation. Goode received head injuries which required hospitalization. On May 14, an agent questioned Bernard at the police department on the reservation. Bernard's mother and a police lieutenant, who both spoke Apache, were also present. Prior to questioning the agent advised Bernard of his Miranda rights and explained each right to Bernard and his mother. Bernard acknowledged he understood his rights. Bernard waived his rights and signed a written waiver form. Bernard never indicated that he did not understand his rights, although he asked his mother and the police lieutenant to explain a few items in Apache. However, these translations were made after the rights were read and waived, and did not involve those rights. The agent questioned Bernard, who responded in English. Bernard made incriminating statements indicating he had assaulted Goode. At the trial, the appellant objected to the government's use of his statements on the ground that they were obtained involuntarily and in violation of his Miranda rights. The motion was denied and Bernard was convicted.

ISSUE

Were statements made by the juvenile admissible in court?

HOLDING

Yes. Language difficulties in this case did not preclude a finding that the minor understood his Miranda rights and voluntarily waived them. He stated that he understood his rights and spoke primarily in English during the questioning by government agents. Although he occasionally spoke Apache with his mother and the officer to clarify some items of uncertainty, he

UNITED STATES v. BERNARD S. *(cont.)*

displayed no evidence of being unable or unwilling to communicate in English.

RATIONALE

To be valid, a waiver of Miranda rights must be voluntarily, knowingly, and intelligently made. Whether there has been a valid waiver depends on the totality of the circumstances, including the background, experience, and conduct of the defendant. Age and language difficulties are components of the totality test. In addition, the burden of showing a valid waiver is on the prosecutor. Although the defendant testified that he did not read or write English, he did testify that he studied English through the seventh grade and that he answered the agent's questions in English. In addition, the agent testified that Bernard indicated he understood each of his rights and the wording of them. The agent also testified that Bernard's mother was made aware of his rights. At no time during the questioning did Bernard indicate he did not understand his rights. In addition, the evidence does not support Bernard's claim that age had a bearing on the waiver of his Miranda rights. Consequently, the evidence seems to indicate Bernard made a voluntary, knowing, and intelligent waiver of his rights.

CASE EXCERPT

"Despite the language difficulties encountered by the appellant, the evidence seems to indicate that he understood his rights and voluntarily, knowingly, and intelligently waived them."

CASE SIGNIFICANCE

The significance of this case lies in the court's decision to again look at the totality of the circumstances in determining whether a juvenile made a knowing and voluntary waiver of his Miranda rights. Although the court did acknowledge the possibility that the juvenile did not speak and understand English well, the juvenile did speak some English during the interrogation and acknowledged that he understood his rights. Further, the juvenile's mother was present for the entire time of the questioning and understood what her child's rights were. Consequently, the officers had no reason to believe they were coercing the juvenile to admit the allegation. In effect, the officers were acting in good faith. Given all of the factors involved in the interrogation, the court ruled the officer's actions were in accordance with the law.

LANES v. STATE

767 S.W.2d 789 (Tex. Crim. App. 1989)

FACTS

Pursuant to a consent order from the juvenile court authorizing the taking of Lanes's fingerprints, a police officer arrested Lanes at his high school and transported him to a police station where he took his fingerprints. The fingerprints linked Lanes to the burglary of a home for which he was subsequently convicted and sentenced to 20 years in prison.

ISSUE

Does the Fourth Amendment of the US Constitution, applicable to the states through the Fourteenth Amendment, apply to the arrest of a child?

HOLDING

Yes. Police officers must have probable cause or a warrant to make an arrest in juvenile proceedings.

RATIONALE

In reviewing the history of juvenile proceedings the court determined that the Supreme Court seemed to utilize a comparative analysis wherein the purposes and goals of the juvenile system were compared to the particular right being asserted. The Supreme Court balanced the function that a constitutional or procedural right served against its impact or degree of impairment on the unique process of the juvenile court and then factored in consideration of the degree of realistic success the juvenile system had obtained. This court used the balancing test in this case. The Texas Juvenile Justice System contains rehabilitation of the child and community protection as its pervasive and uniform themes. The Fourth Amendment provides that all persons shall be secure in their persons against unreasonable searches and seizures. In addition, probable cause has typically been the enforcer of these protections. In this case, the balancing of the best interest of the child was weighed against the best interest of the community. In the past, law enforcement officers could take children into custody if they felt it would be in their best interests. In this case, the court attempted to provide the child with the treatment model of the juvenile system and the procedural safeguards of the adult system. Therefore, it extended the probable cause requirement to juvenile proceedings. In the present case, the officers had an order to take the child's fingerprints, which was lawfully based on probable cause. However, this order did not allow for an arrest of the juvenile. Therefore, absent the probable cause for an arrest, the arrest and subsequent taking of the child's fingerprints were inadmissible.

CASE EXCERPT

"The probable cause requirement rests on the principal that a true balance between an individual—whether youth or adult—and the government depends on the recognition and respect of 'the right to be let alone—the most comprehensive of rights and the right most valued by civilized men.' Today we are proudly able to afford such a right to juveniles."

CASE SIGNIFICANCE

In this case, the court acted on behalf of juvenile defendants by requiring that the police establish probable cause prior to making an arrest. This case is important because it represents the trend toward criminalization in the juvenile court. Although the court acted on behalf of this juvenile defendant by safeguarding his rights, the court also made the juvenile procedural law more formal, like its adult criminal counterpart. Other states have formalized their juvenile law in this fashion in their attempts to move away from the child-saver movement that initiated the juvenile court toward a more formalized quasi-criminal court that handles juveniles. In addition, the court also distinguished between an order for fingerprints and an arrest warrant. The court contended the taking of fingerprints was analogous to a search, not an arrest or seizure. In so holding, the court would have had the officer simply take the fingerprints at the juvenile's high school.

SMITH v. STATE

623 So.2d 369 (Ala. Cr. App. 1992)

FACTS

Three black males stole a car and drove by a home, firing shots into a group of people gathered on the front porch. One person was killed and another injured. After the police were notified, two officers attempted to stop a car occupied by three black males and matching the description which was broadcast. The car made an illegal lane change and sped away when the officers pursued it with their lights on. Several blocks away the car stopped and the occupants ran from the car. Smith, a juvenile, was apprehended about 10 blocks from the

scene of the shooting by another officer on the lookout for the suspects. The officer also found a sawed-off shotgun near the abandoned car that had been stolen earlier. In addition, a fingerprint of Smith's was found on the car. At the trial, one of the codefendants testified that Smith had fired the gun at the victims. Smith testified that he knew the car was stolen when they found it, and that he and one of the codefendants had fired into the group on the porch. He further testified that he did not intend to hurt anyone. Smith contended that his statement at trial should not be allowed into evidence because the police did not comply with a rule that indicates a child taken into custody must not only be informed of his or her Miranda rights but also that he or she has the right to communicate with his or her parents or guardian and that if necessary reasonable means will be provided for him or her to do so. According to the testimony at the suppression hearing, Smith was advised of his rights and asked if he wanted to speak with anyone. Smith indicated he would like to speak with his grandmother. The officer, on cross-examination, indicated he did ask about the car prior to calling the defendant's grandmother.

ISSUE

Was the juvenile's request for his grandmother during questioning the same as a request for legal counsel?

HOLDING

Yes. Statements regarding the shootings and the automobile theft were illegally obtained because the juvenile had invoked his right to remain silent with his request to see his grandmother.

RATIONALE

Before an accused's confession can be received into evidence, the state must show that the statement was made voluntarily and that the suspect was read and understood his or her Miranda rights. In addition, the state must show that the juvenile was told he had the right to communicate with his parent or guardian. The court relied on an earlier case that held that a request to speak with a grandmother is the equivalent of requesting counsel. In some cases, the evidence illegally obtained has been allowed if the error was harmless beyond a reasonable doubt. However, in this case the only evidence linking Smith to the crime was the testimony of a codefendant with an interest in the case, and a fingerprint, which did not link him to the shooting. Consequently, the statements obtained subsequent

SMITH v. STATE *(cont.)*

to Smith's request to speak with his grandmother were inadmissible.

CASE EXCERPT

"Receipt of an illegally obtained confession is harmless if the court can find, based on the circumstances of the case, that admittance of the confession was harmless beyond a reasonable doubt...We will not say that the error was harmless beyond a reasonable doubt."

CASE SIGNIFICANCE

This case is important because it showed that the court was willing to equate a parent with counsel. Although the Supreme Court seemed to move away from this in *Fare v. Michael C.,* the fact that it did not specifically hold that a request to speak with a parent was not equivalent to a juvenile's invocation of his or her Fifth Amendment rights left the door open for the states to decide for themselves. Consequently, many states still distinguish between the juvenile and adult systems by allowing juveniles to have a parent or guardian present during any questioning either by request or as standard procedure. In addition, this court recognized that a grandmother could fulfill the same role as a parent and in many cases often does.

IN RE J.M.

619 A.2d 497 (D.C. Ct. App. 1992)

FACTS

A detective and a team of officers were at the bus station. Their assignment was to question, and presumably search if they had cause or obtained consent, passengers arriving in or passing through Washington, DC, from New York City. A bus arrived, and after the driver announced a 10-minute rest stop, the detective and two other officers boarded the bus dressed in civilian attire. Using the bus loudspeaker, the detective announced their identity and purpose. After questioning several passengers, the detective approached J.M., aged 14, who was seated three-quarters of the way to the rear next to a window. The detective introduced himself and asked J.M.'s point of origin and destination and if he could see his bus ticket. He also inquired if the youth was carrying drugs or weapons. J.M. replied that he was not. The detective asked if he could search J.M.'s bag. J.M. consented, and the search revealed nothing. The detective asked if J.M. had any drugs or weapons

on his person. J.M. replied negatively, and the officer asked if he minded if he patted him down. J.M. turned toward the officer and raised his arms while remaining seated. The detective patted him down and felt a hard object on his right side next to his rib cage. He lifted the shirt and discovered a bag containing crack cocaine taped to J.M.'s body. J.M. was placed under arrest. He acknowledged consenting to the search of his bag, but denied giving consent to pat him down. He indicated that the officer had just started patting him down.

ISSUE

Is consent to search voluntary when given by a 14-year-old traveling alone on a bus?

HOLDING

Yes. The nature of the consent must be determined by the totality of the circumstances in which it occurred. Further, the court must examine all the issues surrounding the consent when it is given without the assistance of counsel.

RATIONALE

When examining the nature of a search and whether or not voluntary consent was given, the totality-of-the-circumstances test is used. The characteristics of the accused become relevant, and may be decisive in these cases. The issue that troubled the court in this case was the defendant's age. However, the court concluded that the special vulnerability of juveniles to intimidation by figures of authority did not justify a presumptive rule invalidating consent of juveniles. J.M. was not seized in this case; however, it remanded the case with instructions that the consent issue must be decided. In doing so, they held that the issue of age must be addressed by the trial judge, which it was not in this case.

CASE EXCERPT

"The crucial test for determining whether a person has been seized is whether, taking into account all of the circumstances surrounding the encounter, the police conduct would 'have communicated to a *reasonable person* that he was not at liberty to ignore the police presence and go about his business.'"

CASE SIGNIFICANCE

This case is important because the court seemingly allowed a 14-year-old to consent to a search absent a parent or an attorney. In examining the totality of the circumstances of the case the court did not find that the juvenile, who was on a bus against a window, was legally seized by the officer's blocking him in his seat. This is significant because the court effectively held that this was equivalent to an officer approaching a juvenile walking on the street. Despite the fact that the court opened the door to allowing consent by a 14-year-old, it did remand the case for reexamination on whether a juvenile at that age can consent.

IN THE INTEREST OF J.L., A CHILD

623 So.2d 860 (Fla. App. 1993)

FACTS
J.L., a juvenile, was charged under petition with delinquency for carrying a concealed firearm. At the suppression hearing the police officer testified that he arrested J.L. after he observed him walking at a normal pace toward the area where a burglary had recently been reported. J.L. was wearing a large coat, which the officer thought was strange, because it was warm that night. The officer asked J.L. to come over to him. According to the officer, J.L. answered his questions truthfully and provided a reasonable explanation of where he was coming from and going. J.L.'s hands were out of his pockets and the officer did not notice a bulge anywhere on J.L.'s clothing. After J.L. answered the officer's questions he was subjected to a pat-down search that yielded a pistol. J.L. was taken into custody.

ISSUE
Does the mere presence of a minor in the area of a reported crime warrant a police investigatory stop?

HOLDING
No. A minor's presence in an area in which a burglary had recently been reported, without other circumstances, does not warrant an investigatory stop and pat-down search of the minor by the police.

RATIONALE
The FACTS in this case did not justify a stop and search. The court contended that an officer may briefly detain and question an individual when that individual's behavior creates a reasonable suspicion of criminal activity. In addition, an officer may conduct a pat-down search when he or she has a reasonable belief that the suspect may be armed. However,

barring reasonable suspicion, police do not have the right to stop and frisk individuals just because they happen to be present in a high crime neighborhood. Consequently, the stop and subsequent search in this case was invalid based on the FACTS to which the officer testified.

CASE EXCERPT
"It is well settled that stopping an individual simply for being present in a particular location, such as a high crime area, is not permitted."

CASE SIGNIFICANCE
This case is important because it extended some of the safeguards of the criminal procedural law to juvenile suspects. The court essentially applied *Terry v. Ohio* (392 U.S. 1 (1968)), which allows officers to detain suspects when they have reason to believe he or she has or is going to commit a crime, and *Sibron v. New York* (392 U.S. 40 (1968)) in which the Supreme Court ruled that officers must have reasonable cause to believe that suspects they pat down are armed. In this latter case, the court upheld the investigatory detention of the juvenile, but not the pat-down search. The court pointed to the officer's own testimony which did not appear to allow for any conclusion that the suspect was in fact armed. In addition, the suspect was cooperative and able to provide legitimate answers to all of the officer's questions.

IN THE INTEREST OF S.A.W.

499 N.W.2d 739 (Iowa App. 1993)

FACTS
Police officers were dispatched to investigate a report of a possible fight in progress. As the officers neared the scene, the dispatcher indicated there had been several reports of gunshots. The officers turned the corner onto a narrow road near the scene and saw a car approaching. The officers stopped the car for investigatory purposes. The officers crowded behind the car with their guns drawn and asked the driver and S.A.W., a juvenile, to get out of the car and place their hands on the hood. An officer patted down the driver and S.A.W. and discovered that S.A.W. had a purse under her jacket. The officer inquired if she had any weapons in the purse; S.A.W. did not respond. The officer felt the purse and discovered a "heavy, semi-large medium style object," which he suspected was a gun. The officer

IN THE INTEREST OF S.A.W. *(cont.)*

asked S.A.W. what was in the purse, but she refused to respond. The officer opened the purse and found a gun. The state filed a petition alleging that S.A.W. had committed a delinquent act.

ISSUE

Based upon reasonable suspicion, are officers justified in stopping a vehicle and searching all occupants and their possessions in an area where a crime is alleged to have taken place?

HOLDING

Yes. Police officers in this case had reasonable suspicion to believe that criminal activity was afoot, and therefore, they had reasonable cause to stop the adult driver and S.A.W.

RATIONALE

S.A.W. contended that the police lacked probable cause to stop her and conduct a pat-down search. In addition, she contended the conduct of the officers was so intrusive as to be tantamount to an arrest. The court relied on *Terry v. Ohio*, which states police officers may briefly detain and frisk a person on less than probable cause. However, reasonable cause is required to permit a stop for investigatory purposes. The validity of the stop must be evaluated based on the totality of the circumstances. The court contended that the possibility of the suspects being afoot, coupled with the report of gunfire, and their proximity to the location of the crime constituted reasonable cause to stop the defendant. In addition, due to the report of a gun being discharged, the officer's actions were not as intrusive as S.A.W. contends. The alleged presence of a firearm constituted a threat to public safety.

CASE EXCERPT

"When an officer is justified in believing that the individual whose suspicious behavior [the officer] is investigating at close range is armed and presently dangerous to the officer, it would appear to be clearly unreasonable to deny the officer the power to take necessary measures to determine whether the person is in fact carrying a weapon and to neutralize the threat of physical harm."

CASE SIGNIFICANCE

In this case, the court elevated the public safety issue over that of individual rights. The court applied the totality-of-the-circumstances test to determine the validity of a detention and subsequent search. First, the court applied an adult case, *Terry v. Ohio*, which allows the investigatory stop of an individual if officers believe the individual might be engaged in or attempting to commit a crime. In this case, the officers had a report of a crime in progress and the juveniles were in the area where the crime allegedly occurred. This constituted reasonable suspicion. Second, the court again relied on *Terry*, which allows for a limited pat-down search of a suspect if the officers have reason to believe the suspect might be armed. *S.A.W.* is significant because the court allowed the mere report of a crime involving a firearm and the suspect's presence in the area to be grounds for a pat-down search. The court pointed to the overwhelming need for public safety as their rationale in support of their finding. In addition, the fact that the suspects were in an automobile, which is inherently mobile, and not responding to the officer's questioning, thereby arousing the officer's suspicion, were likely of some importance in the court's decision. Thus, the court applied adult criminal procedure to juvenile matters.

IN RE STARVON J.

29 Cal.Rptr.2d 471 (Cal. App. 1994)

FACTS

The defendant was involved in a two and one-half–hour crime spree that resulted in the murder of one person, the robberies of 12 people, and the assault of one person with a handgun. When officers arrived at the final crime scene they saw Starvon J., aged 15, walking and crying. She appeared upset and waved over one of the officers, who asked if there was a problem. The defendant indicated her aunt had gone to the store, she had heard some gunfire, and her aunt had not returned since. The officer obtained some information about the defendant's aunt and suggested she wait until they discerned if her aunt was hurt in the shootout. Five minutes later, an individual named Humphries joined the defendant on the sidewalk and they got into an automobile and began to drive away. The officer stopped them, but the defendant told her she had found her aunt and was leaving. They proceeded to the defendant's grandmother's home and unloaded most of the stolen items. Forty-five minutes later Humphries and the minor returned to the crime scene in another car. The defendant told another officer she had lost her ID card near the crime scene and wanted to pass through to retrieve it. The officer said he could not let her pass, but if she came back later he would help her find the card. The defendant and Humphries left. An hour later they returned, but the officer would not let them through, as the investigation was ongoing. The pair returned again and were noticed by another officer who inquired what they were doing. The defendant indicated they were looking for her ID card. While the defendant and Humphries were gone one of the victims indicated that a female matching the minor's description was in the store prior to the robbery and might be a witness. The next time the pair returned to the scene an officer questioned the defendant as to where her aunt lived. After noticing her description the officer called for backup. One of the officers conducted a field interview, but did not ask the minor to get out of the car or place her under arrest. The minor gave the officer the ID card story. The officers searched for the ID, but could not find anything. The officers decided to transport the pair to the station. At no time did the officers inquire about the robbery. In addition, the pair was not placed under arrest. An officer questioned the minor and she provided the ID card story and said she was staying with her aunt. The officers attempted to drive to where her aunt allegedly lived. However, the defendant never identified her aunt's home. In the meantime, the officers discovered that Humphries's boyfriend was one of those who had committed the robbery. The officers went to her home and impounded her car. In the car they found some stolen merchandise. The officers were still unsure of the minor's involvement, and did not place her under arrest. The next day a detective spoke with her and advised her of her rights. The minor waived her rights. The defendant then disclosed her involvement in the crime spree.

ISSUE

Was the incriminating statement by the minor voluntarily given?

HOLDING

Yes. The minor's statements were made voluntarily and there was nothing illegal about the circumstances and length of the minor's detention.

RATIONALE

The court contended that the officers acted reasonably in removing the minor from the crime scene and detaining her. The officers gave her ample time to provide them with the information of why she was in the area. In addition, they attempted to locate her ID card and aunt's home. The court contended that the

placement of the minor in the police car while this was occurring was a lawful detention, made in an effort to clear the minor of suspicion of any wrongdoing. In addition, the transportation to the station house did not amount to an arrest, because the officers did not have anywhere else to take her and she had not been cleared of any wrongdoing. The court also contended the arrest was based on probable cause. The minor was advised of her rights, which she waived. Further, the police did not use any coercive actions, which made the confession of a free and voluntary nature. Consequently, the confession and subsequent arrest were not tainted and were admissible.

CASE EXCERPT

"A voluntary statement obtained following an illegal detention is not automatically suppressed, but is admissible if it is shown that the connection between the illegality and the evidence subsequently obtained is so attenuated as to dissipate the taint."

CASE SIGNIFICANCE

Although there is no specific reference to it in the holding, the court utilized the totality-of-the-circumstances test in determining that the juvenile's confession was voluntary. The case is important because a lengthy detention of a juvenile was allowed because the officers made a good faith effort to locate the juvenile's guardian and confirm her story. A detention of this length would typically not be allowed in the adult criminal system, or would be considered an arrest; however, the different systems have different standards. In the juvenile system the state must act in loco parentis, and the court determined that the police were proceeding under that doctrine in their efforts to locate the juvenile's aunt. The court, in rendering its decision, considered that the police would have had to merely release the juvenile to the streets had they not detained her for the length of time they did. However, the court still discussed the protection of the juvenile's rights by pointing out the efforts the police made to locate the juvenile's aunt and ID card.

IN RE TYRELL J.
876 P.2d 519 (Cal. 1994)

FACTS

On May 21, 1991, Tyrell J., a juvenile, was declared a ward of the court. He was placed on probation subject to a variety of conditions, including that he submit

IN RE TYRELL J. *(cont.)*

to a search of his person and property, with or without a warrant, by any law enforcement officer, probation officer, or school official. On October 3, 1991, an officer was on patrol at a high school football game. A shooting incident involving two local gangs had occurred at a game between the two schools the previous week. Another officer advised that Tyrell J. and his two companions belonged to one of the gangs. Although the temperature was over 80 degrees, one of Tyrell J.'s friends wore a heavy quilted coat. The officer approached the trio and asked them to hold up. The officer pulled away the heavy coat revealing a large hunting knife. The officers then asked all three to walk to a fence 15 feet away. As Tyrell J. walked toward the fence an officer observed him adjust his trousers three times in the crotch area. At the fence the officer conducted a pat-down search of Tyrell J., including the crotch area. The officer felt a soft object approximately three inches in diameter and 12 inches long. The major part of this object was protruding from Tyrell J.'s pants. Although the officer did not believe the object was a weapon, he retrieved it and determined it was a bag of marijuana. The minor was petitioned into court for possession of marijuana.

ISSUE

When a police officer conducts an otherwise illegal search of a minor, may the fruits of the search be properly admitted into evidence against the minor if the minor was subject to a probation search condition of which the officer was unaware?

HOLDING

Yes. When subject to a valid condition of probation which requires submission to warrantless searches by any law enforcement officer, no reasonable expectation of privacy exists over a cache of marijuana in a minor's pants.

RATIONALE

The Fourth Amendment prohibits unreasonable searches and seizures by police officers and other government officials. This constitutional proscription is enforced by the exclusionary rule, which prohibits admission at trial of any evidence obtained in violation of the Fourth Amendment. When a warrantless search is conducted the burden to show cause rests with the government. The Supreme Court has not ruled on the constitutionality of juvenile probation search

conditions. In addition, it has never ruled on the admissibility of evidence seized when the officer was unaware of a probationer's search condition. When a juvenile is declared a ward of the court the court fashions the conditions, taking into account the circumstances of the crime and also the juvenile's social history. This is contrary to how the criminal court operates when sentencing an adult. Therefore, the court contended that a condition that may be unconstitutional for an adult probationer may be permissible for a juvenile under the supervision of the court. Further, the adult defendant may refuse probation terms, whereas the juvenile may not, as the terms are fashioned to rehabilitate that juvenile. Therefore, the court had to determine if Tyrell J. had a reasonable expectation of privacy over the marijuana that was seized. As a general rule adult probationers have a reduced expectation of privacy. The intrusions by the government are based on legitimate government demands. The court contended that juveniles observe this reduced protection as well. The court drew a comparison with other common terms of probation, such as drug testing and school attendance. Therefore, a juvenile probationer does not have a reasonable expectation of privacy when he or she is subject to a search condition. In addition, Tyrell J. had no reason to believe that only police officers who were aware of the search condition would utilize it. Further, to restrict the search provision to only officers who were aware of it would limit the rehabilitation goal of the juvenile court. A juvenile subject to a search condition must think that all officers are going to search him or her; therefore, the condition will deter future criminal acts. In concluding, the court contended this ruling did not limit the exclusionary rule because the officer still took a chance when he seized the item, and the marijuana would have been inadmissible absent the search condition. Therefore, the rule would still deter police misconduct.

CASE EXCERPT

"As we explain, we conclude that because the minor was subject to a valid condition of probation that required him to submit to warrantless searches by 'any' law enforcement officer, he had no reasonable expectation of privacy over a cache of marijuana in his pants."

CASE SIGNIFICANCE

This case is important for several reasons. First, the court initially distinguished between the juvenile court and the adult criminal court by pointing out that adults have a choice to accept probation terms while juveniles do not, based on the premise that the juvenile court was founded on parens patriae and therefore was entrusted with rehabilitating juvenile offenders. However, the court subsequently allowed the search of the juvenile by drawing a comparison to adult probationers and the limited expectation of privacy they enjoy. Ironically, it is the conditional sentence of probation in the adult criminal system that has guided the courts in upholding the warrantless searches of adult probationers. Therefore, this court seemed to make the juvenile system more analogous to the adult criminal system. However, the court later pointed out the underpinning goal of deterrence that the courts hope to achieve by stripping probationers, either adult or juvenile, of their Fourth Amendment rights. The court contended that by deterring the youth from future criminal acts the courts were acting in a rehabilitative manner. Consequently, this case illustrated the quandary the courts are faced with when sentencing a juvenile in a system that is rehabilitative in design, while still striving to offer some protection to the community.

STATE v. SUGG
456 S.E.2d 469 (W. Va. 1995)

FACTS
A Chevron station was robbed by a young African American male. An officer dressed in civilian clothes observed the defendant approximately one-fourth of a mile from the station. The officer drew his gun and ordered Sugg to halt. Sugg fled, but was later apprehended with the assistance of other officers. The officers read Sugg his Miranda rights while he was cuffed on the ground. When the officers lifted Sugg from the ground they discovered a pistol. After Sugg was transported to the station it was determined he was only 17 years old. According to the state, the defendant told an officer he wanted to talk shortly after he arrived. Defense counsel claimed Sugg initially denied involvement in the robbery and only confessed after continued interrogation. The police interrogated Sugg after they determined his age. Sugg was presented with and signed a waiver of his rights. The officers took his statement before they called his parents. The confession was subsequently admitted at the trial. In addition, because of the seriousness of the crime Sugg was transferred to criminal court. He was convicted by a jury of robbery with the use of a firearm.

ISSUE
Was the juvenile's waiver of his Miranda rights valid in the absence of his parents?

HOLDING
Yes. A juvenile may waive his or her Miranda rights even in the absence of parents, as long as the juvenile knowingly, voluntarily, and intelligently waives such rights, viewed in the totality of the circumstances.

RATIONALE
The court recognized that the primary purpose for additional juvenile protection is the likelihood that a juvenile who commits a serious crime may be transferred to the criminal court. In addition, if it appears the primary reason for any delay is to obtain a confession from the juvenile, the confession is then inadmissible. However, at the suppression hearing the defendant did not testify and so all the evidence came from the police and Sugg's parents. Therefore the evidence suggests Sugg wanted to talk to the police without his parents or a lawyer present. In addition, when advised of his right to have a lawyer present or call his parents, he refused. Further, the entire time from transportation to the initial appearance was only two to three hours. Therefore, there was not an unreasonable delay in the defendant's detention. When the waiver of rights was examined, the court relied on the totality-of-the-circumstances test. The defendant had some encounters with the police in the past, he was 17 years old, and the police read him his rights twice. Furthermore, the police encouraged him to call his parents prior to questioning. Despite this the defendant waived his rights and confessed. Almost immediately he was taken before a magistrate, who determined the waiver was knowing and voluntary. Consequently, the confession was admitted.

CASE EXCERPT
"Requiring the presence of parents in every case in which a juvenile is in custody and informed of his rights would be overly protective; would exclude from evidence juvenile statements that are, in fact, knowingly and voluntarily given; and would restrict law enforcement unnecessarily."

CASE SIGNIFICANCE
This case is important because it illustrated that the court often sides with the police when determining whether juveniles can waive their rights themselves. In this case, the court examined the totality of the

STATE v. SUGG *(cont.)*

circumstances and pointed to the defendant's age and criminal history, as well as the length of time he was detained. The court contended that based on the evidence, it could not conclude that the police coerced the defendant into confessing in any way. In addition, the court pointed out the measures the officers took to attempt to get the defendant to have a parent present for his questioning. Consequently, this court ruled that a juvenile can intentionally and knowingly waive his or her rights without his or her parent or counsel present. The case illustrated the growing trend to reduce the age of responsibility in the eyes of the law.

VERNONIA SCHOOL DISTRICT 47J v. ACTON

515 U.S. 646 (1995)

FACTS

Drugs were not considered a major problem in Vernonia School District 47J until the mid- to late 1980s, when teachers and administrators observed a sharp increase in student use. Not only were student athletes included among the users, they were identified as leaders of the drug culture. This caused school district administrators concern because drug use was reasoned to increase the risk of sports-related injury.

Initially, the district responded to the problem by offering special classes, speakers, and presentations designed to deter drug use. It brought in a specially trained dog to detect drugs, but the drug problem persisted. District officials next implemented a drug-testing program. Input was gathered for a proposed Student Athlete Drug Policy and parents gave their unanimous approval. The school board approved the policy for implementation in the fall of 1989. The express purpose of the policy was to prevent student athletes from using drugs, to protect their health and safety, and to provide drug users with treatment assistance. The policy applied to all students participating in interscholastic athletics. Students wishing to participate in a sport had to obtain written consent from their parents and sign a form consenting to being drug tested. Prescription medications were cleared through doctor's authorization.

Male testing consisted of students producing a sample at a urinal, remaining fully clothed with his back to the monitor, who stood approximately 12 to 15 feet behind the student. Monitors were allowed to watch students while they produced the samples, and listened for normal sounds of urination. Girls produced samples in an enclosed bathroom stall, so they could be heard but not observed. Samples were sent to an independent laboratory which routinely tested for amphetamines, cocaine, and marijuana. Only the superintendent, principals, vice-principals, and athletic directors had access to test results, and the results were destroyed after one year. If a sample tested positive, a second test was administered as soon as possible to confirm the result. If the second test was negative, no further action was taken. If the second test was positive, the athlete's parents were notified and the school convened a meeting with the principal at which time the student was given the option of (1) completing a six week drug treatment assistance program that included weekly urinalysis, or (2) suffering suspension from the team for the remainder of the current and next athletic season. A second offense resulted in automatic suspension and reimposition of option (2); a third offense resulted in suspension for the remainder of the current season and the next two athletic seasons.

In the fall of 1991, respondent James Acton, then a seventh-grader, signed up to play football at one of the district's grade schools. He was denied participation, however, because he and his parents refused to sign the testing consent forms. The Actons filed suit, seeking declaratory and injunctive relief from enforcement of the policy on the grounds that it violated the Fourth and Fourteenth Amendments to the United States Constitution and the Oregon Constitution. The district court denied the claims, but the court of appeals reversed, holding that the policy violated both the federal and state constitutions. The school district then appealed to the Supreme Court.

ISSUE

Is the drug testing of student athletes reasonable under the Fourth Amendment?

HOLDING

Yes. The drug testing policy of the school district that applies to student athletes is reasonable under the Fourth Amendment.

RATIONALE

As the text of the Fourth Amendment indicates, the ultimate measure of the constitutionality of a governmental search is reasonableness. This is especially true in a case such as this, where there was no clear practice, either approving or disapproving the type of search at issue, at the time the constitutional provision was enacted. The Court contended whether a particular search meets the reasonableness standard is judged by balancing its intrusion on the individual's Fourth Amendment interests against its promotion of legitimate governmental interests. Where a search is undertaken by law enforcement officials to discover evidence of criminal wrongdoing, the Court has said that reasonableness generally requires the obtaining of a judicial warrant. Warrants cannot be issued, of course, without the showing of probable cause required by the warrant clause. But a warrant is not required to establish the reasonableness of all government searches; and when a warrant is not required, probable cause is not invariably required either. A search not supported by probable cause can be constitutional, when special needs, beyond the normal need for law enforcement, make the warrant and probable-cause requirements impracticable. The Court found in *T.L.O.* such special needs to exist in the public-school context. There, the warrant requirement would unduly interfere with the maintenance of the swift and informal disciplinary procedures that are needed, and strict adherence to the requirement that searches be based upon probable cause would undercut the substantial need of teachers and administrators for freedom to maintain order in the schools. The school search the Court approved in *T.L.O.*, while not based on probable cause, was based on individualized suspicion of wrongdoing. As the Court explicitly acknowledged, however, the Fourth Amendment imposes no irreducible requirement of such suspicion. The Court has upheld suspicionless searches and seizures to conduct drug testing of railroad personnel involved in train accidents, to conduct random drug testing of federal customs officers who carry arms or are involved in drug interdiction, and to maintain automobile checkpoints looking for illegal immigrants and contraband. Fourth Amendment rights, no less than First and Fourteenth Amendment rights, are different in public schools than elsewhere; the reasonableness inquiry cannot disregard the schools' custodial and tutelary responsibility for children. For their own good and that of their classmates, public school children are routinely required to submit to various physical examinations, and to be vaccinated against various diseases. Legitimate privacy expectations are even less with regard to student athletes. School sports are not for the bashful. They require suiting up before each practice or event, and showering

and changing afterward. Public school locker rooms, the usual sites for these activities, are not notable for the privacy they afford. There is an additional respect in which school athletes have a reduced expectation of privacy. By choosing to go out for the team, they voluntarily subject themselves to a degree of regulation even higher than that imposed on students generally. In Vernonia's public schools, they must submit to a preseason physical exam, acquire adequate insurance coverage or sign an insurance waiver, maintain a minimum grade point average, and comply with any rules of conduct, dress, training hours, and related matters that may be established for each sport by the head coach and athletic director with the principal's approval. The Court recognized in *Skinner* that collecting the samples for urinalysis intrudes upon an excretory function traditionally shielded by great privacy. The Court noted, however, that the degree of intrusion depends upon the manner in which production of the urine sample is monitored.

The conditions were nearly identical to those typically encountered in public restrooms, which men, women, and especially schoolchildren use daily. Under such conditions, the privacy interests compromised by the process of obtaining the urine sample were, in the Court's view, negligible. It would be a mistake, however, to think that the phrase "compelling state interest," in the Fourth Amendment context, describes a fixed, minimum quantum of governmental concern, so that one could dispose of a case by answering in isolation the question: Was there a compelling state interest here? Rather, the phrase describes an interest that appears important enough to justify the particular search at hand, in light of other factors, which show the search to be relatively intrusive upon a genuine expectation of privacy. Whether that relatively high degree of government concern was necessary in this case or not, the Court thought it was met. School years are the time when the physical, psychological, and addictive effects of drugs are most severe. Maturing nervous systems are more critically impaired by intoxicants than mature ones are, childhood losses in learning are lifelong and profound, children grow chemically dependent more quickly than adults, and their record of recovery is depressingly poor. As for the immediacy of the district's concerns, the Court was not inclined to question; indeed, the Court could not possibly find clearly erroneous, the district court's conclusion that a large segment of the student body, particularly those involved in interscholastic athletics, was in a state of

VERNONIA SCHOOL DISTRICT 47J v. ACTON (cont.)

rebellion, that disciplinary actions had reached epidemic proportions, and that the rebellion was being fueled by alcohol and drug abuse as well as by the students' misperceptions about the drug culture. Taking into account all the factors considered above, the decreased expectation of privacy, the relative unobtrusiveness of the search, and the severity of the need met by the search, the Court concluded Vernonia's policy was reasonable and hence constitutional.

CASE EXCERPT

"Somewhat like adults who choose to participate in a closely regulated industry, students who voluntarily participate in school athletics have reason to expect intrusions upon normal rights and privileges, including privacy."

CASE SIGNIFICANCE

This case is important because it represented a return to the parens patriae philosophy. The Court contended that the school district is entrusted with providing a safe and healthy school environment for its students. In this case, the Court agreed with the school district that drug use among those juveniles involved in sports had grown and was causing a notable disturbance in the safe and healthy environment of the public school. The Court justified its intrusion upon the juvenile by indicating that it is in a student's best interest to be drug free. This case extended an earlier case, *T.L.O.*, by allowing an intrusion on a juvenile's Fourth Amendment rights absent probable cause or reasonable suspicion. Although this case is not applicable to all juveniles in a school, it opened the door. In using the justification of a student choosing to go out for a team, it would be possible and is likely for school districts to extend the intrusion to any activity a student chooses to do.

BOARD OF EDUCATION POTTAWATOMIE COUNTY v. EARLS

545 U.S. 1015 (2002)

FACTS

The Student Activities Drug Testing Policy adopted by the Tecumseh, Oklahoma, School District requires all middle- and high-school students to consent to urinalysis testing for drugs in order to participate in any extracurricular activity. In practice, the policy has been applied only to competitive extracurricular activities sanctioned by the Oklahoma Secondary Schools Activities Association. Respondent high school students and their parents brought this action for equitable relief, alleging that the policy violated the Fourth Amendment. The district court granted the school district summary judgment. The 10th Circuit reversed, holding that the policy violated the Fourth Amendment. It concluded that before imposing a suspicionless drug-testing program, a school must demonstrate some identifiable drug abuse problem among a sufficient number of those tested, such that testing that group will actually redress its drug problem. The 10th Circuit Court then held that the school district had failed to demonstrate such a problem among Tecumseh students participating in competitive extracurricular activities. The school district appealed to the Supreme Court.

ISSUE

Does the school district's policy of drug testing students involved in extracurricular activities violate the Fourth Amendment?

HOLDING

No. Tecumseh's policy is a reasonable means of furthering the school district's important interest in preventing and deterring drug use among its schoolchildren and does not violate the Fourth Amendment.

RATIONALE

The Court contended that because searches by public school officials implicate Fourth Amendment interests, the Court must review the policy for reasonableness, the touchstone of constitutionality. According to *T.L.O.*, in contrast to the criminal context, a probable cause finding is unnecessary in the public school context because it would unduly interfere with maintenance of the swift and informal disciplinary procedures that are needed. In the public school context, a search may be reasonable when supported by special needs beyond the normal need for law enforcement. Because the reasonableness inquiry cannot disregard the school's custodial and tutelary responsibility for children, a finding of individualized suspicion may not be necessary. In upholding the suspicionless drug testing of athletes, the Court in *Vernonia* conducted a fact-specific balancing of the intrusion on the children's Fourth Amendment rights against the promotion of legitimate governmental interests. Applying *Vernonia*'s principles to the somewhat different FACTS of this case demonstrated that Tecumseh's policy was also constitutional. The Court considered first the nature of the privacy interest allegedly compromised by the drug testing, and the Court concluded that the students affected by this policy had a limited expectation of privacy. Respondents argued that because children participating in nonathletic extracurricular activities are not subject to regular physicals and communal undress they have a stronger expectation of privacy than the *Vernonia* athletes. This distinction, however, was not essential in *Vernonia,* which depended primarily upon the school's custodial responsibility and authority. In any event, students who participate in competitive extracurricular activities voluntarily subject themselves to many of the same intrusions on their privacy as do athletes. Some of these clubs and activities require occasional off-campus travel and communal undress, and all of them have their own rules and requirements that do not apply to the student body as a whole. Each of them must abide by rules, and a faculty sponsor monitors students for compliance with the various rules dictated by the clubs and activities. The Court contended such regulation further diminishes the schoolchildren's expectation of privacy. The Court also considered the character of the intrusion imposed by the policy, and concluded that the invasion of students' privacy was not significant, given the minimally intrusive nature of the sample collection and the limited uses to which the test results were put. The degree of intrusion caused by collecting a urine sample depends upon the manner in which production of the sample is monitored. Under the policy, a faculty monitor waits outside the closed restroom stall for the student to produce a sample and must listen for the normal sounds of urination to guard against tampered specimens and ensure an accurate chain of custody. This procedure is virtually identical to the negligible intrusion approved in *Vernonia.* The policy clearly required that test results be kept in confidential files separate from a student's other records and released to school personnel only on a need-to-know basis. Moreover, the test results were not turned over to any law enforcement authority, nor did they lead to the imposition of discipline or have any academic consequences. Rather, the only consequence of a failed drug test was to limit the student's privilege of participating in extracurricular activities. Finally, the Court considered the nature and immediacy of the government's concerns and the efficacy of the policy in meeting them. The Court concluded that the policy effectively served the school district's interest in protecting its students' safety and health. Preventing drug use by schoolchildren is an important governmental concern. The health and safety risks identified

in *Vernonia* apply with equal force to Tecumseh's children.

The school district provided sufficient evidence to shore up its program. Furthermore, the Court had not previously required a particularized or pervasive drug problem before allowing the government to conduct suspicionless drug testing. The need to prevent and deter the substantial harm of childhood drug use provided the necessary immediacy for a school testing policy. Given the nationwide epidemic of drug use, and the evidence of increased drug use in Tecumseh schools, it was entirely reasonable for the school district to enact this particular drug testing policy.

CASE EXCERPT

"In upholding the constitutionality of the Policy, we express no opinion as to its wisdom. Rather, we hold only that Tecumseh's Policy is a reasonable means of furthering the School District's important interest in preventing and deterring drug use among its schoolchildren."

CASE SIGNIFICANCE

In this case the Court expanded on earlier decisions dealing with school searches, *T.L.O.* and *Vernonia,* by allowing the school district to drug test students who participated in any extracurricular activity. In so holding the Court lowered the standard to justify an intrusion in the school setting. The Court indicated that its foremost rationale was the school district's "custodial responsibility and authority" to the schoolchildren under its care. In *Vernonia* the school district established that the drug problem was a growing concern and likely promulgated by those whose rights were being intruded upon, student athletes. However, in this case the school district applied *Vernonia* in their decision to test anyone involved in an extracurricular activity, despite a lack of evidence that a drug problem was being promoted by that student group. With the Court's holding the door was opened wider in terms of what types of intrusions upon students would be allowed in the public schools.

YARBOROUGH v. ALVARADO

541 U.S. 652 (2004)

FACTS

At the request of police, the parents of Michael Alvarado, 17, drove him to the local police station where he was interviewed about his possible

YARBOROUGH v. ALVARADO (cont.)

involvement in a crime. Though his parents willingly drove their son in for questioning they were denied access to the interview. Neither parent proactively contacted an attorney even when the interview, which was supposed to last only 30 minutes, stretched into two hours. Michael was not under arrest at the time nor was he Mirandized. Nevertheless, based on statements made during that interview, Alvarado was charged several months later and eventually convicted of second-degree murder and attempted robbery. The Ninth Circuit Court of Appeals reversed the conviction arguing that because Alvarado was a juvenile, he have felt compelled to cooperate with police since he was essentially in police custody, therefore he should have been properly Mirandized.

ISSUE

Should police consider factors such as age and prior record when determining whether a suspect is in custody and therefore entitled to Miranda warnings under the Fifth Amendment?

HOLDING

No. Custodial analyses and determinations about when a suspect is actually in custody should not be driven by subjective criteria such as age and criminal history but rather by objective criteria like restrictions on a suspect's freedom of movement. Custody occurs when a suspect decides to stop being cooperative but, due to a possible impending arrest, he or she is no longer free to leave.

RATIONALE

Once a suspect is no longer free to leave they are essentially in police custody and in most cases should be properly Mirandized at that time. In this case, the majority argued that an interview is not an interrogation, Alvarado could have stopped answering questions at any time, stood up and walked out of the interview. He was simply not told about that option and he didn't ask.

CASE EXCERPT

"True, suspects with prior law enforcement experience may understand police procedures and reasonably feel free to leave unless told otherwise. On the other hand, they may view past as prologue and expect another in a string of arrests. We do not ask police officers to consider these contingent psychological factors when deciding when suspects should be advised of their *Miranda* rights."

CASE SIGNIFICANCE

Many juveniles can recite the Miranda warnings verbatim, but when confronted with accusatory questioning by law enforcement kids often (wrongly) feel compelled to cooperate, often to their legal detriment. From an early age children are admonished to be honest, to tell the truth, especially when they've engaged in wrongdoing. But as we saw in *Fare v. Michael C.* (1979), even properly Mirandized suspects talk and cooperate their way into a murder rap. Police interviews of children in the field are much more common than arranged interviews as in Alvarado's case, so it is difficult to estimate how often children submit to police interviews without the benefit of a parent or legal counsel. Rather than asking, "Am I under arrest?", today's youth might be better served by asking, "Am I free to leave, and may I call a parent?" If the answer to both questions is no, they might need a lawyer.

SAFFORD UNIFIED SCHOOL DISTRICT #1 v. REDDING

557 U.S.—(2009)

FACTS

In early October, 2003, a student at Safford Middle School informed assistant principal, Kerry Wilson, that kids were bringing drugs and weapons to campus and that he had gotten sick after taking one of the pills. Several days later the same student contacted Wilson again, handed over a white pill (later identified as Ibuprofen 400, a prescription-strength pain killer strictly prohibited by school policy), and said he got it from another student, Marissa Glines. According to the informant, other students were planning to take the pills at lunch that day. Glines was immediately removed from class and a day planner within her reach was seized. The day planner was later discovered to contain various contraband items including knives, lighters, a permanent marker, and a cigarette. In Wilson's office Glines voluntarily produced several white pills and a blue pill (later identified as an over-the-counter antiinflammatory drug, naproxen). When asked where the blue pill came from, Glines responded, "I guess it slipped in there when *she* gave me the IBU 400s." When asked who Glines was referring to she replied, "Savana Redding." Glines denied any knowledge of the contraband items found in the day planner; she was then subjected to a strip search by the school nurse which included her outer clothing, bra, and underpants. The search revealed no additional pills.

Wilson next removed Savana Redding from class. In the office, Wilson confronted Redding with the contents of the day planner. Redding claimed that the day planner was hers but she had lent it to Marissa Glines a few days earlier. Redding claimed no knowledge of the knives or the pills or any plan to distribute pills to other students. Wilson and an administrative assistant searched Redding's backpack, which turned up nothing. She was then sent to the nurse's office where her jacket, shoes, and socks were searched. She was made to strip to her underwear then told to pull her bra out and to the side and shake it, and to pull out the elastic on her underpants, exposing her breasts and pelvic area to some degree. No pills were found. Redding's mother filed suit against Safford Unified School District #1 and all parties involved in the search of her daughter on the grounds that the strip search violated her daughter's Fourth Amendment rights.

ISSUE
Are a 13-year-old student's Fourth Amendment rights violated when she is subjected to a search of her bra and underpants by school officials acting on reasonable suspicion that she had brought forbidden prescription and over-the-counter drugs to school?

HOLDING
Yes. There was no reason to suspect the drugs presented a danger or were concealed in the students' underwear. But, even though the search was unreasonable, school officials who ordered and conducted the unconstitutional search are entitled to qualified immunity from liability.

RATIONALE
In *New Jersey* v. *T.L.O.* (1985), the Court held that strip search was unjustified under the Fourth Amendment test for searches of students conducted by school officials. When reasonable suspicion exists, school officials may search a student without a warrant and such a search "will be permissible in its scope when the measures adopted are reasonably related to the objectives of the search and not excessively intrusive in light of the age and sex of the student and the nature of the infraction" (*New Jersey* v. *T.L.O.* 469 U.S. 342).

Consistent with the *T.L.O.* ruling, the Court held here that the search of Redding's outer clothing, backpack, shoes and socks, and the day planner was not excessively intrusive; but making her pull out her underwear was embarrassing, frightening, humiliating, and constitutionally unreasonable. Yet even though the search was unconstitutional, school officials in this case could not be sued for their actions as a result of qualified immunity.

CASE EXCERPT
"Here, the content of the suspicion failed to match the degree of intrusion. Wilson knew beforehand that the pills were…equivalent to two Advil or one Aleve…In sum, what was missing from the suspected FACTS…was any indication of danger to the students from the power of the drugs or their quantity, and any reason to suppose that Savana was carrying pills in her underwear. We think the combination of these deficiencies was fatal to finding the search reasonable."

CASE SIGNIFICANCE
The Court ruled that the intrusiveness of the strip search here was not justifiably related to the circumstances and was thus unconstitutional. However, Wilson and other school officials involved in the search were protected from liability because those actions were guided by good intentions and were similar to parents who may overreact to protect their children from harm. Indeed the Court specifically notes, "[i]n so holding, we mean to cast no ill reflection on the assistant principal, for the record raises no doubt that his motive throughout was to eliminate drugs from his school and protect students."

CAMRETA v. GREENE
563 U.S.—(2011)

FACTS
Police arrested Nimrod Greene for suspected sexual abuse of a young boy unrelated to him. During the course of that investigation the victim's parents told police they suspected Greene of molesting his nine-year-old daughter, S.G. Police reported this to the Oregon Department of Human Services which assigned Bob Camreta, a child protective caseworker, to inquire about S.G.'s safety. Several days later Camreta and James Alford, a Deschutes County deputy sheriff, went to S.G.'s elementary school and interviewed her about

CAMRETA v. GREENE *(cont.)*

the allegations. Neither Camreta nor Alford obtained a warrant, nor did they obtain parental consent to interview the child. Initially S.G. denied the allegations, but later admitted that her father had sexually abused her. Greene was prosecuted but the jury failed to reach a verdict in the case and the charges were eventually dropped. A decade later Sarah Greene, S.G.'s mother, filed suit against Camreta and Alford on the grounds that the interview was unconstitutional and a violation of her daughter's Fourth Amendment rights.

ISSUE

May the Supreme Court review a lower court's ruling at the behest of government officials who won final judgment on qualified immunity grounds but could not for this case due to details specific to it.

HOLDING

Yes. The Court may review a lower court's ruling at the behest of a government official granted qualified immunity, but this particular case is moot.

RATIONALE

It is important to stress that this suit was filed 10 years after the initial interview, and S.G.'s standing as a victim in the case had been greatly diminished. Although it was determined that Camreta and Alford had engaged in an unlawful interview, both were granted qualified immunity from liability. In the intervening decade S.G. moved back to Florida and claimed she had no intention of relocating back to Oregon. At the time of this decision S.G. was only months away from her eighteenth birthday and it was highly improbable that she would ever be subject to another unlawful child abuse investigation in Oregon, so the case was vacated.

CASE EXCERPT

"Time and distance combined have stymied our ability to consider this petition... The case has become moot because the child has grown up and moved across the country, and so will never again be subject to the Oregon in-school interviewing practices whose constitutionality is at issue. We therefore do not reach the Fourth Amendment question in this case."

CASE SIGNIFICANCE

Though the case against Camreta and Alford was ultimately vacated, it suggests that even government agents working under the aegis of qualified immunity should heretofore obtain a search warrant when conducting interviews in child abuse cases, especially sensitive cases alleging acts of sexual exploitation. The court specifically instructed government officials to "cease operating on the assumption" that warrantless interviews are permitted. In an age when professions of all types—teachers, daycare workers, physicians, counselors, police—are mandated to report suspected cases of child abuse, this decision strongly suggests that government agents first obtain a warrant or risk exposing themselves to both civil and 42 U.S.C. Section 1983 claims of civil rights violations.

J.D.B. v. NORTH CAROLINA
564 U.S—(2011)

FACTS

Police stopped and questioned petitioner J.D.B., a 13-year-old seventh-grade student, upon seeing him near the site of two home break-ins. Five days later, a digital camera matching the description of one of the stolen items was found at J.D.B's school, and it was seen in his possession. A school resource officer removed J.D.B. from his classroom and delivered him to a closed-door meeting in a school conference room. There J.D.B. was questioned for between 30 and 45 minutes by the SRO (school resource officer); a juvenile detective, Inspector DiCostanzo; the school's vice-principal; and an administrative assistant intern. J.D.B. was not allowed to contact his grandmother, his legal guardian and primary caretaker, nor was he read his Miranda rights or told that he was free to leave the room during questioning.

At first, J.D.B. denied all involvement in the break-ins, but as more evidence against him was disclosed he asked whether he would "still be in trouble" if he returned the "stuff." He was told by Inspector DiCostanzo that while that information would be helpful, "this thing is going to court" regardless. J.D.B. was also warned by DiCostanzo about the prospect of going to juvenile detention. The assistant principal urged J.D.B. to "do the right thing," warning him that "the truth always comes out in the end." Only after J.D.B. confessed was he told that he could refuse to answer questions and that he was free to leave. Asked whether he understood, J.D.B. nodded and provided further details. He eventually wrote out a statement which included how he and friend had committed the break-ins and the location of the other stolen items. When the school day ended, J.D.B. was allowed to leave to catch the bus home. Later, two petitions were filed charging J.D.B. with breaking and entering and with larceny.

J.D.B.'s public defender moved to suppress his statement and the evidence derived therefrom, arguing that he had been interrogated in a custodial setting without benefit of Miranda warnings and that his statements were made involuntarily. Based on the Court's earlier ruling in *Alvarado* (2004), North Carolina contended that a child's age has no place in the custody analysis, no matter how young. The trial court denied the motion and J.D.B. entered a transcript admitting his charges, but he renewed his objection that his statement should have been suppressed. The North Carolina Court of Appeals and the State Supreme Court affirmed the decision that J.D.B.'s age was not relevant to the determination of whether or when he was in police custody.

ISSUE

Is a child's age relevant to a determination about when they are in police custody? Essentially, does a child's age affect their perceptions about if and when they are in police custody and if and when they feel free to leave?

HOLDING

A child's age properly informs the *Miranda* custody analysis, so long as the child's age was known to the officer at the time of police questioning, or would have been objectively apparent to a reasonable officer. Due to the Court's earlier ruling in *Yarborough v. Alvarado* (2004), which advocated the development of objective measures like restrictions on a suspect's freedom of movement over subjective criteria like age to inform when a suspect is in custody. Due to possible misinterpretation the North Carolina Supreme Court may have erroneously excluded age in its custody analysis. Had the North Carolina courts considered age in their analysis, they may have concluded that J.D.B. was indeed in custody for purposes of *Miranda*. The case was remanded back down on the argument that a child's age *is* an appropriate factor to consider when making determinations about how children, as "reasonable people," perceive themselves when in police custody and if and when they feel free to leave.

RATIONALE

This case seeks to resolve the issue of whether J.D.B. was (or only perceived himself to be) in police custody when he was interviewed, taking into account all of the relevant circumstances of the interview, including J.D.B.'s age (13) when the incriminating statements were made. North Carolina argued that age is irrelevant to determinations of when one feels compelled to answer police questions or when they feel free to leave. The US Supreme Court disagreed, ruling that age is an appropriate factor when making determinations about the nature of police interrogations. Police custodial interrogation involve "inherently compelling pressures" that "can induce a frighteningly high percentage of people to confess to crimes they never committed...[and] that risk is all the more acute when the subject of custodial interrogation is a juvenile." Whether a suspect is in custody for *Miranda* purposes is an objective determination involving two discrete inquiries: first, what were the circumstances surrounding the interrogation; and second, given those circumstances, would a reasonable person have felt at liberty to terminate the interrogation and just leave?

CASE EXCERPT

"[H]ow would a reasonable adult understand his situation, after being removed from a seventh grade social studies class by a uniformed school resource officer; being encouraged by his assistant principal to 'do the right thing'; and being warned by a police investigator of the prospect of juvenile detention and separation from his guardian and primary caretaker...Neither officers nor courts can reasonably evaluate the effect of objective circumstances that, by their nature, are specific to children without accounting for the age of the child subjected to those circumstances."

CASE SIGNIFICANCE

According to the majority, it is beyond dispute that children often feel compelled to submit to police questioning when an adult in similar circumstances may feel free to leave. The Court argues that by their very nature, custodial police interrogations produce "inherently compelling pressures," even for adults. Recognizing the coercive nature of custodial interrogation "blurs the line between voluntary and involuntary statements" and further evidences the need to consider age as an important variable in a child's

J.D.B. v. NORTH CAROLINA (cont.)

analysis of custody. This is why the Court ruled in *Miranda* that when a suspect is in police custody, she or he must be warned prior to questioning that they have the right to remain silent, that any statement they make may be used against them, and that they have a right to the presence of an attorney, either retained or appointed.

When is a suspect in police custody and when are they free to leave? Good questions both, irrespective of the suspect's age, but age becomes especially critical when the case implicates the rights and liberties of the very young. For Sotomayor, the critical issue is this: Once the scene is set and the players' lines and actions are reconstructed, the court must apply an objective test to resolve the ultimate inquiry: was there a formal arrest or restraint on freedom of movement of the degree associated with formal arrest? This test need not involve consideration of the "actual mindset" of the particular suspect and police should not be required to "make [subjective] guesses" about circumstances unknowable to them at the time. Still, age is far more than a chronological fact; it "generates commonsense conclusions about behavior and perception." Such conclusions are self-evident to anyone who was once a child and apply broadly to children as a class today.

As to the specific context of police interrogation, the Court observed that events that would "leave one man cold and unimpressed can overawe and overwhelm a lad in his early teens." Drawing on language from its earlier decisions in *Haley v. Ohio* (1948) and *Gallegos v. Colorado* (1962), the Court reasoned that children are incapable of exercising mature judgment and they possess only an incomplete ability to understand the world around them. As a result, they cannot be considered miniature adults. This is not to say that a child's age will be a determinative, or even a significant factor, in every case, but it is a reality that courts cannot simply ignore.

DISCUSSION QUESTIONS

1. Briefly describe what rights are (and are not) afforded to juveniles during encounters with police.
2. Describe the standard of proof police need to make a lawful arrest of a juvenile offender? How and why does that standard differ at school?
3. At what point does a police detention become an arrest? Does the age of the suspect matter in the analysis of police detentions? Describe the conditions under which you would feel compelled to answer police questions and when you would feel free to leave.
4. Why was Michael C. denied the ability to speak with his probation officer? Do you agree with the Court's ruling in this case? Why or why not?
5. Should juveniles be allowed to waive their right to remain silent and make voluntarily statements to police without the benefit of counsel?
6. What have the courts considered the functional equivalent of asking for an attorney?
7. What procedural rights do juveniles give up in the public school setting?
8. What is the justification for status offenses? Should difficult, unwilling students be "forced" to attend public schools under threat of truancy charges? At what age should children be permitted to leave school permanently?
9. Why and under what conditions may school-children be subject to drug testing? Under what conditions and to what extent may students be searched by school officials?
10. What are the controlling cases in police search and seizure cases involving juveniles?

CHAPTER THREE

ENTRY INTO THE COURT SYSTEM

IN RE FRANK H., *337 N.Y.S.2D 118 (1972)*

WANSLEY v. SLAYTON, *487 F.2D 90 (4TH CIR. 1973)*

IN THE WELFARE OF SNYDER, *532 P.2D 278 (WASH. 1975)*

IN RE WAYNE H., *596 P.2D 1 (CAL. 1979)*

IN THE INTEREST OF E.B., *287 N.W.2D 462 (N.D. 1980)*

WASHINGTON v. CHATHAM, *624 P.2D 1180 (WASH. APP. 1981)*

STATE v. MCDOWELL, *685 P.2D 595 (WASH. 1984)*

UNITED STATES v. NASH, *620 F.SUPP. 1439 (S.D.N.Y. 1985)*

CHRISTOPHER P. v. NEW MEXICO, *816 P.2D 485 (N.M. 1991)*

UNITED STATES v. A.R., *38 F.3D 699 (3D CIR. 1994)*

R.R. v. PORTSEY, *629 SO.2D 1059 (FLA. APP. 1994)*

STATE v. K.K.H., *878 P.2D 1255 (WASH. APP. 1994)*

STATE v. LOWRY, *230 A.2D 907 (N.J. 1997)*

INTRODUCTION

Although the pretrial phase of a juvenile proceeding has not been defined by the Supreme Court as a "critical stage" in the process, it is of critical importance to the juvenile justice system. The pretrial phase is often referred to as *intake*. Within intake several important functions are performed by juvenile probation officers. When the police arrest a juvenile delinquent they rarely take the youth into custody. Rather, they often release the juvenile to his or her parents and forward the police report to the juvenile court office. Once the police report arrives, either the prosecutor assigned to juvenile cases or a juvenile probation officer reviews the case to decide how to best handle the matter. First-time, low-risk offenders are frequently offered diversion. Diversion is an opportunity for the youth to meet with a probation officer and informally handle the matter. After a juvenile has been informed of his or her rights and has admitted to an offense, he or she is given a sanction or placed on a contract by the juvenile probation officer. If the juvenile fulfills the diversion agreement the case is not filed by petition

in juvenile court. More serious offenses and repeat offenders are typically prosecuted in juvenile court and not offered diversion.

When petitioned into court, a juvenile still typically meets with a juvenile probation officer or intake worker at the probation department prior to going before the court. The purpose of this meeting is to determine the juvenile's status and obtain a brief background. In addition, the juvenile's rights are explained as well as the charges against him or her. A probation officer also typically meets with any juveniles who have been taken into custody as well as their parents in an effort to determine if the juveniles should remain in detention or should be placed in a less secure alternative, such as their parents' custody. This function of the juvenile probation department is critical to the efficiency of the juvenile court; however, it is not mandatory that juveniles attend the intake meeting. After meeting with the juvenile probation officer, the youth and his or her parents go before the juvenile court, where the probation officer still has the ability to recommend that the court informally adjust the case if he or she feels it is appropriate. This allows for the juvenile to complete a period of supervision after which the case is dismissed. However, the juvenile's plea of true is recorded, which is analagous to a guilty plea in the adult system, and if he or she does not successfully complete the period of supervision he or she is formally adjudicated of the charge.

Although these functions are critical to the juvenile court process the courts have not defined them as "critical stages" in the proceedings. Despite this, the courts have still heard cases and rendered decisions that govern pretrial procedures. In reference to the diversion process, the courts have determined a juvenile does not have a right to be diverted. In addition, if a juvenile is offered a diversion and refuses, the prosecutor may charge an offense other than that specified in the diversion meeting. Further, the courts have allowed diverted offenses to be considered in a juvenile's prior history when they are dispositioned for subsequent offenses.

The courts have also examined the intake process and not defined it as a critical stage of the juvenile proceedings. Consequently, juveniles do not have the right to be represented by counsel at the intake meeting. However, a juvenile does not have to participate in the intake conference. If a juvenile chooses to participate in the intake conference, any statements made to the probation officer during the conference are solely admissible for a placement decision and not for prosecution in juvenile or adult criminal court. If the courts opt to detain a juvenile pending an adjudicatory hearing, a probable cause determination by a magistrate is required within a reasonable time. Furthermore, if the prosecutor or the court feels it may be appropriate to waive a juvenile to criminal court for prosecution, the state can compel a juvenile to submit to a psychological evaluation for the purpose of determining if the juvenile is appropriate for the transfer. However, the information obtained in the evaluation cannot be used in the prosecution of the juvenile's case, nor can the court compel the juvenile to discuss the offense for which he or she is currently before the court. These court decisions have guided juvenile probation departments in their development of policy and procedures for handling juveniles during the pretrial phase of a juvenile proceeding. In this chapter we review some of the leading cases dealing with juvenile pretrial procedures.

IN RE FRANK H.

337 N.Y.S.2d 118 (1972)

FACTS

The petition in this case alleges that Frank H., a juvenile, while acting in concert with one other individual, who was also apprehended, was in a 1971 Pontiac with no registration, which belonged to Robbins Reef Buick Corporation. The car was alleged to have been stolen. Frank H. and his parents met with an intake officer prior to going before the court. When Frank H. first appeared before the court he was assigned counsel. His attorney made a motion to vacate the petition and send the case back to intake for consideration de novo on the ground that Frank H. had been denied his constitutional right to counsel at the intake stage of the family court proceeding.

ISSUE

Does a juvenile have a constitutional right to counsel at intake?

HOLDING

No. The intake conference is not a critical stage in the juvenile justice proceeding; therefore, a juvenile does not enjoy the constitutional right to counsel during intake.

RATIONALE

The initial intake conference occurs before a petition is ordered drawn and prior to the holding of a family court hearing. The probation service is authorized to confer with any person seeking to originate a juvenile delinquency or person in need of supervision proceeding under Article 7 of the Family Court Act, with the potential respondent, and with other interested persons concerning the availability of filing a petition under said article and to attempt to adjust suitable cases before a petition is filed. The court contended there are more social than legal issues involved in the intake process. An adjustment is not mandatory and the rules only specify that the probation department cannot prevent any person from having access to the court if he or she insists a petition be filed. In addition, no person can be compelled to appear at the conference, produce any papers, or visit any place. Intake is not a legal term with the exception of juvenile and family courts. The court contended it has been derived from the field of social welfare and in welfare the client has complete freedom of choice. Both he or she and the agency have the choice of whether to accept or deny services. This is not the case at court intake. The Supreme Court provided for a juvenile's right to counsel in *In Re Gault* [387 U.S. 1 (1967)]. However, it did not answer whether the intake stage was a critical stage of the proceedings wherein the juvenile's right to counsel would attach. However, Section 735 of the Family Court Act provides that no statement made during a preliminary conference may be admitted into evidence at a fact-finding hearing or, if the proceeding is transferred to criminal court, at any time prior to a conviction. The intent was to preserve the spirit of cooperation at a preliminary conference such as intake and guard against self-incrimination, a prohibition in *Gault.* The court concluded that to require counsel at intake would be an intolerable burden on an already overburdened court.

CASE EXCERPT

"The minor who is subject to the possibility of a transfer order should not be put to the unfair choice of being considered uncooperative by the juvenile probation officer and juvenile court because of his refusal to discuss his case with the probation officer, or of having his statements to that officer used against him in subsequent criminal proceedings. Such a result would frustrate the rehabilitative purpose of the Juvenile Court Law."

CASE SIGNIFICANCE

This case is important because it reflected the Court's desire to keep the juvenile court system separate and distinct from the adult criminal court. Intake is an important stage in the juvenile court process because it allows the probation department to explain the charges against juveniles to them and their parents. In addition, it allows the department to gather information for the purposes of determining placement and whether it may be appropriate to informally adjust the case. These functions are designed to speed up the handling of cases in juvenile court. In this case, the court pointed out that juveniles are not compelled to participate in the intake process. In addition, the juvenile's or his or her parents' comments during the process are not admissible as evidence in any of the important stages in the juvenile court proceedings. Consequently, the court determined the intake process is not a critical stage of the juvenile court proceedings,

and thus the constitutional rights supplied by *Gault* do not attach.

WANSLEY v. SLAYTON

487 F.2d 90 (4th Cir. 1973)

FACTS

Wansley filed a writ of habeas corpus while serving time in prison for the rape and robbery of a woman and several other crimes when he was 17 years old. After being arrested, Wansley was interrogated by the police without counsel or a parent present. His mother was notified and upon her arrival at the police station she was greeted by Wansley's juvenile probation officer. The probation officer informed her of the charges against her son and then escorted her to the holding cell where Wansley was detained. When she arrived she asked Wansley whether he had committed the crimes. Wansley replied that he had. Due to his age Wansley was under the jurisdiction of the juvenile court at the time he made the statement in the presence of his probation officer. Upon being transferred to criminal court, Wansley's probation officer testified at his trial as to the contents of the conversation at the holding cell. After numerous trials, Wansley was convicted and received sentences of life in prison and 20 years.

ISSUE

Can spontaneous statements made by a juvenile in the presence of his or her juvenile probation officer, while under the exclusive jurisdiction of the juvenile court, be used against him or her in a trial as an adult?

HOLDING

Yes. When a 17-year-old makes spontaneous admissions to his or her mother in the presence of a juvenile probation officer while subject to the jurisdiction of the juvenile court, the probation officer's testimony with regard to those statements at the juvenile's criminal trial does not violate the juvenile's right to due process and is therefore admissible.

RATIONALE

The probation officer's actions with regard to his informing the mother of the charges and accompanying her to see her son were routine. The state supreme court found the testimony admissible because the spontaneous admission resulted from an unprompted

WANSLEY v. SLAYTON (cont.)

question by the juvenile's mother, not from questioning by the police or the probation officer. The district court held to the contrary, recognizing that the admissibility of evidence at state court trials is ordinarily not cognizable on federal habeas corpus and that the rule in *Miranda* was not applicable, but concluded that the admission of such evidence offended fundamental fairness because it arose out of a violation of the witness role as a juvenile court officer, a parens patriae. It relied on several cases in doing so. However, this court pointed out that those cases had instances where the confession had been given in responses to police interrogation, unlike the situation here. What are involved are statements secured by police questioning and confrontation. The probation officer was also put through intense cross-examination, in which defense counsel raised the issue that the juvenile was talking about another incident. However, that determination is one left for the jury.

CASE EXCERPT

"When the mother saw her son she inquired whether he was guilty and he spontaneously replied in the affirmative. The officer who was standing near the mother testified to the conversation between mother and son. It is this conversation, the admission of which the District Court found constitutionally proscribed.... The State Supreme Court, on appeal, found the testimony admissible, stating (171 S.E.2d 678 at p. 684): "Suffice it to say, in rejecting this contention, that counsel overlook, or brush aside the fact that Wansley's spontaneous admission resulted from an unprompted question asked by his mother, not from questioning by the police or any other person.""

CASE SIGNIFICANCE

This case is important for several reasons. First, it established that a juvenile probation officer's responsibility is first to the state and then to the juvenile under his or her supervision. This clarified the juvenile probation officer's role as a peace officer. Second, it distinguished what type of information the court will allow a probation officer to testify to. Typically, information that is revealed to a probation officer in pretrial proceedings such as intake conferences is not admissible. However, this court differentiated the information obtained in this case because the juvenile's mother, not the probation officer, asked the questions. The court concluded that the mother would have no interest in seeing the juvenile prosecuted, which would distinguish her from the police or a probation officer.

IN THE WELFARE OF SNYDER

532 P.2d 278 (Wash. 1975)

FACTS

The record reflects that prior to this action Snyder, a 16-year-old child, resided with her parents in their home. As Snyder entered her teen years a pattern developed where she was frequently rebelling against her parents, forcing them to become more disciplinarian in their parenting methods. These hostilities by all parties led to a collapse in the parent/child relationship. On June 18, 1973, Mr. Snyder, having concluded the juvenile court might be able to assist him in controlling his daughter, removed her from the home and delivered her to the Youth Services Center. The child was placed in the center. The next day, in an attempt to avoid returning home, the child filed a petition alleging she was a dependent child. On June 23, the child was placed in temporary custody of the Department of Social and Health Services and an attorney was appointed for her. On October 12, the court held that allegations against the child's parents were incorrect and she should be returned home. The child was returned home and she remained until November 16. At that time the child sought the help of the Youth Services Center. The individual in charge of the intake program at the center filed a petition alleging the child was incorrigible. A hearing was held on December 3 at which the court decided the child should be placed in a foster home pending the outcome of a fact-finding hearing. At that hearing, which was held on December 10 and 11, the commissioner found that the child was incorrigible and continued the matter for one week so that the family could meet with a counselor. On December 18, after reviewing the comments of the counselor, the commissioner decided the child was to be placed in a foster home under the supervision of the probation department and that she and her parents were to continue counseling, subject to subsequent review. The parents immediately filed a motion for revision of the commissioner's decision.

ISSUE

Is there substantial evidence in the record, taken as a whole, to support the juvenile court's determination that Snyder is incorrigible?

HOLDING

Yes. The juvenile court held correctly in finding the child incorrigible.

RATIONALE

According to Washington law a child is incorrigible when he or she is beyond the power and control of her parents by reason of her own conduct. In reviewing the record, the court found evidence in sufficient quantum to persuade a fair-minded, rational person of the truth of a declared premise. The court pointed out that in order to act in the welfare of the child it has typically placed a great deal of weight on what the trial court has decided. The juvenile court relied on the testimony of the child and family members along with the determination of the professionals in reaching its decision. Consequently, the court found the juvenile court's decision to be supported by substantial evidence and therefore affirmed. Cynthia's obstinate state of mind can be best understood by considering her clear and unambiguous testimony in response to her attorney's direct examination.

CASE EXCERPT

"Q: Your petition alleges that you absolutely refuse to go home and obey your parents, is that correct?

A: Yes....

Q: The position then, why don't you state that for the Court?

A: I refuse to go back there. I just won't do it.

MR. SANDERS [ATTORNEY FOR PARENTS]: I object to the whole line of testimony. I think it is irrelevant whether she refuses to go back home. That is not an issue in the case.

THE COURT: Overruled.

A: I just absolutely refuse to go back there. I can't live with them [her parents]."

CASE SIGNIFICANCE

This case is important because it reflected the juvenile court's parens patriae philosophy. The juvenile court has the ability to adjudicate a child delinquent for an act that would not be a crime if committed by an adult. These offenses are known as status offenses. In this case the juvenile court found the child to be incorrigible or beyond the control of her parents. The court removed the child from her parents' home and ordered the child and her parents to attend counseling. In doing so, the court acted in the best interests of the child. In addition, this case also demonstrated the juvenile court's jurisdiction over

parents. This jurisdiction (in loco parentis for parents) is common in many state juvenile codes.

IN RE WAYNE H.

596 P.2d 1 (Cal. 1979)

FACTS

A black male robbed a gas station with a pistol and escaped with fifty-four dollars. The station attendant was able to describe the suspect's clothing. Just before the robbery an attendant at another station in the area had noticed the suspicious movements of a gray Chevrolet containing two persons, one wearing a hat like that described by the attendant who was robbed. Responding to the robbery, an officer observed a gray Chevrolet traveling at high speed away from the crime scene. After the Chevrolet ran a stop sign the officer pursued the vehicle. When the passenger threw a pistol out the window, the officer stopped the vehicle and arrested the occupants. Wayne H., aged 16, was identified as the passenger. He matched the description given by the attendant and fifty-four dollars was found on the floorboard of the passenger side of the vehicle. The suspects were taken to the police station and held overnight. The next day a detective questioned Wayne H., who denied any involvement and provided an alibi. Wayne H. was taken to juvenile hall where he was interviewed by a probation officer. The probation officer gave Wayne H. Miranda warnings and explained that the results of the interview would bear on the determination of whether or not he would be detained and whether juvenile fitness proceedings would be recommended. Wayne H. again denied involvement. At the end of the interview the officer announced that he intended to recommend detention and a fitness hearing. Wayne H. then responded that "he did this one." At the ensuing jurisdictional hearing Wayne H.'s statement to the probation officer was admitted over his objection. Wayne H. was found true of the charges.

ISSUE

Is the information acquired by a probation officer at intake admissible in a subsequent adjudication or criminal trial?

HOLDING

No. It was an error to admit as evidence of guilt an incriminating statement that the minor made to the probation officer at intake.

IN RE WAYNE H. (*cont.*)

RATIONALE

The cases that the court reviewed stressed the law's interest in encouraging complete candor between a defendant and his or her probation officer. Consequently, admissions or statements made to probation officers in social reports or intake interviews have typically been inadmissible. The purpose of the interview is to assemble all the available information relevant to an informed disposition of the case if guilt is determined, or to assist in the evaluation of the juvenile's fitness for treatment as a juvenile. These decisions, courts have concluded, should be based on the most complete knowledge of the defendant's background that is possible. The defendant's description of the alleged offense, and his acknowledgment of guilt and demonstration of remorse, may significantly affect decisions about any punishments that the court may impose. Therefore, the minor should be advised any statements he or she makes will be used only for the information of the court in a probationary hearing. The court did not believe defendants would talk as freely if they believed their statements could be used against them in criminal proceedings. The court concluded that the subsequent use of statements made by a juvenile to a probation officer in a Section 628 interview would frustrate important purposes of that statute, and of the juvenile court law. Therefore, the court holds that such statements are not admissible as substantive evidence, or for impeachment, in any subsequent proceeding to determine criminal guilt, whether juvenile or criminal. However, such statements may be admitted and considered in hearings on the issues of detention and fitness for juvenile treatment.

CASE EXCERPT

"We conclude that the subsequent use of statements made by a juvenile to a probation officer in a section 628 interview would frustrate important purposes of that statute, and of the Juvenile Court Law generally. We therefore hold that such statements are not admissible as substantive evidence, or for impeachment, in any subsequent proceeding to determine criminal guilt, whether juvenile or adult. Such statements may, of course, be admitted and considered in hearings on the issues of detention and fitness for juvenile treatment."

CASE SIGNIFICANCE

This case stressed the rehabilitative nature of the juvenile court. The juvenile justice system is fundamentally designed to rehabilitate juveniles who are brought to its attention. An important component of any rehabilitative effort is the assessment provided to the court by a juvenile probation officer. The court encourages the juvenile to be honest with the probation officer during intake as well as a social history interview. The court takes this position because the intent of the juvenile system is rehabilitative first versus the punishment and community safety priorities that are elevated in the adult criminal system. In addition, the information attained by the probation officer in these interviews is invaluable to the court as it attempts to individualize a disposition that will rehabilitate the juvenile who has come to its attention. Consequently, the court puts the goal of rehabilitating the juvenile ahead of the state's interest in prosecuting him or her. In addition, if the court were to allow the information attained at either the intake meeting or social history interview to be used as evidence, it would have to allow the juvenile to have counsel present and thereby make those stages of the process critical stages in the proceedings. However, the court determined, as have most states, those stages should remain informal in nature and fundamentally designed to rehabilitate.

IN THE INTEREST OF E.B.

287 N.W.2d 462 (N.D. 1980)

FACTS

E.B., a 15-year-old living with his mother, was involved in an informal adjustment before a juvenile supervisor in 1978, at which time he admitted the unruly act of truancy during the 1977–1978 school year and was placed on probation. The following year a petition was filed alleging that E.B. was habitually truant from school. He missed a total of 18 days of school, six and one-half of which were unexcused, between September 5, 1978, and January 30, 1979. E.B.'s attorney moved to dismiss the petition on the ground that the section of the Juvenile Court Act was unconstitutionally vague. The court denied the motion.

ISSUES

Is the Juvenile Court Act's section too vague for the fair administration of justice? Does the state have to prove a child's absences from school were willful? Do six and one-half days of unexcused absences constitute habitual truancy?

HOLDING

No, no, and yes. The statute providing that an unruly child meant a child who was habitually and without justification truant from school was not unconstitutionally vague. The state was not required to prove the juvenile's absences were voluntary or willful or that there was no justification for the absences. The evidence supported determination that the juvenile had been habitually and without justification truant from school.

RATIONALE

The relevant section of the Juvenile Court Act provides that *unruly child* means a child who "[i]s habitually and without justification truant from school; In any of the foregoing is in need of treatment or rehabilitation." The court relied on the applicable principles for determining whether a statute is void for vagueness. The underlying principle is that no person shall be held criminally responsible for conduct which he or she could not reasonably understand to be proscribed. The court did not find argument that the words habitually and without justification were too vague to provide adequate standards. In doing so it relied on several other state court decisions on similar matters. The court also pointed out that the law requires children to attend school every day, unless said child's parent excuses him or her. The court did not intend to define what conduct is willful and not willful. The court placed this burden on the defendant. The court also agreed that based on the record and the history involving this child that the court made an accurate determination in ruling the child truant, despite his only having six and one-half days of unexcused absences.

CASE EXCERPT

"If the child does not attend, and his or her parent did not give permission for the absence—the child's absence is marked unexcused. This is the exact conduct meant to be proscribed, whether the reason for the absence was oversleeping or something else. We are hard-pressed to see how oversleeping is not volitional conduct, unless the fatigue producing the oversleeping is due to illness or other conditions beyond the juvenile's control."

CASE SIGNIFICANCE

This is an important case because it was representative of truancy cases in most states. The court was asked to further define the truancy statute and what

constitutes delinquency. Truancy statutes in most states are somewhat vague, as the defendant contended this one was. The rationale behind this vagueness is to leave up to individual school districts the decision of whom to charge with an offense. The court clearly did not want to interfere with the school district's ability to make such determinations. If the court were to define a set number of absences that constituted truancy, school districts would be forced to petition all those students who reached the prescribed amount of absences. However, the court determined that school districts may have good reason for not petitioning juveniles to be charged for truancy, despite many absences. By intervening, the court would interfere with the informal nature of school discipline, which the court was not prepared to do.

WASHINGTON v. CHATHAM

624 P.2d 1180 (Wash. App. 1981)

FACTS

Chatham, a juvenile, appealed his juvenile court assault conviction. The charge arose from an altercation between a group of several adult golfers and several juveniles including Chatham. During the altercation, one of the golfers sustained a serious and permanent eye injury caused by blows struck by Chatham. The appeal involves a juvenile's right to a diversion, as that term is used in the state's Juvenile Justice Act of 1977. The act establishes a comprehensive system for the disposition of juveniles. One such disposition is a juvenile diversion program in which eligible juvenile offenders perform community services as opposed to prosecution. In the present case, a member of the prosecuting attorney's staff phoned the chairperson of the diversion program and relayed the facts of the case. The chairperson declined because the serious nature of the charge did not fall within the committee's eligibility standards for diversion.

ISSUE

Do juveniles have a constitutional right to diversion?

HOLDING

No. Although a juvenile has a right to be considered for diversion, he or she does not have the constitutional right to be guaranteed admission into a diversion program.

WASHINGTON v. CHATHAM *(cont.)*

RATIONALE

Because the juvenile in this case was a first-time offender and not charged with a felony, he had a right to have his case referred to a diversionary unit. The juvenile code grants the diversion unit the authority to exercise sound discretion and to reject a case referred to it for diversion. The diversion unit must provide the reasons for refusal in writing according to the statute. Because this did not occur in this case a hearing was held to determine the reasons for rejecting the juvenile's referral. At the hearing, the chairperson testified this was the only case she could remember in which there was not a written explanation provided as to why the juvenile was not granted a diversion. However, she also testified that the diversion unit did not take cases that involved a serious injury or weapons, as this case did. Therefore the juvenile court determined the error was formalistic and not prejudicial. This court contended that the case was referred and denied according to reasons that were neither arbitrary nor capricious. Therefore, the actions of the committee and subsequent actions of the court did not violate due process.

CASE EXCERPT

"The juvenile's statutory right to have his or her case referred to a diversion unit does not guarantee that the unit will enter into a diversion agreement with the juvenile. Diversion is not always an appropriate disposition, even in first offender juvenile cases...Diversion represents the intent to preserve a species of informal adjustment for those youngsters whose offenses have been so few and so minor that involvement with a court would be counterproductive. The intent is to foster community accountability boards, a means for straightening out youthful offenders that has proved both popular and effective in the past."

CASE SIGNIFICANCE

This case is important for two reasons. First, the court held that a juvenile does not have a constitutional right to a diversion. Diversion has become popular and more formalized in recent times as juvenile justice practitioners have attempted to reduce the workload for the juvenile court by keeping less serious offenders away from the court process, while still holding them accountable informally through the diversion process. In addition, if a juvenile completes a diversion program the offense is typically kept off his or her record so as to avoid the stigma that goes along with having a history

with the court. In this case, the court allowed the decision of who is appropriate for diversion and who is not to be left to those individuals working in the individual jurisdictions. However, the court did uphold the part of the statute that said each juvenile does have the right to be considered for diversion. Consequently, every first-time offender charged with a crime by the police does have to be considered for diversion. However, the court did leave the methods of consideration up to each individual jurisdiction.

STATE v. MCDOWELL

685 P.2d 595 (Wash. 1984)

FACTS

A police report was sent to the King County prosecutor's office recommending that McDowell be charged with reckless endangerment. The case was screened and diverted to a diversion unit. McDowell met with a diversion staff member, but decided to reject the diversion program. The complaint was referred back to the prosecutor's office and an information charging McDowell with second-degree assault was filed. McDowell moved to dismiss the felony information because of prosecutorial vindictiveness, but the motion was denied. McDowell was found guilty of second-degree assault and was subsequently sentenced within the standard range for second-degree assault.

ISSUES

When a juvenile refuses to enter a diversion program on a complaint alleging a misdemeanor and the case is referred back to the prosecutor, does the prosecutor have discretion to file a felony information? If the juvenile is subsequently found guilty of the felony, is the sentencing court's discretion limited to imposing terms allowed under a diversion program?

HOLDING

Yes and yes. Under the circumstances of this case, the prosecutor's discretion was properly exercised. Furthermore, McDowell's sentence was valid.

RATIONALE

Existing Washington case law, suggests that actual vindictiveness is required to invalidate a prosecutor's adversarial decisions made prior to trial. The court found no rationale to presume that abuse of prosecutorial discretion is more likely when juveniles are brought to justice than when adults are prosecuted. Nor did the court conclude that the statutory scheme of the juvenile diversion system presents any special potential for abuse. The screening function that the prosecutor fulfills prior to diversion is merely to determine if cases are legally sufficient, not to determine the actual charges that would be brought. Only after a failure in, or refusal to enter, the diversion program does a prosecutor exercise his or her discretion for charging. Consequently, the court contended that presuming improper motivation for the prosecutor's filing decisions whenever an information differed from the original complaint would restrict the prosecutor's ability to make necessary pretrial adversarial decisions. Therefore, the court found no violation of McDowell's due process rights. In addition, the court did not assume that the legislature, by enacting a provision circumscribing judicial sentencing power, intended to remedy potential prosecutorial abuse. Consequently, there was no error in McDowell's sentence.

CASE EXCERPT

"Once a legally sufficient complaint is determined to require filing, such as when the juvenile refuses the offer of diversion, the prosecutor's charging discretion must be exercised. Common sense dictates that the original complaint and screening procedure will be reviewed and evaluated before an information is filed. For any number of reasons, whether it be new evidence or new conclusions about the significance of the allegations in the complaint, the charge actually filed might differ from the offense alleged in the initial complaint. Nothing in this procedure suggests that retaliatory motivation on the part of the prosecutor will underlie the charging decision."

CASE SIGNIFICANCE

This case is important because it allowed prosecutors to charge cases as they see fit, not as recommended by police officers. The court did not want the police to make charging decisions. That is solely the role of the prosecutor. In making the decision to refer a case for diversion a prosecutor is merely determining if the juvenile and the charge brought against him or her meet the criteria for diversion. The prosecutor typically examines the seriousness of the offense and discerns whether the juvenile has a prior history with the court. The prosecutor is not determining what specific crime has been alleged, merely if the case has merit. To require the prosecutor to make such a

decision would unduly burden him or her, which is fundamentally what the diversion process is designed to undo. Consequently, the court held that filing a more serious charge than that recommended by the police was not vindictive, but within the law.

UNITED STATES v. NASH

620 F.Supp. 1439 (S.D.N.Y. 1985)

FACTS

Nash, a juvenile, was arrested for attempted armed bank robbery. He was advised of his rights and driven to FBI headquarters. Upon arrival, Nash was taken to an interview room and advised of his rights again. He then signed a waiver of his rights, which caused the agents to become aware of his age. They contacted his mother and advised her of the arrest and the charges against her son. She indicated she was unable to come to court. It is unclear whether this notification took place before or after Nash made the statement at issue in the motion, or whether Mrs. Nash was advised of her son's rights. Nash was subsequently processed and taken before a magistrate. Nash was in custody for two to three hours before making a confession and eight to nine hours before seeing a magistrate. Some of the delay was due to interviews by pretrial services and the interview of the codefendant by his probation officer.

ISSUE

Were the notification procedures and time delay before the first court appearance justifiable, thereby allowing incriminating statements made by the juveniles to be admissible in court?

HOLDING

No. The requirements of the Federal Juvenile Delinquency Act concerning admonition of legal rights, notification of a responsible adult, and presentment to a magistrate were not satisfied; therefore, any postarrest statements made prior to presentment to the magistrate must be suppressed.

RATIONALE

Section 5033 of the Federal Juvenile Delinquency Act provides: "Whenever a juvenile is taken into custody for an alleged act of juvenile delinquency, the arresting officer shall immediately advise such juvenile of his legal rights, in language comprehensible to a juvenile, and shall immediately notify the Attorney General

UNITED STATES v. NASH *(cont.)*

and the juvenile's parents, guardian, or custodian of such custody. The arresting officer shall also notify the parents or guardian of the rights of a juvenile and of the nature of the alleged offense. The juvenile shall be taken before a magistrate forthwith. In no event shall the juvenile be detained for longer than a reasonable period of time before being brought before a magistrate." The court interpreted the second part of the section to cover weekends and holidays. The court contended that under normal circumstances the "forthwith" language is to be followed by the arresting officers. The court also pointed out that the defendant's parents were accessible and the officers could have waited to take a statement from the juvenile until such time as the juvenile's mother could be there. The mother indicated she would be unable to come to court; however, an alternate interview time could have been arranged. The government attempted to argue a totality-of-the-circumstances defense to admitting the statements; however, the court found to the contrary. The court again pointed to the notification, and the unreasonable delay before going before a magistrate that was readily available on a weekday morning. In addition, the court struck down the government's contention that the youth was streetwise, by saying that he may have been, but nonetheless he was a juvenile.

CASE EXCERPT

"We are not persuaded by the Government's arguments. In fact, looking at the total circumstances of this case, we are more convinced that these statements must be held inadmissible. The Government's notification did not, and could not, effectuate the purpose of the statute. The 7–9 hour delay before presentment was unreasonable given the availability of a magistrate on that weekday morning."

CASE SIGNIFICANCE

This case is important because it clarifies the language dealing with pretrial detention procedure in the Federal Juvenile Delinquency Act. The court held that the police must make every effort to have a juvenile's parent or guardian present for any questioning and make sure that the parent or guardian is aware of his or her child's rights prior to any questioning. This is consistent with other cases in which the courts have taken a totality-of-the-circumstances approach. In this case, the court determined the officers did not make reasonable efforts to advise the juvenile's mother of his

rights or make arrangements to have her present for questioning. In addition, the court also clarified the meaning of the word "forthwith" in the act. The court determined that a juvenile who is detained should be presented to a magistrate as soon as it is humanly possible. The court made clear that they did not want a juvenile unreasonably detained when a magistrate is available. This clearly is distinct from the adult criminal system, in which the state may detain an individual for a reasonable period of time, which the Court has determined to be up to 48 hours, not counting a weekend or holiday.

CHRISTOPHER P. v. NEW MEXICO
816 P.2d 485 (N.M. 1991)

FACTS

Christopher P., a juvenile, was charged in the children's court division of a district court with two counts of first-degree murder and conspiracy to commit first-degree murder. At the same time, the children's court attorney filed a motion to transfer the case to the adult division of the district court. The transfer proceedings were bifurcated. During the initial stages of the transfer proceedings, the children's court judge determined there were reasonable grounds to believe Christopher P. committed the delinquent acts. The subsequent stage of the proceedings addressed whether he was amenable to treatment as a child through available facilities. Prior to this portion of the transfer proceedings, the children's court judge ordered that Christopher P. submit to a psychological evaluation to aid the court in its amenability determination. Over objection of the juvenile's counsel, the court ordered the child to discuss the alleged delinquent acts with the psychologist conducting the evaluation. The court also ordered that any information about the alleged incident discussed during the examination could be used only for the amenability portion of the transfer hearing and for no other purposes. During the evaluation, Christopher described his activities before and during the alleged offenses and the feelings he experienced. The record reflects that the psychologist's testimony during the amenability proceedings included specific references to the child's statements and that, at least in part, the psychologist relied on the child's statements in reaching his conclusion that Christopher was not amenable to treatment as a child. Christopher P. was transferred to criminal court.

ISSUE

Was the juvenile's Fifth Amendment privilege against self-incrimination violated when the court ordered him to discuss the alleged crimes during a psychological evaluation to determine whether he could benefit from treatment in the juvenile justice system?

HOLDING

Yes. The juvenile's Fifth Amendment privilege was violated by the court's order compelling him to discuss alleged offenses with a psychologist, without advice of counsel, during a psychological evaluation ordered by the court for the purpose of determining whether he would benefit from treatment in the juvenile justice system.

RATIONALE

Christopher P. did not challenge the court's authority to order him to submit to a psychological evaluation for the purpose of aiding the court in determining amenability. Instead he argued the court's authority to require him to discuss specifics of the alleged offense. The state argued the Fifth Amendment was not applicable to the transfer proceeding because it was not adversarial and its only purpose was to determine the forum in which the juvenile would be tried. The court contended the state's characterization diminished the impact of the proceeding on the juvenile. The court pointed to the legislative intent of the Juvenile Code, which is to remove children committing delinquent acts from adult consequences and provide the most appropriate and distinct dispositional options for the treatment and rehabilitation of the children. In addition, the legislature wanted to provide judicial and other procedures in which the juveniles are assured a fair hearing and their constitutional rights are enforced. Further, children are afforded the same basic rights as adults. The court also pointed to *Kent* [383 U.S. 541 (1966)], where the Supreme Court held that the transfer hearing was a "critically important" stage of the proceedings. Therefore, the court deemed transfer proceedings must measure up to the essentials of due process and fair treatment. The court also pointed to *Gault*, in which the Supreme Court held the Fifth Amendment applicable to adjudicatory proceedings in juvenile court. In this case, not only was the child compelled to make inculpatory statements for purposes of the transfer proceedings, his exposure was maximized by the presence of the prosecution during the psychologist's examination. This court felt that although the statements made by the juvenile were barred from trial, it is unlikely that the prosecution would not have gained new insight and information from the child's statements. Consequently, this court held the transfer proceeding is a critical stage in the child's involvement in the justice system and therefore the Fifth Amendment applied.

CASE EXCERPT

The Fifth Amendment "not only protects the individual against being involuntarily called as a witness against himself in a criminal prosecution but also privileges him not to answer official questions put to him in any other proceeding, civil or criminal, formal or informal, where his answers might incriminate him in future criminal proceedings…While the court's order here barred use of the inculpatory statements in further proceedings, it is difficult to imagine how the prosecution could have failed to gain new insights and information from the child's statements."

CASE SIGNIFICANCE

This case is important because it clarified procedure in transfer hearings. The courts often order a juvenile to submit to a psychological evaluation for the purposes of determining his or her mental fitness and amenability to treatment. In this case, the court also ordered the juvenile to discuss the alleged offense with the psychologist in the presence of the prosecutor. Although the court did not allow the information about the offense to be used in the criminal trial, it did allow the information to become the knowledge of the state. This court contended that to be in violation of *Gault*, which prohibits self-incrimination at the adjudicatory stage of the proceedings. Although the transfer hearing is not an adjudicatory hearing, it is a critical stage in the process, as defined in *Kent*. Consequently, the same rules apply.

UNITED STATES v. A.R.

38 F.3d 699 (3d Cir. 1994)

FACTS

A.R., aged 17, and a group of companions allegedly spotted a white Pontiac in a hotel parking lot and decided to steal it. A.R. approached the car, pointed a gun at the head of the woman in the driver's seat, and told her to get out because he was taking the car. The driver and her passenger got out of the car. A.R. and a

UNITED STATES v. A.R. *(cont.)*

female juvenile got into the car and sped away. They were apprehended following a high-speed chase, and A.R. was charged. After he was in custody, the authorities filed charges against him for a number of armed robberies committed the day before. He was taken to the juvenile detention center where he underwent a psychological evaluation and a psychiatric evaluation. Both were conducted at the request of the district attorney, for use in a hearing to determine whether A.R. should be certified as an adult. These reports were not intended for use at subsequent criminal proceedings. The reports concluded that A.R. was in need of a highly secure facility and that the juvenile system could not offer him anything more at this point. A.R. contended that he was not given Miranda warnings prior to the evaluations, nor was his attorney given notice they were going to occur. The record contained no explicit factual findings concerning the truth of the allegations in the report. A trial was held to determine whether A.R. should be transferred to criminal court. Both reports were admitted into evidence and A.R. also introduced his own psychologist. The court ultimately transferred A.R. to criminal court.

ISSUE

Did the process of psychological and psychiatric evaluations used in this case violate the juvenile's Fifth Amendment right to remain silent and his Sixth Amendment right to have counsel present during questioning?

HOLDING

No. Psychiatric evaluations for the purpose of determining adult transfer status are not critical stages of the proceedings, and thus are not subject to the protections of the Fifth and Sixth Amendments of the United States Constitution.

RATIONALE

The court contended that the focus of the Fifth Amendment is upon the nature of the statement or admission and upon the exposure to which it invites, not the type of proceeding in which it is made. The court indicated that other courts have typically addressed adult certification hearings as civil in nature, because they result only in a decision upon the status of the individual. As such, the hearing court is entitled to assume the juvenile committed the offense for the purpose of the hearing. Further, while the evidence

introduced at the hearing must be consistent with due process and fundamental fairness, it need not be in compliance with the federal rules of evidence. In addition, while the burden of proof is on the government, that burden is only the preponderance of the evidence. Therefore, this hearing paralleled a competency hearing. These types of reports are commonly used in those proceedings. Therefore, the failure to administer Miranda warnings did not violate A.R.'s Fifth Amendment rights, because the information attained was not being used to incriminate him. As for A.R.'s claim that he did not have counsel present during the evaluations, this court did not see the evaluation as a critical stage in the process. No significant rights were at stake in the evaluation itself. At the transfer hearing the juvenile had the right to counsel, as well as the right to attack the methods employed by the evaluators. In addition, the evaluation was not a legal confrontation that could only be fully understood after consultation with counsel. Further, the merits of the case were not an issue, because the trial court, for purposes of the transfer hearing, could assume the juvenile was guilty. Therefore, the court did not believe counsel would serve a functional purpose at a psychiatric evaluation the results of which were used, as was necessarily the case here, only in making the neutral determination whether a juvenile should stay within the juvenile justice system or be treated as an adult.

CASE EXCERPT

"Simply stated, counsel would serve no functional purpose at a psychiatric evaluation the results of which are used, as is necessarily the case here, only in making the neutral determination whether a juvenile should stay within the juvenile justice system or be treated as an adult. A.R., therefore, had no Sixth Amendment right to counsel in connection with the evaluations."

CASE SIGNIFICANCE

This case is important because it allowed the state to compel a juvenile to submit to a psychiatric or psychological evaluation for the purposes of determining whether he or she is amenable to treatment and whether he or she should be transferred to adult criminal court. Courts have previously not allowed the state to compel juveniles to submit to these types of evaluations and discuss the present offense. However, in this case the evaluator's sole purpose was to determine if the juvenile should be transferred to criminal court. Consequently, the evaluator would be examining elements such as maturity and level of sophistication. Therefore the court allowed the evaluations to be utilized and conducted without counsel present. In holding this way, the court established that the evaluation itself is not a critical stage in the proceedings.

R.R. v. PORTESY

629 So.2d 1059 (Fla. App. 1994)

FACTS

R.R., a juvenile, was charged with arson and taken into custody by the police. Shortly afterward, a detention hearing was held in the judge's chambers. Present in the chambers with the judge were an assistant public defender representing R.R., and an assistant state attorney. R.R. was continued detained and was not physically present at the hearing in the judge's chambers. R.R.'s communication with his counsel and the court was by videophone. The public defender had previously objected to the use of the procedure in other juvenile cases. R.R. filed a petition objecting to the use of the videophone and the fact that he was not allowed to be physically present at his hearing.

ISSUE

Are technology-assisted distance detention hearings constitutional if the juvenile is not physically present but is allowed to participate via video hookup?

HOLDING

No. Absent rule or statute that allows such proceedings, there is no authority for the court to hold a detention hearing with the juvenile's presence secured only by videophone. The juvenile's presence is required in the absence of a waiver or a specific finding that the juvenile's mental or physical condition precluded his presence.

RATIONALE

R.R. pointed out that Florida Rule of Juvenile Procedure 8.100 required his presence at the detention hearing and argued that it meant that he be physically present before the judge with counsel. R.R. argued that the videophone procedure used in this case did not satisfy the requirement of physical presence, and further noted that no rule or statute authorized the procedure. The court agreed with R.R. and interpreted the law to mean that a juvenile is to be physically present at all hearings held under the juvenile rules, except where

there has been a waiver of the right to be present or the court makes specific findings regarding the child's physical or mental condition that precludes physical presence. Neither of those exceptions existed in the present case. The court did not intend to offer any view on the feasibility of using such technology to improve the efficiency of the court system. The court merely did not want to rule on such technological innovations at this level. It was its contention that those matters should be left to the Florida Supreme Court or the Florida legislature. Consequently, absent a rule from one of those entities, the use of the videophone violated the juvenile rule.

CASE EXCERPT

"By this decision we do not intend to offer any view on the feasibility of using such technology to improve the efficiency of the court system. Nor do we intend to discourage the investigation and use of innovative techniques that can enhance the efficiency of court procedure. We only hold that the use of video-telephones for juvenile detention hearings is a substantial change in policy which...should be developed and approved through the rule-making authority of the Florida Supreme Court or through the legislative process."

CASE SIGNIFICANCE

This case is important because it reflected the court's unwillingness to construct new law. The court did not say that the use of the videophone was not a necessary evolution of the times; what it did say was that the Florida statute did not allow for such measures to be used in a hearing. In so ruling, the court put the burden of making the decision of whether these technological devices will be used on the state legislature. Many jurisdictions are using technological devices to improve judicial efficiency. In this holding, the court maintained that the legislature must construct law that allows the use of these devices. Absent such law the defendant has a right to be physically present at all hearings, unless he or she waives that right.

STATE v. K.K.H.

878 P.2d 1255 (Wash. App. 1994)

FACTS

K.K.H., a juvenile, was arrested for possession of stolen property and placed in the Department of Youth Services Detention Center later the same day. Less

STATE v. K.K.H. *(cont.)*

than 24 hours after K.K.H.'s arrest, the prosecutor telephoned a superior court judge, was placed under oath, and read the police department's reports regarding the case to the judge. Defense counsel was present with the prosecutor when the call was made, but the judge denied his request to participate in the call. The judge found adequate basis upon which to find probable cause to believe K.K.H. committed the crime for which he had been arrested. A detention review hearing was scheduled. Prior to the hearing the prosecutor filed an information and the hearing was continued to the following day. At the hearing K.K.H. was ordered detained. The appearance, which was his first, occurred 96 hours after his arrest.

ISSUE

Is there a time within which a juvenile must be given a probable cause hearing, and what are the appropriate procedures for establishing probable cause when the juvenile is detained?

HOLDING

Yes. The constitutional time frame for such a determination is generally within 48 hours, not the 96-hour delay in this case. Procedures for determining probable cause may vary by jurisdiction as long as they can withstand constitutional scrutiny.

RATIONALE

The Washington law reads that any juvenile who has been taken into custody and detained must receive a judicial determination on the issues of probable cause no later than 48 hours following the juvenile's arrest. This is designed to reflect the Supreme Court's decision in *Riverside v. McLaughlin* (500 U.S. 44 (1991))]. Therefore, the juvenile's challenge failed. The court rejected his argument for a 24-hour limit on the time between arrest and probable cause determination. Washington law requires a judicial determination of probable cause, not a hearing. K.K.H. challenged the telephone procedure that was used in this case. However, the court pointed out that nothing in the rule required that the juvenile's counsel be permitted to participate. The court relied on *Gerstein* [*v. Pugh* (420 U.S. 103 (1975))], which does not define the probable cause determination as a critical stage in the process. Therefore, the telephone conference between prosecutor and judge met the constitutional requirements defined by the Supreme Court.

CASE EXCERPT

"We assume for purposes of our analysis that, by whatever method the probable cause determination is made, it complies with JuCR 7.3(a) to the extent it is made within 48 hours of arrest. Moreover, we assume that in addition to occurring within 48 hours of arrest, the probable cause determinations are not unreasonably delayed."

CASE SIGNIFICANCE

This case is important because it reflected the wide amount of discretion states have in determining probable cause to detain a juvenile. The purpose of the probable cause stage of a proceeding is to judicially determine whether there is a fair probability a crime has occurred. Although some states allow for hearings on such matters, in which there is cross-examination, absent a constitutional requirement there is no need for such hearings to occur. The only requirement is that the case be presented to a magistrate within 48 hours of the detention, which is analogous to the adult criminal system.

STATE v. LOWRY

230 A.2d 907 (N.J. 1997)

FACTS

Two police officers patrolling in a marked police car observed a new Mustang with three occupants parked in a deserted area. The area was known as a location where stolen cars were dropped. The officers became suspicious and began to investigate. On the way to the car one of the officers noticed a man with something in his hand about to exit the car. The officer told him to stop and the man got back in the car and closed the door. Upon approaching the car an officer noticed one of the passengers attempt to hide cigarettes. When the suspect rolled down the window the officer detected the odor of marijuana. The officers then asked the other passengers to exit the car, which they did. The officers noticed some more cigarettes and seized them. The officers then made arrests. Lowry, age 17, the driver of the car, moved to suppress evidence seized as a result of an allegedly illegal search of a parked car in which it was seized. The defendant based the motion on the fact that the search was warrantless and not incident to a valid arrest.

ISSUE

Is the Fourth Amendment right applicable to juveniles?

HOLDING

Yes. The rights of privacy, security, and liberty against unreasonable searches and seizures are applicable to juveniles in accordance with reason and due process of law.

RATIONALE

The court cited a prior case which applied the Fourth Amendment to all persons regardless of age. The court did point out how the juvenile justice system does not guarantee all the rights afforded adults to juveniles because it is intended to operate in the best interests of the child. However, the rights guaranteed under the Fourth Amendment are not those that are withheld. The court relied on the historical development of the law, which indicates the rule is not only applicable to all, but also fundamental to the concept of due process. The court contended that the Juvenile Court Act was designed to remove juveniles from the harshness of the criminal justice system, not to deprive them of any rights. The court also justified its decision by pointing to the parens patriae philosophy and indicating that in order to better rehabilitate juveniles, official misconduct must not go undeterred. Consequently, the right of privacy applies to all regardless of age. However, in this case the court ruled that the warrantless search and subsequent arrests were reasonable and justified, as the police were following typical police procedure in their investigation of the three individuals.

CASE EXCERPT

"Not only did the police officers have a right to investigate under the aforementioned circumstances, they had a *duty* to investigate, and in the proper exercise of their responsibility these officers observed through the car windows the crimped cigarettes...Observing this evidence, fully disclosed and in plain view of the police officers, whether or not in artificial light, is not a search. A search implies some exploratory investigation and a prying into hidden places for that which is concealed."

CASE SIGNIFICANCE

This case is important because the court went to great lengths to justify why the Fourth Amendment applies to juveniles. The court did point out that juveniles are not afforded all rights provided to adults; however, they are afforded Fourth Amendment protections. The court contended that to allow officer misconduct, which is prohibited in the adult criminal system by the exclusionary rule, would fly in the face of the rehabilitative ideal of the juvenile justice system. However, in this case the officers acted upon reasonable suspicion and located evidence of crime. Consequently, the search and subsequent arrest did not violate the juveniles' Fourth Amendment rights.

DISCUSSION QUESTIONS

1. What due process rights do juveniles have when they are charged in juvenile court?
2. Why is the intake process not considered a critical stage in juvenile court proceedings?
3. Is it permissible to impose fines and court costs on juveniles?
4. What procedures take place at intake and why are they important?
5. Many studies show that pretrial detention is one of the best predictors of deep penetration into the juvenile justice system. Why should that be?
6. What rights are juveniles afforded in the intake conference?
7. Are truancy statutes written vaguely?
8. What is the purpose of diversion?
9. What rules govern the use of diversion procedures?
10. What are positives and negatives associated with court-ordered psychiatric evaluations prior to adjudication?

CHAPTER FOUR

DETENTION

BENJAMIN STEINER, UNIVERSITY OF NEBRASKA – OMAHA
RIANE MILLER, UNIVERSITY OF SOUTH CAROLINA

BALDWIN V. LEWIS, *300 F.SUPP. 1220 (WISC. 1969)*

MARTARELLA V. KELLEY, *349 F.SUPP. 575 (S.D.N.Y. 1972)*

COX V. TURLEY, *506 F.2D 1347 (6TH CIR. 1974)*

MOSS V. WEAVER, *535 F.2D 1258 (5TH CIR. 1976)*

MARTIN V. STRASBURG, *689 F.2D 363 (2D CIR. 1982)*

D.B. V. TEWKSBURY, *545 F.SUPP. 896 (D. OR. 1982)*

IN THE INTEREST OF DARLENE C., *301 S.E.2D 136 (S.C. 1983)*

SCHALL V. MARTIN, *104 U.S. 2403 (1984)*

RENO V. FLORES, *507 U.S. 292 (1993)*

HORN BY PARKS V. MADISON COUNTY FISCAL COURT, *22 F.3D 653 (6TH CIR. 1994)*

INTRODUCTION

A juvenile detention center is analogous to a county jail in the adult criminal system. It is not the same as a youth correctional facility, much like a jail is not the same as a prison; jails are typically operated by county sheriffs, whereas prisons are typically operated by the state or federal government. Juvenile detention is fundamentally designed for short-term confinement. However, in some jurisdictions, this is not what typically occurs.

The decision to detain is one of the initial determinations in the juvenile justice system and the first in the juvenile court. When juveniles are taken into custody, the juvenile court must determine whether they should be held in detention or whether it is appropriate to return them to their parents' home pending the next hearing. This is a critical decision because it involves a child's liberty, as there is no right to bail in the juvenile justice system. In making this decision, the juvenile judge will often consider factors such as the probability the offense was committed, the seriousness of the offense, the likelihood the juvenile will return for the next hearing, the suitability of the parents and their home, and the protection of current or future victims. This information is typically supplied to the juvenile court by the juvenile probation department. However,

some jurisdictions allow defense counsel to be present for the detention hearing. This can, and often does, lead to an adversarial argument of probable cause as well as the issue of detention.

In the past, juveniles were typically housed with adults in jail facilities. Although they were often segregated, most jurisdictions did not have separate facilities for juveniles. Now, most jurisdictions have their own juvenile detention centers or contract with another locale that does. As with the other stages of juvenile justice proceedings, court cases have guided the applicable laws and procedures that govern how detention decisions are made. Initially, juveniles were most often returned to their parents' homes. However, over time, juveniles began to be placed in preventative detention under the doctrine of parens patriae. The courts justified this by determining that a child was a risk to him- or herself. This conclusion was reached by using such rationale as that the juvenile was out of control, would commit further delinquent acts, or might not return for his or her next hearing. However, as detention was used more regularly, official misconduct increased in frequency. This was not necessarily the fault of those individuals making detention decisions, but perhaps a fault of the system for not establishing clear guidelines for juvenile justice practitioners to follow. Consequently, the courts were called upon to intervene.

Initially, the courts held that juveniles had a right to due process in the determination of whether they should be held in detention pending adjudicatory hearing. The courts followed this by encouraging against, and in some jurisdictions eliminating, the holding of juveniles in adult facilities. In addition, the courts provided that detention could be used to detain status offenders, but the detention had to be for rehabilitative purposes. In the 1960s and 1970s, juveniles' civil liberties became more of a concern and the procedures for detention became more defined. Among the procedures the courts required were the notification of the juvenile's parents, a judicial determination of probable cause within a reasonable period of time, and adequate facilities with a treatment component to house juveniles. Absent these procedures, pretrial detention was often ruled unconstitutional.

The states responded and developed procedures that complied with the courts' mandates. As has been the case in other areas of the juvenile justice system, the procedures have largely mirrored those of the adult criminal justice system. Court decisions have guided states and juvenile court systems in their development of policy and procedures for handling juveniles who are confined in pretrial detention. In this chapter, we review some of the leading cases dealing with juvenile detention.

BALDWIN v. LEWIS

300 F.Supp. 1220 (Wisc. 1969)

FACTS

Baldwin, a 17-year-old, was taken into custody on suspicion of having committed arson. Baldwin was held by a Detention Authorization Form which, in Baldwin's case, gave no reason for the detention. The next day, prior to his mother's arrival, Baldwin appeared before a social worker who had been designated by the children's court to determine whether juveniles should be detained at the detention center. Baldwin was ordered detained and a Detention Authorization Form was again used, on which the worker checked the following sections: (1) It is reasonably believed that a child has committed an act which if committed by an adult would be a felony; and (2) the child is almost certain to commit an offense dangerous to himself or the community before the court disposition or transfer to an institution or another jurisdiction. There was nothing in the record that alluded to the facts on which the worker based his conclusions. Two days later, Baldwin went before a judge to determine if he should be held and was ordered detained. At that hearing, Baldwin's attorney argued that since nearly a month had occurred between the alleged act and Baldwin's arrest there should have been a judicial determination of probable cause prior to his arrest. The court indicated the only matter that was to be considered at this hearing was whether the juvenile should be detained pending the next hearing. Baldwin's attorney argued for release or, at the least, a bail amount. The court asked what the probation department's opinion on the matter was, and the social worker indicated he thought Baldwin should be detained. The state argued for detention indicating that the Children's Code did not provide for bail in juvenile matters. The court then ruled that it would be in the best interest of the juvenile and the community if Baldwin were detained. The Detention Authorization Form was again used to detain the juvenile, only the judge also signed it this time. The next day a writ of habeas corpus was filed. The circuit court determined the detention hearing was not properly conducted and ordered a new hearing. The circuit court subsequently held that hearing and determined the state was not required to show probable cause to believe the petitioner had committed an act which would have been a crime if he was an adult because the Wisconsin statutes did not contain such a requirement. Consequently, the actions of the state were within the statutory requirements. The circuit court also ordered Baldwin held in detention without bail.

ISSUES

Must probable cause exist before a juvenile may be taken into custody on suspicion of having committed a violation of the law which would constitute a crime if committed by an adult? Must the determination of probable cause be made by a judicial officer prior to arrest? Did the officers at the time of the arrest have knowledge of facts sufficient to establish probable cause? Was the petitioner entitled to a hearing on the existence of probable cause for his continued detention subsequent to his arrest? Does the petitioner have a constitutional right to bail?

HOLDING

Yes, yes, no, yes, and no. The juvenile was denied due process of law, in violation of the Fourteenth

BALDWIN v. LEWIS (cont.)

Amendment during his detention hearings before both the children's court and the circuit court. The writ of habeas corpus was justifiably granted.

RATIONALE

In reference to the probable cause requirement, the court cited numerous cases in which the Fourth Amendment has been interpreted to require probable cause prior to an arrest. The court pointed out that this rule has been applied to the states through the due process clause of the Fourteenth Amendment. The court contended that when the juvenile was taken into custody he was in effect under arrest. The court relied on the Ninth Circuit's decision in *Gilbert v. United States*, 366 F.2d 923 (1966) when making this ruling. However, the court pointed out that the police officer making an arrest does not need to have a judicial officer make a probable cause determination prior to the arrest if the officer has knowledge of sufficient facts to establish probable cause. The court also indicated that based on the reports that were taken in this case, the police had probable cause to make an arrest. In addition, it was unclear how much time it took to establish probable cause. Therefore, the lapse in time between the act and arrest may have been warranted. The court also held that the petitioner was entitled to a probable cause hearing after his arrest. The court applied *In re Gault*, 387 U.S. 1 (1967) in stating that a juvenile has the same right to due process as an adult. In this case, defense counsel was not even allowed to examine the materials for which the state and the court based its decision for continued detention. Consequently, this court felt that the juvenile's right to fundamental fairness had been infringed. The court ordered the juvenile released. The court did take up the issue of a juvenile's right to bail; however, it was the court's finding that the Wisconsin code, when observed correctly, was more than an adequate substitute for bail.

CASE EXCERPT

"In order to satisfy the constitutional requirements of due process, a detention hearing held pursuant to §48.29 must include a determination as to whether there is probable cause to believe (1) that an act has been committed which if committed by an adult would be a crime, and (2) that the juvenile in custody has in fact committed such act. The Wisconsin Children's Code, when applied in a manner consistent with due process, affords a juvenile an adequate substitute for bail."

CASE SIGNIFICANCE

This case is important because the court required that juveniles be afforded the due process protections applied to the states through the Fourteenth Amendment. In doing so, the court indicated that there must be a judicial determination of probable cause within a reasonable amount of time after a juvenile's arrest. This holding brought juvenile procedure in line with adult criminal procedure, where a probable cause determination by a magistrate is required within 48 working hours after arrest. This decision afforded juvenile defendants a constitutional right and moved the juvenile court in this state away from the informal nature it had operated under prior to this ruling.

MARTARELLA v. KELLEY

349 F.Supp. 575 (S.D.N.Y. 1972)

FACTS

Martarella, a juvenile, was declared a person in need of supervision (PINS) pursuant to New York state law. A suit was filed on behalf of Martarella and two other juveniles alleging that the temporary detention in three of the maximum-security juvenile facilities operated by New York City deprived the juveniles of due process and equal protection because they were not provided with treatment during their detention. In addition, the suit alleged that the treatment within the facilities constituted cruel and unusual punishment, and that because they were held with juvenile delinquents their rights had been further violated.

ISSUES

May PINS be constitutionally confined in the maximum-security centers named in this suit? Does the detention of PINS with juvenile delinquents violate the equal protection clause?

HOLDING

No and no. Conditions at one facility violated the Eighth Amendment, and the detention centers did not provide adequate treatment for children who were not true temporary detainees and thereby violated their right to due process. However, joint custody with juvenile delinquents is not unconstitutional.

RATIONALE

The court contended that juveniles who have been adjudicated as PINS are runaways, truants, or ungovernable within their home. These acts, for which they may be brought to the attention of the court, detained at centers, and subsequently held in custody for long periods of time, would not be considered crimes if committed by an adult. However, when the state imposes detention, it does so as parens patriae. When doing this, the state meets the requirements of due process and prohibition of cruel and unusual punishment outlined in the Constitution. However, adequate treatment must be provided to the detainee. The court contended that however benign the reasons for which the PINS were held in custody, and whatever the sad circumstances that prompted their detention, they were held in penal conditions, and thus should be given the same access to treatment as detained juvenile delinquents. In the present facilities, only the Manida facility did not meet the required conditions. The court contended that while they favored the separation of PINS and juvenile delinquents, they were bound by an earlier decision, *Sostre v. McGinnis*, 442 F.2d. 178 (2d Cir. 1971). In *Sostre*, the court determined it needed to become more informed before it could make a responsible use of judicial review to declare a punishment unconstitutional under the Eighth Amendment.

CASE EXCERPT

"There is no doubt that the Eighth Amendment's prohibition of cruel and unusual punishment is not restricted to instances of particular punishment inflicted on a given individual but also applies to mere confinement to an institution which is 'characterized by conditions and practices so bad as to be shocking to the conscience of reasonably civilized people.' There can be no doubt that the right to treatment, generally, for those held in non-criminal custody (whether based on due process, equal protection or the Eighth Amendment, or a combination of them) has by now been recognized by the Supreme Court, the lower federal courts, and the courts of New York."

CASE SIGNIFICANCE

This case is important because it dealt with the detention of nondelinquent youth. The court pointed out how this state, as well as others, allowed for the detention of juveniles who are adjudicated of status offenses to be held in detention centers under the doctrine of parens patriae. Essentially, the courts place these juveniles in detention because they are considered a risk to themselves. This case is also important because

it illustrated some of the concerning aspects of this practice. In addition, the court found one of the facilities to violate the Eighth Amendment because of the conditions to which the juveniles were subjected. This was important because at this time, many jurisdictions did not have standards for housing juvenile detainees and this case, as well as related cases decided in other states, forced states to develop such standards. Furthermore, the court determined that these youth have a due process right to receive treatment while in custody. This clearly demonstrated the difference between the adult criminal justice system and the juvenile justice system, as the court ordered that if these youth were going to be detained they were to be provided rehabilitative measures, given that was the justification for the detention. However, the court did not overturn the law, which does allow for the detaining of PINS with delinquent youth. Despite this, the court did use strong language encouraging against the custom.

COX v. TURLEY
506 F.2d 1347 (6th Cir. 1974)

FACTS

Cox, a 16-year-old, was arrested for a curfew violation and taken to the Madison County Jail, where he was held on the order of a nonlawyer judge in charge of juvenile affairs. Cox requested to phone his father, but the request was denied. Cox was then placed under the custody of the jailer without any type of hearing. The arresting officer did not notify Cox's parents or release the boy with a written promise to appear, as provided by the Kentucky statute. On the fifth day after the arrest, the nonlawyer judge had Cox brought before him. There is no record of what was said other than the boy was told to get a haircut, shave his beard, and reappear before the nonlawyer judge a week later. Cox was then released to his father. Cox complied with the order and was again released to his father pending juvenile court proceedings. Cox's father filed suit.

ISSUE

Were Cox's constitutional rights violated when he was denied a telephone call to his parents, his parents were not notified by the arresting officer, and he was detained in the general jail population for five days without a probable cause hearing?

COX v. TURLEY (*cont.*)

HOLDING

Yes. The refusal of officers to permit the minor to make a telephone call to his parents when he was taken to jail, and refusal of the arresting officer to notify the boy's parents as required by Kentucky statutes, together with the minor's confinement with the general jail population for five days without a probable cause hearing, constituted cruel and unusual punishment in violation of the minor's constitutional rights.

RATIONALE

The court contended that the due process clause requires that notice of the charges must be given to the accused at the earliest practical time and, in any event, sufficiently in advance of scheduled court proceedings so that reasonable opportunity to prepare will be afforded. Further, the court held that the notice of charges must set forth the alleged misconduct and particularity. This was applied to juvenile matters in *Gault*. The court determined that the treatment of the boy in this case was that of gross misconduct. The court was of the opinion that the constitutional rights of the boy were violated in several ways. By failing to arraign the boy, and keeping him in custody, denying him any rights to communicate with his parents, and without releasing the boy to his parents in accordance with the Kentucky statutes, and by failing to give notice of the cause of his arrest within the earliest practicable time, he was deprived of his liberty in violation of the Fourth and Fifth Amendments of the Constitution. In reaching their conclusion, the court relied on *United States v. Hegstrom,* 178 F. Supp. 17 (1959), an earlier Second Circuit decision.

CASE EXCERPT

"The boy was deprived of his constitutional rights under the due process clause by reason of confinement with the general jail population without a charge lodged against him, without being arraigned, and without being taken before any judicial officer at the earliest practicable time…and without being given any notice of his alleged offense. Moreover, the officer's refusal to permit the boy to make a telephone call to his parents when he was taken to jail, and the refusal of the arresting officer to notify the boy's parents, as commanded by the Kentucky statutes, together with his confinement with the general jail population without a probable cause hearing, constituted cruel and unusual punishment."

CASE SIGNIFICANCE

This case is important because it applied *Gault* to pretrial detention proceedings. In *Gault,* the Court applied most of the due process rights guaranteed adults to juvenile cases (see chapter 6 for a full brief). In this case, the court held that a juvenile's parents must be notified when he or she is taken into custody. In addition, the court maintained that there must be a judicial determination of probable cause within a reasonable amount of time. By affording juveniles these rights, the court continued the trend the Supreme Court began with *Kent v. United States,* 383 U.S. 541 (1966) and *Gault,* that of formalizing the juvenile court. This is important because prior to these cases juveniles could be held for indeterminate periods of time, provided there was justification under parens patriae. Although these decisions weakened parens patriae, they provided juveniles with rights that protect them from official misconduct like that in this case.

MOSS v. WEAVER

535 F.2d 1258 (5th Cir. 1976)

FACTS

Moss, a juvenile, filed a class action suit challenging the juvenile court judges' practice of imposing pretrial detention upon accused juvenile delinquents without determining whether there was probable cause to believe that the accused had committed an offense.

ISSUE

Does pretrial detention of a juvenile without a determination of probable cause violate the Fourth Amendment?

HOLDING

Yes. Pretrial detention without a probable cause determination violates the Fourth Amendment requirements of due process.

RATIONALE

Under Florida law, a juvenile taken into custody on a charge of violating criminal law must be brought before the court for a pretrial detention hearing within 48 hours, where the court determines whether to release or detain him or her pending a formal adjudicatory hearing. The applicable statute specified three factors for the judge to consider: (1) whether detention was necessary to protect the person or property of the child or others; (2) whether a parent or guardian was available and able to provide adequate care and supervision for the juvenile; and, (3) whether the parent or guardian convincingly assured the court of the juvenile's future presence at the adjudicatory hearing. There is also agreement that the seriousness of the alleged offense is frequently taken into consideration in practice. If the juvenile is detained, bail is not made available. The court relied on two cases from the Supreme Court in rendering its decision. In *Gerstein v. Pugh*, 420 U.S. 103 (1975), the Court required a finding of probable cause before a man could be held on an information. In addition, in *Cooley v. Stone*, 134 U.S. App. D.C. 317, 414 F. 2d 1213 (1969), the Court held that the Fourth Amendment's prohibition on penal custody without probable cause applied to juveniles and adults alike. The court in the present case also resolved the welfare of the child argument by indicating that a detention on that basis is allowed, but only if there is probable cause to believe the juvenile has committed the crime for which he or she is being held. The court observed that the finding of FACTS and circumstances to warrant a reasonable man to believe that a suspect has committed a crime is central to the Fourth Amendment's protections against official abuses of power.

CASE EXCERPT
"Pretrial detention is an onerous experience, especially for juveniles, and the Constitution is affronted when this burden is imposed without adequate assurance that the accused has in fact committed the alleged crime. Florida may properly direct its juvenile court judges to make a decision about the child's welfare when they consider whether he should be released pending his adjudicatory hearing. But if they do not find release desirable on that basis, the Fourth Amendment's principles dictate that they must not detain him unless they also find probable cause to believe him guilty."

CASE SIGNIFICANCE
The importance of this case lies in the court's affording a protection to juvenile defendants which brought the juvenile court more in harmony with the adult criminal court. The court required the juvenile magistrate to find probable cause to hold a juvenile in pretrial detention pending an adjudicatory hearing. However, the difference between the adult criminal court and juvenile court was still discernible when the court pointed out that juveniles are not allowed the right to

bail. In addition, the court upheld the Florida statute that outlines the factors to be considered in making such a decision. That statute is similar to those in other states and reflects the parens patriae philosophy of the juvenile court, which only allows for the detention of juveniles who have committed serious offenses or juveniles whose parents are unable to supervise or care for them adequately.

MARTIN v. STRASBURG
689 F.2d 363 (2d Cir. 1982)

FACTS
A habeas corpus class action suit was filed in district court on behalf of Martin and other youths who would be held or were currently being held in juvenile detention under the provision of the New York Family Court Act, which authorized preventative detention of youths accused of juvenile delinquency. The act required that in order to detain a youth, there must be either substantial probability that he or she would not reappear in court on the proscribed date or serious risk that he or she might commit an act before that date which, if committed by an adult, would constitute a crime.

ISSUE
Does the preventative detention of juveniles under the New York Family Court Act violate the due process rights of juveniles who are detained?

HOLDING
Yes. The provision of the New York Family Court Act for preventative detention violates the due process clause of the Fourteenth Amendment.

RATIONALE
The court contended the statutory scheme was analogous to that of an adult proceeding. Essentially, a juvenile can be detained after the filing of a petition and prior to a fact-finding hearing. However, juveniles are entitled to a probable cause hearing within three to six days and an expedited fact-finding hearing. After examining the process, the court determined that the vast majority of the juveniles ordered detained were subsequently released in a couple of weeks. The court contended that predispositional detention is designed for community protection and based on limited information, whereas postdispositional detention is based on more information and designed for welfare

MARTIN v. STRASBURG (cont.)

and treatment. The court relied on *In re Winship* 397 U.S. 358 (1970) in stating that the presumption of innocence and the requirement that guilt be proven beyond a reasonable doubt are important elements of due process. The court contended due process would be greatly diminished in the protections it affords if individuals could routinely be incarcerated pending trial. The court asserted that even the most persuasive demonstration of innocence cannot prevent the deprivation of liberty if incarceration precedes, rather than follows, the adjudication of criminal liability. Consequently, pretrial detention cannot be imposed for anticrime purposes pursuant to substantively and procedurally unlimited statutory authority when, in all likelihood, most detainees will either not be adjudicated guilty or will be sentenced to confinement after the adjudication of guilt.

CASE EXCERPT

"The statutory scheme and practice under it violate the Due Process Clause of the Fourteenth Amendment in that the period of pre-trial detention is utilized principally to impose punishment before adjudication of the alleged criminal acts. The presumption of innocence and the requirement that guilt be proven beyond a reasonable doubt are important elements of Due Process itself, which would be gravely diminished in the protection they afford if individuals can be routinely incarcerated pending trial."

CASE SIGNIFICANCE

This case is important for two reasons. First, the court overrode the statute, which allowed for the preventative detention of juveniles pending an adjudicatory hearing. The state contended that this is analogous to the adult criminal system. However, juveniles are not afforded bail. Consequently, the court contended that the preadjudication detention violated juveniles' right to be found guilty beyond a reasonable doubt by imposing punishment prior to that finding. Second, the court researched the cases in which the juveniles were detained pending an adjudicatory hearing and determined that the majority of the juveniles were either found not guilty or released at the next hearing. This is significant because it reflected the court's willingness to educate themselves on the larger issue and act in the interest of the child in juvenile matters, as opposed to interpreting the statute, which would be the likely outcome in adult criminal court.

D.B. v. TEWKSBURY

545 F.Supp. 896 (D. Or. 1982)

FACTS

A civil action was brought by D.B. and other children who were confined in the Columbia County Correctional Facility (CCCF), a jail used to house adults in St. Helens, Oregon. The suit challenged the confinement claiming it unconstitutional.

ISSUE

Does holding juveniles in adult jails for punishment, pending adjudicatory hearings, or if they are status offenders violate their constitutional rights?

HOLDING

Yes. Detaining juvenile pretrial detainees in jail under certain circumstances constitutes punishment, and thus, violates the due process clause of the Fourteenth Amendment. Confinement of runaway children or children out of parental control in jails constitutes punishment and violates their due process rights. Lodging a juvenile in modern adult jail, pending adjudication of criminal charges, is fundamentally unfair so as to violate his or her due process rights.

RATIONALE

The court found CCCF to be designed for the purposes of confinement. The facility was a maximum-security institution that only provided for the basic needs of the individuals who were lodged there. The facility was not responsive to the needs of children and their families in any way. Confinement in CCCF only served to punish children. The court did not find this to be consistent with simple detention, rehabilitation, or even the protection of society. Consequently, the defendants' due process rights against pretrial punishment were violated by their confinement in the CCCF. The court indicated that the detention of a runaway or out-of-control child is sometimes necessary for treatment or even for the protection of society. However, confinement in a jail facility, with the criminal stigma that attaches, constitutes punishment. Therefore, holding a status offender in such a facility violates his or her due process rights under the Fourteenth Amendment. The court contended that juvenile proceedings are in the nature of guardianship under the doctrine of parens patriae. Consequently, it is in the interest of providing fundamental fairness that rights available to adults charged with crimes may sometimes be denied to juveniles if the denial is offset by a special solicitude designed for children. However, when the constitutional rights for children are not offset by a special solicitude but by lodging them in adult jails, it is fundamentally unfair. When the children found guilty of committing criminal acts cannot be lodged in adult facilities, it is fundamentally unfair to hold children accused of committing criminal acts in adult jails. Consequently, lodging children in adult jails violated the juveniles' due process rights.

CASE EXCERPT

"A state does not acquire the power to punish a person—adult or child (assuming a child is convicted of committing a crime)—until after it has secured a formal adjudication of guilt in accordance with due process of law. A runaway child or a child out of control, as an addict or an insane person, may be confined for treatment or for the protection of society, but to put such a child in a jail—any jail—with its criminal stigma—constitutes punishment and is a violation of that child's due process rights under the Fourteenth Amendment to the United States Constitution. No child who is a *status* offender may be lodged constitutionally in an adult jail. When children who are found *guilty* of committing criminal acts cannot be placed in adult jails, it is fundamentally unfair to lodge children *accused* of committing criminal acts in adult jails."

CASE SIGNIFICANCE

This case is important because it is representative of the intent behind the juvenile justice system's creation, that of keeping juvenile matters separate from adult matters. Confining juveniles in adult jails was standard practice in many states and jurisdictions until recent times when juvenile detention centers were constructed. This court's holding forced jurisdictions to either construct their own detention centers or contract with existing facilities in other locations. In addition, the court contended that the housing of status offenders in adult facilities violated the Eighth Amendment, given the fact that they have not even committed a delinquent act. However, the court did point out the necessity to occasionally confine status offenders because it is in their best interest. In addition, the court supplied the rationale for its decision by stating that the purposes of juvenile detention facilities are to rehabilitate juveniles as well as to protect society, not merely to mete out punishment.

IN THE INTEREST OF DARLENE C.

301 S.E.2d 136 (S.C. 1983)

FACTS

The family court found Darlene C., a 16-year-old, to be a runaway child, and ordered her to be placed in the North Augusta Girls' Home and to receive counseling. The court also ordered that if the defendant failed to abide by its mandate, she would be found in contempt. Two days later Darlene C. ran away again. The family court issued a rule to show cause as to why appellant should not be held in contempt of court for violating the previous court order. Darlene C. appeared at the rule to show cause but offered no defense, and the judge held her in contempt. Although the law does not allow for status offenders to be placed in detention, the judge ruled her status to be delinquent for violating the court order. The court sentenced her as a delinquent to commitment in a detention center for an indeterminate period of time not to exceed her twenty-first birthday.

ISSUE

Can a juvenile who commits criminal contempt by running away in violation of a court order be given a disposition reserved for delinquents who have committed offenses that would be crimes if committed by an adult?

HOLDING

Yes. Family courts may exercise their contempt power in such a manner that a status offender will be incarcerated in a secure facility.

RATIONALE

The court contended that, although it had held that juvenile offenders may be punished only as prescribed by the South Carolina Children's Code, the Code specifically provided that it should be interpreted in conjunction with all relevant laws and regulations. Therefore, the court could look to its inherent powers as well as the Children's Code. All courts possess the inherent power to punish those in contempt. The court contended the power is essential to the preservation of order in judicial proceedings, and the enforcement of the courts' judgments, orders, and writs. The court upheld the lower court's decision to hold the defendant in contempt. The court recognized the legislative intent but maintained that the legislature did not provide for

IN THE INTEREST OF DARLENE C. (*cont.*)

an adequate way of dealing with runaway youth. The contempt power allows for adequate measures to be taken. However, the court maintained that only under the most egregious circumstances should family courts exercise their contempt power in such a manner that a status offender would be incarcerated in a secure facility. The record must show that all less restrictive alternatives have failed in the past. The court also required that the defendant actually meet the elements for contempt and be aware that he or she could face detention time if he or she violated the court's order. However, when the court directed its attention to the disposition, it held that the family court erred in sentencing the girl as a delinquent. The court merely had the power to punish contemnors, not adjudicate them delinquent.

CASE EXCERPT

"Only under the most egregious circumstances should family courts exercise their contempt power in such a manner that a status offender will be incarcerated in a secure facility. Before a chronic status offender is placed in a secure facility, the record must show that all less restrictive alternatives have failed in the past. Additionally the following elements should exist: (1) the existence of a valid order directing the alleged contemnor to do or refrain from doing something and the court's jurisdiction to enter that order; (2) the contemnor's notice of the order with sufficient time to comply with it; and in most cases, (3) the contemnor's ability to comply with the order; and (4) the contemnor's willful failure to comply with the order. Furthermore, the record must reflect the juvenile understood that disobedience would result in incarceration in a secure facility."

CASE SIGNIFICANCE

This case is important because the court allowed for the judiciary to hold a juvenile in contempt of court for violating a court order. The federal government has taken great measures to compel states to deinstitutionalize status offenders, and many states have written their juvenile codes so that status offenders are not placed in detention. However, frustrated judges have used the contempt powers of the court to hold these juveniles accountable by placing them in secure confinement for violating court orders. In this case, the court upheld that procedure. However, the court did not allow the lower court to punish the juvenile as a delinquent. Instead, the court held that the juvenile could only be punished as a contemnor, which

typically carries with it a less severe punishment than that of being adjudicated delinquent.

SCHALL v. MARTIN
104 U.S. 2403 (1984)

FACTS

Martin was arrested on December 13, 1977, and charged with first-degree robbery, second-degree assault, and criminal possession of a weapon based on an incident in which he, with two others, allegedly hit a youth on the head with a loaded gun and stole his jacket and sneakers. Martin had possession of the gun when he was arrested. He was 14 years old at the time, and, therefore, came within the jurisdiction of New York's family court. The incident occurred at 11:30 at night, and Martin lied to the police about where and with whom he lived. He was consequently detained overnight. A petition of delinquency was filed, and Martin made his initial appearance in family court on December 14th, accompanied by his grandmother. The family court judge, citing the possession of the loaded weapon, the false address given to the police, and the lateness of the hour as evidence that there was a lack of supervision, ordered Martin detained. A probable-cause hearing was held five days later, and probable cause was found to exist for all the crimes charged. At the fact-finding hearing, Martin was found guilty of the robbery and criminal possession charges. Between the initial appearance and the completion of the fact-finding hearing, he had been detained for a total of 15 days. On December 21st, 1977, while still in preventive detention pending his fact-finding hearing, Martin filed a habeas corpus class action suit on behalf of those persons who were, or during the pendency of this action would be, preventively detained pursuant to the Family Court Act.

ISSUE

Is the preventive detention of a juvenile charged with a delinquent act constitutional?

HOLDING

Yes. The Family Court Act section allowing preventive detention is valid under the due process clause of the Fourteenth Amendment.

RATIONALE

The Court contended preventive detention under the statute served the legitimate state objective, held in common with every state, of protecting both the juvenile and society from the hazards of pretrial crime. That objective is compatible with the fundamental fairness demanded by the due process clause in juvenile proceedings, and the terms and condition of confinement under the Act are compatible with that objective. Pretrial detention need not be considered punishment merely because a juvenile is subsequently discharged subject to conditions or put on probation. Additionally, even when a case is terminated prior to fact finding, it does not follow that the decision to detain the juvenile pursuant to the Act amounts to a due process violation. The procedural safeguards afforded by the Family Court Act to juveniles detained prior to fact finding provide sufficient protection against erroneous and unnecessary deprivations of liberty. Notice, a hearing, and a statement of facts and reasons are given to the juvenile prior to any detention, and a formal probable cause hearing is then held within a short time thereafter, if the fact-finding hearing is not itself scheduled within three days. The Court contended that there was no merit to the argument that the risk of erroneous and unnecessary detention is too high despite these procedures because the standard for detention is fatally vague. The Court further contended there was nothing inherently unattainable about a prediction of future criminal conduct. Such a prediction was an experienced one based on a host of variables that cannot be readily codified. Moreover, the postdetention procedures, habeas corpus review, appeals, and motions for reconsideration provided a sufficient mechanism for correcting on a case-by-case basis any erroneous detention.

CASE EXCERPT

"The 'legitimate and compelling state interest' in protecting the community from crime cannot be doubted. We have stressed before that crime prevention is 'a weighty social objective,' and this interest persists undiluted in the juvenile context. The juvenile's countervailing interest in freedom from institutional restraints, even for the brief time involved here, is undoubtedly substantial as well. But that interest must be qualified by the recognition that juveniles, unlike adults, are always in some form of custody. Children, by definition, are not assumed to have the capacity to take care of themselves. They are assumed to be subject to the control of their parents, and if parental control falters, the State must play its part as *parens patriae*."

CASE SIGNIFICANCE

This case is important because it allowed for the pretrial detention of a juvenile charged with an act of delinquency. In so holding, the Court opened the door for many states to begin implementing preventive detention in juvenile matters. This is distinguishable from the adult criminal system because juveniles are not afforded the right to bail. Once they are detained, they remain so until their next hearing. What distinguished this case from earlier ones is that the Family Court Act under review provided for specific procedures that must be followed for a juvenile to be detained. According to the Court, these procedures provide adequate safeguards to a juvenile's due process rights. In addition, there are ample measures a juvenile can take to challenge pretrial detention. However, juvenile cases do not typically move as quickly as the Court illustrated in this case. Much like the adult criminal court, the juvenile court has become overburdened, which has contributed to greater length between hearings. Consequently, juveniles are detained for much longer periods of time. This case also marked a change in the juvenile court. In previous cases, the Supreme Court awarded juveniles rights and protections. However, in this case, the best interests of society seem to have been elevated over the best interests of the child. The Court put societal protection ahead of the rehabilitative goal of the juvenile court, solidifying the juvenile justice system's shift from the rehabilitative to the crime control model.

RENO v. FLORES

507 U.S. 292 (1993)

FACTS

Congress has given the attorney general broad discretion to determine whether, and on what terms, an alien arrested on suspicion of being deportable should be released pending a deportation hearing. In general, an alien should not be detained or required to post bond except on a finding that he is either a threat to national security or a poor bail risk. In the case of arrested alien juveniles, however, the Immigration and Naturalization Service (INS) cannot release a juvenile on bail or their own recognizance. The INS must be sure that someone will care for the juvenile during the resolution of their deportation proceedings. This situation becomes complicated when a juvenile is arrested alone. In 1984, responding to the increased flow of

RENO v. FLORES (cont.)

unaccompanied juvenile aliens into California, the INS Western Regional Office adopted a policy of limiting the release of detained minors to a parent or lawful guardian, except in unusual and extraordinary cases, when the juvenile could be released to a responsible individual who agrees to provide care and be responsible for the welfare and well-being of the child. In July of the following year, the respondents filed an action in the District Court for the Central District of California on behalf of a class, consisting of all aliens under the age of 18 who are detained by the INS Western Region because a parent or legal guardian fails to personally appear to take custody of them.

ISSUE

Do juveniles, suspected of being deported, have a fundamental right to freedom from physical restraint?

HOLDING

No. The INS policy is a reasonable response to the difficult problems presented when the Service arrests unaccompanied alien juveniles.

RATIONALE

The Court observed that the respondents' claim regarding their fundamental right to physical restraint is not at issue in this case, since the child is not shackled or in chains. The Court argued that the issue at hand is whether a child, for whom the government is responsible, who does not have an available parent or legal guardian, should be placed in the custody of a private custodian rather than a government-operated or government selected child-care institution. The Court reasoned that if there is a fundamental right to be released into a noncustodial setting, then there is no reason why it would apply only in the context of government custody incidentally acquired in the course of law enforcement. It would presumably apply to state custody over orphans and abandoned children as well. Yet the Court pointed out that no court has ever held that a child has a constitutional right not to be placed in a decent and humane custodial institution if there is available a responsible person unwilling to become the child's legal guardian but willing to undertake temporary legal custody. In reaching their decision, the Court relied on *Schall v. Martin* 104 U.S. 2403 (1984), in which they held that juveniles, as opposed to adults, are always in some form of custody, and where the custody of the parent or guardian fails, the government may exercise custody itself or appoint someone else to do it.

CASE EXCERPT

"Where a juvenile has no available parent, close relative, or legal guardian, where the government does not intend to punish the child, and where the conditions of governmental custody are decent and humane, such custody surely does not violate the Constitution. It is rationally connected to a governmental interest in preserving and promoting the welfare of the child and is not punitive since it is not excessive in relation to that valid purpose."

CASE SIGNIFICANCE

This case is important because it applies the Court's rationale used in deciding *Schall v. Martin* to cases involving alien juveniles without a parent or guardian, a growing problem in the United States. Alien juveniles may be detained simply because they do not have a parent or legal guardian to take custody of them. Similar to *Schall*, the Court pointed to the diminished rights of juveniles versus adults, and the government's responsibility to provide for the care and welfare of juveniles in the absence of a capable and willing guardian who will do so.

HORN BY PARKS v. MADISON COUNTY FISCAL COURT
22 F.3d 653 (6th Cir. 1994)

FACTS

Horn, age 17, pleaded guilty to a robbery charge in the Madison County District Court. He was committed to the Cabinet of Human Resources and released to the custody of his parents pending placement under the condition that he remain within arm's reach of his parents. Five days later, Horn's parents reported that he had left home and his whereabouts were unknown. A complaint was signed and a pick-up order issued by a judge. The following day Horn turned himself in to his caseworker and was taken to a detention center. The detention center was an adult jail, newly opened, and designated for use as an intermittent juvenile holding facility where juvenile offenders could be held under statutorily prescribed conditions for a period not to exceed 24 hours. Horn was processed into the facility with his caseworker present. Both she and the jail deputy later testified Horn appeared in a good mood and coherent. Horn was taken to his cell and routine checks were performed about every 15 minutes. Five minutes after a check, where Horn appeared to be okay, he was found hanging from the bunk in his cell with a bed sheet tied around his neck. He subsequently suffered from brain damage and paralysis confining him to a wheelchair. His family filed suit, holding the county was negligent in his care.

ISSUES

Did the actions of the county detention facility staff amount to deliberate indifference to the juvenile's medical needs? Are juvenile detainees as a group at such high risk for suicide as to constitute a special class requiring special consideration based strictly on their age?

HOLDING

No and no. The failure of jail officials to take more than ordinary precautions to protect juvenile defendants from suicide did not constitute deliberate indifference to Horn's medical needs. Actions by such employees were consistent with the policies in place within the detention facility. Even though the Juvenile Justice Act discourages the placement of juveniles in facilities primarily dedicated to adult inmate care, the actions of the staff in this case did not amount to negligence. This is true even if juveniles as a class are determined to be prone to suicide.

RATIONALE

The court assumed that the appellant would have been able to establish that his temporary lodging in the Madison County Detention Center was technically in violation of the Juvenile Justice Act because an acceptable alternative placement was available. However, the court could not find anything in the record showing the center's nature contributed in any way to the appellant's suicide attempt or resulting injury. The record demonstrated that the appellant was scrupulously shielded from the deleterious influences associated with adult facilities. The court pointed to the statutory guidance for the holding procedures and the special care the intake worker and staff took to protect the juvenile from the perils of adult confinement. The appellant's theory that he would have been better cared for in a juvenile facility because the staff would have been better equipped to handle him was just that, theory. It was speculation and the court did not find support for it in the record.

The court pointed out that in order to demonstrate deliberate indifference, the appellant would have had to show the conduct for which liability attached to be more culpable than mere negligence. In addition, it would have had to demonstrate deliberateness tantamount to intent to punish. The court contended that was not the case here.

CASE EXCERPT

"We assume appellant would have been able to establish his temporary lodging in the Madison County Detention Center was technically violative of the Juvenile Justice Act because an acceptable alternative placement was available. However, the record is devoid of proof tending to show that the center's nature, being a secure adult facility as opposed to a secure juvenile facility, contributed in any way to appellant's suicide attempt or resultant injury. In fact, the record unequivocally demonstrates appellant was scrupulously shielded from the deleterious influences associated with adult facilities."

CASE SIGNIFICANCE

This case is important because it illustrated that some states still allowed for the jailing of juveniles in adult facilities. In this jurisdiction, special measures were in place so as not to subject a juvenile to long-term confinement in an adult facility. Nevertheless, confinement in an adult facility was still allowed. In addition, the court determined that jail officials did not have to provide the juvenile with any special treatment. Although the court discouraged the placing of the juveniles in adult facilities, it did not overturn the state's ability to utilize such a facility, nor did it require special attention be given to those juveniles confined there. This was important because it contradicted the separation of juveniles and adults intended by the juvenile court.

DISCUSSION QUESTIONS

1. Do juveniles have a right to a hearing on pretrial detention?
2. Do juveniles have a right to treatment?
3. What have the courts said constitutes cruel and unusual punishment in reference to detention?
4. Describe the court-made rules that govern placing juveniles in adult jail.
5. What is the justification for holding juveniles in pretrial detention?

6. Do juveniles have a right to bail?

7. Is it constitutional to detain arrested juveniles who are aliens?

8. What was the Supreme Court's rational behind allowing for the preventative detention of juveniles charged with a delinquent act?

9. Under what circumstances has the court ruled that a status offender may be incarcerated in a secure facility?

10. During the detention stage of juvenile proceedings, what rights are guaranteed to juveniles under the due process clause?

CHAPTER FIVE

WAIVER TO CRIMINAL COURT

BENJAMINE STEINER, UNIVERSITY OF NEBRASKA – OMAHA
RIANE MILLER, UNIVERSITY OF SOUTH CAROLINA

KENT v. UNITED STATES, *383 U.S. 541 (1966)*

UNITED STATES v. HOWARD, *449 F.2D 1086 (D.C. CIR. 1971)*

PEOPLE v. FIELDS, *199 N.W.2D 217 (MICH. 1972)*

FAIN v. DUFF, *488 F.2D 218 (5TH CIR. 1973)*

UNITED STATES EX REL. BOMBACINO v. BENSINGER, *498 F.2D 875 (7TH CIR. 1974)*

BREED v. JONES, *421 U.S. 519 (1975)*

IN RE MATHIS, *537 P.2D 148 (OR. APP. 1975)*

RUSSELL v. PARRATT, *543 F.2D 1214 (8TH CIR. 1976)*

UNITED STATES v. J.D., *517 F.SUPP. 69 (S.D.N.Y. 1981)*

MATTER OF SEVEN MINORS, *664 P.2D 947 (NEV. 1983)*

STATE v. MUHAMMAD, *703 P.2D 835 (KAN. 1985)*

R.H. v. STATE, *777 P.2D 204 (ALASKA APP. 1989)*

PEOPLE v. P.H., *582 N.E.2D 700 (ILL. 1991)*

C.M. v. STATE, *884 S.W.2D 562 (TEX. APP. 1994)*

LASWELL v. FREY, *45 F.3D 1011 (6TH CIR. 1995)*

STATE v. VERHAGEN, *542 N.W.2D 189 (WIS. APP. 1995)*

O'BRIEN v. JOHN MARSHALL, *SUPERINTENDENT, 453 F.3D 13 (U.S. APP. 2006)*

STATE v. DIXON, *967 A.2D 1114 (VT. 2008)*

INTRODUCTION

The waiver of juvenile court jurisdiction, which is also referred to as transfer, bind-over, and certification, is the end of the line for juvenile offenders. When a juvenile is waived, the juvenile court's jurisdiction is transferred to the adult criminal court, where he or she is then subject to criminal prosecution and sanctions. Juvenile waiver was theoretically designed to allow juvenile courts to move a juvenile offender who had committed a serious offense or who had exhausted the juvenile courts' resources to adult criminal court where, if convicted, he or she would be punished more severely. However, over time, use of the waiver has evolved into something far different from what was theoretically conceived.

The process of waiving a juvenile to criminal court for prosecution is one of many criminalization trends in the juvenile courts. In the 1970s and 1980s, as society became disenchanted with the ability of the criminal justice system to reduce or prevent crime, the "get tough" movement gained prominence. This disenchantment carried over to the juvenile justice system. Since the creation of the juvenile court at the beginning of the twentieth century, juveniles have been dealt with separately and differently, largely on the assumption that youth are both less culpable and more amenable to treatment. By the 1970s, this assumption was being questioned, both by the public and politicians alike. One result was an increase in the use of the juvenile waiver to transfer juveniles to criminal court, where, presumably, the range of sanctions is greater.

The process of waiver to adult criminal court has been closely scrutinized and shaped by the courts. As with most juvenile justice system issues, no formalized structure to the waiver process existed prior to the

1960s. Juveniles could be waived for many different offenses and without hearings or the constitutional protections that attach. Consequently, there was occasional, and in some jurisdictions frequent, misuse of judicial discretion. However, during this period, the use of the waiver was still rare. In the 1960s, when the civil liberties of juvenile defendants became of concern, the waiver process was one of the first issues the Supreme Court chose to address. The Court eventually determined that the waiver of a juvenile defendant to criminal court was a "critical stage" in the juvenile court process, which afforded juveniles specific due process rights during waiver hearings. Thus, in rendering their decision, the Court established procedures for transferring juveniles to criminal court that the state courts were to follow. Accordingly, many states wrote procedures for transferring juveniles to criminal court into their juvenile codebooks. Interestingly enough, this Supreme Court decision on the behalf of juvenile offenders may have actually contributed to the increase in juveniles waived to criminal court, as the courts became more familiar with the procedure.

The lower courts have also defined how waiver procedures are to occur in their respective states. Some of the more notable changes to the procedure are the requiring of a hearing and a statement of reasons supporting the transfer, a defined set of criteria within a waiver statute, and a requirement of a clear and convincing standard that is to be met before a juvenile is waived. In addition, the courts have also ruled on the admissibility of psychiatric or psychological testimony, the importance of the elements that are to be considered, and the amount of discretion a judge is granted in making the decision to waive jurisdiction. Juveniles were also afforded protection from double jeopardy when the courts prohibited trying a juvenile in adult criminal court once they have been adjudicated of the same offense in juvenile court. Furthermore, the courts have determined a juvenile need not be present at a waiver hearing if he or she is represented by counsel at that hearing. These decisions, as well as many others, have made the issue of waiving juveniles to criminal court one of the most challenging issues confronting the court system today.

Currently, there are several ways that a juvenile can be transferred to criminal court. Judicial waiver laws are the legal mechanism under which juvenile court judges may, at their discretion, waive juvenile court jurisdiction in juvenile cases, effectively transferring them to adult criminal court. Statutory exclusion or legislative waiver laws are the transfer method in which state legislatures have excluded certain offenses from juvenile court jurisdiction. In states that have statutory exclusion laws, all juveniles of a legally prescribed minimum age who are charged with a legislatively excluded offense are automatically tried in criminal court. Direct file transfer laws authorize prosecutors the discretion to file certain juvenile cases in either juvenile or criminal court under concurrent jurisdiction status. Similar to statutory exclusion laws, direct file laws can only be applied for certain offenses and for juveniles of particular ages. Although the states have recently made the process for moving a juvenile offender to criminal court easier, the use of the judicial waiver has actually tapered off. Although it is currently being used more frequently today than 20 years ago, its use has slowed since its peak in the early 1990s. Whether this is a result of the research showing its ineffectiveness, increased use of statutory exclusion or direct file transfer laws, or the courts' decision to limit its practice remains a question. However, it is clear that decisions handed down from the courts regarding this controversial practice have played a major role in the waiver's conception, definition, and possibly even its use. In this chapter, we review the leading cases that have guided the development of the waiver of juveniles to adult criminal court for prosecution.

KENT v. UNITED STATES
383 U.S. 541 (1966)

FACTS

Kent, age 16, was arrested in connection with charges of housebreaking, robbery, and rape. As a juvenile, he was subject to the exclusive jurisdiction of the District of Columbia Juvenile Court, unless after full investigation, that court should waive jurisdiction over him and transfer him for trial to the United States District Court for the District of Columbia. Kent's counsel filed a motion in the juvenile court for a hearing on the question of waiver, and for access to the juvenile court's social service file, which had been accumulated on Kent during his probation for a prior offense. The juvenile court did not rule on these motions. Instead, it entered an order waiving jurisdiction, with the recitation that this was done after the required full investigation. Kent was indicted in district court and moved to dismiss the indictment on the ground that the juvenile court's waiver was invalid. The district court overruled the motion, and Kent was tried. He was convicted on six counts of housebreaking and robbery, but acquitted on two rape counts by reason of insanity. On appeal, Kent raised, among other things, the validity of the juvenile court's waiver of jurisdiction; the United States Court of Appeals for the District of Columbia Circuit affirmed, finding the procedure leading to waiver and the waiver order itself valid. Kent sought review in the Supreme Court.

ISSUE

Do juveniles have any due process rights in cases in which jurisdiction is transferred from juvenile court to criminal court?

HOLDING

Yes. A transfer of jurisdiction in a juvenile hearing is a "critically important" stage in the judicial process. Therefore, the juvenile is entitled to the following due process rights: (1) a hearing; (2) to be represented by counsel at such hearing; (3) to be given access to records considered by the juvenile court; and (4) to a statement of the reasons in support of the waiver order.

RATIONALE

The Court indicated that the theory of the District's Juvenile Court Act, like that of other jurisdictions, is rooted in social welfare philosophy rather than in the corpus juris. Juvenile court proceedings are designated as civil rather than criminal. The juvenile court is theoretically engaged in determining the needs of the child and of society rather than adjudicating criminal conduct. The objectives are to provide measures of guidance and rehabilitation for the child and protection for society, not to fix criminal responsibility, guilt, and punishment. The state is parens patriae rather than prosecuting attorney and judge. However, the Court noted that the admonition to function in a parental relationship is not an invitation to procedural arbitrariness. Because the state is supposed to proceed in respect of the child as parens patriae and not as adversary, courts have relied on the premise that the proceedings are civil in nature and not criminal, and have asserted that the child cannot complain of the deprivation of important rights available in criminal cases. It has been asserted that he or she can claim only the fundamental due process right to fair treatment. The Court contended it was clear beyond dispute that the waiver of jurisdiction is a critically important action determining vitally important statutory rights of the juvenile. The statutory scheme makes this plain. The juvenile court is vested with original and exclusive jurisdiction of the child. This jurisdiction confers special rights and immunities. He or she is, as specified by the statute, shielded from publicity. He or she may be confined, but with rare exceptions not jailed along with adults. He or she may be detained, but only until 21 years of age. The Court is cautioned by the statute to give preference to retaining the child in the custody of his or her parents unless his or her welfare and the safety and protection of the public cannot be adequately safeguarded without removal. The child is protected against consequences of adult conviction such as the loss of civil rights, the use of adjudication against him or her in subsequent proceedings, and disqualification for public employment. The net, therefore, was that the petitioner, then a boy of 16, was by statute entitled to certain procedures and benefits as a consequence of his statutory right to the exclusive jurisdiction of the juvenile court. In these circumstances, considering particularly that decision as to waiver of jurisdiction and transfer of the matter to the district court was potentially as important to the petitioner as the difference between five years' confinement and a death sentence, the Court concluded that, as a condition to a valid waiver order, the petitioner was entitled to a hearing, including access by his counsel to the social records and probation or similar reports which presumably were considered by the court, and to a statement of reasons for the juvenile court's decision. The Court contended meaningful review required that the reviewing court should actually review the waiver. It should not be remitted to assumptions. It must have before it a statement of the reasons motivating the waiver including, of course, a statement of the relevant facts. It may not assume that there are adequate reasons, nor may it merely assume that a full investigation has been made. Accordingly, the Court held that it was incumbent upon the juvenile court to accompany its waiver order with a statement of the reasons or considerations therefore. The Court did not read the statute as requiring that this statement must be formal or that it should necessarily include conventional findings of fact. Instead, the Court contended that the statement should be sufficient to demonstrate that the statutory requirement of full investigation had been met, and that the question had received the careful consideration of the juvenile court, and it must set forth the basis for the order with sufficient specificity to permit meaningful review.

KENT v. UNITED STATES *(cont.)*

The Court did not agree with the court of appeals' statement attempting to justify denial of access to these records, that counsel's role is limited to presenting to the Court anything on behalf of the child, which might help the Court in arriving at a decision; it is not to denigrate the staff's submissions and recommendations. On the contrary, if the staff's submissions include materials that are susceptible to challenge or impeachment, it is precisely the role of counsel to denigrate such matters. There is no irrefutable presumption of accuracy attached to staff reports. If a decision on waiver is critically important it is equally of critical importance that the material submitted to the judge, which is protected by the statute only against indiscriminate inspection, be subjected, within reasonable limits having regard to the theory of the Juvenile Court Act, to examination, criticism, and refutation. While the juvenile court judge may, of course, receive ex parte analyses and recommendations from his staff, he may not, for purposes of a decision on waiver, receive and rely upon secret information, whether emanating from his staff or otherwise.

CASE EXCERPT

"We conclude that an opportunity for a hearing which may be informal, must be given the child prior to entry of a waiver order. Under *Black* [*Black v. United States*, 355 F. 2d 104 (1965)], the child is entitled to counsel in connection with a waiver proceeding, and under *Watkins* [*Watkins v. United States*, 343 F. 2d 278, 282 (1964)], counsel is entitled to see the child's social records. These rights are meaningless—an illusion, a mockery—unless counsel is given an opportunity to function. The right to representation by counsel is not a formality. It is not a grudging gesture to a ritualistic requirement. It is of the essence of justice."

CASE SIGNIFICANCE

This case is important for several reasons. First, it was the first time the Supreme Court provided oversight to juvenile court proceedings. Although the Court had previously heard *Haley v. Ohio*, 332 U.S. 596 (1948), that case dealt with police actions, not those of the juvenile court. In this case, the Court defined the waiver of a juvenile to criminal court as a critically important decision and thus a critical stage in juvenile proceedings. In doing so, the Court held that a juvenile court had to put a specific finding in writing outlining why the juvenile should be transferred to adult criminal court. In addition, the Court determined that in view of the fact that this stage was a critical one in the proceedings, certain rights should be afforded the juvenile. Specifically, the Court ordered that a juvenile has the right to an actual hearing on the matter, to be represented by counsel at that hearing, to be provided access to the records considered by the juvenile court, and to the aforementioned statement of reasons if the court decides to waive jurisdiction. This decision is important because it eliminated the arbitrary way in which some states waived juveniles into adult criminal court. However, this case also marked the beginning of the criminalization movement in the juvenile court. By affording juveniles certain rights, the Court actually began formalizing the juvenile court, making it more like its adult criminal counterpart and less like the informal court governed by parens patriae.

UNITED STATES v. HOWARD

449 F.2d 1086 (D.C. Cir. 1971)

FACTS

Howard, age 17, and three other males entered and robbed a drugstore and its employees. During the course of the robbery, an officer, Kelley, appeared on the scene. One of the robbers fired a shot at Kelley and then forced an employee to walk in front of the group toward the front of the store so they could escape. As they were walking, Sweitzer, an employee of the store, struggled with the man who shot at the officer. During the course of the struggle, Sweitzer was shot and fatally wounded. Howard was later identified as the man who fired the shot. Howard had a substantial juvenile record including two robbery adjudications. At the time the current offense occurred, he was an escapee from the receiving home where he had been placed. In addition to the current offense, two other robbery charges from several days earlier had been filed against him. A waiver hearing was held. At the hearing, several experts ranging from doctors to state employees testified. The majority of the testimony favored retaining Howard in the juvenile system and placing him at a secure treatment facility. Nevertheless, the juvenile court waived jurisdiction. The judge's opinion focused on the seriousness of the alleged offenses. The decision occurred at the same time the Supreme Court was deciding *Kent*. The district court recessed to study and apply the *Kent* decision to the case it was reviewing. However, the district court affirmed the juvenile court's decision to transfer Howard to criminal court.

ISSUE

Must a transfer hearing involve a full review of all relevant issues related to fitness for transfer?

HOLDING

No. As long as the court conducts a full hearing and exercises all relevant options, proper consideration is deemed to have been given before transfer to a criminal court.

RATIONALE

Howard challenged the validity of his waiver on the ground that the juvenile court did not fully explore the possibilities for his rehabilitation as required by statute and by decisions of this court and the Supreme Court. The court contended that the full investigation required by statute cannot be mere ritual. The court pointed to previous decisions it had rendered as well as *Kent* 383 U.S. 541 (1966), where the Supreme Court held that the decision to waive must be accompanied by a statement of the reasons or considerations therefore. The court interpreted that the statement should be sufficient to demonstrate that the statutory requirement has been met. In the present case, the juvenile court held extensive hearings on Howard's prospects for rehabilitation, as well as facilities available to contain him. Despite the discrepancies in the testimony, the juvenile court had all the information when it rendered its decision. The juvenile court was allowed to rely on the fact that Howard was nearing 18 years of age and would therefore only be subject to jurisdiction for three more years. Therefore, the juvenile court deemed Howard would be in need of more long-term care, and thus the decision to transfer. This court did not find that the juvenile court abused its discretion in reaching that decision.

CASE EXCERPT

"The court could reasonably conclude, on the basis of testimony and appellant's past record, that even assuming a juvenile like appellant could be rehabilitated if provided with rehabilitation programs over a longer period of time, the short span available to the Juvenile Court as to this appellant would be insufficient to ensure success in any rehabilitative endeavor."

CASE SIGNIFICANCE

This case is important because it was one of the first cases to apply the Supreme Court's holding in *Kent*. Thus, this case demonstrated how the *Kent* decision could be interpreted and applied to the waiver of a juvenile to adult criminal court. In *Kent*, the Court determined the waiver hearing was a critical stage in the proceedings, and thus protections are afforded to a juvenile defendant undergoing that process. In this case, Howard challenged the juvenile court's decision to waive jurisdiction because he felt the juvenile court did not fully explore the possibilities for rehabilitation in the juvenile system, and there was substantial testimony favoring his retention there. However, in reviewing the record and applying *Kent*, the court determined that the juvenile court was only required to hold a hearing on the matter of waiver and provide a statement of reasons in support of its decision to waive jurisdiction. In this case, the juvenile court did hold extensive hearings on the matter and also noted the seriousness of the offense as well as the juvenile's age as the primary reason for its decision to waive Howard to adult criminal court.

PEOPLE v. FIELDS

199 N.W.2d 217 (Mich. 1972)

FACTS

On August 16, 1968, the court ruled on a motion by the prosecuting attorney to waive jurisdiction of Fields, age 16, for uttering and publishing of checks and breaking and entering. The court ruled that a prima facie case had been made based on the evidence that was presented. The court also ruled on whether Fields would be rehabilitated through the facilities of the juvenile court. The three tests that applied were the nature of the offense and whether the juvenile court was appropriate, whether the juvenile court had made use of every available disposition available to it, and whether the minor had shown a maturation beyond the calendar age which made the minor unwilling to accept treatment as a minor. The court ruled that the nature of the offense was obviously of such adult character as to make the juvenile court inappropriate. In addition, the planning and carrying out of the crime indicated mature character. Therefore, the juvenile court was inappropriate. Further, the juvenile had been on probation for years and subject to some of the treatment of the juvenile court. In addition, he was 17 and

PEOPLE v. FIELDS *(cont.)*

married. Therefore, his maturation was beyond that of a typical juvenile.

ISSUE

Does a lack of standards in a transfer statute make the statute unconstitutional?

HOLDING

Yes. The statute regarding transfer is unconstitutional because of lack of standards.

RATIONALE

Fields filed an appeal based on whether the statute allowing probate courts to waive jurisdiction over certain juveniles was void on its face. The attack was based solely on the theory that the statute was void because it lacked standards for determining whether or not probate court should waive jurisdiction. The court contended that the probate court carefully considered all the factors when rendering its decision to transfer Fields. However, when the statute was examined, the court was unable to find any statutory guidelines except the age of the child and nature of the offense. The court relied on an earlier decision, *Devereaux v. Township Board of Genesee,* 211 Mich 38 (1920), that a statute invalid for want of standards according to the constitutional rule cannot be validated by any rule of the court which, although in itself well within the constitutional powers of the court, undertakes to supply what the statute does not. The court contended the legislature must establish suitable and ascertainable standards whereby such persons are to be deemed adults and treated as such subject to the processes and penalties of the criminal law.

CASE EXCERPT

"If the Legislature is to treat some persons under the age of 17 differently from the entire class of such persons, excluding them from the beneficient processes and purposes of our juvenile courts, the Legislature must establish suitable and ascertainable standards whereby such persons are to be deemed adults and treated as such subject to the processes and penalties of our criminal law. The statute is unconstitutional because it lacks standards."

CASE SIGNIFICANCE

This case is important because it reflected some of the state courts' desire to extend *Kent* 383 U.S. 541 (1966) and reduce the possibility of arbitrary waiver of a juvenile to adult criminal court. In this case, the court not only required the hearing and statement of reasons for waiver that resulted from *Kent,* but it also invalidated a statute that only called for an examination of a juvenile's age and the seriousity of the offense. Therefore, the court contended that the juvenile court acted in concert with the applicable law, but the law was not valid. Many states have established certain criteria for determining whether a juvenile should be transferred to adult criminal court. In addition to age and seriousness of the offense, the courts often examine other factors such as the juvenile's history, his or her amenability to treatment, and how the offense was carried out. The Supreme Court has never ruled on the necessity to consider these factors; however, this case reflected what many state courts have done to ensure that a formal set of criteria is considered in making the decision to waive jurisdiction.

FAIN v. DUFF

488 F.2d 218 (5th Cir. 1973)

FACTS

Fain, age 16, was arrested for breaking into the home of a woman and raping her. Eleven days later, Fain was adjudicated delinquent by a juvenile court. He was subsequently committed to the Division of Youth Services for an indeterminate period of time. The state urged the court to stay the commitment, but the court refused. Nine days after the juvenile proceeding, a grand jury indicted Fain with the criminal offense of rape. Fain's argument that his prosecution for rape would violate the former jeopardy clause of the Fifth Amendment was rejected by the state courts. Fain then obtained a writ of habeas corpus. The state appealed the granting of the writ.

ISSUES

Did the district court have jurisdiction to entertain Fain's application for a writ of habeas corpus? Was the district court correct in determining that the actions of the state of Florida violated the double jeopardy clause of the Fifth Amendment, made applicable to the states by the Fourteenth Amendment? Was the district court correct in determining that the actions of the state of Florida violated the Fourteenth Amendment and notions of fundamental fairness?

HOLDING

Yes, yes, and yes. Fain would be placed in double jeopardy if, after adjudication in a juvenile court, he would again be tried in criminal court.

RATIONALE

The court contended that although Fain was in the custody of a juvenile facility, if he were to be released he would immediately be subject to custody in an adult facility. The court based its determination on the testimony of the juvenile center's authorities when they indicated they were not releasing him for that very reason. Therefore, the court held that they had the right to hear the case. As for the matter of jeopardy, the court contended that the juvenile court can seriously affect a defendant's liberty. The court indicated that although the punishment imposed was rehabilitative in nature, it was still punishment. Fain would therefore be subject to a second punishment for the same offense. The court contended that the problem in this case lay in the fact that the state failed to indict Fain before they adjudicated him. Regarding the issue of fundamental fairness, the court found that although the juvenile court judge was informed of the state's intent to indict, the indictment had not been handed down. Therefore, the juvenile court judge was well within his discretion to adjudicate and dispose of Fain as a juvenile. The court held that the actions of the state violated Fain's right against double jeopardy.

CASE EXCERPT

"Fain's commitment to the division resulted from his having been found delinquent. And his being found delinquent resulted from his having violated a criminal law of the State of Florida. Thus, a violation of the criminal law may directly result in incarceration. This is a classic example of 'jeopardy.' The state's argument that the purpose of the commitment is rehabilitative and not punitive does not change its nature...A court proceeding which may result in incarceration places a person, adult or juvenile, in jeopardy. Fain's mere status as a juvenile, although it may subject him to the jurisdiction of an entirely different court system, cannot deprive him of rights that adults enjoy in the criminal justice system."

CASE SIGNIFICANCE

This case is important because it extended yet another right guaranteed to adults to juveniles. In this case, the juvenile was adjudicated of an offense in juvenile court

and dispositioned accordingly. During that process, and subsequent to the adjudication, the state indicted Fain in adult criminal court for the same offense. The court contended that this constituted double jeopardy, prohibited by the Fifth Amendment. In so holding, the court applied this protection to juvenile defendants. The court based its rationale for this on the fact that the juvenile court can seriously affect an individual's liberty, and thus an adjudication is analogous to that of a conviction in terms of determining jeopardy. In addition, the court also allowed a juvenile to file a writ of habeas corpus. The court contended the juvenile system can still substantially affect an individual's liberty and thus a juvenile has a right to file a writ. The implication of this decision is that states must now decide at the charging stage of the process if they are going to try a juvenile in juvenile court or motion to waive that juvenile to adult criminal court prior to an adjudication hearing.

UNITED STATES EX REL. BOMBACINO v. BENSINGER

498 F.2d 875 (7th Cir. 1974)

FACTS

Bensinger and two other young men were charged by petition in juvenile court with the offense of aggravated battery. The victim subsequently died, and the state moved to have the cases transferred to criminal court. After Bensinger objected, the juvenile court judge heard oral arguments, but did not receive any evidence. The motion was granted and Bensinger and his codefendants were transferred to criminal court. The juveniles were subsequently indicted for murder, and Bensinger was convicted of voluntary manslaughter, while the other two juveniles were acquitted. Bensinger was sentenced to one to five years, and committed to the Department of Corrections.

ISSUES

Is a juvenile judge required to give a statement of the reasons for a transfer? Does a transfer hearing require the presentation of evidence?

HOLDING

No and no. The court of appeals found nothing in the procedure of the transfer that was fundamentally unfair, and therefore the transfer of jurisdiction was valid.

UNITED STATES EX REL. BOMBACINO v. BENSINGER (cont.)

RATIONALE

The court contended that there is uncertainty about the impact of the due process clause on the procedure used by the state in determining whether to transfer a juvenile to criminal court. The court found respectable authority for the notion that the determination may be left entirely to the prosecutor's discretion. Under this view, procedural safeguards would not be constitutionally required unless the state elected to provide for judicial participation in the transfer decision. The court held that since the Illinois procedure under review did not provide that the juvenile judge could object to a decision by the state to transfer, for purposes of their decision they assume that the proceeding is of such critical importance to the juvenile that any fundamental procedural unfairness in that proceeding will require a subsequent conviction to be set aside. The court did not find any such unfairness. As to the petitioner's objections, the court found it significant that no evidence was heard; however, they did not find anything in the record to show that the court refused to hear such evidence. In addition, the court did not find a requirement that a statement of reasons must be given by the juvenile court when rendering a decision to transfer a juvenile to criminal court. The court contended that a statement of reasons in any procedural context must be evaluated in the light of the function such a statement would perform. Unlike Kent 383 U.S. 541 (1966), the present case involves a statutory scheme in which the role of the judge was confined to supervising the exercise of prosecutorial discretion and the undisputed fact the judge was given, after the oral argument he heard, sufficient opportunity to consider whether objection was appropriate. The absence of a statement of reasons cannot be deemed fundamentally unfair.

CASE EXCERPT

"A statement of reasons is less necessary when the person affected is represented, as was petitioner in this case, by competent counsel. We are well aware of the significant value of a statement of reasons in the decisional process of any case because such a statement always reduces the risk that the decision may be, or may appear to be, arbitrary. Nevertheless, there are so many aspects of the judicial process in which critical decisions have traditionally been made without explanation, that we could not properly hold that a statement is constitutionally mandated simply as a safeguard against real or apparent arbitrariness."

CASE SIGNIFICANCE

This case is important because it provided the framework for a transfer scheme which is known as prosecutorial discretion or direct file. Under this type of transfer scheme, the prosecutor may file a case in juvenile or adult court absent a hearing. This distinguishes this case from Kent, in which the method of transfer was judicial. In that case, the purpose of the waiver hearing was to determine if the juvenile should in fact be transferred. Consequently, the court must provide a statement of reasons for the transfer. In this case, the statute did provide for a waiver hearing, but its purpose was merely to supervise the exercise of the prosecutor's discretion. Now, many states allow this method of transfer, most without a hearing.

BREED v. JONES

421 U.S. 519 (1975)

FACTS

A petition was filed alleging that Jones, then 17 years of age, had committed acts, which if committed by an adult, would constitute the crime of robbery. The following day, a detention hearing was held, at the conclusion of which Jones was ordered detained pending a hearing on the petition. The jurisdictional or adjudicatory hearing was conducted. After taking testimony from two prosecution witnesses and Jones, the juvenile court found that the allegations in the petition were true, and it sustained the petition. The proceedings were continued for a dispositional hearing, pending which the court ordered that the respondent remain detained. At a later hearing, the juvenile court indicated its intention to find the respondent not amenable to the care, treatment, and training program available through the facilities of the juvenile court. Jones's counsel orally moved to continue the matter on the ground of surprise, contending that the respondent was not informed that it was going to be a transfer hearing. The court continued the matter for one week, at which time, having considered the report of the probation officer assigned to the case and having heard her testimony, it declared Jones unfit for treatment as a juvenile, and ordered that he be prosecuted as an adult. Thereafter, Jones filed a petition for a writ of habeas corpus in juvenile court, raising the same double jeopardy claim now presented. Upon the denial of that petition, Jones sought habeas corpus relief in the California Court of Appeal, Second Appellate District. Although it initially stayed the criminal prosecution pending against the respondent, that court denied the petition. After a preliminary hearing, Jones was ordered held for trial in superior court, where an information was subsequently filed accusing him of having committed robbery, while armed with a deadly weapon. Jones entered a plea of not guilty, and he also pleaded that he had already been placed once in jeopardy and convicted of the offense charged. By stipulation, the case was submitted to the court on the transcript of the preliminary hearing. The court found the respondent guilty of robbery in the first degree and ordered that he be committed to the California Youth Authority. No appeal was taken from the judgment of conviction. Jones, through his mother as guardian *ad litem,* filed the instant petition for a writ of habeas corpus in the United States District Court for the Central District of California. In his petition, he alleged that his transfer to criminal court pursuant to and subsequent trial there placed him in double jeopardy. The district court denied the petition, rejecting Jones's contention that jeopardy attached at his adjudicatory hearing. The court of appeals reversed, concluding that applying double jeopardy protection to juvenile proceedings would not impede the juvenile courts in carrying out their basic goal of rehabilitating the erring youth, and that the contrary result might do irreparable harm to or destroy their confidence in our judicial system. The court therefore held that the double jeopardy clause is fully applicable to juvenile court proceedings.

Turning to the question whether there had been a constitutional violation in this case, the court of appeals pointed to the power of the juvenile court to impose severe restrictions upon the juvenile's liberty, in support of its conclusion that jeopardy attached in Jones's adjudicatory hearing. It rejected Jones's contention that no new jeopardy attached when he was referred to superior court and subsequently tried and convicted, finding continuing jeopardy principles advanced by Jones inapplicable. Finally, the court of appeals observed that acceptance of Jones's position would allow the prosecution to review in advance the accused's defense and, as here, hear him testify about the crime charged, a procedure it found offensive to our concepts of basic, even-handed fairness. The court therefore held that once jeopardy attached at the adjudicatory hearing, a minor could not be retried as an

adult or a juvenile absent some exception to the double jeopardy prohibition, and that there was none here.

ISSUE

Does the double jeopardy clause of the Fifth Amendment protect a juvenile from being prosecuted as an adult after undergoing adjudication proceedings in juvenile court?

HOLDING

Yes. A juvenile who has undergone adjudication proceedings in juvenile court cannot be tried on the same charge as an adult in a criminal court because to do so would constitute double jeopardy.

RATIONALE

The Court observed that jeopardy describes the risk that is traditionally associated with a criminal prosecution. Although the constitutional language, jeopardy of life or limb, suggests proceedings in which only the most serious penalties can be imposed, the clause has long been construed to mean something far broader than its literal language. At the same time, however, the Court held that the risk to which the clause refers is not present in proceedings that are not essentially criminal. Although the juvenile court system had its genesis in the desire to provide a distinctive procedure and setting to deal with the problems of youth, including those manifested by antisocial conduct, the Court's decisions in recent years have recognized that there is a gap between the originally benign conception of the system and its realities. With the exception of *McKeiver v. Pennsylvania,* 403 U.S. 528 (1971), the Court's response to that perception has been to make applicable in juvenile proceedings constitutional guarantees associated with traditional criminal prosecutions. In so doing, the Court has evinced awareness of the threat, which such a process represents to the efforts of the juvenile court system, functioning in a unique manner, to ameliorate the harshness of criminal justice when applied to youthful offenders. That the system has fallen short of the high expectations of its sponsors and in no way detracts from the broad social benefits sought or from those benefits that can survive constitutional scrutiny. The Court contends it is simply too late to conclude, as did the District Court in this case, that a juvenile is not put in jeopardy at a proceeding whose object is to determine whether he has committed acts that violate a criminal law and whose potential consequences include both the stigma inherent in such a

BREED v. JONES *(cont.)*

determination and the deprivation of liberty for many years. The Court deals here, not with the formalities of the criminal adjudicative process, but with an analysis of an aspect of the juvenile court system in terms of the kind of risk to which jeopardy refers. Under the Court's decisions, there is no persuasive distinction in that regard between the proceeding conducted in this case pursuant to and a criminal prosecution, each of which is designed to vindicate the very vital interest in enforcement of criminal laws. The Court therefore concluded that Jones was put in jeopardy at the adjudicatory hearing. Jeopardy attached when Jones was put to trial before the trier of the facts—that is, when the Juvenile Court, as the trier of the facts, began to hear evidence.

CASE EXCERPT

"Respondent was put in jeopardy at the adjudicatory hearing. Jeopardy attached when respondent was 'put to trial before the trier of the facts,' that is, when the Juvenile Court, as the trier of the facts, began to hear evidence. We cannot agree with petitioner that the trial of respondent in Superior Court on an information charging the same offense as that for which he had been tried in Juvenile Court violated none of the policies of the Double Jeopardy Clause. For, even accepting petitioner's premise that respondent 'never faced the risk of more than one punishment,' we have pointed out that 'the Double Jeopardy Clause...is written in terms of potential or risk of *trial* and conviction, not punishment.'"

CASE SIGNIFICANCE

This case is important for several reasons. First, it marked the second time the Supreme Court had issued certiorari for a juvenile case involving the waiver of a juvenile to adult criminal court. In doing so, it was evident that the Court did indeed consider this to be a critical stage in the proceedings, as they held in *Kent*. Second, the Court extended the Fifth Amendment protection against double jeopardy to juvenile defendants. The Court followed the lead of several states that had already done so, and made the law applicable to all. Although the Court acknowledged that the juvenile court is civil in nature, they extended a basic right to juvenile defendants in the interest of providing fundamental fairness, as they had in several cases before. The Court contended that jeopardy attached because a juvenile can suffer a significant loss of a liberty as a result of both juvenile and adult court impositions. The Court contended that in extending certain rights they were ensuring that juvenile defendants' rights were protected while maintaining the informal nature of the juvenile court. However, by extending this right and others, the Court actually criminalized the juvenile court.

IN RE MATHIS
537 P.2d 148 (Or. App. 1975)

FACTS

Mathis, age 16, was charged by petition in juvenile court. The petition alleged murder and robbery. Mathis had a long history of problems with drugs, alcohol, truancy, and running away. In addition, Mathis had been under psychiatric care for about seven or eight months prior to the filing of the petition. At the transfer hearing, two psychiatrists testified that Mathis would probably require counseling for three to four years. The juvenile court judge transferred Mathis to criminal court, indicating that the evidence strongly supported the offenses that were alleged, and that the juvenile's age and need for long-term care also justified transfer of jurisdiction.

ISSUE

Is a decision to transfer a juvenile to criminal court proper if based on the strength of the evidence, the juvenile's age, and the need for long-term care?

HOLDING

Yes. If based on the strength of the evidence, the juvenile's age, and the need for long-term care, a decision to transfer a juvenile to criminal court is constitutional.

RATIONALE

The court pointed out that although Mathis did not have a prior juvenile record and thus had not been afforded the services the juvenile system can provide, he had been provided with extended efforts by his school as well as psychiatric services for the past seven months. In addition, the court pointed to the fact that Mathis was 16 years old and therefore, according to testimony, would only be confined for three years if retained in the juvenile system. Further, he would be over the average age of juveniles confined in juvenile institutions. The court also took into account the factual considerations of the case. It felt that the case against Mathis was strong. Therefore, the court found that transfer to criminal court was not only in the best interest of Mathis, but the community as well.

CASE EXCERPT

"Thus, it appears that for a situation like we have at bar, where the juvenile at first may need the type of juvenile care that MacLaren affords, but will outgrow it and may still need more institutional care, and undoubtedly more years of supervision of parole nature if not institutional care, the methods exist for meeting these various needs. But the variety of the methods is only possible if the juvenile's case is tried in adult court with resultant commitment to the Corrections Division. Perhaps, as the trial judge noted, an adult court criminal trial will result in exoneration. But if it does not, the juvenile can be served with his age group peers while still a juvenile if the facts justify it, and with the public still protected by his further confinement or supervision after juvenile age if the facts then justify that approach."

CASE SIGNIFICANCE

This case is important because it signified what factors juvenile courts take into account when making the decision to transfer a juvenile to criminal court. In this case, the juvenile was charged with a serious crime. However, he had never been afforded any services in the juvenile justice system, which is a factor that is considered in making the decision to waive jurisdiction. The court decided to transfer the juvenile, thereby elevating the principle of the offense over the best interests of the child. The court also made reference to Mathis's age, 16, which made him older than many juveniles in custody and only eligible for confinement for three years. In elevating the principle of the offense to the most important factor taken into account, the juvenile court moved away from the rehabilitative nature of the juvenile court toward the punishment-driven adult criminal court.

RUSSELL v. PARRATT

543 F.2d 1214 (8th Cir. 1976)

FACTS

The daughter of the owner of an automobile witnessed Russell attempting to break into her father's automobile. A police officer was called and Russell, a 17-year-old boy, was interrogated after he was located in a nearby store. The car owner declined to press charges and the officer decided not to pursue the matter; however, he did fill out an informational with Russell's address. The officer also noted that Russell appeared to be in a deranged mental condition, although he answered the officer's questions. When the officer returned to the station, he learned that the body of an eight-year-old boy had been located near Russell's address. Two officers went to the residence where Russell lived and indicated that they wanted to take Russell to the station to discuss the automobile break-in. Russell was subsequently charged with first-degree murder. The prosecuting attorney chose to treat Russell as an adult, per his own unreviewable discretion.

ISSUES

Was due process violated by the county attorney's having unreviewable discretion, without applicable standards to charge a juvenile as an adult? Did the juvenile knowingly and intelligently waive his rights to counsel and self-incrimination?

HOLDING

No and yes. The county attorney's unreviewable decision to charge the juvenile as an adult did not violate the juvenile's due process rights. The juvenile knowingly waived his rights.

RATIONALE

Russell relied on the *Kent* decision in arguing the first issue. However, the court contended that although *Kent* indicates that when the question is one of waiver of juvenile court jurisdiction, and it is to be decided by a judge, the juvenile is entitled to a hearing on the matter and the assistance of counsel in that matter, that was not the case here. The case at hand did not involve a judicial proceeding, but a traditional exercise of discretion within the executive branch. Therefore, absent legislative direction, the court would not equate a prosecutorial decision with judicial proceedings. As to Russell's second claim, the court could not find anything in the record to indicate that the defendant did not know what he was doing when he waived his rights.

CASE EXCERPT

"But we do not here confront judicial proceedings. Rather, we have simply a traditional exercise of discretion within the executive branch, and while we recognize that the prosecutor's decision has a substantial

RUSSELL v. PARRATT *(cont.)*

impact on the course of subsequent proceedings, we cannot equate the prosecutorial decision with judicial proceedings, absent legislative direction."

CASE SIGNIFICANCE

This case is important because it upheld the constitutionality of prosecutorial discretion or direct file as a method of waiving a juvenile to adult criminal court. Many states have added this method of waiver to their statutes in an effort to bypass the juvenile court jurisdiction and subsequent hearing guaranteed by *Kent* 383 U.S. 541 (1966). In this method of waiver, the prosecutor has the unreviewable discretion to charge a youth in adult or juvenile court. Some states have limited the offenses for which the prosecutor may do this, as well as the juvenile's age at which discretionary transfer can occur, but most do not require a hearing of any type as long as the offense satisfies those two criteria. Again, in this case, the principle of the offense was elevated over the best interests of the child, as prosecutors cannot be expected to know a juvenile's history and background.

UNITED STATES v. J.D.

517 F.Supp. 69 (S.D.N.Y. 1981)

FACTS

Three juveniles were arrested and charged with attempted robbery. Six days later, an information was filed charging the juveniles with conspiracy, attempted bank robbery, carrying of firearms during the commission of a felony, and possession of an unregistered firearm. The government sought to transfer the juveniles to criminal court. As a preliminary step toward its consideration and determination, the government sought an order committing the juveniles to the custody of the attorney general for observation and study by an appropriate agency on an outpatient basis. The intent of the study would be to ascertain the juveniles' background, personal traits, capabilities, prior record, intellectual development, and psychological maturity. The agency would then report its findings to the government, defense counsel, and the court for the purpose of assisting in the transfer decision. The defense counsel challenged the study on the basis that juveniles might be forced to make self-incriminating statements. The defense also challenged the statute on the ground that it did not contain clear guidelines for the judge to follow in rendering his decision.

ISSUES

Was the statute providing for commitment for study constitutional? Did the statute, as applied to these juveniles, violate their Fifth Amendment rights?

HOLDING

Yes and yes. The statute governing the commitments for study is constitutional, but the statute as applied to these juveniles was unconstitutional because it violated the juveniles' Fifth Amendment privileges against self-incrimination.

RATIONALE

The court contended that the statute itself was constitutional, but that the application sought by the government in this case would violate the juveniles' Fifth Amendment rights. The court pointed to the Supreme Court's decision in *In re Gault* 387 U.S. 1 (1967). In *Gault,* the Court ruled that juvenile defendants are entitled to the Fifth Amendment's protection against self-incrimination in juvenile proceedings, despite the noncriminal nature of those proceedings. This court contended that *Gault* applies to all juvenile proceedings, including transfer proceedings. The court illustrated that if transferred, juveniles are subject to longer periods of confinement, and therefore, their liberty is very much at stake. Therefore, the Fifth Amendment applied in this case. As to the issue of the psychological testing itself, the court contended that there was much discrepancy in the case law. However, in the present case, the government sought to compel the juveniles to submit to the examinations. The defense had not submitted any psychological defenses in the case. Therefore, the court concluded that as to all areas of proposed inquiry with the exception of the juveniles' intellectual development, psychological maturity, and mental defects, insofar as the government sought to rely upon the defendants themselves to supply information relevant to the transfer motion, the government sought to compel incriminatory statements. The court believed this was in violation of the juveniles' Fifth Amendment rights. The court granted the commitment order, but under conditions that the evaluation would only examine mental defects, intellectual capability, and psychological maturity. In addition, to safeguard the juveniles' rights the government was not allowed to use the defendants' statements in the evaluation in the course of the hearing.

CASE EXCERPT

"In *Gault*, the court ruled that juveniles are entitled to the Fifth Amendment's protection against self-incrimination in juvenile proceedings themselves, despite the non-criminal nature of those proceedings . . The court looked to the purposes of the privilege, and in particular its goal of preventing the state 'whether by force or by psychological domination, from overcoming the mind and will of the person under investigation and depriving him of the freedom to decide whether to assist the state in securing his conviction.' Both of these grounds support the applicability of the Fifth Amendment to transfer proceedings as well as to juvenile proceedings themselves. The defendants would be open to a far longer period of incarceration if the transfer motion were to be successful than if they were to be proceeded against as juveniles. Their liberty is therefore very much at stake."

CASE SIGNIFICANCE

This case is important because it limited the government's ability to gather evidence to assist its case to transfer juveniles to adult criminal court. In this case, the government sought to have the juveniles committed to the attorney general to evaluate their background, personal traits, capabilities, prior record, intellectual development, and psychological maturity. In challenging this, the defense contended that the juveniles would be ordered to undergo evaluation for a crime of which they had not been convicted, and subsequently be compelled to provide statements that might incriminate them. The court balanced the needs of the government with safeguarding some of the children's rights, a trend that has become prevalent as constitutional rights have been applied to juvenile matters. The court allowed the commitment of the juveniles, but limited the evaluation to basic psychological testing. In addition, the statements provided by the juveniles in the evaluation could not be used in the hearing, merely the evaluator's findings.

MATTER OF SEVEN MINORS

664 P.2d 947 (Nev. 1983)

FACTS

This case consolidated the facts from cases of seven different juveniles focusing on the issue of transfer decisions. The juveniles all had different offense levels, ranging from residential burglary to pickpocketing while engaging in prostitution. Several of the juveniles had prior records and some had been committed to juvenile institutions. Some of the others had minor or no juvenile justice system involvement.

ISSUE

What are the appropriate criteria and standard of proof necessary for a transfer decision?

HOLDING

The appropriate criteria for transfer of juveniles from juvenile to criminal court are threefold: (1) the nature and seriousness of the charges; (2) the persistency and seriousness of past adjudications of criminal behavior; and (3) subjective factors such as age, level of maturity, and family relationships. All of these criteria should be weighed using the clear and convincing standard of proof.

RATIONALE

The court contended that the transfer process was based upon the sound idea that there is no arbitrary age at which all youths should be held fully responsible as adults for their criminal acts and that there should be a transition period during which an offender may or may not be held criminally liable, depending on the nature of the offender and the offense. The court also pointed out that other than requiring a full investigation, the statute placed no limits on the discretion of the juvenile courts in such matters. The court contended that the juvenile court had long been focused on the best interest of the child versus the best interests of society. The court was of the opinion, however, that when the two clash, the best interests of society should prevail. Therefore, in making decisions, the juvenile court must make a rational discrimination, based on the best interests of the state, between youth who should properly be kept in the juvenile court system and youth who should be sent to criminal court. That being said, the court contended that if punishment and deterrence were guiding principles, more youth should be retained in the juvenile system. The juvenile system could adequately punish the youth and hopefully rehabilitate them to the point they were deterred from committing future acts. The adult system, on the other hand, may not punish them due to a judge's unwillingness to subject a youth to prison, or may in fact make them worse by placing them with adults. The court also indicated that juveniles should not be transferred unless public safety and welfare clearly and convincingly required it.

MATTER OF SEVEN MINORS (cont.)

CASE EXCERPT

"With community protection as the guiding principle to be considered in transfer proceedings, subjective evaluations and prognostications as to whether a given youth is or is not likely to respond favorably to juvenile court treatment will no longer be the court's primary focus in transfer proceedings; rather, the dispositive question to be addressed by the court is whether the public interest requires that the youth be placed within the jurisdiction of the adult criminal courts."

CASE SIGNIFICANCE

This case is important for several reasons. First, the court observed that there should be standards for determining if a juvenile should be transferred to adult criminal court. Those standards or criteria should be the nature and seriousness of the charges, the persistency and seriousness of past adjudications of criminal behavior, and subjective factors such as age, level of maturity, and family relationships. These criteria were similar to those used by many other states. In addition, the court dictated that these standards should be applied to each individual juvenile and each juvenile should be treated diversely. This is clearly consistent with the "best interest of the child" rationale on which the juvenile court was founded. Second, the court contended that the juvenile court needed to meet a clear and convincing standard in determining that a juvenile should be transferred to criminal court. In so holding, the court forced the juvenile court to thoroughly justify its decision to transfer. The court justified this by indicating that the juvenile system can adequately punish juvenile offenders, and more juveniles should be retained in juvenile court then transferred to the adult criminal court, where their punishment may not necessarily be more severe, and where their propensity to commit crime may be intensified by contact with adult offenders. In so holding, the court elevated the individual differences of juveniles over the principle of the offense in terms of a juvenile court's decision to transfer a juvenile to adult criminal court.

STATE v. MUHAMMAD

703 P.2d 835 (Kan. 1985)

FACTS

Muhammad, age 17, was arrested for allowing her friends and family to take items from the store where she worked without paying for them. The state filed a motion to waive jurisdiction. At the waiver hearing, neither Muhammad nor her parents appeared, although her court-appointed attorney was present. The attorney indicated that Muhammad was not present because she had been mistakenly arrested in a nearby county. The court proceeded with the hearing despite Muhammad's absence and she was waived to criminal court.

ISSUE

Was the defendant denied due process rights when the court waived jurisdiction to the criminal court without the juvenile being present?

HOLDING

No. When the juvenile is notified of the hearing, given the right to be present, and is represented by counsel, due process and fair treatment requirements are met, even if the juvenile does not appear.

RATIONALE

Muhammad did not contest whether there was evidence to support her transfer to criminal court, nor did she attack the constitutionality of the Kansas law. Her sole claim was that under the facts of this particular case, she was denied her right to due process when the hearing was held absent her presence. In *Kent* 383 U.S. 541 (1966), the Supreme Court defined the waiver hearing as a critical stage in the process. They further indicated that at each stage that is critical, a child must be afforded numerous safeguards. The court in the present case determined that only a few other courts had considered the question of whether a juvenile has the absolute right to be present at a waiver hearing. The court indicated there was a split in those decisions. From what had been said, it appeared obvious that a juvenile waiver proceeding is a critically important proceeding that requires a hearing, notice, and an opportunity to be present in person or by counsel or both. The court contended that Kansas law required an attorney at every stage of the proceedings. However, the court also noted that a juvenile may waive his or her appearance if such a waiver is knowingly or voluntarily made. The question then became whether or not the court could waive appearance for the juvenile if his or her attorney was allowed to act on his or her behalf. This court held that it could.

CASE EXCERPT

"While a waiver hearing involves a substantial right subject to the requirements of due process, it is not adjudicatory in nature in that it does not result in any determination of guilt or innocence or in confinement or punishment. It is merely a preliminary process to determine the type of adjudicatory procedure to be carried out at a later date. As indicated earlier the statutes require that the juvenile must be represented and that the attorney be present for the hearing."

CASE SIGNIFICANCE

This case's importance lies in the fact that the court held that a juvenile need not be present at a critical stage in the proceedings if he or she has an attorney acting on his or her behalf. The court equated a juvenile's inability to appear, for whatever reason, to that of an attorney appearing on behalf of a client per the client's choice. In so holding, the court stripped juveniles of their right to confront the testimony against them and aid in their own defense as long as their counsel is present to act on their behalf and represent their interests. The court contended that its only responsibility is to provide notice of the hearing, which it did in this case.

R.H. v. STATE

777 P.2d 204 (Alaska App. 1989)

FACTS

R.H. and another juvenile burglarized an office and stole a pistol, the owner's manual to the pistol, some ammunition, and an extra clip. The pair learned how to operate the gun and decided to rob a taxicab driver in an effort to obtain money for drugs. The boys also made plans to kill the driver of the cab. They flagged down a cab and asked to be taken to a destination. The driver proceeded to the location and stopped the cab. R.H. fired four shots into the back of the driver. As R.H. fired the shots, the driver threw a wad of money into the back seat. After firing the shots, R.H. went through the driver's pockets and then dragged him out of the car. He then proceeded to shoot him one more time in the head. The boys then left the scene in the cab. Two days later the police interviewed R.H., who gave a videotaped confession to the murder and prior burglary. The state then petitioned to waive jurisdiction of R.H. to criminal court. The state requested a psychiatric evaluation of R.H., arguing that expert testimony concerning R.H.'s psychological condition would be relevant in determining his amenability to

treatment. R.H. opposed the evaluation. After hearing arguments, the judge ordered R.H. to submit to the evaluation. However, the judge took elaborate precautions to safeguard R.H.'s privilege against self-incrimination and his right to counsel. A panel of two psychiatrists and one psychologist evaluated R.H. R.H. did not object to the state having probable cause to believe he committed the offense, or to the seriousness of the offense. In addition, he conceded he had a substantial juvenile record. However, based on the findings of the evaluations, which indicated there were no facilities available to deal with someone like R.H., the judge transferred him to criminal court.

ISSUES

Do the involuntary psychiatric evaluations of a juvenile for use in waiver proceedings violate the Fifth Amendment to the Constitution? Do the involuntary psychiatric evaluations of a juvenile for use in waiver proceedings violate the Sixth Amendment to the Constitution?

HOLDING

Yes and no. The juvenile's privilege against self-incrimination was violated by the court. The juvenile's Sixth Amendment right to counsel was not violated because his counsel was permitted to accompany him and consult with him throughout the evaluation process.

RATIONALE

The court distinguished between competency hearings and waiver hearings indicating that they are not neutral proceedings. Instead, the waiver hearing is a fully adversary proceeding in which the burden of establishing a juvenile's lack of amenability to treatment is on the state. In addition, the court observed that waiver proceedings do not only affect the forum where the issue of guilt is to be adjudicated. The juvenile waiver proceeding is the only means by which the state can seek to prosecute a child as an adult. Consequently, the stakes of such a proceeding are high. The court went on to distinguish between the possible penalties available at the juvenile and criminal levels. They concluded that the juvenile would suffer a much more severe punishment at the adult level. The court contended that admission of the psychiatric evidence against R.H. as an adult thereby exposed him to potential punishment far more severe than could otherwise have been placed upon him. Therefore, the state's reliance on the court-compelled evidence at the waiver hearing was not in

R.H. v. STATE *(cont.)*

the best interests of R.H. The court went on to indicate that the use of psychiatric evidence was not necessary to further the state's interest in waiving a juvenile to criminal court. The court recommended more weight be placed on prior record and offense seriousness. The court contended these factors would typically carry more weight than expert testimony. Psychiatric evidence should typically be left to the discretion of the defense and should not be compelled. The court concluded that the testimony of the experts resulted in harmful error, as it most likely was influential in the decision to transfer.

CASE EXCERPT

"In contrast to competency proceedings, juvenile waiver hearings are hardly 'neutral proceedings.' Rather, they are fully adversary proceedings in which the burden of establishing a child's probable unamenability to treatment is formally allocated to the state . . . A juvenile waiver proceeding is the only available avenue by which the state may seek to prosecute a child as an adult. Consequently, the stakes involved in such proceedings are high. Accordingly, we conclude that the superior court erred in compelling R.H. to submit to a psychiatric evaluation for the purpose of determining his amenability to treatment as a child."

CASE SIGNIFICANCE

This case is important because the court effectively eliminated the use of psychiatric or psychological evaluations in waiver hearings, unless they are presented by the defense. The court contended that a state-compelled evaluation violates the juvenile's right to self-incrimination, which is guaranteed them by *In re Gault*, 387 U.S. 1 (1967) (see chapter 6). It is important to note that there is substantial differences across state statutes as to whether state-compelled evaluations can be used in these hearings. However, in this case, the court clearly distinguished between the waiver hearing and a hearing that is held to determine mental competency. The court justified this distinction because of the punishments that are imposed as a possible result of the two hearings. The court also indicated that the decision to waive jurisdiction should be based more on prior record and offense seriousness, both of which were present in this case, than on expert testimony. In other words, facts should be given greater weight than opinion.

PEOPLE v. P.H.

582 N.E.2d 700 (Ill. 1991)

FACTS

P.H., a juvenile, was arrested and charged with two counts of attempted murder, two counts of aggravated battery, two counts of aggravated battery with a firearm, and one count of armed violence. Pursuant to the gang transfer provision, the state filed a motion to permit prosecution of P.H. in criminal court. The gang transfer statute requires that a minor be charged as an adult if the minor has prior felony adjudications and is subsequently charged with commission of a felony in furtherance of gang activity. The circuit court denied the state's motion holding the gang transfer provision unconstitutional in that it violated separation of powers.

ISSUE

Is the gang transfer provision of the statute constitutional?

HOLDING

Yes. The gang transfer provision of the statute is constitutional. It does not violate constitutional provisions on separation of powers, double jeopardy, equal protection, or due process.

RATIONALE

In reviewing the separation of powers challenge, the court contended that the gang transfer provision was an infringement upon the inherent powers of the judiciary, not the juvenile. In reaching this decision, the court contended that juveniles have neither a common law nor a constitutional right to adjudication under the Juvenile Court Act. As to the challenge of double jeopardy, the court did not agree with P.H.'s contention that the transfer hearing was tantamount to an adjudicatory hearing. P.H. believed his contention was supported by *Breed*, 421 U.S. 519 (1975); however, the court indicated that the reasonable standard applied in *Breed* applied to proof of the allegations of delinquency, not to the decision to transfer. In tackling the equal protection challenge, the court found no equal protection violation despite the fact that the two groups of offenders, because of their age, were alike. Equal protection does not preclude different treatment for like persons where there is a rational basis for doing so. The court believed that standard was met here. The Juvenile Court Act seeks to rehabilitate juvenile offenders, thereby benefiting the juvenile and society. The act was not designed to protect those juveniles who well knew the consequences of their actions and still chose to engage in criminal conduct. It is these offenders the gang transfer mechanism was aimed to affect. Therefore, the court contended the statute was constitutional.

CASE EXCERPT

"We do not interpret the absence of an express standard of proof as requiring a reasonable doubt standard. We believe it to be a more reasonable inference that the standard of proof required by the 'gang-transfer' provision parallel that in other transfer proceedings. Even accepting that the standard is reasonable doubt, such proof of the requirements for transfer under the 'gang-transfer' provision does not convert the proceeding into an adjudication. Under the 'gang-transfer' provision, unlike an adjudicatory hearing, there is no requirement that the State present evidence of the minor's delinquency."

CASE SIGNIFICANCE

The importance of this case lies in the gang transfer statute. In response to a recent increase in gang crime, many states are adding gang transfer provisions to their existing waiver statutes. In allowing this transfer solely on the basis of the juvenile committing a gang crime, the court effectively upheld the statute and allowed the state to transfer a juvenile who committed the same crime as another juvenile just because he or she did so in furtherance of gang activity. The court justified its decision using the theory of individualized treatment of juvenile offenders on which the juvenile court was founded. Consequently, the court contended that there is a difference between a gang-involved juvenile who commits a crime and another juvenile who commits that very same crime.

C.M. v. STATE
884 S.W.2d 562 (Tex. App. 1994)

FACTS

C.M. and a friend were walking through a public housing project when they came across Garcia and others spray painting graffiti on a wall. Garcia and his associates belonged to a rival gang of the one in which C.M. belonged. Garcia had also assaulted C.M. one week prior to the night in question. C.M. confronted Garcia and a fight ensued. Both boys were 15 years old, but Garcia was twice C.M.'s size. During the course of the fight, C.M. shot Garcia with a pistol he produced from his pocket. Garcia died at the hospital. C.M. was charged with intentionally and knowingly causing the death of Garcia. He was transferred to criminal court to stand trial. During the waiver hearing, a probation officer and a clinical psychologist both testified that C.M. would have a better chance for rehabilitation if he stayed in the juvenile justice system. C.M. challenged the judge's decision to transfer him to criminal court.

ISSUE

Did the judge err in ordering C.M. transferred to criminal court?

HOLDING

No. There was sufficient evidence for the trial court to make the decision to transfer C.M. to criminal court.

RATIONALE

The requirements for transferring a juvenile to criminal court are that (1) the child is alleged to have committed a felony; (2) the child was 15 years of age or older at the time the offense occurred; and (3) after a full investigation and hearing, the juvenile court determines that there is probable cause to believe the child committed the offense alleged and that because of the seriousness of the offense or the background of the child, the welfare of the community requires criminal proceeding. In making the transfer determination, the trial court appropriately considered the factors set forth, and made the following findings of fact: (1) the offense was against a person; (2) the offense was committed in an aggressive and premeditated manner; (3) there was sufficient evidence upon which a grand jury could be expected to return an indictment; (4) C.M. was sufficiently mature and sophisticated to confer with his attorney and assist with his own defense; (5) there were no prior offenses; and (6) it was unclear whether the public would be adequately protected if C. M. were not transferred to criminal court. Most important, the trial court found that because of the seriousness of the offense, the welfare of the community required the transfer. Therefore, the court found there was sufficient evidence for the trial court to decide that this matter would be better handled in criminal court.

C.M. v. STATE *(cont.)*

CASE EXCERPT

"When the factual sufficiency of a transfer is challenged, the reviewing court must consider all of the evidence to determine if the finding is so against the great weight and preponderance of the evidence as to be manifestly erroneous or unjust. The trial judge is the sole fact finder in a pre-trial hearing and its ruling will not be overturned absent an abuse of discretion."

CASE SIGNIFICANCE

This case is important for a number of reasons. First, the transfer criteria that the court must apply were clearly laid out. These criteria are similar to those found in other states' juvenile codes. In addition, the trial court made findings pertaining to each of the criteria when it made its decision to waive jurisdiction. Second, the trial court transferred the juvenile against the recommendation of the probation officer and a psychiatrist who had evaluated the youth. This reflects a trend to elevate the principle of the offense over the individual differences juvenile defendants possess. In addition, the court made clear that the trial court elevated the safety of the public over the best interests of the child when the trial court determined it was unclear whether the juvenile system could adequately protect the public.

LASWELL v. FREY

45 F.3d 1011 (6th Cir. 1995)

FACTS

Laswell, age 16, and two others were arrested for robbery and double murder. Laswell was charged only with two counts of complicity to commit first-degree robbery at the time of her initial appearance and arraignment in juvenile court. Laswell was represented by counsel at the hearing. At the hearing, Laswell was advised of the charge against her, advised of her constitutional rights, including the right to an attorney, the right to remain silent, the right to confront witnesses against her, the right to appeal the determination of the court, and the right to examine any reports filed with the court and to question whoever made those reports. Laswell subsequently admitted to the charges and a disposition hearing was set. Between the time of the admission and the disposition, the Commonwealth added two counts of murder and moved to transfer

jurisdiction to criminal court. Laswell was informed of this at her disposition hearing. Defense counsel objected that jeopardy attached. The court denied the objection and at a youthful offender hearing Laswell was waived to criminal court and indicted by a grand jury. She subsequently filed a writ of habeas corpus arguing that the first hearing had been an adjudication hearing and the subsequent criminal hearings would violate the double jeopardy clause.

ISSUE

Was the preliminary hearing an adjudication hearing and, if it was, would the subsequent criminal hearings held after the transfer hearing constitute double jeopardy?

HOLDING

No. Admitting to the charges in the preliminary hearing did not automatically transform a detention hearing into an adjudication; therefore, there was no double jeopardy in the criminal proceeding.

RATIONALE

After reviewing the law, the court determined that an adjudication requires a determination of truth or falsity of the allegations, and that a determination of truth requires more than the simple verbal admission at the detention hearing at issue in the present case. At the outset of the initial hearing, the juvenile court indicated the purpose of the hearing was to determine if Laswell should remain in detention and not to determine the truth of the allegations. The court contended that because no inquiry was made to determine if the plea was voluntarily made, and because no inquiry was made as to the nature of the charges, the proceedings could not later be transformed from a determination of probable cause for detention into an acceptance of a valid guilty plea. The court agreed with the district court when it found that Laswell was simply trying to fashion a guilty plea after the fact based on the events subsequent to her admission. The court contended that the juvenile court was merely determining probable cause when they inquired whether Laswell admitted or denied the offenses at the initial hearing. The establishment of probable cause was merely for detention purposes. At that time, and under the circumstances, it was insufficient to determine guilt, and thus jeopardy did not attach at the hearing.

CASE EXCERPT

"The Court is persuaded that, because no inquiry was made of the veracity of the charges or admission, because no inquiry was made to determine if the 'plea' was voluntarily made, and because no inquiry was made as to the nature of the charges, that the proceedings cannot later be transformed from a determination of probable cause for detention into an acceptance of a valid guilty plea. While the statement 'I admit them' alone is sufficient to support the finding of probable cause, absent other protection of the defendant and a specific acknowledgment and acceptance of a plea by the court—on the record or in a written order—the statement is insufficient to change the very nature of the proceedings into an adjudication hearing."

CASE SIGNIFICANCE

This case is important because the court determined that a detention hearing is not analogous to an adjudicatory hearing. Therefore, any protections against double jeopardy a juvenile is entitled to after they are adjudicated, do not apply at the detention hearing. In this case, however, the juvenile court did accept the juvenile's plea and set the matter for a dispositional hearing, which would lead one to believe an adjudication of guilt had been entered. However, the court ruled that the entering of an adjudication at that time was not appropriate because the juvenile court made clear the sole purpose of the hearing was to determine probable cause and subsequently whether the juvenile should remain detained. Consequently, the implications of this case could go beyond that of the waiver issue.

STATE v. VERHAGEN

542 N.W.2d 189 (Wis. App. 1995)

FACTS

Verhagen was charged with the battery of a youth counselor at the Ethan Allen School for Boys where Verhagen was committed as a juvenile offender. The criminal court had exclusive jurisdiction for the offense unless it determined the child should be transferred to the juvenile court in a reverse waiver proceeding. Verhagen made an initial appearance in criminal court and then challenged the criminal court's jurisdiction on constitutional and statutory grounds. The Court denied these challenges. Verhagen filed for a

substitution of judge, and the matter was reassigned to a different judge. Following a probable cause determination, the judge addressed the reverse waiver question by requiring the parties to each bear the burden of proof. The judge ruled that the state had carried its burden. Verhagen challenged the judge's allocation of burden of proof.

ISSUE

Did the criminal court improperly assign a portion of the burden of proof to Verhagen in the reverse waiver proceeding and consequently did the criminal court err in retaining jurisdiction?

HOLDING

No. A juvenile defendant has the burden of proof in a reverse waiver proceeding and therefore, the criminal court did not err in retaining jurisdiction of the juvenile.

RATIONALE

The applicable statute (Section 970.032) mandates the criminal court shall maintain jurisdiction unless the court finds the following conditions are satisfied: (1) that, if convicted, the child could not receive adequate treatment in the criminal justice system; (2) that transferring jurisdiction to the court assigned to exercise jurisdiction under Ch. 48 would not depreciate the seriousness of the offense; and (3) that retaining jurisdiction is not necessary to deter the child or other children from committing violations of S. 940.20(1) or 946.43 or other similar offenses while placed in a secured correctional facility, as defined in S.48.02(15m). The court concluded that the statute did not specify who carries the burden of proof and reasonable minds could differ on this issue. The court pointed out that the statute did not require the juvenile to bring a motion, but that the hearing was part of the normal proceedings. The court then applied a five-factor analysis in determining which party had the burden. The five factors were policy considerations, judicial estimate of probabilities, the natural tendency to place the burden on the party seeking change, the fairness factor, and convenience. The court contended the legislature clearly favored criminal jurisdiction over juvenile jurisdiction, or it would not have enacted the legislation. The court also decided that the unusual situation would be to transfer jurisdiction. In addition, the law tended to place the burden on the party seeking the change. Further, a

STATE v. VERHAGEN *(cont.)*

transfer of jurisdiction would constitute an exception or a negative to the normal method of operation. Last, the juvenile would more readily have the facts to support transfer at his or her disposal. Consequently, the burden rested with the juvenile. In addition, the court contended that the judge had the discretion to retain jurisdiction and acted upon that discretion.

CASE EXCERPT

"Absent express legislative direction on the question, we employ a five-factor analysis in determining which party has the burden of proof. The five factors are: (1) special policy considerations, (2) the judicial estimate of probabilities, (3) the natural tendency to place the burdens on the party desiring change, (4) the fairness factors, and (5) convenience."

CASE SIGNIFICANCE

This case is important because it determined where the burden of proof lies in a reverse waiver proceeding. Many states have statutorily excluded certain offenses from the juvenile court's jurisdiction. However, some of those states have in place a mechanism for the criminal court judge to reverse the waiver and transfer the juvenile back to juvenile court to be processed there. In this case, the court determined that the burden to prove why a juvenile should be transferred back down to juvenile court lies with the juvenile. The court contended that the more likely and preferred result is retention of the juvenile in criminal court. The court also pointed out that the burden typically rests with the party who seeks the change of venue, much like the burden rests with the state in a judicial waiver proceeding. In addition, the court contended the juvenile would be better able to provide evidence in support of the reverse waiver than the state, who clearly would wish to prosecute the juvenile in criminal court. Consequently, the court contended that the burden of proof in a reverse waiver proceeding rests with the juvenile.

O'BRIEN v. JOHN MARSHALL, SUPERINTENDENT

453 F.3d 13 (U.S. App. 2006)

FACTS

O'Brien was convicted of first-degree murder in Middlesex County, Massachusetts, and sentenced to life in prison. In January 2002, O'Brien filed his federal habeas petition, raising both Fifth Amendment and due process issues. In order to try O'Brien as an adult, the Commonwealth had to prove, by a preponderance of the evidence, that he was both a significant danger to the public and not amenable to rehabilitation within the juvenile justice system. O'Brien's Fifth Amendment claim is that in the transfer proceeding that led to his subsequent trial as an adult, the state court judge relied upon O'Brien's silence in deciding that O'Brien was not amenable to rehabilitation within the juvenile justice system.

ISSUE

Did the court's reliance on a juvenile's silence regarding his need for treatment in a transfer hearing violate his Fifth Amendment right against self incrimination?

HOLDING

No. The transfer court did not infer guilt from the juvenile's silence. The Fifth Amendment does not preclude considering a defendant's attitude, whether or not characterized as silence, in determining that he was not likely to be rehabilitated and should be tried as an adult.

RATIONALE

The court assumed that the judge's transfer decision was in part based on his inferences about the juvenile's make-up, which were drawn from his failure to say or do things suggesting a desire for rehabilitation. The court also observed that if the transfer hearing were treated as a criminal trial, the procedures used would have raised problems that would need careful consideration. However, the court relied on the Supreme Court's decision in *Estelle v. Smith*, 451 U.S. 454 (1981), where the Court held that the Fifth Amendment did not apply in a state court hearing to determine whether the defendant was competent to stand trial, so long as the evidence (information obtained by a psychiatrist without a Miranda warning) was used only for the competency hearing. The court observed that transfer hearings are very similar to competency hearings because neither resolves questions pertaining to guilt, but instead address whether a defendant should be exempt from criminal prosecution due to who they are. O'Brien also argued that the use of his silence in the transfer decision punished him be denying him his juvenile status, and that had he made any self-incriminating statements, they could have been used against him at the criminal trial. The court again pointed to *Estelle*, in which the Supreme Court noted that there may have been a problem if incriminating information, extracted involuntarily from the defendant in a competency hearing, were then to be used against him in a criminal trial. Indeed, for federal juvenile transfer hearings, the statute provides formal protection against this risk. However, the court observed that the problem would rarely arise in Massachusetts practice where the juvenile is not supposed to be questioned about his guilt at all in the transfer evaluation, but the court did note that O'Brien may have been correct in saying that the prosecution at the criminal trial could have been aided by his explanations as to why he needed treatment, if he had made such admissions in the transfer hearing. Yet the court rejected O'Brien's claim because he never asked the court to protect him against potentially self-incriminating statement that would have been made to a therapist and used at trial.

CASE EXCERPT

"In *Estelle v. Smith*, 451 U.S. 454 (1981), the Supreme Court said that the Fifth Amendment did not apply in a state court hearing to determine whether the defendant was competent to stand trial--so long as the evidence (information obtained by a psychiatrist without a *Miranda* warning) was used only for the competency hearing. Juvenile court transfer hearings closely parallel competency hearings…Given *Estelle*, we hold that the Fifth Amendment did not preclude the state court judge from taking account of O'Brien's attitude, whether or not characterized as silence, in determining that he was not likely to be rehabilitated and should instead be tried as an adult."

CASE SIGNIFICANCE

This case is important because it permits courts to use juvenile's silence during transfer hearings as part of a rationale for transferring them to adult criminal court. The case also aligns a transfer hearing with a competency hearing, which would suggest that all procedural rules that are applicable to competency hearings could be applied to transfer hearings. However, the court also observed that if the juvenile would have raised a concern regarding self-incrimination during the transfer proceeding, the case may have resulted in a different outcome. Thus, the court did acknowledge that the issue could be subject to a different interpretation, given slightly different circumstances.

STATE v. DIXON
967 A.2d 1114 (VT. 2008)

FACTS

Dixon was charged with second-degree murder after he allegedly shot a man who was having sexual relations with his mother. Dixon's mother suffered from bipolar disorder and drug and alcohol abuse and the family had an extensive history with the state Department of Children and Families (DCF). Dixon and his sister had been temporarily removed from his mother's care on several prior occasions. There was not a dispute as to Dixon's mother's condition, or as to whether Dixon believed the victim was taking advantage of his mother. It was also believed that Dixon shot the victim during a struggle that ensued when the victim attempted to wrestle the shotgun away from Dixon. In Vermont, second-degree murder is an offense for which a juvenile would be automatically prosecuted in criminal court. Dixon moved to transfer his case to juvenile court. After a contested hearing at which conflicting expert testimony was introduced, the trial court denied his motion. In making its conclusions, the trial court considered the factors outlined in *Kent* for evaluating when a case should be transferred from juvenile court, as well as three non-*Kent* factors; system breakdown and the role of DCF, public accountability and understanding, and deterrence. The court observed that most of the factors they considered supported retaining Dixon in district court, although a few factors did favor transfer to juvenile court. The court ultimately concluded that a transfer to juvenile court would be inappropriate because defendant had not met his burden of showing that transfer was warranted. The court also noted that in light of all the relevant factors-particularly the extraordinary seriousness of the charged crime, its effect on the community, and the juvenile court's inability to mandate prolonged treatment for defendant-the court concluded that the case should remain in district court.

ISSUE

Did the district court's decision to deny transfer to the juvenile court constitute an abuse of discretion?

HOLDING

Yes. The trial court erred in weighing the non-*Kent* [*Kent v. United States*, 383 U.S. 541 (1966)] factor "system breakdown" against the defendant. The trial

STATE v. DIXON *(cont.)*

court erred by using the non-*Kent* criteria "the ability of the public to follow the case through the judicial system" against the juvenile. The trial court further erred in weighing the *Kent* criteria, prosecutive merits of the charge, against the juvenile.

RATIONALE

The court observed that they have left transfer decisions to the discretion of trial courts, and refused to set any predetermined limits on that discretion. The court also noted that they have never found a case in which a trial court abused its discretion by refusing to transfer a case to juvenile court. Regarding the current case, the court advised that the case must be considered alongside the factual setting that contributed to the defendant's actions. The court concluded that the trial court erred in weighing the non-*Kent* factor system breakdown against the defendant. The record reflects that trial court acknowledged that DCF had failed to serve the juvenile to date, yet the trial court still penalized the juvenile for the failings of the state agency because the agency had told the defendant that the agency was working to get him and his sister out of the home. The court found this to be unreasonable and an abuse of the trial court's discretion. The court also found that the trial court's use of the non-*Kent* criteria the ability of the public to follow the case through the judicial system was inappropriate. The court observed that the legislature has determined that a primary purpose of the juvenile court system is to protect juveniles from the "taint of criminality" that inevitably results from the publicity and permanence of convictions in the district court. The trial court did not account for the important policies underlying the legislative provisions. Regarding the *Kent* criteria, the court contended that the trial court erred in weighing the factor, prosecutive merits of the charge, against the juvenile. The court observed that *Kent*, and this factor, arose in a case in which transfer from juvenile court to criminal court was sought. In the current case, the reverse was true. In cases where juveniles seek transfer from criminal court to juvenile court, the prosecutive merit question will always be settled by the court's finding of probable cause, a finding that occurs before the reverse transfer hearing.

CASE EXCERPT

"First, we conclude that the district court erred in weighing the non-*Kent* factor titled 'System Breakdown' against defendant... The record discloses that defendant and his sister had been left almost entirely to fend for themselves. Their pleas for help from the adults in positions of authority in their lives had had no effect on the 'deplorable' living situation. And yet the court weighed this factor against transfer to juvenile court... This was not a proper consideration, and was not entitled to independent weight as a matter of law. The Legislature has determined that a primary purpose of the juvenile court system is to protect juveniles from the 'taint of criminality' that inevitably results from the publicity and permanence of convictions in the district court."

CASE SIGNIFICANCE

This case is important because it is one of the first times a higher court has held that a trial court abused its discretion in a transfer proceeding. The case is also important because the court, in rendering it decision, nullified one of the criteria set forth in *Kent* for reverse waiver hearings; the prosecutive merit of the charge. Although the court did not find that the trial court erred in its application of any of the other *Kent* criteria, the court did infer that the trial court might consider certain pieces of information related to several of those criteria more carefully. Finally, the court also advised that the trial court was correct to consider some other factors besides those identified in *Kent* (i.e., system breakdown), but incorrect to consider others (i.e., public accountability and understanding). Thus, the court still seemingly supported the individualized treatment of cases and the context surrounding them, but also within some limits. Importantly, the court did not dictate here how the trial court should rule. They simply remanded the case so that the trial court could exercise its discretion to make new findings if necessary in light of the evidence already introduced and the standards announced in this opinion.

DISCUSSION QUESTIONS

1. Why is a transfer a critically important stage in the proceedings?
2. What rights does a juvenile have in a transfer hearing?
3. In reference to transfer hearings, what have the courts said regarding double jeopardy?
4. Based on court rulings, have transfers become easier or harder since *Kent*?

5. What factors do the courts look at when making the decision to transfer?

6. What have the courts said regarding psychological and psychiatric testimony in terms of transfer hearings?

7. Who has the burden of proof in a reverse waiver hearing, and why?

8. What factors should the courts focus on when making the decision on a reverse hearing waiver?

9. In reference to transfer hearings, must a juvenile judge give a statement of the reasons for a transfer?

10. What have the courts ruled regarding the constitutionality of gang transfer provisions?

609.377 609.3785
60238

CHAPTER SIX

ADJUDICATION IN JUVENILE COURT

IN RE GAULT, *387 U.S. 1 (1967)*

IN RE WINSHIP, *397 U.S. 358 (1970)*

MCKEIVER v. PENNSYLVANIA, *403 U.S. 528 (1971)*

IVAN v. CITY OF NEW YORK, *407 U.S. 203 (1972)*

UNITED STATES v. TORRES, *500 F.2D 944 (2D CIR. 1974)*

GOSS v. LOPEZ, *419 U.S. 565 (1975)*

IN RE JESSE MCM., *164 CAL.RPTR. 199 (CAL. APP. 1980)*

IN THE INTEREST OF C.T.F., *316 N.W.2D 865 (IOWA 1982)*

IN RE MONTRAIL M., *601 A.2D 1102 (MD. 1992)*

BOYD v. STATE, *853 S.W.2D 263 (ARK. 1993)*

IN RE MARVEN C., *39 CAL.RPTR.2D 354 (CAL. APP. 1995)*

IN RE CAREY, *615 N.W.2D 742 (MICH. APP. 2000)*

INTRODUCTION

Adjudication hearings are designed to establish responsibility for alleged delinquent acts. Youth referred to juvenile court may be adjudicated delinquent after admitting to a charge, or after the court finds sufficient evidence to conclude, beyond a reasonable doubt, that the juvenile committed the act alleged in the petition. In 1998, some 630,189 juveniles were adjudicated delinquent. This outcome represents 63 percent of the more than one million cases brought before a judge in that year (Stahl 2001).

When the first juvenile court was established in Cook County, Illinois, in 1899, it was founded upon the philosophy of parens patriae, which stressed informality and discretion over due process and strict adherence to the rule of law (Platt 1977). For example, lawyers were not appointed to defend the legal interests of juveniles, judges were not bound by formal rules of evidence, and cases were routinely decided by a preponderance of the evidence. In effect, juveniles enjoyed no legal rights in early adjudication hearings. Between 1899 and the mid-1960s, juvenile court judges wielded tremendous power over the lives of troubled youth and were afforded a great deal of deference in how they crafted juvenile dispositions (e.g., sentences).

Because juvenile proceedings were founded upon civil law, criminal procedures and constitutional protections that today we take for granted were routinely denied to children accused of delinquent acts.

Formality and the imposition of legal rights were seen as anathema in early adjudication proceedings. In effect, they were seen as obstacles that could hinder the rehabilitative process. For example, the appointment of counsel and the right to remain silent were seen as ways to help juveniles defy personal responsibility for their actions. Informality, on the other hand, and subtle pressures to admit wrongdoing, were seen as the first steps toward true reformation. Judges therefore resisted attempts to formalize juvenile proceedings, arguing that the mission of the court was to treat (e.g., "fix") wayward youth, not punish them. However, legal advocates argued that the informality of juvenile adjudication hearings only served to ensure a finding of guilty. Despite the sporadic attacks on the nature of juvenile proceedings, the doctrine of parens patriae was defended in various court rulings throughout the early 1900s. For example, in the case of *Commonwealth v. Fisher*, 213 Pa. 48 (1905), the Pennsylvania Supreme Court ruled that informal judicial intervention was both a legitimate state interest and a moral duty: "The design [of juvenile proceedings] is not punishment, nor…imprisonment, any more than is the wholesome restraint which a parent exercises over his child.… There is no probability, in the proper administration of law, of the child's liberty being unduly invaded. Every statute is designed to give protection, care, and training to children as a needed substitute for parental authority…and is but a recognition of the duty of the state, as the legitimate guardian and protector of children where other guardianship fails."

This affirmation of the parens patriae philosophy was used to quash subsequent challenges to judicial proceedings for more than 60 years. However, in 1966, the so-called benevolent intentions of the parens patriae philosophy were tested in the case of *Kent v. United States* (see chapter 5). Here, the US Supreme Court began to express concern about the lack of due process protections accorded to juveniles. More important, it began to question whether the informal nature of juvenile proceedings might actually be detrimental to the "best interests of the child." For example, Justice Abe Fortas noted, "[t]here is evidence, in fact, there may be cause for concern that the child receives the worst of both worlds; that he gets neither the protections accorded to adults nor the solicitous care and regenerative treatment postulated for children." The *Kent* case, then, can be considered a watershed ruling insofar as it marks the point at which the Supreme Court began to abandon its hands-off policy toward juvenile proceedings. Though the *Kent* decision did not actually impose major structural or procedural reforms on juvenile court operations, it did set the stage for more vigorous intervention in the coming years. For example, in 1967 the Supreme Court decided the case of *In re Gault,* which resulted in the extension of several basic constitutional rights to juveniles, including the right to counsel, notification of the charges, the ability to confront and cross-examine witnesses, and protections against self-incrimination. In 1970, the Court decided the case of *In re Winship,* ruling that adjudication hearings must conform to the same burden of proof as adult hearings (e.g., beyond a reasonable doubt).

Yet despite these significant reforms, the Supreme Court stopped short of creating a mirror image of the adult criminal justice system. For example, in the case of *McKeiver v. Pennsylvania,* the Court ruled that juveniles do not have a constitutional right to trial by jury. Today, this is one of the fundamental differences between juvenile and adult proceedings. It should be noted, however, that several states actually do provide juveniles with the right to a jury trial in certain cases.

REFERENCES

Platt, A. (1977). *The Child Savers: The Invention of Delinquency,* 2nd edition. Chicago, IL: University of Chicago Press.

Stahl, A. (2001). *Delinquency Cases in Juvenile Courts, 1998.* Washington, DC: Office of Juvenile Justice and Delinquency Prevention.

IN RE GAULT

387 U.S. 1 (1967)

FACTS

On June 8, 1964, the Gila County Sheriff arrested 15-year-old Gault and a friend for allegedly making obscene phone calls to a neighbor. Gault was on probation at the time and he was taken to a detention facility. His parents, who were both at work at the time of the arrest, were not notified of their son's whereabouts well later that evening. At his trial, Gault was not represented by counsel, he was denied formal notice of the charges pending against him, the state's chief witness (the victim, Mrs. Cook) never appeared in court to testify, he was adjudicated delinquent, but no official transcript of the proceedings were made. Gault was sentenced to a state training school "for the period of his minority," or six years. Had he been an adult at the time of the offense, the maximum penalty he could have received would have been a fine of fifty dollars or a jail sentence of not more than two months. The boy's parents filed a petition for habeas corpus, but the superior court and the Arizona Supreme Court affirmed the conviction. The case was then appealed to the US Supreme Court.

ISSUE

Are juveniles entitled to formal due process protections during the adjudication phase of delinquency proceedings?

HOLDING

Yes. The US Supreme Court ruled that juveniles are entitled to certain due process rights during delinquency proceedings where there is a possibility of

IN RE GAULT (cont.)

confinement in a locked facility. These rights include (1) the right to adequate notice of the charges; (2) the assistance of counsel, retained privately or appointed by the state; (3) the right to confront and cross-examine prosecution witnesses; and (4) the right to remain silent as well as privilege against self-incrimination.

RATIONALE

The application of procedural safeguards in this case was justified on two grounds. First, the Court noted that judicial proceedings against Gault were akin to a "kangaroo court." Second, the Court argued that Gault's sanction was much more severe than what an adult would have received for the same offense. In combination, these two factors resulted in the denial of both due process and equal protection. Despite the semantic differences, juvenile training schools are the equivalent of adult prisons—both result in deprivation of liberty. Thus, the Constitution requires that juveniles be tried in accordance with the guarantees outlined in the Bill of Rights.

CASE EXCERPT

"A boy is charged with misconduct. The boy is committed to an institution where he may be restrained of liberty for years. It is of no constitutional consequence—and of limited practical meaning—that the institution to which he is committed is called an Industrial School. The fact of the matter is that, however euphemistic the title, a 'receiving home' or an 'industrial school' for juveniles is an institution of confinement in which the child is incarcerated for a greater or lesser time... In view of this, it would be extraordinary if our Constitution did not require the procedural regularity and the exercise of care implied in the phrase 'due process.' Under our Constitution, the condition of being a boy does not justify a kangaroo court."

CASE SIGNIFICANCE

Gault is considered a landmark case in juvenile justice because it was one of the first successful challenges to the benevolent effect of juvenile proceedings. Prior to this decision, delinquency proceedings were considered purely civil matters, and thus not subject to the same due process requirements as adult criminal cases. The significance of this change cannot be overstated because civil proceedings involving juveniles were guided by the philosophy of parens patriae. Parens patriae, or the power of the state to act as one's parent,

allowed government officials wide latitude to intervene in the lives of wayward youth and to craft dispositions that would "cure" them of their wicked ways. In addition to skewing the power relationship between state and child, supporters of parens patriae vehemently argued that procedural constraints and due process protections were anathema to the purposes of rehabilitation. In effect, supporters of parens patriae argued that no harm could befall children under an informal juvenile justice system since juvenile dispositions were always crafted with an eye toward advancing the "best interests of the child." With this said, it should be noted that the language used by the Court in this decision clearly indicated that it had no desire to vacate the major tenets of parens patriae. Rather, it sought to provide more formal due process protections to juvenile defendants in order to protect them from unbridled discretion and well-intended state intervention. It is also important to keep in mind that the procedural protections extended to juveniles under the *Gault* decision apply only in those cases likely to result in the deprivation of liberty. In short, they do not automatically apply in all adjudication hearings.

IN RE WINSHIP
397 U.S. 358 (1970)

FACTS

This case involved a 12-year-old boy who broke into a locker and stole $112 from a woman's purse. The petition charging Winship noted that this crime, "if done by an adult, would constitute the crime or crimes of larceny." Winship was found guilty at his initial trial and subsequently placed in a New York training school for a term of confinement not to exceed six years. Winship appealed his conviction, arguing that the trial judge erred in his decision to convict upon the basis of a preponderance of the evidence rather than the more stringent standard of proof beyond a reasonable doubt. Had the higher standard been in effect, trial transcripts indicate that the trial judge might not have been able to establish guilt in this case. Nevertheless, the appellate court affirmed the decision without opinion, and Winship appealed to the Supreme Court.

ISSUE

Does the due process clause of the Fourteenth Amendment require proof beyond a reasonable doubt during the adjudication phase of delinquency proceedings?

HOLDING

Yes. In adjudication hearings that may result in the possibility of commitment to a locked facility, the standard of proof shall be proof beyond a reasonable doubt.

RATIONALE

The Supreme Court held that the due process clause, which helps to protect adults during criminal prosecutions, also extends to juveniles accused of delinquent acts. In arriving at its decision, the Court argued that New York State's standard of proof in juvenile proceedings—a preponderance of the evidence—was open to inaccurate findings of guilt. While the Court recognized that adjudication hearings were designed to be informal, it argued that (1) despite the rhetoric of the juvenile court, a delinquency adjudication is still a conviction; (2) deprivation of liberty and the stigma of a delinquency record still attach; and (3) juvenile training schools are the functional equivalents of adult prisons. In short, juveniles have a great deal at stake during adjudication hearings. For these reasons, the Court concluded that juveniles are constitutionally entitled to a higher level of protection than a mere preponderance of the evidence.

CASE EXCERPT

"The reasonable doubt standard plays a vital role in the American scheme of criminal procedure. It is a prime instrument for reducing the risk of convictions resting on factual error...Moreover, use of the reasonable doubt standard is indispensible to command the respect and confidence of the community in applications of the criminal law. It is critical that the moral force of the criminal law not be diluted by a standard of proof that leaves people in doubt whether innocent men are being condemned."

CASE SIGNIFICANCE

The significance of the *Winship* ruling, like the earlier decision in *Gault,* is its emphasis on greater due process protections for juvenile defendants. Though the Court recognized that juvenile proceedings are civil in nature, and the proper standard of proof in such cases is a preponderance of the evidence, the Court argued that juvenile proceedings may result in the deprivation of liberty. Thus, a higher standard of proof—beyond a reasonable doubt—is required to guard against inaccurate findings of guilt. However, it should be noted that this higher standard of proof

does not immediately apply to all juvenile defendants. What it says is that all juvenile proceedings in which a juvenile "is charged with an act that would constitute a crime if committed by an adult" (i.e., not a status offense) are subject to the higher standard of proof. Juvenile proceedings that do not fall into this specific category are governed by the preponderance standard because they generally do not result in the deprivation of liberty.

MCKEIVER v. PENNSYLVANIA
403 U.S. 528 (1971)

FACTS

In May 1968, McKeiver, then aged 16, was charged with robbery, larceny, and receiving stolen goods, all of which were considered felonies under Pennsylvania law. Though the transcript is somewhat unclear, it appears that the "robbery" consisted of the defendant taking twenty-five cents from a group of teenagers. At the time of his adjudication hearing, McKeiver was represented by counsel. He requested a jury trial, but this request was denied. At his trial, McKeiver was adjudicated delinquent for having violated a law of the Commonwealth of Pennsylvania, and he was placed on probation. As in *Winship,* the appellate court affirmed the decision without opinion and McKeiver appealed to the Supreme Court.

ISSUE

Do juveniles have a right to trial by jury during the adjudication phase of delinquency proceedings?

HOLDING

No. Juveniles do not have a constitutional right to trial by jury.

RATIONALE

The Supreme Court's decision to deny juveniles the right to trial by jury was grounded upon three major principles. First, the Court argued that it did not want to turn juvenile hearings into a fully adversarial process. To do so, it argued, would effectively end "the idealistic prospect of an intimate, informal protective proceeding." Second, the Court noted that because bench trials typically result in accurate determinations of guilt, jury trials are not an absolute necessity in delinquency proceedings. Third, the Court claimed that it was reluctant to impose federal requirements for jury trials in

MCKEIVER v. PENNSYLVANIA *(cont.)*

juvenile proceedings because doing so could prevent states from experimenting with different methods of adjudication. Justice Blackmun, who delivered the decision in *McKeiver,* argued, "[i]f in its wisdom, any State feels the jury trial is desirable in all cases, or in certain kinds, there appears to be no impediment to its installing a system embracing that feature. That however, is the State's privilege and not its obligation." Yet Blackmun goes on to state that the creation of such a mirror image of the adult criminal justice system might have the effect of negating "every aspect of fairness, of concern, of sympathy, and of parental attention that the juvenile court system contemplates."

CASE EXCERPT

"There is a possibility, at least, that the jury trial, if required as a matter of constitutional precept, will remake the juvenile proceedings into a fully adversarial process and will put an effective end to what has been the idealistic prospect of an intimate, informal protective proceeding... If the formalities of the criminal adjudicative process are to be superimposed upon the juvenile court system, there is little need for its separate existence. Perhaps that ultimate disillusionment will come one day, but for the moment we are disinclined to give impetus to it."

CASE SIGNIFICANCE

The *McKeiver* case is significant not because it extended constitutional protections in juvenile proceedings but because it denied juveniles a right that is routinely afforded to adult criminal defendants. That is, the *McKeiver* ruling said that juveniles are not entitled to trial by jury during an adjudication hearing or at any stage of a juvenile proceeding. The imposition of a jury trial requirement, the Court argued, would be detrimental insofar as it (1) would help transform juvenile proceedings into a more fully adversarial process; (2) would involve delay, formality, and the possibility of a public hearing; and (3) would not remedy existing defects in the system, nor would it greatly strengthen the fact-finding function. With this said, it should be noted that some states do provide juveniles the right to jury trial during adjudication. However, this is done under state law; it is not a constitutional requirement. In addition, trial by jury is just one of several constitutional rights that is currently denied to juveniles. Others include (1) the right to a public trial; (2) the right to bail; and (3) the right to grand jury indictment.

IVAN v. CITY OF NEW YORK

407 U.S. 203 (1972)

FACTS

Petitioner Ivan was adjudicated delinquent in the family court of Bronx County, New York, for forcibly stealing a bicycle at knifepoint. However, Ivan was adjudicated by a preponderance of the evidence some three months before the US Supreme Court handed down its ruling in *Winship,* which required the more stringent standard of proof beyond a reasonable doubt. On direct appeal, the appellate division reversed the lower court's ruling on the ground that proof beyond a reasonable doubt should be retroactively applied. In effect, the case was remanded back to the trial court to be retried. The New York Court of Appeals reversed this decision, holding that *Winship* requirements ought not to be applied retroactively, and the US Supreme Court granted certiorari.

ISSUE

Should the *Winship* decision, which requires juvenile court judges to employ the proof beyond a reasonable doubt standard during adjudication hearings, apply retroactively to all cases currently under appeal?

HOLDING

Yes. The *Winship* ruling applied retroactively to all juvenile cases currently pending appeal with regard to this issue.

RATIONALE

The question at issue was whether this new standard of guilt should be applied retroactively to cases in which a juvenile was previously adjudicated delinquent on the basis of a preponderance of the evidence. The Court ruled that yes, the new constitutional doctrine should be given complete retroactive effect. However, it should be noted that "complete retroactive effect" does not imply that all juveniles previously adjudged delinquent by a preponderance of the evidence are automatically granted a new trial. Instead, only those cases currently under appeal on this issue were to be retried.

CASE EXCERPT

"Plainly, then, the major purpose of the constitutional standard of proof beyond a reasonable doubt announced in Winship was to overcome an aspect of a criminal trial that substantially impairs the truth-finding function, and Winship is thus to be given complete retroactive effect."

CASE SIGNIFICANCE

The case is significant because the juvenile in question had been adjudicated a delinquent by a preponderance of the evidence. At the time of appeal the Supreme Court had not yet handed down its decision in *Winship*. Thus, the question remained: Should the *Winship* decision—which required proof of guilt beyond a reasonable doubt—be applied retroactively? The Court held that the requirement of proof beyond a reasonable doubt should be applied retroactively to all cases in the appeals process. So, although this case was important, its actual significance was both time and case sensitive.

UNITED STATES v. TORRES

500 F.2d 944 (2d Cir. 1974)

FACTS

Sixteen-year-old Torres was arrested on federal charges of unlawfully possessing a photographic negative of a one-dollar bill. At the time of his arrest, Torres was serving time in a New York training school for an unrelated offense. At his initial hearing in district court, Torres was advised by his lawyer that he should agree to be treated as a juvenile rather than being tried in criminal court as an adult. For this to happen, however, Torres was required to sign an agreement waving his right to a jury trial. Torres agreed and signed the waiver. Some time later, Torres had a change of heart. At the adjudication hearing, Torres's counsel argued that the boy in fact had a right to trial by jury under the Sixth Amendment, and the federal statute requiring him to waive this right in order to be tried as a juvenile was unconstitutional. The trial judge disagreed and Torres was adjudicated delinquent on the charge that he had made an unauthorized photographic image of the face side of a one-dollar federal reserve note. The case was appealed.

ISSUE

Are juveniles who are tried in federal court entitled to a trial by jury?

HOLDING

No. Juveniles are not constitutionally entitled to trial by jury in the federal system.

RATIONALE

It is clear that the controlling case here is *McKeiver v. Pennsylvania*. In that case, the United States Supreme Court ruled that juveniles, even those facing the possibility of placement in a locked facility, are not constitutionally entitled to a trial by jury. However, Torres maintained that the *McKeiver* ruling applied only to adjudication hearings in state courts, not the federal court system. Moreover, Torres claimed the provision of the Federal Juvenile Delinquency Act that requires juveniles to waive their right to jury trial in order to be tried as juveniles was unconstitutional—a violation of the Sixth Amendment. The circuit court disagreed: "The principles applied in McKeiver are applicable to the Federal Juvenile Delinquency Act...[and] the requirement that proceedings under the Act shall be tried without a jury does not violate the Sixth Amendment or due process standards of fundamental fairness." The court reasoned that federal juvenile proceedings are not "materially different" than those proceedings one might expect to encounter in state courts. Thus, jury trials for juvenile defendants are not a constitutional requirement in federal proceedings.

CASE EXCERPT

"A juvenile has no comparable constitutional right to a trial by jury in proceedings under the Federal Juvenile Delinquency Act. Whether or not such proceedings should be tried without a jury was for Congress to determine...Congress did not so provide. Instead, it permitted the juvenile to choose between the relative beneficent and rehabilitative juvenile delinquency proceedings in which he was not entitled to a jury and prosecution as an adult with trial by jury."

CASE SIGNIFICANCE

As noted earlier, the Supreme Court ruled in *McKeiver v. Pennsylvania* that juveniles do not have the right to trial by jury in state court. The *Torres* decision is significant because it extended *McKeiver's* reach from state delinquency proceedings to include federal proceedings as well.

GOSS v. LOPEZ

419 U.S. 565 (1975)

FACTS

This class action suit was brought on behalf of nine teenagers who were suspended from the Columbus,

GOSS v. LOPEZ *(cont.)*

Ohio Public School System (CPSS) for 10 days for engaging in disruptive misconduct at school. The suit alleges that CPSS school administrators unconstitutionally suspended the students with little or no due process protections (e.g., a suspension hearing) and enjoins Columbus school administrators to remove all references to the suspensions from the students' records. At the time, CPSS policy required that in cases of suspension or expulsion, school administrators must contact the student's parents within 24 hours and provide a reason for the action taken. In cases of expulsion, the student or his parents were granted the opportunity to appeal the school's decision to the Board of Education. However, no such review process was available for suspended students. Thus, the suit alleged that the suspended students in question were unconstitutionally denied their right to education without a hearing of any kind, in violation of the due process clause of the Fourteenth Amendment. The case was appealed to the Supreme Court.

ISSUES

Do students facing temporary suspension from a public school system have substantial property and liberty interests requiring protection under the due process clause of the Fourteenth Amendment?

HOLDING

Yes. Students facing temporary suspension have legitimate property and liberty interests that qualify for protection under the due process clause of the Fourteenth Amendment. The due process clause requires that students facing temporary suspension must be provided with (1) oral or written notice of the charges against them; (2) in a timely manner; and (3) whenever possible, notice should be given prior to the actual suspension. If the student denies the allegation, he or she is entitled to (4) an explanation of the evidence authorities have; and (5) an opportunity to present his or her side of the story.

RATIONALE

Justice White, who delivered the opinion for the Court, argued that suspension is considered a necessary tool to maintain order in schools. But "it would be a strange disciplinary system in an educational institution if no communication was sought by the disciplinarian with the student in an effort to inform

him of his dereliction and to let him tell his side of the story in order to make sure that an injustice is not done." In short, White argued, "[s]ecrecy is not congenial to truth-seeking and self-righteousness gives too slender an assurance of rightness." In ordering the establishment of minimal safeguards to protect the rights of suspended students, the Court sought to "provide a meaningful hedge against erroneous action" at the hands of school officials. The Court took notice of the fact that some colleges and employers at the time routinely asked applicants if they had ever been suspended or expelled from school. An affirmative response to such a question, the Court argued, could have long-term, negative consequences. With this said, the Court expressly sought to avoid the burdens of making the review hearing a fully adversarial process. In addition, the Court recognized that in some cases, prior notice and hearings are impractical. That is, some students can be removed from school immediately because their presence may constitute a continuing danger to persons or property or an ongoing threat of disruption to the academic process. In such cases, notice and a rudimentary hearing should follow as soon as possible.

CASE EXCERPT

"To impose in each such case even truncated trial-type procedures might well overwhelm administrative facilities in many places and, by diverting resources, cost more than it would save in educational effectiveness. Moreover, further formalizing the suspension process and escalating its formality and adversarial nature may not only make it too costly as a regular disciplinary tool but also destroy its effectiveness as part of the teaching process."

CASE SIGNIFICANCE

This case is significant because it helped to formalize the nature of school disciplinary procedures by saying that school administrators must provide minimal safeguards of due process to ensure (1) that students who receive suspensions are actually guilty of the alleged act(s); and (2) that the punishment is commensurate with the violation. While some might view these formal procedures as cumbersome and unnecessary, the Court argued that they are in fact necessary since many states have made education a fundamental right (e.g., liberty and property interests) through mandatory attendance policies.

IN RE JESSE MCM.

164 Cal.Rptr. 199 (Cal. App. 1980)

FACTS

Jesse McM., a 17-year-old, was charged by an amended petition with two counts of sodomy and two counts of committing lewd and lascivious acts upon a child. Following a jurisdictional hearing the court found the allegations of the amended petition to be true and committed the child to the California Youth Authority for a maximum period of five years. Jesse McM. appealed, first on the grounds that he had been denied a public trial, and second, that the court had erred in allowing a friend of his mother's to be present in the courtroom. The case was appealed to the California Court of Appeals.

ISSUE

Does a juvenile have a right to a public trial?

HOLDING

No. A juvenile does not have a right to a public trial.

RATIONALE

The court relied on a prior case which held that the rule that disparate treatment may be accorded to persons charged with crimes and persons charged with juvenile misconduct. When the California Supreme Court decided that case they relied on the Supreme Court's decision in *McKeiver*. Consequently, the court found that it was evident from the language that a public trial in juvenile court was neither mandated nor, in most instances, even desirable. Further, the court pointed out that even in some criminal trials the court had the discretion to close the court to protect a witness or ensure fairness to a party. In this case, two young males had to testify to sensitive issues and it seemed the court acted appropriately when it did close the courtroom. The court also indicated that the lower court's decision to allow Jesse's mother's friend in the courtroom was appropriate given the nature of the case and the likely ordeal it would put the mother through.

CASE EXCERPT

"In this instance, it was necessary for two boys, aged nine and ten, to testify to delicate and revolting facts. Under such circumstances, even if Jesse's request for a public trial had been made in a more timely fashion and his mother had joined in said request, we find that the situation nevertheless was one where it was appropriate for the court to exercise its discretion by denying Jesse's request for a public trial."

CASE SIGNIFICANCE

This case is significant in that the court acknowledged that juvenile defendants are not afforded the same rights and privileges as adult criminal defendants. While criminal defendants have a constitutional right to a public trial, this right does not extend to the juvenile court. It is within the discretion of the judge whether to close a juvenile proceeding.

IN THE INTEREST OF C.T.F.

316 N.W.2d 865 (Iowa 1982)

FACTS

A petition was filed alleging C.T.F., a juvenile, committed a delinquent act, second-degree burglary. A deputy clerk mailed an original notice, with an attachment of the petition, to both the juvenile and his father. The notice indicated they would be notified at a later date of the time and place of the hearing on the petition. The juvenile's father filed an application on behalf of the juvenile for an appointment of counsel. The juvenile court appointed an attorney to represent the juvenile. Three months and 10 days after the filing of the original petition C.T.F.'s attorney filed a motion to dismiss the petition, alleging the juvenile's right to a speedy trial had been abridged. The juvenile court scheduled a hearing on the petition almost a month later. The court orally overruled the motion on the basis that a juvenile does not have a right to a speedy trial in a delinquency proceeding. No evidence was offered in support of the motion. The juvenile was subsequently adjudicated delinquent, and he appealed to the Iowa Supreme Court.

ISSUES

Do juveniles have a constitutional or a statutory right to a speedy trial in a juvenile delinquency proceeding?

HOLDING

Yes and no. A juvenile has a constitutional, but not a statutory, right to a speedy trial.

IN THE INTEREST OF C.T.F. *(cont.)*

RATIONALE

The court contended that a juvenile court proceeding is not a prosecution for a crime, but rather a special proceeding that serves as an ameliorative alternative to a criminal prosecution. The court pointed to much case law to support this contention. The court also pointed to state law, which only provides for a speedy trial or indictment when the defendant is being charged with a public offense. The court contended a delinquency petition is not a public offense. Consequently, a juvenile is not amenable to criminal prosecution unless he or she is transferred to district court. However, the court pointed to the Supreme Court's decision in *Gault,* which allowed for a case-by-case determination of the applicability of constitutional rights available in juvenile proceedings predicated on fair treatment, tempered by the nature of the juvenile hearing. This case had been applied in several cases, but none addressed the issue of a speedy trial for juveniles. However, this court interpreted the Constitution and state constitution to provide for a speedy trial for juveniles, when the *Gault* test was applied. The court contended that charging a juvenile with a delinquent act results in stress for the juvenile and his or her family. In addition, not having a speedy trial can hurt both sides of the adversarial process. Consequently, the court held that juveniles have a constitutional right to a speedy trial. However, in this case the juvenile failed to prove his right to a speedy trial was violated, and therefore the juvenile court's decision was affirmed.

CASE EXCERPT

"The State maintains that even if the juvenile has a constitutional right to a speedy trial there is no evidence in the record that the right was violated in this case. The State bases its contention on the four-factor test enunciated by the United States Supreme Court in *Barker v. Wingo,* 407 U.S. 514…for determining whether an accused has been denied the right to a speedy trial under the sixth amendment [sic]. In *Barker* the Court stated that under the circumstances of each case the following factors must be considered: (1) the length of the delay; (2) the reason for the delay; (3) whether the accused asserted the right; and (4) whether the accused was prejudiced by the delay."

CASE SIGNIFICANCE

As in the previous case, this case is significant in that the court acknowledged that juvenile defendants are not afforded the same rights and privileges as adult criminal defendants. While defendants, criminal and juveniles, have a constitutional right to a speedy trial, that right is driven by contextual factors.

IN RE MONTRAIL M.

601 A.2d 1102 (Md. 1992)

FACTS

Montrail M., Harold S., and Matio C., all juveniles, were arrested by Ohio police for having in their mutual possession nine vials of crack cocaine. Because the vials appeared to be packaged for sale, the boys were also charged with the additional crime of intent to distribute. At the adjudication hearing, each defendant was adjudicated delinquent on the two drug offenses (e.g., possession and intent to distribute). At the disposition hearing, the trial court remanded the defendants to the custody of the Department of Juvenile Services. On appeal, the boys argued that the trial court had erred in its decision to adjudicate on multiple counts of delinquency, because both drug offenses arose from a single act. They further argued that their disposition was more punitive than it would have been had they been allowed to merge the two offenses into a single adjudication. In short, they argued that the crimes for which they were adjudicated were so similar in nature as to amount to a violation of the double jeopardy clause of the Fifth Amendment.

ISSUES

Does the "merger doctrine" (e.g., situations in which lesser offenses are merged into the greater offense) apply to juvenile cases?

HOLDING

Yes. The merger doctrine applies to juvenile proceedings and does not violate prohibitions of double jeopardy.

RATIONALE

Both the possession of narcotics and the intent to distribute narcotics arose out of a single incident. Under the merger doctrine, lesser included offenses are merged, which precludes multiple punishments for the same offense. The Fifth Amendment also bars multiple punishments for the same offense. However, neither the merger doctrine nor the Fifth Amendment bar separate adjudications of delinquency when only one sanction is eventually imposed. Thus it is appropriate to hold separate delinquency adjudication hearings.

CASE EXCERPT

"There was one 'punishment' imposed, and absent a separate sanction for each adjudication, the principles of merger were not violated. The Petitioners urge, however, that as long as both adjudications stand, they are 'punished' over and above that reflected in the disposition announced. Therefore, they seek to have the adjudication as to simple possession stricken, and they would accomplish that through the doctrine of merger. But, we have determined, that even though merger occurs, both adjudications persist, and the objectives the Petitioners seek, the vacating of the simple possession adjudication, is not attained by the merger doctrine on which they rely."

CASE SIGNIFICANCE

This case is significant insofar as it placed juveniles on the same level as adult defendants on the issues of merger of offenses and double jeopardy. As noted in the Supreme Court's decision in *Breed v. Jones* (421 U.S. 519 (1975)), protections against double jeopardy apply in all juvenile proceedings. However, the United States Supreme Court has not yet adequately addressed the issue of merger in juvenile adjudication hearings.

BOYD v. STATE

853 S.W.2d 263 (Ark. 1993)

FACTS

While in police custody, 17-year-old Stacy Boyd was questioned by Little Rock (Arkansas) detectives about a burglary at a local pawnshop. Though police advised Boyd of his *Miranda* rights, he voluntarily waived his rights and offered up incriminating statements to police. He was subsequently certified as an adult, transferred to adult court, and tried for the crimes of burglary and theft. At his criminal trial, Boyd moved to suppress his earlier statements. His motion was denied and he was convicted of the two felonies. On appeal, Boyd argued that Arkansas law clearly states that anyone under the age of 18 is a juvenile, and a juvenile may not voluntarily waive his or her right to counsel unless a custodial parent agrees to the waiver in writing. Since his mother had not agreed to the waiver in writing, Boyd argued that he could not have legally waived his rights. The

appellate court affirmed the lower court's ruling and the Arkansas Supreme Court agreed to hear the case.

ISSUE

When juveniles are tried as adults, do they still fall under the procedural rules of the juvenile court?

HOLDING

No. When juveniles are tried in adult court, they are subject to the procedural rules and penalties of the adult court system.

RATIONALE

The Arkansas Supreme Court affirmed the lower courts' decision, ruling that Boyd had, unfortunately, misconstrued the statute in its entirety. That is, Boyd's argument rested on the assumption that the requirement for parental consent also applies to proceedings in adult court. That assumption was wrong. The section of the juvenile code that required parental consent is limited only to proceedings in the juvenile division of the chancery court. Had he read a little further he would have seen that the statute goes on to state that when a case involves a juvenile 16 years or older, "and the alleged act would constitute a felony if committed by an adult, the prosecuting attorney has the discretion to file a petition in juvenile court alleging delinquency, or to file charges in circuit court and to prosecute as an adult." However, due to the parent consent issue, it is important to note that Boyd's statements could not have been introduced as evidence in juvenile proceedings and thus *necessitated* his prosecution in adult court. The following case excerpt is drawn from the dissenting opinion of Justice Newburn.

CASE EXCERPT

"If the Court's opinion is correct, when a juvenile like Boyd waives the right to counsel without the required guidance and confesses, the prosecutor choosing whether to charge the juvenile in a juvenile court or in a circuit court must file felony charges in circuit court or risk suppression of the confession for noncompliance with [the parental consent statute]. A statute designed to protect juveniles thus will result in their being subjected to greater punishment, and the rehabilitative goals of the Juvenile Code will be subverted."

CASE SIGNIFICANCE

This case centers on the voluntary waiver of Miranda rights, particularly the right to remain silent and not

BOYD v. STATE (*cont.*)

answer questions during interrogation. Arkansas law required consent of a juvenile's parent or guardian in order to establish a voluntary waiver of such rights. Consent is not required, however, when a juvenile is certified for adult trial. Instead, voluntary waiver of Miranda is determined by other criteria—for example, did the juvenile make statements to the police knowingly, intelligently, and voluntarily? If so, any information obtained during questioning is admissible in court.

IN RE MARVEN C.

39 Cal.Rptr.2d 354 (Cal. App. 1995)

FACTS

Marven C. was charged in juvenile court with murder and discharging a firearm at an occupied vehicle. Both offenses stemmed from an apparent dispute between rival gangs. The incident began with verbal insults, escalated when a gun was brandished, and culminated into a two-vehicle chase through the back streets of a Los Angeles suburb. During the pursuit, Marven C. is alleged to have fired a weapon several times at members of the rival gang, eventually leading to the death of one teenage boy. Because Marven C. was a Guatemalan immigrant, there was some dispute as to his actual age. However, it seems clear that at the time of his crime he was between 13 and 14 years old. Marven C. was found delinquent on both counts, declared a ward of the state, and sent to the California Youth Authority for a period not to exceed 29 years to life. At his appeal, he claimed that the prosecutor in his original trial had failed to show clear proof that Marven knew and appreciated the wrongfulness of his actions.

ISSUE

In cases where a statute clearly presumes that a minor under the age of 14 is incapable of committing a crime, does the state have the burden of establishing that the juvenile in question did in fact know and appreciate the wrongfulness of his or her actions?

HOLDING

Yes. The state carries the burden of proof to show that, based on factors such as age, experience, conduct, and knowledge, a juvenile under the age of 14 has the capacity to appreciate the wrongfulness of his or her actions.

RATIONALE

Although it is clear from the court's ruling that the burden of proof to show that a minor appreciated the wrongfulness of an act rests with the state, factors such as "age, experience, conduct, and knowledge" are imprecise terms that are open to a great deal of interpretation. Moreover, the court never attempted to put a precise definition on the meaning of these terms. Instead, it relied heavily on the facts of the case to show that Marven C. knew what he was doing and that he appreciated the wrongfulness of his actions. In effect, the court allowed the facts speak for themselves:

CASE EXCERPT

"The evidence established that appellant carried a concealed weapon to the school and displayed it to Ivan, pulling it from 'his stomach.' When a school security guard appeared, the blue Mustang departed. Thereafter, appellant fired three shots at the occupants in the Subaru on three separate occasions as the cars drove in the area of school. Each time, appellant leaned far out of the car window to fire the gun . . . the manner in which this was conducted, the speed with which it was conducted, firing and departing the scene, all do impute a knowledge of the wrongfulness of the act. Shooting at someone several times in a public place to kill them would not be something that even a two-year-old would think would be all right. A minor as street-smart as this individual has shown himself to be leave him to the imputation of knowledge of the wrongfulness of his acts."

CASE SIGNIFICANCE

This case is significant because it says that in order to overcome the assumption of immaturity, the state must provide evidence to the contrary. That is, the state must show that a juvenile under the age of 14 was capable of knowing the wrongfulness of his or her actions. Here, the court argued that substantial evidence exists to show that the defendant knew the wrongfulness of his acts. In criminal cases, the state bears the burden of establishing knowledge (and in certain cases, intent) of the wrongfulness of an offender's act. This is also true in juvenile cases; however, a prosecutor's ability to demonstrate issues such as intent and knowledge is often inversely related to the defendant's age.

IN RE CAREY

615 N.W.2d 742 (Mich. App. 2000)

FACTS

A petition was filed alleging that Carey had committed second-degree sexual conduct. Shortly after filing the petition, the prosecutor moved to have Carey evaluated concerning both his competency to stand trial and his criminal responsibility. Two psychiatrists testified at the hearing, both were allowed to testify about Carey's ability to function within the legal system, but neither were allowed to testified about his competency to stand trial. Both agreed that his full range IQ test results were somewhere between 52 and 65 (i.e., the lowest one percentile of people his age). One psychologist indicated that Carey was only aware that he had done something wrong in simple terms: "[h]is mother was angry with him and [respondent] stated he wouldn't do it again because his Mom was upset with him." It was unclear whether he would be able to assist counsel in his own defense. On May 15, 1998, the court concluded that the defendant was not competent to stand trial because he would not be able to understand the nature of the proceedings. However, on New Year's Eve of that same year, the court issued an opinion in which it ruled the issue of competency was not relevant to the adjudication phase of juvenile proceedings. Carey appealed to the state court of appeals.

ISSUES

(1) Does due process require that a competency determination be made before a juvenile of questionable competence is subjected to the adjudication phase of a delinquency proceeding, and (2) if such a right exists, should adult provisions of the Mental Health Code apply to juvenile competency proceedings?

HOLDING

Yes and yes. The due process clause requires that a juvenile be competent to understand the nature of the proceedings against them and to assist counsel in their own defense. In making this determination, the provisions of the Mental Health Code applicable to adult competency in criminal trials can serve as a guide for juvenile competency determinations.

RATIONALE

The court pointed to Michigan case law which indicated that juvenile proceedings need not conform with all the requirements of criminal trials, but essential requirements of due process and fair treatment must be met. The court also pointed to a criminal case (*People v. Newton*, 179 Mich. App 484 [1989]), in which it was ruled that the conviction of a legally incompetent individual violated due process. The court pointed to many other states that have applied competency determinations to a juvenile's due process rights. The court contended that the juvenile court's adjudication hearing was similar in nature to a criminal trial and that many of the rights guaranteed a juvenile, such as right to counsel, are meaningless if the juvenile cannot function within the courtroom process. Consequently, competency is tantamount to due process being observed. The court also opined that the Mental Health Code's already established procedures for determining competency in criminal matters were sufficient for answering the same inquiries in juvenile court.

CASE EXCERPT

"We believe that the Mental Health Code provisions for competency determinations can provide a useful guide for the trial courts in this context. As summarized above, they provide a standard of competency and a process by which questions of competency can be raised and determined. We hold that, in the absence of other applicable rules or statutes, these provisions should be used to assure that the due process rights of a juvenile are protected."

CASE SIGNIFICANCE

This case is significant in that the court acknowledged that juvenile defendants have a right to a competency hearing, just as criminal defendants do in adult court. The key here was the court's determination that there was a potential loss of liberty at stake, and thus the due process clause was implicated. Due process requires the opportunity for a competency hearing when the facts so dictate.

DISCUSSION QUESTIONS

1. More than 20 years after the *Gault* decision, research by Barry Feld (1988) suggested that about half of all youth charged with acts of delinquency appear in court without the assistance of counsel. Why is that? You can find Feld's arguments

in an article entitled, *In re Gault Revisited: A Cross-State Comparison of the Right to Counsel in Juvenile Court*; the article appears in the journal *Crime & Delinquency* (Volume 34, Issue 4, pages 393–424).

2. Juvenile proceedings are grounded in civil law and the burden of proof in civil cases is a preponderance of the evidence. So why did the Supreme Court rule in *Winship* that adjudication hearings require proof beyond a reasonable doubt?

3. Did *Winship* imply that all juveniles previously adjudicated delinquent by a preponderance of the evidence are automatically granted new trials? In effect, did *Winship* have a complete retroactive effect on all adjudications prior to 1970?

4. Having read the *Goss v. Lopez* decision, how does the Supreme Court balance students' interests in an education with the interests of a school to suspend (or expel) them for disruptive behavior? What steps are school officials required to take under either scenario to ensure due process has been met?

5. According to the 1980 decision in *In re Jesse McM.*, juveniles do not have the right to a public trial. Considering the procedural changes that have occurred in adjudication hearings over the past 35 years, is it possible that this ruling will be overturned in the near future?

6. Consider the facts in the case of *Boyd v. State.* Should Boyd have been allowed to voluntarily waive his Miranda rights? Without his incriminating statements to police, might he not have been certified as an adult?

7. *In the interest of C.T.F.* helps us to better understand the meaning of speedy trials as they pertain to juvenile matters. Which factors are appropriate to consider when determining whether an accused has been denied the right to a speedy trial under the Sixth Amendment?

8. Compare and contrast the dispositional outcomes discussed in *In re Gault* and *In re Marven C.* In light of these differences, would you say that the juvenile court judges today are more or less punitive than they were, say, 30 years ago?

9. Though the record is unclear, Marven C. was believed to be between 13 and 14 years old at the time of his offense. If California law had allowed him to be certified as an adult, should he have rightfully been tried as one?

10. How do your states' Mental Health Codes and procedures determine competency in criminal and delinquency matters?

CHAPTER SEVEN

DISPOSITION

BOARD OF MANAGERS OF ARKANSAS TRAINING SCHOOL FOR BOYS v. GEORGE, *377 F.2D 228 (8TH CIR. 1967)*

UNITED STATES EX REL. MURRAY v. OWENS, *465 F.2D 289 (2D CIR. 1972)*

BAKER v. HAMILTON, *345 F.SUPP. 345 (W.D. KY. 1972)*

STATE IN THE INTEREST OF D.G.W., *361 A.2D 513 (N.J. 1976)*

THOMPSON v. CARLSON, *624 F.2D 415 (3D CIR. 1980)*

STATE v. QUIROZ, *733 P.2D 963 (WASH. 1987)*

IN RE MARCELLUS L., *278 CAL.RPTR. 901 (CAL. APP. 1991)*

IN RE BIHN L., *6 CAL.RPTR.2D 678 (CAL. APP. 1992)*

MATTER OF SHAWN V., *600 N.Y.S.2D 393 (A.D. 1993)*

P.W. v. STATE, *625 SO.2D 1207 (ALA. CR. APP. 1993)*

IN RE JAMONT C., *17 CAL.RPTR.2D 336 (CAL. APP. 1993)*

G.A.D. v. STATE, *865 P.2D 100 (ALASKA APP. 1993)*

A.S. v. STATE, *627 SO.2D 1265 (FLA. APP. 1993)*

UNITED STATES v. JUVENILE NO. 1, *38 F.3D 470 (9TH CIR. 1994)*

STATE IN THE INTEREST OF T.L.V., *643 SO.2D 290 (LA. APP. 1994)*

EDDINGS v. OKLAHOMA, *445 U.S. 104 (1982)*

THOMPSON v. OKLAHOMA, *487 U.S. 815 (1988)*

STANFORD v. KENTUCKY, *492 U.S. 361 (1989)*

ROPER v. SIMMONS, *543 U.S. 551 (2005)*

GRAHAM v. FLORIDA, *560 U.S.—(2010)*

MILLER v. ALABAMA, *567 U.S.—(2012)*

INTRODUCTION

Once juveniles are adjudicated delinquent, they proceed to the next phase in the process, the disposition hearing. Disposition hearings are the functional equivalent of sentencing in adult criminal cases. In most cases, adjudication and disposition hearings are conducted separately—that is, they are "bifurcated" phases in juvenile proceedings. The lag time between the two hearings gives probation officers time to collect social history data on the adjudicated delinquent. Social history data typically include information gleaned from the child, his or her parent(s), school officials, and social service agencies, especially those in the mental health field (Lawrence 1998, 183). This information is then compiled into a predispositional report that is presented to the judge in an effort to assist him or her in crafting a sentence commensurate to the crime.

Dispositional hearings are typically less formal than adjudication hearings because over time judges develop a working knowledge of the "going rate" for certain offenses (Walker 2001). That is, they acquire a sense of the relative worth of certain kinds of offenses which, in turn, allows them to dispose of cases quickly and in a more routinized manner. This is not to say that all juvenile dispositions are bureaucratic and impersonal. To the contrary, predispositional reports typically offer a highly individualized account of an offender's social history, which gives judges the information needed to tailor treatments specific to the offender's perceived needs. In addition, some dispositional hearings may involve testimony from the probation officer who prepared the report, and juveniles, through their attorneys, may challenge the facts and information contained therein. With this said, research suggests that the most important determinates of an offender's disposition are the seriousness of the instant offense and the juvenile's prior record (Bartollas and Miller 2001, 125).

After considering the predispositional report, judges have a variety of different disposition alternatives to choose from. For example, based on the evidence (or lack of it), a judge may opt to dismiss the charges against the juvenile. This rarely happens, though it is possible. A second option is diversion. In such cases the formal disposition is set aside in order to allow the juvenile the opportunity to undergo treatment in a community-based program. If the juvenile successfully completes the assigned program the charges may be dropped. If, on the other hand, he or she fails to complete the assigned program, diversion efforts may be abandoned and the juvenile can be sentenced on the original adjudication finding.

A third option is probation. Probation is the most widely used disposition in juvenile court. Recent data reveal that more than half (59 percent) of all adjudicated delinquents are placed on probation (Drowns and Hess 2000, 341). In most cases probation is used in conjunction with various conditions and rules. Though probation conditions can vary widely, common conditions include obeying all laws, regular school attendance, nighttime curfews, and prohibitions on the use of drugs and alcohol. More restrictive conditions may include mandatory participation in a treatment program, the imposition of a search clause (discussed later in this chapter), prohibitions against associating with certain people, and mandatory community service or financial restitution to victims (also discussed later).

A fourth option is placement of the juvenile in a community residential facility such as a mental health or drug and alcohol treatment facility. In cases of parental abuse or neglect, juveniles may also be placed in foster care until more permanent living assignments can be arranged. By and large these dispositions are short-term and placements occur in nonsecure facilities. Serious offenders, however, may be placed in secure facilities commonly referred to as training schools.

Training schools are the functional equivalent of adult correctional institutions. In most cases they are operated by the state and vary in their level of supervision from minimum to maximum security. Based on historical concerns about labeling and differential association (e.g., the potential for juveniles to learn bad habits from more experienced offenders), placement decisions are guided by the philosophy of "least restrictive" alternatives. That is, juveniles are placed in the least restrictive settings possible based on the level of treatment needed and the level of danger they present to the community. In most cases confinement in a locked facility is considered a disposition of last resort, and is typically reserved for youth who have committed serious or violent offenses. Though some dispositions include a fixed term of confinement, most are indeterminate, and will vary based on the offender's behavior while incarcerated or the degree to which they participate in rehabilitative programming. In most cases juveniles are released from state custody between the ages of 18 and 21, although recent legislation allows some states to retain custody over juvenile offenders beyond the age of majority under a "blended sentence" or concurrent jurisdictional arrangement (Siegel 2002).

REFERENCES

Bartollas, C., and S. Miller. (2001). *Juvenile Justice in America,* 3rd edition. Upper Saddle River, NJ: Prentice Hall.

Drowns, R., and K. Hess. (2000). *Juvenile Justice,* 3rd edition. Belmont, CA: Wadsworth/Thompson Learning.

Lawrence, R. (1998). *School Crime and Juvenile Justice.* New York: Oxford University Press.

Siegel, L. (2002). *Juvenile Delinquency: The Core.* Belmont, CA: Wadsworth/Thompson Learning.

Walker, S. (2001). *Sense and Nonsense About Crime and Drugs: A Policy Guide,* 5th edition. Belmont, CA: Wadsworth/Thompson Learning.

BOARD OF MANAGERS OF ARKANSAS TRAINING SCHOOL FOR BOYS v. GEORGE

377 F.2d 228 (8th Cir. 1967)

FACTS

This case involved a class action suit brought on behalf of African American juveniles against Arkansas juvenile justice officials for operating and maintaining racially segregated training schools. The suit sought interlocutory and permanent injunction against the state's policies of maintaining racially segregated training schools and sending boys to either one of two training schools (e.g., Arkansas Training Schools for Boys at Pine Bluff and Wrightsville) solely on the basis of race. Plaintiffs alleged that the maintenance of racially segregated facilities violated the due process and equal protection clauses of the Fourteenth Amendment insofar as it deprived African American youth of their equal right to treatment, privileges, and opportunities solely on the basis of their race or color. The case was decided by the US Court of Appeals after the Board of Managers lost in US District Court.

ISSUE

Is it discriminatory for juvenile justice officials to place youth into what appear to be equal juvenile disposition facilities solely on the basis of race?

HOLDING

Yes. It is unconstitutional for judges to place youth in separate juvenile training schools when such placement is made solely on the basis of race.

RATIONALE

At the time of this ruling Arkansas law was clear that a training school "is not, and shall not be a part of the penal system"; rather, training schools were designed for "training and educational" purposes. As such, the US Court of Appeals ruled that Arkansas training schools are an integral part of the state's educational system. Further, given the Supreme Court's ruling in *Brown v. Board of Education* (347 U.S. 483 [1954]), the state of Arkansas' "responsibilities are equal to any other public institutions of learning." In short, the court argued, the doctrine of maintaining "separate but equal" juvenile facilities is "inherently unequal" and thus unconstitutional. The court of appeals went on to require the Arkansas Board of Managers to prepare a plan and a timetable within which it was to ensure the complete desegregation of its juvenile facilities.

CASE EXCERPT

"By legislative fiat these schools are an integral part of the educational system in the State of Arkansas. Their responsibilities are equal to any other public institution of learning in educating young people to assume useful roles in society. In the field of public education the doctrine of 'separate but equal' has no place. Separate educational facilities are inherently unequal."

CASE SIGNIFICANCE

This ruling is significant because the court found that it is unconstitutional to use race as a factor to maintain segregated dispositional placement facilities. Although the court did imply that it might be permissible to operate separate facilities while at the same time grouping together "like peers," such grouping practices may not be made on the basis of race. This ruling is consistent with the Supreme Court's earlier decision in *Brown v. Board of Education* regarding separate but equal educational facilities. However, in this case, the federal court of appeals noted that racial discrimination will not be tolerated in dispositional placement matters or in any other area of formal processing.

UNITED STATES EX REL. MURRAY v. OWENS

465 F.2d 289 (2d Cir. 1972)

FACTS

Murray, a 15-year-old, was adjudicated delinquent in New York Family Court for the commission of first-degree rape and first-degree robbery, acts which would constitute class B felonies if committed by an adult. Pursuant to Section 758 of the New York Family Court Act, the trial judge ordered Murray to be committed for three years to the Elmira Reception Center, a medium-security adult facility for males between the ages of 16 and twenty-one. On appeal, the New York Supreme Court dismissed the rape charge but affirmed the decision to place Murray in an adult correctional institution. Murray then filed a writ of habeas corpus in federal court alleging that Section 758 "arbitrarily singles out 15-year-olds for disparate treatment." That is, juveniles 14 and under may not be sent to Elmira, while youth 16 years and older are afforded the right to trial by jury; only 15-year-olds can be denied a jury trial and sent to Elmira.

ISSUE

Is it unconstitutional to sentence a juvenile to an adult correctional facility upon being adjudged a delinquent in juvenile court without the benefit of a jury trial?

HOLDING

No. The New York Act permitting 15-year-olds to be placed in adult correctional institutions after

UNITED STATES EX REL. MURRAY v. OWENS *(cont.)*

adjudication in juvenile court is not a violation of due process, and is therefore constitutional.

RATIONALE

Upon reviewing this case the US District Court initially ordered Murray to be released unless the state committed him to a juvenile correctional facility or granted him a new trial by jury. The US Court of Appeals, however, reversed this decision, arguing that the Supreme Court's ruling in *McKeiver v. Pennsylvania* (403 U.S. 528 (1975)) actually foresaw instances similar to the case at hand. Although the court of appeals conceded that the Supreme Court did not specifically address this particular question, its ruling heavily implied that jury trials are not constitutionally required even in cases where juveniles may be sent to adult correctional institutions. As for the issue of disparate treatment, the court ruled that it is reasonable for states to shunt "criminally mature" 15-year-olds out of training schools and into adult correctional facilities since failure to do so could have adverse effects on younger children as well as the objectives and proper functioning of training schools.

CASE EXCERPT

"We think the conclusion is inescapable that the Supreme Court in no way implied that jury trial were constitutionally required if the ultimate disposition following an adjudication of delinquency was the same as for older offenders."

CASE SIGNIFICANCE

This case is significant because the court held that due process does not require that juveniles be afforded a jury trial or the right to incarceration in juvenile facilities. Historically, housing juveniles in adult prisons was frowned upon for fear that the juveniles would be adversely affected by the adult inmates. Here, the court focused less on the effect on the juvenile offender in the adult prison and more on the potential impact of the juvenile offender on younger offenders housed in juvenile facilities.

BAKER v. HAMILTON

345 F.Supp. 345 (W.D. Ky. 1972)

FACTS

This case involved a class action lawsuit brought on behalf of Baker, a 17-year-old boy, and 60 other similarly situated juveniles against Hamilton, the Sheriff of Jefferson County, Kentucky, and Judge David Thompson, Chief Trial Commissioner of the Juvenile Court Division. The suit alleged that Judge Thompson had developed an unconstitutional policy of holding juveniles in county jail pending disposition hearings and sentencing juveniles to brief periods of confinement in jail as a means of "shock treatment." The plaintiffs sought declaratory, injunctive, and damage relief under Title 42 U.S.C. Section 1983 for violations of the Eighth and Fourteenth Amendments. While court transcripts indicate that no juveniles were held in the jail for a period of longer than 30 days, the jail conditions were described as deplorable, decrepit, and disgraceful. The jail contained an average of about 400 inmates ranging from serious felons to misdemeanants awaiting trial. Records indicated that the jail had poor ventilation and many broken windows, light bulbs needed replacing, locks were inoperable, and the cells themselves were five feet by nine feet long and contained two bunks each. In addition, for egregious violation, some offenders, including juveniles, were sent to solitary confinement, which was described as even more "horrible" than conditions in the general population. Judge Thompson defended his policy of detaining minors in the adult jail on the grounds that the juveniles sent there were tough and physically mature and had created past disturbances in the juvenile detention center, and hardened, sophisticated juveniles should have the opportunity to "observe the realities that confront them when they reach adulthood if they do not change their ways."

ISSUE

Is it constitutional to hold juveniles in an adult jail pending their dispositional hearing or as part of their postadjudication disposition?

HOLDING

No. Holding juveniles in an adult jail during predispositional matters or as part of a postadjudication disposition, even for brief periods of time, constitutes a violation of the Fourteenth Amendment in that it punishes juveniles like adults without affording them due process rights routinely afforded to adults. Moreover, the practices in this particular case constituted a violation of the Eighth Amendment given the cruel and inhumane living conditions as well as the lack of rehabilitative programs.

RATIONALE

The ruling in this case hinged on the fact that Kentucky law specified that juveniles may only be placed in adult jails pending predispositional matters if (1) no other facilities are available to accommodate juveniles; and (2) they are separated from the adult inmate population. In addition to the Eighth Amendment violation, the US District Court ruled that three separate violations had occurred: (1) the judge had other holding/placement options available but purposefully failed to make use of them; (2) the sheriff purposefully refused to separate juveniles from the adult population as required by law; and (3) the practice of placing juveniles in the adult jail was meted out as a form of punishment, all in violation of the Fourteenth Amendment.

CASE EXCERPT

"No matter how well intentioned the Juvenile Court Judge's acts are in this respect, they cannot be upheld where they constitute a violation of the Fourteenth Amendment."

CASE SIGNIFICANCE

This case is significant because it sought to end the practice of placing juvenile offenders in adult jails during pre- and postdispositional matters. Today, federal law prohibits agencies that receive federal funding from housing juveniles and adults together in the same detention facility. However, some jurisdictions (particularly those in rural areas) continue the practice due to a lack of resources and a basic inability to maintain separate institutions. In such cases, states must ensure physical separation between juvenile and adult residents. In this case, no such effort was made.

STATE IN THE INTEREST OF D.G.W.

361 A.2d 513 (N.J. 1976)

FACTS

D.G.W., a juvenile, along with three codefendants, was adjudicated delinquent for his participation in the breaking and entering of several residences and school buildings and the theft and destruction of property therein which was estimated to be in the thousands of dollars. At his disposition hearing, the trial judge placed D.G.W. on probation for one year and added, as a condition of probation, that the juvenile make restitution to the victims. The specific amount of restitution was to be "worked out" between the offender

and the probation department of that county. The probation department developed a list of damages at one school building totaling $626. For his part in that offense, D.G.W. was ordered to pay one-fourth that amount, or $156.50. D.G.W. appealed.

ISSUE

Is it constitutional for juvenile court judges to include restitution as a condition of juvenile probation?

HOLDING

Yes. The New Jersey Supreme Court ordered that the addition of restitution as a condition of probation is constitutional so long as reasonable safeguards are built into the process. Reasonable safeguards, in this case, included (1) the compilation and presentation of a report prepared by the probation department to determine the extent of the damage caused by the offender; (2) a summary hearing in order to present the results of the report to the juvenile; and (3) the opportunity for the juvenile to object to the findings of that report at the dispositional hearing.

RATIONALE

The court rendered its decision as to the constitutionality of restitution rather quickly. Its major concerns lay in the kinds of protections that are required in order to protect the liberty and property interests of juveniles. Specifically, the court was concerned about (1) the amount of damages the juvenile may be held responsible for; (2) the method of determining the value of damaged goods; (3) the share of payment to be imposed in cases involving multiple offenders; and (4) a reasonable method of repayment that realistically assesses the offender's ability to pay. The court ruled that a probation department should be responsible for conducting an investigation and compiling a list of damages caused by the offender. The method used to determine the value of actual losses should be reasonable (e.g., cost of repair or replacement, market or depreciated value, appraisal, etc.). The share of repayment should be proportionate to the offender's level of responsibility. Finally, the amount of restitution should be reasonably based on the offender's ability to pay.

CASE EXCERPT

"A vast amount of damage, let us say by vandalism, minor implication of the particular juvenile involved, perhaps his domination by a juvenile gang 'leader'

STATE IN THE INTEREST OF D.G.W. *(cont.)*

primarily responsible for the damage, or other factors would have to be considered by the court if projected. Thus even though the less implicated juvenile offender might be appropriately adjudged as delinquent, his relative culpability for the damage inflicted should be considered by the court."

CASE SIGNIFICANCE

This decision is significant in that the appellate court ruled that juvenile court judges may not completely delegate away decision-making authority for restitution, or any other probation condition, to court personnel. Although probation officers and other judicial staff may continue to provide information such as damage assessments and an offender's ability to pay restitution, the setting of probation conditions, including restitution agreements, is a judicial function that must be overseen and ultimately approved by the court itself unless otherwise clearly allowed by law.

THOMPSON v. CARLSON
624 F.2d 415 (3d Cir. 1980)

FACTS

Thompson, then 17 years old, was convicted in federal court of assault with intent to rape and received an eight-year sentence under the Youth Corrections Act (YCA). The Act allowed Thompson to serve his time in an adult facility, but mandated that he be segregated from other adult inmates. While serving time on the assault charge, Thompson was convicted of first-degree murder of an inmate who was stabbed by several other inmates while Thompson acted as a lookout. For his participation in the murder, Thompson was sentenced to a consecutive term of life imprisonment. However, this time, the sentencing judge sent him to an adult facility where he was to be held in the general prison population without the benefit of protective segregation. Thompson filed a writ of habeas corpus alleging that his confinement was illegal because he was entitled to segregation from adult offenders at least until the completion of his original sentence for assault.

ISSUE

If a juvenile offender is tried and convicted of a second offense as an adult, does the second conviction supersede a previous sentence that provides special protective considerations for juvenile inmates?

HOLDING

Yes. Juvenile offenders who commit new crimes while incarcerated may have their sentences reviewed and amended if the original sentencing judge finds that the individual in question would no longer benefit from special treatment afforded to juveniles.

RATIONALE

The purpose of the Youth Corrections Act was "to provide a better method of treating young offenders convicted in federal courts in the vulnerable age bracket [16 to 22 years old], to rehabilitate them and restore normal behavioral patters." At the time of his murder conviction, Thompson was 20 years old. However, the sentencing judge was given an opportunity to reevaluate the original assault sentence in light of the new offense. He determined that continued service of the original sentence under the conditions offered by the YCA (e.g., protective segregation) was no longer beneficial. Thus, Thompson's life sentence for murder as an adult superseded his prior protected status, making him eligible for transfer to the adult prison population.

CASE EXCERPT

"Most of the causes which contribute to antisocial conduct of youth offenders in the period between adolescence and maturity disappear when the youth reaches full maturity. The problem is to provide a successful method and means for treatment of young men between the ages of 16 and 22 who stand convicted in our Federal courts and are not fit subjects for supervised probation a method and means that will effect rehabilitation and restore normality, rather than develop recidivists."

CASE SIGNIFICANCE

Citizens often complain about the "revolving door" of juvenile justice. Much of this anger is directed at juvenile court judges, who are criticized for treating young offenders with "kid gloves." There is a degree of truth in this criticism; however, this case demonstrated that sentenced offenders who commit additional crimes while serving time for a previous conviction can and often do face serious consequences. Here, the court ruled that adult sanctions could be imposed upon a juvenile who commits additional crimes while in state custody and who is now certifiable as an adult. The court further ruled that in a case of conflict (e.g., an adult punishment that is handed down to an inmate who is currently serving time in a juvenile institution), the adult sentence takes precedence over the punishment imposed by the juvenile court.

STATE v. QUIROZ

733 P.2d 963 (Wash. 1987)

FACTS

Quiroz, a juvenile, arrived at the diversion unit prior to his appointment and was given a form entitled Advice About Diversion. He read the form and then discussed it point by point with a probation officer who then entered into the diversion agreement with Quiroz. The advice agreement made specific reference to the juvenile's right to consult an attorney and his right to a trial if he did not believe he committed the alleged offense. In addition, it made reference to the fact that it could serve to enhance a child's future penalty. The probation officer testified that had Quiroz wanted a lawyer or a more detailed explanation of the charges against him or his possible options, she would have referred him to an attorney. Nevertheless, Quiroz then signed the diversion agreement and a waiver of counsel form. After he was adjudicated delinquent, Quiroz appealed to the state appellate court.

ISSUE

May a juvenile court judge take into account a youth's prior diversion and use it to enhance a subsequent delinquency disposition?

HOLDING

Yes. A juvenile court judge may take into account prior diverted offenses when sentencing a juvenile.

RATIONALE

Washington law provides for very structured sentencing which weighs the severity of an offense as well as a juvenile's prior history. In the present case, Quiroz's two prior misdemeanors, which were diverted, increased his sentence from 20 to 40 days. The state supreme court has defined the way in which diversion units must follow certain procedures. The juvenile must be informed of his or her right to counsel and that he or she must waive that right to enter into a diversion contract. Further, the advice form and the fact that the diversion becomes part of the juvenile's history must be explained to the juvenile. In this case, the court believed that the written notice given to the juvenile prior to his signing the diversion agreement, which

indicated that he could consult with counsel, met the conception of fair play. However, the court did say that much confusion may have been spared by sending an advisement of rights to the juvenile and his or her parent before the day of the appointment. Further, since the agreement warned the juvenile about its future usage in court hearings and he signed said agreement, it was constitutional to use the diversion to enhance future sentences.

CASE EXCERPT

"The [diversion] agreement warned the juveniles of its effect on their criminal histories, and therefore, the juveniles cannot complain that they were unaware of its consequences. Therefore, because the agreement warned about the possibility of its future use, and because the agreement itself was not the same as a conviction, its future use did not violate their constitutional rights."

CASE SIGNIFICANCE

This case is important because the court upheld the statute allowing juvenile courts to use a prior diverted offense in determining a juvenile's prior record when sentencing the juvenile for a new offense. Washington, like some other states, uses a presumptive sentencing scheme. Consequently, any prior offense is sure to earn the juvenile defendant a disposition enhancement. Diversion is an attempt to deal with a juvenile outside of the legal process. In this case, the juvenile had previously successfully completed the diversion program. Therefore, the prior charge was never formally filed. However, the court still allowed the previously diverted offense to be utilized in determining the juvenile's prior history. In justifying this, the court pointed to the language in the diversion contract, which informs juveniles that diversion will be taken into account at any future dispositional hearings for new offenses. Diversion is designed to keep first-time, low-risk offenders away from the harshness of the court; it is not designed to provide chances to repeat offenders. The Washington statute is consistent with this ideology.

IN RE MARCELLUS L.

278 Cal.Rptr. 901 (Cal. App. 1991)

FACTS

Marcellus L., a minor on probation, was sitting on the front steps of what a Richmond (California) police

IN RE MARCELLUS L. (cont.)

officer described as "a house where crack cocaine is sold." Because it was around noon on a weekday and Marcellus L. looked "very young," the officer decided to investigate to see if Marcellus was truant from school. Prior to questioning the suspect, the officer conducted a cursory pat-down search and discovered that Marcellus L. was in possession of 1.68 grams of crack cocaine. He was arrested. At trial, Marcellus L. moved to suppress the drug evidence arguing that the officer (1) had no articulable facts justifying the pat-down search; (2) was not pursuing a valid probationary purpose; and (3) was not even aware that Marcellus was on probation at the time of the search. The state countered that because Marcellus L. was on probation with a search condition, he had no grounds to challenge the search since he had effectively waived his Fourth Amendment protections. The superior court denied the suppression motion and the defendant appealed to the California appellate court.

ISSUE

When a juvenile accepts a disposition of probation with a search clause, do they in effect consent to unlimited searches by peace officers, even in cases where no probable cause exists to conduct a pat-down search?

HOLDING

Yes. If considered in a contextual vacuum, this search would be deemed invalid. However, because Marcellus L. was on probation at the time, he had in effect given up his right to privacy under the Fourth Amendment, and thus had no right to challenge the search.

RATIONALE

The court ruled that juvenile probationers have only limited Fourth Amendment protections against searches by a peace officer. These exceptions include (1) searches conducted for the purposes of harassment; and (2) other improper searches that lack any legitimate law enforcement aim. The frisk in question involved only a minimal invasion of privacy and was conducted for purposes of officer safety; thus it could not be classified as harassment. Moreover, California law states that a defendant who agrees to the standard probation search clause in order to obtain the benefits of probation has voluntarily waived "whatever claim of privacy he might otherwise have had." The purpose of limiting probationers' privacy, the court reasoned, is to deter future offending and to discover whether the

probationer is obeying the terms of probation. Because the officer in question was investigating a school attendance matter, there was no harassment or other improper motive for the search.

CASE EXCERPT

"What is critical is that the juvenile probationer has been admitted to probation upon a legitimate search condition....and has absolutely no reasonable expectation to be free from the type of search here conducted...Appellant's expectation of privacy cannot reasonably be said to extend to searches conducted by officers who are ignorant of his probationary status."

CASE SIGNIFICANCE

This case is significant because the court clearly stated that probationers, even juveniles, have no reasonable expectation of privacy and must submit to searches any time, any place, irrespective of the legality of the search. The court further noted that it would be burdensome—to the point of rendering the search clause meaningless—if a peace officer had to have first-hand knowledge of a juvenile's probationary status before conducting a search. In other words, police efforts to deter crimes would be severely undermined if they had to have personal knowledge of every juvenile who is on probation before conducting a search. Thus, the court found that even if the search had been conducted illegally, the fact that the defendant was on probation and was aware of the search condition made any evidence seized admissible in future proceedings.

IN RE BIHN L.

6 Cal.Rptr.2d 678 (Cal. App. 1992)

FACTS

On the morning of March 7, 1991, a California police officer stopped a vehicle for operating with an obscured registration tag. The vehicle contained several juveniles, among them Bihn L., who was on probation for car theft. As part of his probation agreement, Bihn L. was required to submit to warrantless searches by a peace officer at any time. As the officer ran the vehicle registration, he noticed that the three juvenile passengers appeared very young. The officer asked the passengers where they attended school and they provided answers. Acting on a hunch that the juveniles were not being truthful, the officer contacted school officials and was advised that none of the three passengers was enrolled at the school they had named. Assuming that the juveniles were truants, the officer ordered them out of the vehicle and proceeded to conduct pat-down searches. Under Bihn L.'s coat the officer discovered a loaded pistol. At trial, the officer admitted that he had been unaware that Bihn L. was on probation. Nevertheless, Bihn was adjudicated delinquent and committed to a juvenile rehabilitation center. He appealed.

ISSUE

Is it constitutional for a court to admit evidence subsequent to an otherwise illegal police search in cases when a juvenile is required, as part of probation, to submit to warrantless police searches "any time, day or night"?

HOLDING

Yes. In cases where a juvenile is subject to a valid search condition as part of his or her probation agreement, incriminating evidence seized by police is admissible in court, even in situations where the officer lacks probable cause to search and was unaware of a search condition.

RATIONALE

In denying the motion to suppress the incriminating evidence used at trial (e.g., the gun), the court reasoned that Bihn "knew, by a direct and valid order of the juvenile court, that he was subject to a warrantless search at any time or place by any probation or police officer." In short, since Bihn was aware of the search condition, he knew the risk he was taking by carrying a concealed weapon. Thus, the fact that the officer was unaware of the search condition, as well as the officer's lack of probable cause to conduct the search, was irrelevant to the case at hand. The court recognized that if Bihn had not been on probation—that is, had he not been subject to the search condition—the evidence might very well have been suppressed as a result of the Fourth Amendment's protections against unreasonable search and seizure. However, since Bihn had agreed to the search condition as part of his probation, which itself was accepted in lieu of a more secure placement, he had effectively agreed to limit his own right to privacy.

CASE EXCERPT

"In short, if there were any circumstance in which the minor could reasonably have expected his decision to carry a loaded pistol to remain private from the police, this was certainly not such a circumstance: Riding in a car only four months after he had acknowledged a probation search condition in an order arising out of admitted vehicle thefts."

CASE SIGNIFICANCE

This case is significant insofar as it said that juveniles who consent to a search condition as part of their probation effectively waive their Fourth Amendment right to privacy. The reason for this is that probation, unlike parole, is a privilege, and greater intrusion by government officials is justified in order to maintain the privilege of community supervision. Thus, any incriminating evidence gathered by police in such situations can and should be admitted in court because juveniles often agree to such searches as conditions of their probation.

MATTER OF SHAWN V.

600 N.Y.S.2d 393 (A.D. 1993)

FACTS

Shawn V., a juvenile, was adjudicated delinquent after he admitted to committing petit larceny. At his disposition hearing, psychiatric experts testified that Shawn V. had serious emotional and behavioral problems which rendered him not only a threat to himself but to the community at large. Given his increasingly violent behavior over the years, the court placed him in a State Division for Youth facility for 12 months. He appealed the placement order arguing that the court had abused its discretion in determining that a secure facility was the "least restrictive" alternative available.

ISSUE

In light of historical efforts to adopt "least restrictive placements" for juvenile offenders, is it proper for judges to consider issues of public safety when crafting juvenile dispositions?

HOLDING

Yes. Juvenile proceedings have historically sought placements that are in the best interests of the child. Dispositions crafted on the basis of least restrictive placements facilitate this outcome insofar as they limit the potential for labeling and psychological harm. However, least restrictive placements must also be balanced against the need to ensure public safety.

MATTER OF SHAWN V. *(cont.)*

RATIONALE

During the disposition hearing the court heard from various experts who testified that Shawn V. was a danger both to himself and others. He had been expelled from several schools for aggressive, assaultive, and antisocial behaviors. More important, a psychologist's report indicated that past acts of sexual aggression toward female students put Shawn into a high-risk category for committing a sex offense. Based on this assessment, as well as testimony from other experts, the court ruled that placing Shawn in a community residential facility was unwise.

CASE EXCERPT

"Here, a review of psychiatric, psychosocial, social and educational reports...establish...that respondent has serious emotional and behavioral problems which render him not only a threat to himself, but to others in the community...All of the professionals who evaluated respondent strongly recommend secure placement and indicated that direct placement in the community was unwise because it may easily result in continued antisocial conduct. Significantly, the examining psychologist's report indicated that certain tests administered to respondent revealed him to be at risk for committing a sex offense."

CASE SIGNIFICANCE

This case offers an example of the dynamic tension created by the juvenile justice system's mandate to impose dispositions that satisfy both the best interests of the child and the public's right to safety. Historically, concerns about the child's best interests have outweighed issues of public safety. Today, however, these concerns have been reversed. That is, factors such as seriousness of the crime and concerns about public safety have superseded concerns about labeling and secondary deviance.

P.W. v. STATE

625 So.2d 1207 (Ala. Cr. App. 1993)

FACTS

P.W. was adjudicated a serious juvenile offender for his participation in illegal acts of theft, burglary of a motor vehicle, and possession of burglary tools. Court records indicate that P.W. had been to juvenile court 28 times and had accumulated $1,065 in court costs and restitution, none of which he had paid. At his disposition hearing, the trial judge gave P.W. two weeks to pay a substantial fine plus court costs or he would be committed to the Alabama Department of Youth Services. P.W. refused to pay and was subsequently incarcerated. At his appeal, P.W. argued that he should not have been ordered to pay court costs and fines in the amount of $1,494 because he was an indigent.

ISSUES

Is it appropriate for judges to impose fines and court costs on juveniles? If yes, is it appropriate to incarcerate a juvenile who fails to pay?

HOLDING

Yes and no. It is well within the discretion of juvenile court judges to levy reasonable fines and court costs against juvenile offenders, although ability to pay must be taken into consideration in cases of indigence. However, it is unconstitutional to incarcerate juveniles for failure to pay court costs and fines.

RATIONALE

The appellate court recognized that in most cases juveniles do not have the ability to repay substantial fines, and pushing the financial burden of such a sanction onto parents would minimize the rehabilitative intent of the sanction. The court further recognized that it is unconstitutional to incarcerate indigents for failure to pay fines, court costs, or restitution. However, it affirmed P.W.'s placement on the grounds that he was not incarcerated because of indigence. Instead, he was incarcerated for displaying a nonrepentant attitude and failing to comply with a valid court order. In effect, the appellate court ruled that the trial judge was offering P.W. one last chance to demonstrate some sign of remorse indicating that he accepted personal responsibility for his actions.

CASE EXCERPT

"If anything, it appears to this Court that the juvenile court was merely trying to impress this juvenile with the 'hardness' of the 'brick wall' he had just hit, for, from the record, it appears that no one harbored even the slightest hope that the accumulated court costs would be paid. In determining disposition, the juvenile court was certainly entitled to consider the juvenile's record of past compliance or noncompliance with the previous orders of the court."

CASE SIGNIFICANCE

This case dealt with the constitutionality of imposing fines as a disposition and the imposition of court costs on juvenile offenders. Dispositions such as this are rarely used in juvenile cases because labor laws often preclude children under a certain age from earning wages. With few financial assets at their disposal, the burden of fines and court costs typically fall on the child's parents, thus diminishing the rehabilitative effect on the offender. Though the court upheld this particular ruling, it went on to argue that it would be unconstitutional to incarcerate indigent offenders merely for their failure to pay such fines and court costs. This ruling is consistent with the Supreme Court's decision in *Bearden v. Georgia,* 461. U.S. 660 (1983), which declared that indigent probationers could not have their probation revoked for failure to pay fines and court costs because doing so would violate the equal protection clause of the Fourteenth Amendment.

IN RE JAMONT C.

17 Cal.Rptr.2d 336 (Cal. App. 1993)

FACTS

Jamont C., a juvenile, challenged the breadth of a probation search clause imposed upon him by the Superior Court of Santa Clara, California. The condition required Jamont C. to "submit his person, property, residence, or any vehicle owned by said minor or in said minor's control to search and seizure at any time of the day or night by any peace officer, school official, with or without a Warrant." Jamont claimed that this probation condition was unconstitutional on the grounds that it permitted unreasonable intrusion upon his Fourth Amendment rights without individualized suspicion that he was engaged in, or was about to engage in, delinquent activities.

ISSUE

Did the probation search condition, which permitted searches and seizures by law enforcement or school officials without individualized suspicion, violate the juvenile's Fourth Amendment right to privacy?

HOLDING

No. Although juveniles do not have a right to refuse probation, nonconsensual searches are permissible in the absence of individualized suspicion. However, such searches are only permissible insofar as the individual's right to privacy is outweighed by the government's interest in promoting the health and welfare of minors.

RATIONALE

The appellate court found that the Fourth Amendment rights of adult probationers who are subject to a valid search condition are not violated by searches that take place in the absence of a warrant or individualized suspicion. In effect, adult probationers consent to these kinds of searches "in exchange for the benefit of avoiding a prison term." However, it also found that adults have the right to refuse probation and related search conditions; juveniles do not have such a right. Nevertheless, the appellate court ruled that the imposition of intrusive probation search conditions on a juvenile is permissible because the state maintains an interest in promoting the health and welfare of minors. It reasoned that juvenile probation "goes beyond the mere prevention of criminal activity and enters the arena of social guidance." As such, the state's interest in "guiding juvenile delinquents along the path to productive citizenship justifies relaxing the barriers to effective supervision of these juveniles," and individualized suspicion requirements would thwart those efforts.

CASE EXCERPT

"The question here is whether, with respect to juvenile probationers, the state's interests justify permitting searches pursuant to lawful probation search conditions in the absence of some objective measurable quantity of individualized suspicion. We conclude that such searches are justified by the state's interest in promoting the health and welfare of minors."

CASE SIGNIFICANCE

This case helped to bolster the legitimacy of probation search conditions by arguing that such searches were consistent with the state's interest in promoting the health and welfare of minors. What makes the case particularly significant is the fact that the search condition was extremely broad, including not only the juvenile himself, but his property, residence, and any vehicle under his direct control at the time of contact. Despite this broad language, the court upheld the condition arguing that juveniles on probation have limited protections under the Fourth Amendment and such limitations are justified by the fact that probation is a privilege, not a right.

G.A.D. v. STATE

865 P.2d 100 (Alaska App. 1993)

FACTS

G.A.D., a 13-year-old, was adjudicated a delinquent for sexually abusing his three-year-old brother. He was sent to the Jesse Lee Home, a residential juvenile sex offender treatment program in Anchorage, Alaska. After 10 months in the program, G.A.D. failed to show improvement. He then committed a new offense by trying to escape from the home. At his hearing on the escape, the judge consulted with various state experts familiar with G.A.D.'s case. All agreed that he should be placed in a secure environment that offered more aggressive treatment programming. According to a clinical therapist, G.A.D. continued to "groom" other Jesse Lee residents for sexual activity, and he failed to perceive the seriousness of his conduct. Thus, she recommended against sending G.A.D. to foster care. His probation officer concurred with this assessment. However, the probation officer went on to recommend against placing G.A.D. in a similar residential placement (the Kenai Care Center) because (1) the rules at the Kenai Center were more lenient; (2) the therapy was less intensive; and (3) Kenai residents attended school in the community, which posed a greater threat to the public. As a result of this damaging testimony, and because there were no other treatment options available, the court placed G.A.D. in the McLaughlin Youth Center. G.A.D. opposed his placement, arguing that the state had failed to show that institutionalization at McLaughlin was required—that no less restrictive alternative existed that could achieve rehabilitation and protect the public.

ISSUE

In crafting juvenile dispositions, does the right to public protection triumph over concerns about least restrictive placement?

HOLDING

Yes. The right to public safety prevails when the state is able to demonstrate that less restrictive placement is likely to fail.

RATIONALE

The court ruled that in cases regarding the potential institutionalization of juveniles, the state bears the burden of proving, by a preponderance of the evidence, that less restrictive placement options will not satisfy the competing goals of rehabilitation and public protection. In this case, the testimonial evidence offered by G.A.D.'s mother, his therapist, his probation officer, and his guardian ad litem, all of whom recommended institutionalization, met that burden. Moreover, the court reasoned that placement in a less secure facility could endanger the public, and the sex offender treatment offered at McLaughlin was similar, and perhaps more appropriate, to that which was offered at the Jesse Lee Home.

CASE EXCERPT

"A minor's history of failed placements and continued violations of the law can justify the superior court's decision to institutionalize the minor... On the other hand, the least restrictive alternative rule does not require that a child be allowed to fail at each [successively more restrictive] level of placement before placement in the next restrictive level may be made... Rather, the court can institutionalize a minor if the State presents substantial evidence that lesser measures will likely fail."

CASE SIGNIFICANCE

Similar to the dilemma posed in *Matter of Shawn V.,* this case represented the court's attempt to balance the dual goals of least restrictive dispositional placement and the need to ensure public safety. Although institutionalization is often seen as a last resort, the decision to place G.A.D. in the more secure environment was made easier given the fact that there were no significant differences in treatment between the less restrictive and more restrictive programs. In fact, the only major difference noted by the judge was the environment in which the treatment occurred. Thus, the court opted for the more secure placement in light of G.A.D.'s prior escape attempt and the fact that experts familiar with his case argued in favor of the more secure setting. This case was also interesting because rural states such as Alaska typically have few placement options at their disposal.

A.S. v. STATE

627 So.2d 1265 (Fla. App. 1993)

FACTS

A.S., a minor, was convicted of aggravated battery for engaging in a schoolyard fight in which the victim, another classmate, suffered a broken nose. As part of his sentence, A.S. was made to pay restitution in the amount of $4,986.60 for medical expenses incurred by the victim's parents. Though this judgment was rendered against the juvenile, the judge reasoned that A.S.'s mother was at least partially responsible for the child's action. He therefore ordered her to pay roughly half of the medical expenses—$2,500 of the $4,986.60. The basis for this decision came from a Florida statute that read, in part, "[t]he liability of a parent under this paragraph shall not exceed $2,500 for any one criminal episode. A finding by the court, after a hearing, that the parent has made diligent good faith efforts to prevent the child from engaging in delinquent acts shall absolve the parent of liability for restitution under this paragraph." A.S. appealed.

ISSUE

Should parents of juveniles who commit delinquent acts be required to pay restitution even though they appear to be "good" parents?

HOLDING

No. Parents of adjudicated delinquents cannot be held partially responsible for restitution under a statute permitting transferred liability, unless the court can justify such action based on evidence showing that the parents have not made a good faith effort to raise the child.

RATIONALE

The appellate court affirmed that it is constitutional for a court to assess a reasonable amount of restitution as part of a delinquency finding. However, it reversed the ruling in this case because the court had failed to show a lack of "good faith effort" on the mother's part. In fact, the evidence clearly indicated that, aside from this one incident, A.S. had an otherwise "unblemished record." Testimonial evidence offered on appeal showed that A.S. was a well-behaved, compliant honor-roll student. However, his parents were divorced, his father lived out of state, and his mother had a string of failed relationships. Aside from the failed relationships, however, which said nothing of her skills as a parent, the mother appeared to have been doing a fine job raising her son.

CASE EXCERPT

"If all the evidence shows that the child is otherwise well-behaved, then surely it should be enough for the parent to show merely that she had accomplished the 'normal parenting tasks' to escape liability for restitution under this statute. To do otherwise would be to impose strict liability on parents for all delinquent acts of their minor children. If the legislature had intended that result, it would have chosen a different text than the one it had adopted at the time."

CASE SIGNIFICANCE

This case is significant because it held that, under certain circumstances, parents could be assessed a reasonable amount of restitution as part of a delinquency finding. However, the Florida statute in this case only permitted such action when the juvenile court was able to make a finding of lack of good faith effort on the parents' part before transferring liability. If no such finding could be made, the court ruled that parents could not be held accountable for their children's actions. Keep in mind this ruling is state-specific, and to some extent, statute-specific. That is, the United States Supreme Court has not decided whether or not parental good faith exceptions are constitutionally valid defenses in juvenile restitution cases.

UNITED STATES v. JUVENILE NO. 1
38 F.3d 470 (9th Cir. 1994)

FACTS

In 1992 juveniles No. 1 and No. 2 broke into the house of an elderly woman on the Umatilla, Oregon, Indian Reservation. They had been drinking heavily and entered the home in search of money and more alcohol. The homeowner, an elderly woman, confronted the juveniles. They knocked her to the floor, piled flammable material on her stove, set it on fire, and ran away. Unable to move without her walker, she lay on the floor until rescued by neighbors. The two juveniles pleaded guilty in US District Court to misdemeanor assault charges and were sentenced to probation. One of the conditions of their probation was that they were prohibited from possessing firearms until they were 21 years old. The juveniles appealed, arguing that participation in a "hunt" with firearms is a religious tenet of the Umatilla tribe—a rite of passage from boyhood to manhood—and that prohibiting the possession of firearms amounted to a violation of their First Amendment right to freedom of religion.

ISSUE

Did the probation condition prohibiting the possession of firearms violate the juveniles' First Amendment right to freedom of religion?

UNITED STATES v. JUVENILE NO. 1 *(cont.)*

HOLDING

No. The probation condition prohibiting the possession of firearms until the juveniles reached age 21 was reasonable insofar as it helped to further the statutory goals of punishment, deterrence, and public protection.

RATIONALE

In reaching its decision, the court paused to reflect on both the seriousness of the instant offense and the juveniles' history of alcoholism. In the instant offense, "[t]he juveniles assaulted an elderly woman, set her house on fire and left her to die." In addition, according to the presentence report, both juveniles began drinking at an early age, and both were plagued by alcohol abuse. Thus, the court reasoned, "[g]iven their history of alcohol abuse and the seriousness of their offense, it is not unreasonable to impose a condition of probation which keeps firearms out of their hands until they are 21 years of age." Moreover, the court argued that this prohibition did not severely hamper the juveniles' religious freedoms under the First Amendment because they would still be allowed to participate in tribal hunts. Though such a prohibition does impinge somewhat on religious rites, the court found that the condition of this probation was both appropriate and reasonably related to public protection.

CASE EXCERPT

"We cannot say that the district court abused its discretion in making this choice. The juveniles may still participate in tribal hunts. They may even take part in killing game, by using a bow and arrow or any other weapon which is not a firearm... Even if an Indian boy's participation in a tribal hunt is a religious rite of passage, the district court's firearm prohibition order, impinging that rite to the extent it does, is a valid condition of probation because it serves the broader purposes of the [Federal Sentencing Reform Act of 1984]."

CASE SIGNIFICANCE

This case is significant because it found that in cases involving Native American juveniles, the First Amendment right to freedom of religion is not absolute. Here, a controversial probation condition was imposed upon the youth that conflicted with a tribal custom requiring young men to participate in a religious hunt with firearms. The condition, however, did not preclude their participation in the hunt, but it did prohibit the boys from possessing or using firearms under any circumstances until the age of twenty-one. The appellate court upheld this ruling arguing that in light of the juveniles' reckless behavior during the previous hunt, the condition barring possession and use of firearms was constitutionally valid, even though it interfered with constitutionally protected religious freedoms.

STATE IN THE INTEREST OF T.L.V.

643 So.2d 290 (La. App. 1994)

FACTS

T.L.V. and another juvenile devised a plan to obtain money by snatching a woman's purse. Laying in wait near a Shreveport, Louisiana shopping mall, T.L.V. and several other youth scanned the parking lot for a potential victim. The youth selected 75-year-old Elizabeth Jackson and hit her over the head, causing a serious wound that required 21 stitches. Jackson was knocked to the ground and her arm was broken. Witnesses saw the youth flee the scene and enter a nearby apartment. At the behest of the local police, the apartment manager made contact with the resident of that unit and delivered a message requesting that T.L.V. and the others turn themselves in. T.L.V. and his mother went to the police station, and he confessed to participating in the purse snatching. He later pled guilty in juvenile court and was sentenced to the Louisiana Department of Public Safety and Corrections for three years on the purse snatching charge and one year on the battery charge; the sentences were to be served consecutively. T.L.V. appealed, arguing that (1) the juvenile court's disposition improperly deviated from the state's sentencing guidelines; and (2) the sentences were excessive and should be run concurrently rather than consecutively.

ISSUE

Was the sentence excessive when compared with the state's sentencing guidelines used in adult criminal court?

HOLDING

No. Juvenile courts are not required to model dispositions based on felony sentencing guidelines that were established for adult offenders.

RATIONALE

In upholding the original dispositions, the appellate court noted that under "normal" circumstances, two or more offenses arising out of the same act would typically be served concurrently. However, concurrent sentencing is not a statutory obligation, and the decision to run the sentences either concurrently or consecutively is left to the discretion of the sentencing judge. In order to craft the most appropriate disposition, judges must consider a variety of factors, such as the gravity or dangerousness of the offense, the viciousness of the crime, the harm done to victims, and the defendant's apparent disregard for the property of others. The court also noted that this crime was planned in advance, and T.L.V. "resorted to violence and inflicted severe injuries when his elderly victim proved less complacent than he had hoped."

CASE EXCERPT

"Defendant, had he been an adult, would have faced up to ten years on the attempted purse snatching and up to five years for the simple battery. The disposition imposed is in the far lower range of what an adult would have faced…Under the circumstances of this case, it does not appear that the disposition is a needless infliction of pain and suffering, nor that it is grossly out of proportion to the seriousness of the offense."

CASE SIGNIFICANCE

This case is significant because it found that juvenile courts are not bound by adult sentencing guidelines. That is, when faced with the dilemma of balancing the needs of the juvenile with the need for public safety, sentencing guidelines are just that—guidelines—and are not mandatory. Thus, the lower court's decision, in this particular case, was not excessive. Though the court ruled that adult sentencing guidelines did not apply to juvenile dispositions in this case, it should be noted that several states have created juvenile sentencing guidelines in an effort to reduce sentencing disparities.

EDDINGS v. OKLAHOMA

445 U.S. 104 (1982)

FACTS

On April 4, 1977, Eddings, age 16, and several younger companions ran away from their Missouri homes traveling in a vehicle owned by Eddings's brother. In the vehicle were a shotgun and several rifles stolen from Eddings's father. Sometime during the trip, Eddings momentarily lost control of the vehicle. He was subsequently signaled to pull over by an officer of the Oklahoma Highway Patrol. Eddings did so, and as the officer approached the vehicle, Eddings pointed a loaded shotgun out of the window and fired, killing the officer. Finding that Eddings was not amenable to rehabilitation in the juvenile justice system, the state of Oklahoma certified him as an adult and prosecuted him on first-degree murder charges. Eddings entered a plea of nolo contendere to the charge and he was found guilty. At his sentencing hearing the state alleged three aggravating circumstances that warranted the death penalty: The murder was especially heinous, the crime was committed to avoid arrest, and the defendant constituted a continuing threat to society. The defense argued that several mitigating circumstances (e.g., a turbulent family life, beatings by a harsh father, and severe emotional disturbance) warranted a sentence less than death. The trial judge upheld all of the aggravating circumstances but found, as a matter of law, the he could not consider any of the mitigating circumstances except the defendant's age. As a result of this ruling, Eddings was sentenced to death. The case was eventually heard by the US Supreme Court.

ISSUE

Are trial courts required to consider mitigating circumstances such as family life, emotional disturbance, and past abuse during sentencing in capital cases?

HOLDING

Yes. Total exclusion of mitigating factors during the sentencing phase of capital cases is improper. Trial courts must consider any and all mitigating factors offered; however, judges are permitted to determine the weight and relevance of those factors.

RATIONALE

In a 5–4 decision, the US Supreme Court held that the trial judge had erred in his decision to exclude the various mitigating circumstances offered at Eddings's trial. The majority found that in capital cases involving juveniles, evidence of a turbulent family life, severe corporal punishment at the hand of a parent, and emotional disturbance are "particularly relevant" in determining whether to impose the death sentence. Though the Court did not specify how lower courts should weigh this evidence, judges were required to consider all mitigating factors prior to the imposition of the death sentence. Based on its own ruling in *Lockett v. Ohio* (438 U.S. 586, 606

EDDINGS v. OKLAHOMA *(cont.)*

[1978]), the Supreme Court vacated Eddings's death sentence on the grounds that it was imposed without "the type of individualized consideration of mitigating factors...required by the Eighth and Fourteenth Amendments in capital cases."

CASE EXCERPT

"Eddings was a youth of 16 years at the time of the murder. Evidence of a difficult family history and of emotional disturbance is typically introduced by defendants in mitigation...In some cases, such evidence may be properly given no weight. But when the defendant was 16 years old at the time of the offense there can be no doubt that evidence of a turbulent family history, of beatings by a harsh father, and of severe emotional disturbance is particularly relevant."

CASE SIGNIFICANCE

Though the Court did not address the question of *how* judges should weigh the importance of certain kinds of mitigating evidence in capital cases, it did require them to consider such evidence (in writing) prior to sentencing. For example, the Court noted that factors such as age and social history of a juvenile are relevant and such evidence must be given serious consideration. But what makes the *Eddings* decision significant is the fact that the Supreme Court narrowed judges' discretion on which mitigating factors they will or will not consider prior to sentencing.

THOMPSON v. OKLAHOMA

487 U.S. 815 (1988)

FACTS

Thompson, a 15-year-old boy, was one of four defendants charged in the brutal slaying of Keene, Thompson's brother-in-law. Keene, whose body was recovered from a river, appeared to have been beaten, shot twice, and his throat, chest, and abdomen cut. Court records indicate that Thompson allegedly killed Keene for physically abusing Thompson's sister. Because of his age, Thompson was considered a child under Oklahoma law, but the prosecutor sought and was granted a motion to try the case in adult court. At trial, Thompson, along with his three codefendants, were convicted of first-degree murder and sentenced to death. The case was eventually heard by the US Supreme Court.

ISSUE

Is it cruel and unusual to sentence a juvenile to death for a crime that was committed when the juvenile was 15 years old?

HOLDING

Yes. The Eighth and Fourteenth Amendments of the US Constitution prohibit the execution of a juvenile whose crime took place when the juvenile was 15 years old.

RATIONALE

In the *Thompson* case the Court's decision was split 5–3, with one abstention. Justice Stevens, writing on behalf of four of the justices, argued that the execution of a juvenile whose offense took place when he or she was under the age of 16 "would offend evolving civilized standards of decency" and thus violate the prohibitions against cruel and unusual punishment under the Eighth and Fourteenth Amendments of the Constitution. Justice O'Connor, writing her own concurring opinion, argued that (1) although it cannot be conclusively demonstrated, most Americans would oppose the execution of any person for a crime they committed under the age of 16; and (2) states that allow such "dubiously constitutional" proceedings to move forward may not have fully considered the propriety of such executions. Thus, the Court reversed the judgment and remanded the case with instructions to vacate Thompson's death sentence.

CASE EXCERPT

"In short, we are not persuaded that the imposition of the death penalty for offenses committed by persons under 16 years of age has made, or can be expected to make, any measurable contribution to the goals that capital punishment is intended to achieve. It is, therefore, 'nothing more than the purposeless and needless imposition of pain and suffering,' *Coker v. Georgia*, 433 U.S. at 433 U.S. 592, and thus an unconstitutional punishment."

CASE SIGNIFICANCE

The *Thompson* case is significant because the Court helped to clarify the age limit at which juveniles may *not* be sentenced to death. The majority opinion was that "it would offend civilized standards of decency to execute a person who was less than 16-years-old at the time of his or her offense." While this decision was somewhat helpful, more pressing questions remained unanswered. For example, could a person who was a juvenile at the time of his or her offense be executed at all, and if so, at what age *would* the imposition of a death sentence be constitutional? These questions remained unanswered until the following year, when the Court revisited this issue in *Stanford v. Kentucky.*

STANFORD v. KENTUCKY
492 U.S. 361 (1989)

FACTS
In granting certiorari to this case, the Supreme Court consolidated the facts of two separate but similar cases. Stanford, a 17-year-old, was charged with first-degree murder, sodomy, robbery, and receiving stolen property for a crime committed at a gas station. Given his age, Stanford was eligible to have his case heard in juvenile court. However, in light of the seriousness of the crime and the unsuccessful attempts of the juvenile justice system to treat Stanford for past acts of delinquency, the prosecutor was allowed to try the case in adult court. At trial, Stanford was convicted on all four felonies and sentenced to death plus 45 years. The second case involved Wilkins, a juvenile charged with first-degree murder of a convenience store attendant, armed criminal action, and carrying a concealed weapon. At the time of his crime Wilkins was 16 years and 6 months old. Under Missouri law, Wilkins could not automatically be tried as an adult, so prosecutors sought and were granted permission to try him in adult court. At his trial Wilkins pleaded guilty to all charges. At the sentencing hearing, both the prosecutor and Wilkins himself urged the court to impose a death sentence. Both sides got their wish. The case was eventually heard by the US Supreme Court.

ISSUE
Is it cruel and unusual to impose a death sentence on a juvenile whose crime was committed when the offender was 16 or 17 years old?

HOLDING
No. The Constitution does not prohibit states from imposing a death sentence on a juvenile who was 16 or 17 years old at the time the crime was committed.

RATIONALE
In another 5–4 split decision, the Supreme Court ruled that the imposition of a death sentence for crimes committed at age 16 or 17 is not cruel and unusual punishment. In so ruling, the Court addressed the question it had failed to resolve in its earlier ruling in *Thompson v. Oklahoma*—is it constitutional to put juveniles to death? It ruled that "the imposition of capital punishment on an individual for a crime committed at age 16 or 17 years of age does not constitute cruel and unusual punishment under the Eighth Amendment." Thus, it is clear from this ruling that (1) the minimum age at which juveniles may constitutionally be put to death is 16 years old; and (2) juveniles 15 years old and younger may not be put to death. In writing the majority opinion, Justice Scalia took the opportunity to address the Court's earlier opinion regarding the so-called evolving standards of decency expressed in *Thompson.* According to Scalia, there is no consensus against the execution of 16- or 17-year-olds. As evidence, he pointed to the fact that 37 states permit capital punishment and less than half of those states (15) decline to impose such sentences upon children under the age of 16 years old. This, he argued, is a far cry from a "national consensus"; and besides, the Court was not telling the states what they should do, it was merely informing them what they *may* do.

CASE EXCERPT
"We discern neither a historic nor a modern societal consensus forbidding the imposition of capital punishment on any person who murders at 16 or 17 years of age. Accordingly, we conclude that such punishment does not offend the Eighth Amendment's prohibition against cruel and unusual punishment."

CASE SIGNIFICANCE
The *Stanford* decision is significant because it clearly addressed the questions the Court refused to answer in *Thompson v. Oklahoma.* Taken together, then, the two cases—*Thompson* and *Stanford*—say that imposing a death sentence upon a juvenile who was 15 years old or younger at the time the crime was committed constitutes cruel and unusual punishment and is therefore unconstitutional. However, imposing a death sentence upon a juvenile who was 16 years old or older at the time of the crime is constitutional. It is important to note that the Supreme Court did not say that states *must* impose a death sentence; rather, it

STANFORD v. KENTUCKY *(cont.)*
simply provided upper and lower age limits on when they may.

ROPER v. SIMMONS

543 U.S. 551, (2005)

FACTS

Christopher Simmons, age 17, and a 15-year-old accomplice, Charles Benjamin, were convicted of murdering 46-year-old Shirley Crook. Before committing the act, Simmons told his friends he wanted to kill someone and he concocted a plan with three of them. On the night of September 9, 1993, only Simmons and Benjamin entered the home via an open window. They subdued Mrs. Crook and bound her hands, mouth and eyes with leather straps and duct tape. The boys then drove Mrs. Crook in her own minivan to a state park where the bindings on her feet and hands were reinforced with electrical wire and she was dumped from a bridge into the Meramec River. Her body was later recovered by fishermen; the cause of death was drowning. After bragging to friends about the crime, Simmons and Benjamin were arrested. While in police custody Simmons confessed to the crime and revealed that he knew Shirley Crook from an earlier encounter with her involving a car accident. That's why, he claims, he had to kill her: "because the bitch seen my face." Simmons was charged with burglary, kidnapping, theft, and first-degree murder. Due to his age, he was charged and convicted as an adult and sentenced to death. In 2002 Simmons filed a habeas corpus petition with the Missouri State Supreme Court arguing that the US Supreme Court's decision in *Atkins* v. *Virginia*, 536 U.S. 304 (2002), which prohibited the execution of a mentally retarded person, establish the same constitutional prohibition on the execution of a juvenile who was under age 18 when the crime was committed. The Missouri State Supreme Court agreed and Simmons's death sentence was set aside and replaced with a sentence of life in prison without parole (LWOP). Clearly, the US Supreme Court granted certiorari here to resolve a question about death penalty for juveniles. But, as Justice Scalia notes in his dissent, this case is also about the Missouri State Supreme Court overstepping its judicial authority.

ISSUES

(1) Once the US Supreme Court holds that a particular punishment is *not* "cruel and unusual," can a lower court reach a different conclusion based on its own analysis of evolving standards? (2) Is the imposition of a death sentence on a person who commits murder at age 17 cruel and unusual and thusly in violation of the Eighth and Fourteenth Amendments?

HOLDING

(1) No, but in this case the Court agreed. (2) Yes. In a 5–4 decision the Court ruled that executing minors for crimes committed as juveniles is cruel and unusual and thus a violation of the Eighth and Fourteen Amendments.

RATIONALE

The majority argued that "evolving standards of decency" in America have reached a point at which the death penalty, at least for juveniles, is no longer defensible. In 2005, 30 states prohibited the death penalty, either barring it outright or made it a legislative impossibility for juveniles. In the other 20 states executions were rare. If there had been any discernible evolution in standards since *Atkins* it was in the consistent direction toward abolishment. Capital punishment has always been reserved for offenders whose crimes are "most deserving of execution." But juveniles, as a class, are less developed—physically and emotionally—than adults, and more easily influenced by group dynamics predisposing them to risk and mistakes. In spite of the obvious cruelty of Simmons's actions, the majority still felt it would be cruel to "extinguish his life and his potential to attain a mature understanding of his own humanity."

Due to developmental changes in the human brain from adolescence through the mid-20s, juveniles are not and cannot be cognitively compared to adults. Much like the mentally ill, juveniles are not always fully in control of their mood, emotions, or behaviors, which often renders them less blameworthy than adults when they make mistakes and less liable for their actions. This is precisely why we deny them certain adult privileges such as voting, working, driving, smoking, drinking, leaving school, getting married, entering into contracts, joining the military, and gambling. We deny those privileges because "it's for their own good"; they're not mature enough to make those important decisions, *yet*.

Finally, the majority argues that the weight of world opinion is against us on this issue. By now all industrialized, democratic nations had banned capital punishment from crimes involving youthful offenders, and most outlawed it for adults too; the United States was an aberration among the international community.

CASE EXCERPT

"Respondent and his *amici* have submitted, and petitioner does not contest, that only seven countries other than the United States have executed juvenile offenders since 1990: Iraq, Pakistan, Saudi Arabia, Yemen, Nigeria, the Democratic Republic of Congo, and China. Since then each of these countries has either abolished capital punishment for juveniles or made public disavowal of the practice. In sum, it is fair to say that the United States now stands alone in a world that has turned its face against the juvenile death penalty."

CASE SIGNIFICANCE

As a public policy issue, *Roper* is easily among the most significant cases in juvenile justice. It banned the death penalty for juveniles entirely and for the foreseeable future. It summarily overturned all death sentences imposed on juvenile offenders since *Eddings* (1982) and another 16 years past the ruling in *Stanford* (1989). Simmons and similarly situated convicts had their sentences commuted to LWOP. More importantly, the decision riled up the policy debate about the kinds of sentences that *are* both fair and appropriate for juveniles. Why, for example, if we cannot "extinguish" convicts until they attain a mature understanding of their own humanity, do we sentence them to life *without* parole? On the other hand, defenders of capital punishment rightly argue, since when do "we" (the US) care about the international community?

GRAHAM v. FLORIDA

560 U.S. .—(2010)

FACTS

Terrence Graham was 16 years old when he was convicted of armed burglary and attempted armed robbery. He served a year-long sentence and was released. Six months later, Graham was tried and convicted of a violent, armed, home invasion robbery and sentenced to life in prison without parole. On appeal, Graham attempted to assure the court that his prison experiences left him a reformed man. "I made a promise to God and myself," he said, "that if I get a second chance, I'm going to do whatever it takes to get to the [National Football League]." The crux of his legal appeal was that on its face, the imposition of a life sentence on a juvenile without the possibility of parole violates the Eighth Amendment because it constitutes cruel and unusual punishment. Both the Florida District Court of Appeals and the Florida Supreme Court disagreed.

ISSUE

Does the imposition of a life sentence without parole (LWOP) on a juvenile convicted of a nonhomicide offense violate the Eighth Amendment's prohibitions against cruel and unusual punishment?

HOLDING

Yes. The Eight and Fourteenth Amendment's cruel and unusual punishments clause does not permit a juvenile offender to be sentenced to life in prison without parole for crimes involving anything less than homicide.

RATIONALE

Based on precedence set down in *Atkins* and *Roper*, this decision was arrived at quite easily and in much the same way: (1) LWOP is an exceptionally harsh penalty that should be reserved only for cases involving juveniles charged with homicide; (2) juveniles, as a class, are categorically less culpable than the average criminal and thereby less deserving of the most severe punishments; (3) juveniles are more capable of change than adults—they cannot yet be said to possess an "irretrievably depraved character"; (4) there is a national consensus against LWOP; and 5) LWOP for juveniles for nonhomicidal crimes also has been "rejected the world over."

CASE EXCERPT

"To justify life without parole on the assumption that the juvenile offender forever will be a danger to society requires the sentencer to make a judgment that the juvenile is incorrigible. The characteristics of juveniles make that judgment questionable. It is difficult even for expert psychologists to differentiate between the juvenile offender whose crime reflects unfortunate yet transient immaturity, and the rare juvenile offender whose crime reflects irreparable corruption (*Roper v. Simmons*, 543 U.S. 560)."

GRAHAM v. FLORIDA (cont.)

CASE SIGNIFICANCE

This ruling extended the Court's logic in *Roper*. It is part of a series of cases that limit the severity of juveniles punishments. Today we know more than ever about adolescent brain development and its impact on teen behavior. Much of that research suggests that juveniles, as a class, are not fully formed human beings and probably won't finish developing until their mid-twenties. At the time this book went to press, the Court was pondering two cases involving life sentences for juveniles. The justices sounded closely split and uncertain over whether to set new constitutional limits on the imposition of prison terms for young murderers. If the justices abolished life terms for anyone under age 18, this could affect the sentences of some 2,300 prisoners nationwide, including Christopher Simmons.

MILLER v. ALABAMA

567 U.S.—(2012)

FACTS

This case was decided concurrently with another case, *Jackson v. Hobbs*. Both cases involve 14-year-old boys who were convicted of murder and statutorily sentenced to mandatory terms of life in prison without the possibility of parole. In the present case, Kuntrell Jackson and two other boys decided to rob a video store. On the way to committing the robbery, Jackson learned that one of the boys, Derrick Shields, was carrying a sawed-off shotgun in his coat sleeve. While Jackson waited outside, the other two accomplices entered the store, pointed the gun at the clerk, and demanded money. The clerk refused. When the clerk threatened to call the police Shields shot and killed her. All three boys fled on foot empty-handed. Jackson was subsequently charged as an adult and convicted of robbery and murder. Due to mandatory sentencing laws in Alabama at the time, the judge did not have the discretion to impose a sentence other than life in prison without the possibility of parole. In essence, state law mandated that Jackson die in prison even if the judge or jury would have thought that his age and the nature of his offense made a lesser sentence (i.e., life *with* the possibility of parole) more appropriate.

ISSUE

Does the imposition of a life without parole sentence on a juvenile violate the Eighth Amendment's prohibition against cruel and unusual punishment?

HOLDING

For the most part, as currently practiced, yes. The Eighth Amendment's prohibition against cruel and unusual punishment guarantees that individuals will not be subject to excessive sanctions. That right follows from the principle of justice that punishment for a crime should be graduated and proportioned to both the offender and the offense. Therefore, the Eighth Amendment forbids a sentencing scheme that *mandates* life in prison without possibility of parole for juvenile homicide offenders.

RATIONALE

Consistent with previous rulings in *Roper* and *Graham*, the Court here again noted that because juveniles have diminished culpability and greater prospects for reform, they are less deserving of the most severe punishments. In short, children lack maturity and often possess an underdeveloped sense of responsibility; they are more vulnerable to negative influences and often lack the ability to extricate themselves from crime-producing settings; and their traits are less fixed, meaning that their actions should not be considered evidence of irretrievable depravity. In addition to these now familiar arguments the Court also pointed out that among the 29 jurisdictions mandating life without parole for children, about half do so without regard to age. This means that juvenile offenders are automatically transferred to adult court with little to no opportunity (but for those states that permit reverse waivers) to seek transfer back to juvenile court. Indeed, many of those states, including Idaho and Nebraska, set no minimum age for who may be transferred to adult court in the first place, thus applying life-without-parole mandates to children of any age. Moreover, many of these same states place the transfer decision exclusively in the hands of prosecutors by state statute and those statutes are typically silent on matters of standards, protocols, or appropriate considerations for prosecutors to follow. Even when states give transfer-stage discretion to judges, judges rarely have full information about the child or the circumstances of his or her offense at the pretrial transfer decision stage. At the time of this decision, fifteen states made life without parole discretionary for juveniles. Only 15 percent of all life-without-parole sentences came from those jurisdictions, while the other 85 percent came from states that mandated such sentences. Therefore, the Court held that the mandatory imposition of life without parole on juvenile killers is inconsistent with the individualized sentencing requirments previously outlined in *Roper* and *Graham*.

CASE EXCERPT

"Such mandatory penalties, by their nature, preclude a sentencer from taking account of an offender's age and the wealth of characteristics and circumstances attendant to it. Under these schemes, every juvenile will receive the same sentence as every other—the 17-year-old and the 14-year-old, the shooter and the accomplice, the child from a stable household and the child from the chaotic and abusive one. And still worse, each juvenile (including these two 14-year-olds) will receive the same sentence as the vast majority of adults committing similar homicide offenses—but really, as *Graham* noted, a *greater* sentence than those adults will serve."

CASE SIGNIFICANCE

This decision, while significant, offers only a narrow ruling on the process by which juveniles may be sentenced to life without parole. Rather than barring this class of sentence entirely (as was done in *Roper* regarding the juvenile death penalty, and life without parole for nonhomicide cases in *Graham*), the Court simply stated that it is unconstitutional to make such sentences mandatory. Indeed, it leaves open the possibility that such sentences could still be imposed. The Court sent both cases back to their respective state courts to make the kind of individualized sentencing decision that the new ruling demands. What sentencing judges now must do, when a youth is convicted of murder, is to assess the age of that individual, their childhood and life experiences, the degree of responsibility the youth was capable of exercising, and the youth's chances for rehabilitation. Only if the judge then concludes that life without parole is proportionate to the offense in question, given all of the factors that mitigate the youth's guilt, can s/he impose such a sentence. Unfortunately, the decision provided no specific guidelines on how judges can/should proceed in making such determinations. Because of this, judges are expected to experience great difficulty distinguishing between a juvenile whose crime reflected "unfortunate yet transient immaturity" and "the rare juvenile offender whose crime reflects irreparable corruption."

DISCUSSION QUESTIONS

1. The ruling in *Baker v. Hamilton* implies that it might be constitutional for juveniles to be housed in an adult jail if no other juvenile facility is available and they are separated from the adult inmate population. What does it mean to be separated? Is it simply physical separation, or are there other criteria that must be met?

2. Critics of the juvenile court have argued that probation is not an effective deterrent to delinquency. After reading *In re Marcellus L.*, would you agree or disagree with the contention that probation is little more than a "slap on the wrist"? If it's so ineffective why do we utilize it so frequently?

3. Rural states like Idaho and Alaska have comparatively few alternatives to choose from when placing adjudicated delinquents. After reading the case of *Matter of Shawn V.*, do you feel the federal government has an obligation to help rural states establish more placement alternatives?

4. Review the case of *State in the Interest of D.G.W.* When a juvenile is ordered to pay restitution for property damage, what is the most appropriate way to assess damages? Should damages be calculated using the original purchase price, the cost of replacement, or the depreciated cost?

5. Can you think of a situation in which parents of a juvenile who commits a delinquent act should be made to pay restitution? Review the case of *A.S. v. State*.

6. Should the right to public protection trump concerns about least restrictive placements for juvenile sex offenders? Review the case of *G.A.D. v. State*. How many placement options were available in Kenai, Alaska at the time?

7. If judges may impose fines and court costs on juveniles who, as a class, are generally considered "indigent," is it appropriate to incarcerate juveniles who fail to pay?

8. Compare the differing opinions of Justices Kennedy and Scalia on the "evolving standards of decency." How do the justices arrive at such divergent opinions when considering the exact same data?

9. Rulings like *Atkins, Roper*, and *Graham* are a radical departure from public policy of the 1980s; do these decisions follow a common philosophical theme? If so, describe it. How and why have our perceptions of youth changed?

10. In March 2012, the Supreme Court heard oral arguments in the cases of Kuntrell Jackson and Evan Miller, both 14-year-old killers sentenced to life without parole. Do you agree with this most recent decision and if so why?

CHAPTER EIGHT

CONDITIONS OF CONFINEMENT

BENJAMINE STEINER, UNIVERSITY OF NEBRASKA – OMAHA
RIANE MILLER, UNIVERSITY OF SOUTH CAROLINA

INMATES OF THE BOYS TRAINING SCHOOL v. AFFLECK, *346 F.SUPP. 1354 (D.R.I. 1972)*

MORALES v. TURMAN, *383 F.SUPP. 53 (E.D. TEX. 1974)*

NELSON v. HEYNE, *491 F.2D 352 (7TH CIR. 1974)*

CRUZ v. COLLAZO, *450 F.SUPP. 235 (D.P.R. 1978)*

C.J.W. BY AND THROUGH L.W. v. STATE, *853 P.2D 4 (KAN. 1993)*

STATE EX REL. SOUTHER v. STUCKEY, *867 S.W.2D 579 (MO. APP. 1993)*

HORN BY PARKS v. MADISON COUNTY FISCAL COURT 22 F.3D 653 (6TH CIR. 1994)

TUNSTALL EX REL. TUNSTALL v. BERGESON, *5 P.3D 691 (WASH. 2000)*

INTRODUCTION

The idea of confining youth in facilities was borrowed from England. As early as the mid-1500s, England established the Bridewell Institution to handle youthful miscreants. The undergirding theory of Bridewell was to teach the confined youth skills and trades that they could use upon their release, and in so doing instill a sense of discipline that would make the youth conform to the norms of society. In the United States, institutions for juveniles started opening in the early 1800s. With the beginning of the Industrial Revolution came a growth in what was dubbed the "dangerous class": typically homeless or street kids who, possibly out of need, committed minor delinquent acts and instilled fear in the minds of society. Consequently, the use of formal controls began to be employed as the once strong social control of the family began to break down.

One way in which the courts controlled these wayward youth was through the use of institutions. These early institutions, called houses of refuge, largely borrowed from the Bridewell philosophy by attempting to instill discipline in youth and teach them skills. The idea followed the parens patriae philosophy in which the state maintains a responsibility to care for its youth. Therefore, if a family could not take care of or provide for its children, the state would intervene and attempt to act in the juveniles' best interests.

Although the intents of these facilities and those who founded them were noble, they often fell short of their desired results. The facilities had little oversight, and misuses of power were common. Youth were often held for long periods of time for minor or status offenses. In addition, they were often subjected to poor conditions and acts of brutality, meted out in the belief that the youth merely needed discipline that they were not receiving at home. Over time, and with the establishment of the juvenile court in 1899, conditions improved. Although juveniles were still sent to institutions for minor or status offenses as well as delinquent acts, there began to be more formalized procedures. In addition, the interventions that were being implemented were not solely based on discipline, but therapeutic theory as well. However, despite these positive strides, there was still a lack of professionalism and oversight of the facilities. In addition, inadequate funding was allocated toward juvenile institutions; thus, these youth were often held in old school buildings and adult correctional facilities. Eventually, following the lead of the adult system, the courts became involved. Civil litigation and habeas corpus petitions began to be filed on behalf of the youth confined in facilities as they began to challenge the conditions and treatment to which they were subjected. Similar to other areas in juvenile justice, the courts played a major role in shaping the procedures and establishing guidelines for juvenile facilities to follow.

Following the path of challenges in the adult system, juvenile cases began to come to the attention of the courts in the 1960s. Some decisions ruled that conditions violated juveniles' due process right to rehabilitation. The courts, under the auspices of the parens patriae philosophy, determined that juvenile delinquents had a constitutional right to be rehabilitated. In addition, the courts examined the conditions and treatment juveniles were subjected to in facilities. This contributed to the formalization and development of standards for juvenile institutions. Specifically, the courts prohibited the use of corporal punishment, standardized medication distribution, and applied a due process protection to juveniles waived to adult criminal court by affording them a right to an education. These are just some of the measures the courts have taken that govern the manner in which the state can treat confined juveniles. In this chapter, we review the leading cases that have guided the standards for the conditions of confinement for juveniles.

INMATES OF THE BOYS TRAINING SCHOOL v. AFFLECK

346 F.Supp. 1354 (D.R.I. 1972)

FACTS

Five juveniles sought a preliminary injunction to cease confinement of juveniles in an adult correctional institution, a former women's reformatory. In addition, the juveniles challenged the conditions of confinement in the training school. The juveniles who were committed to the training school were held for several reasons: adjudicated delinquent, pending trial, declared wayward by the court, found to be dependent or neglected, or voluntarily committed by their parents. After escapes and disciplinary problems in the school

became prevalent, the youth were sent to institutions known as Annex B, Annex C, Annex C cellblock, and the maximum security building of the adult correctional institution. These transfers occurred without prior notice or an administrative or judicial hearing. The juveniles sought to stop isolation of any juvenile in a room for more than two hours without a psychiatrist's certificate, and in any event, for more than 24 hours in a seven-day period. Additionally, the juveniles sought rights such as education, drug treatment, vocational counseling, and the like.

ISSUES

Did conditions of confinement at the training school violate the prohibition of cruel and unusual punishment offered by the Eighth Amendment? Did the confinement of juveniles in a former women's reformatory violate the equal protection and due process clauses of the Constitution?

HOLDING

Yes and yes. At the training school for boys, isolation of juveniles in cold, dark isolation cells containing only a mattress and a toilet constituted cruel and unusual punishment. Confinement of juveniles in a former women's reformatory were antirehabilitative and in violation of due process and equal protection.

RATIONALE

The court pointed out that many of the boys at the training school were there for what they were, not what they did. In addition, the court illustrated that the purpose of confinement of juveniles is instructive and reformative, not punitive. An adjudication is not the same as a conviction, as the child is not seen as criminal. The court pointed out that juveniles are afforded all of the procedural safeguards of adults except those that may contradict rehabilitative ideals, such as a trial by jury. Therefore, due process in the juvenile justice system requires that the postadjudication stage adhere to the rehabilitation philosophy. However, the court considered this case in the context of those children adjudicated delinquent, as society has a right to be protected from these juveniles as well. In reference to Annex B, the court found that the conditions there were antirehabilitative and therefore a violation of both equal protection and due process of law. In examining maximum security, the court was disturbed by the testimony of two boys who were confined in maximum security and indicated that they had learned little

INMATES OF THE BOYS TRAINING SCHOOL v. AFFLECK
(cont.)

more than how to become better criminals. Further, the boys stated that they were threatened by attacks and that they did not participate in any rehabilitative programming. Although the court recognized that some juveniles may be detrimental to the operation of a facility, they argued that there must be some better way of dealing with them. With regard to Annex C and Annex C cellblock, the court found that the only reason people were housed there was for punishment. Therefore, due to the fact that little or no rehabilitation occurred, these two areas were in violation of due process. As to the other claims of the juveniles, the court could not find conclusive evidence to sustain their claims. The court concluded by emphasizing that its judgment did not reflect on the defendants' choice of theory of rehabilitation techniques. The court realized that the defendants had been handicapped by a lack of adequate facilities and personnel to deal with the juveniles in their care. Therefore, the issue was not the good or bad faith of the defendants, but rather the issue of protection of the constitutional rights of the boys confined in the defendants' facility.

CASE EXCERPT

"Rehabilitation, then, is the interest which the state has defined as being the purpose of confinement of juveniles. Due process in the adjudicative stages of the juvenile justice system has been defined differently from due process in the criminal justice system because the goal of the juvenile system, rehabilitation, differs from the goals of the criminal system, which include punishment, deterrence and retribution. Thus due process in the juvenile justice system requires that the post-adjudicative stage of institutionalization further this goal of rehabilitation."

CASE SIGNIFICANCE

This case is important because it reflected the court's willingness to uphold the rehabilitative ideal on which the juvenile justice system was founded. The court acknowledged that there are juveniles who come to the attention of the juvenile court who are a danger to society and who may need to be confined. However, the court held that these and all other delinquent youth who are confined are entitled to treatment aimed at rehabilitation. The court did not attempt to specify the type of treatment, but ordered that youth are to be afforded some type of treatment. Consequently, the court held that the conditions at several of the institutions run by the defendants in this case were antirehabilitative in nature. Specifically, the sole purpose of these institutions was punishment, which is in violation of the juveniles' due process rights to rehabilitation. In addition, the facilities at one of the institutions violated the Eighth Amendment by failing to provide treatment and by imposing conditions that were cruel and unusual.

MORALES v. TURMAN

383 F.Supp. 53 (E.D. Tex. 1974)

FACTS

Two attorneys attempted to hold a conference in private with several children who were committed to the Texas Youth Council facilities. Access to their clients was denied and the attorneys filed a civil action. The attorneys filed a motion for a preliminary injunction seeking to enjoin the Texas Youth Council and their agents from interfering with the children's right to confer privately with counsel and from impeding in any manner their correspondence with counsel through the mail. The primary concern was that the youth had not been afforded due process during their adjudication hearings, rights that were guaranteed to them in *In re Gault*, 387 U.S. 1 (1967). The results of questionnaires revealed that many juveniles had not yet received full rights, and the suit expanded to include the question of procedural due process during an adjudication hearing. In addition, several of the questionnaires that were returned contained allegations of abuse within the institution. The judge approved a number of unique investigative requests by the plaintiffs to get into the institutions and determine whether practices within those institutions violated the prohibition of cruel and unusual punishment clause of the Eighth Amendment. Some of these requests included the interviewing of juvenile inmates for the purpose of determining how they were treated in the facilities and the granting of permission for participant observation teams of professionals to observe conditions of confinement in some selected institutions. A trial was held two years after the original motion was filed by the attorneys.

ISSUE

Did the Texas Youth Council engage in policy and practices that violated the Eighth Amendment's prohibition against cruel and unusual punishment?

HOLDING

Yes. Juveniles confined in the facilities of the Texas Youth Council have a right to proper treatment. Some of the practices and procedures of the Texas Youth Council constituted cruel and unusual punishment.

RATIONALE

The court drew a comparison between those who were committed to mental hospitals in civil proceedings and juveniles who were committed to the Texas Youth Council. In doing so, the court relied on a recent decision that held that any person involuntarily committed to a state mental hospital has a constitutional right to receive such individual treatment as will give him or her reasonable opportunity to be cured or improve his or her mental condition. The basis for commitment of a juvenile to the Texas Youth Council, which was to rehabilitate and reenter the juvenile into society, was clearly grounded in the parens patriae philosophy. Therefore, the court reasoned that juvenile must be given treatment. In addition, the court also found that schools under the jurisdiction of the Texas Youth Council, particularly Mountain View and Gatesville, had been the scenes of widespread physical and psychological brutality. In the emergency interim relief order, several practices found to be in violation of the Eighth Amendment's prohibition of cruel and unusual punishment were enjoined on the grounds that such practices were so severe as to degrade human dignity; were inflicted in a wholly arbitrary fashion; were so severe as to be unacceptable to contemporary society; and finally, were not justified in serving any purpose. Some of the practices found by the court to violate the Eighth Amendment were the widespread practice of beating, slapping, kicking, and otherwise physically abusing juveniles in the absence of any exigent circumstances; the use of tear gas and other chemical crowd-control devices in situations not posing an imminent threat to human life or an imminent and substantial threat to property; the placing of juveniles in solitary confinement or other secured facilities in the absence of any legislative or administrative limitation on the duration and intensity of the confinement and subject only to the unfettered discretion of a correctional officer; the requirement that inmates maintain silence during periods of the day merely for the purpose of punishment; and the performance of repetitive, nonfunctional, degrading, and unnecessary tasks. Some of those tasks included requiring a juvenile to pull grass without bending his knees on a large tract of ground not intended for cultivation or any other purpose; forcing him to move dirt with a shovel from one place on the ground to another and then back again many times; and making him buff a small area of the floor for a period of time exceeding that in which any reasonable person would conclude that the floor was sufficiently buffed. In conclusion, the court found that the practices of the Texas Youth Council constituted cruel and unusual punishment and that the juveniles were denied their due process right to treatment. The two facilities mentioned in the rationale were ordered closed by the court.

CASE EXCERPT

"It is clear that the Eighth Amendment's proscription applies to the state as well as to the federal government. Moreover, the protection applies to persons who have not been convicted of crimes, such as juveniles involuntarily committed to the state's institutions. Under the parens patriae theory, the juvenile must be given treatment lest the involuntary commitment amount to an arbitrary exercise of governmental power proscribed by the due process clause."

CASE SIGNIFICANCE

This case is important for several reasons. First, the court contended that juveniles are to be afforded an opportunity to rehabilitate. The court pointed to the Juvenile Code, clearly grounded in the parens patriae philosophy, which maintains that the state has a responsibility to rehabilitate delinquent youth. The court contended this is analogous to the treatment of the mentally ill. The court held that all delinquent juveniles, even those that warrant confinement, have a constitutional right to rehabilitative measures. Second, the court ordered the investigation of practices that were occurring within several facilities, a relatively new practice that had begun in some adult facilities during the same time. Even in the present day, this is a rare occurrence. Based on the findings of the investigation, the court actually closed two of the facilities by holding that their practices violated the Eighth Amendment rights of the juveniles who were confined there. This is significant because the courts will typically make orders that must be followed when investigating a state agency; however, it is rare that they will find conditions so in violation of the Eighth Amendment that they warrant the closing of the facility.

NELSON v. HEYNE

491 F.2d 352 (7th Cir. 1974)

FACTS

A suit was filed against the Indiana Boys' School alleging unconstitutional practices and policies. The school was a medium-security state correctional institution for boys ages 12 to 18. Of those, it was estimated that one-third were noncriminal offenders. The boys resided in 16 cottages, and the facility included a school, gymnasium, and administration building. The average length of incarceration at the school was about six and one-half months. The maximum capacity of the school was 300; however, the population was usually around 400. In addition, two staff members had observed beatings. During the beatings, a fraternity paddle that was 12 inches long and one-half to two inches thick was used. The testimony of the juveniles indicated that children weighing 160 pounds were struck five times on their clothed buttocks by a staff member, often by one who weighed 285 pounds. The beatings often caused painful injuries. The complaint alleged that the defendants' practices and policies violated the Eighth and Fourteenth Amendment rights of the juveniles under their care. The plaintiffs moved for a temporary restraining order to protect them from, inter alia, defendants' corporal punishment and the use of tranquilizing drugs.

ISSUES

Does corporal punishment inflicted with a paddle constitute cruel and unusual punishment? Is the use of a tranquilizing drug administered intramuscularly by staff, without trying medication short of drugs and without adequate medical guidance and prescription, cruel and unusual punishment? Do juveniles have a right to treatment under the due process clause of the Fourteenth Amendment and the Indiana Juvenile Court Act?

HOLDING

Yes, yes, and yes. Practices in the Indiana Boys' School constituted conditions that violated the Eighth and Fourteenth Amendments.

RATIONALE

The court pointed out that it was not disputed that juveniles who misbehaved, attempted escape, or violated certain school rules were beaten routinely by guards under the defendants' supervision. However, there was no evidence that suggested formal procedures were in place to govern the administration of the beatings. Typically, they occurred after a decision was made by two or three staff members. In addition, expert testimony introduced at the trial indicated that the beatings did not serve as useful punishment or as treatment, and it could actually breed counter hostility resulting in a more aggressive child. Consequently, the court concluded that the beatings were unnecessary and excessive. In addition, witnesses for both the school and the juveniles testified that tranquilizing drugs, specifically Sparine and Thorazine, were occasionally administered to the juveniles for the purpose of controlling excited behavior, and not for psychotherapeutic treatment. The registered nurse and licensed practical nurse prescribed intramuscular dosages of the drugs upon recommendation from the staff under standing orders by the physician. Neither before nor after injections were the juveniles examined by medically competent staff members to determine their tolerances. The court held only that the use of disciplinary beatings and tranquility drugs in the circumstances shown by this record violated the plaintiffs' Fourteenth Amendment rights protecting them from cruel and unusual punishment. The court did not suggest that penal and reform institution physicians could not prescribe necessary tranquilizing drugs in appropriate cases. The court's concern was with the actual and potential abuses under policies where juveniles are beaten with an instrument causing serious injuries, and drugs that are administered to juveniles intramuscularly by staff without trying medication short of drugs and without adequate medical guidance and prescription. The court also relied on the history of a juvenile's right to treatment beginning in the social reform movement. In doing so, they held that juveniles have the right under the Fourteenth Amendment due process clause to rehabilitative treatment. In so holding, the court relied on the testimony of experts at the trial that indicated the classification system being used at the school was not adequate treatment and may not have been treatment at all. The court went on to say that treatment includes the right to minimum acceptable standards of care and treatment for juveniles and the right to individualized treatment and care.

CASE EXCERPT

"The uncontradicted authoritative evidence indicated that the practice does not serve as useful punishment or as treatment, and it actually breeds counter-hostility resulting in greater aggression by a child. For these reasons we find the beatings presently administered are unnecessary and therefore excessive. In our view, the 'right to treatment' includes the right to minimum acceptable standards of care and treatment for juveniles and the right to *individualized* care and treatment. When a state assumes the place of a juvenile's parents, it assumes as well the parental duties, and its treatment of its juveniles should, so far as can be reasonably required, be what proper parental care would provide. Without a program of individual treatment the result may be that the juveniles will not be rehabilitated, but warehoused, and that at the termination of detention they will likely be incapable of taking their proper places in free society; their interests and those of the state and the school thereby being defeated."

CASE SIGNIFICANCE

This case is important for a number of reasons. First, it was one of the first times a court ordered that a type of treatment was not appropriate and possibly not even treatment at all. The court pointed out that juveniles have a due process right to treatment or rehabilitation, as has been the case in many states. The courts have typically justified this with the parens patriae philosophy the juvenile justice system was founded on. However, in this case, the court examined the type of treatment that was being employed at the facility and determined that because it did not meet certain standards it violated the juveniles' due process rights. Therefore, the court effectively held that treatment must meet certain standards to be considered treatment and not be in violation of the Fourteenth Amendment. Second, the court ruled that beatings, which were controlled to an extent, violated the juveniles' Eighth Amendment right prohibiting cruel and unusual punishment. This is important because it reflected a time when corporal punishment of this type was prevalent in schools and facilities until the courts stepped in and determined that it violated the juveniles' rights. Further, the court also ruled on the administration of psychotropic medications. The court did not determine that these types of medications could not be used on juveniles. However, it did hold that there must be standards in place for the administration and prescription of such medications. Otherwise, their use violated the juveniles' right to be secure from cruel and unusual punishment, which is guaranteed to them by the Eighth Amendment.

CRUZ v. COLLAZO
450 F.Supp. 235 (D.P.R. 1978)

FACTS

Cruz, a minor, was within the custody of the Secretary of the Department of Social Services of the Commonwealth of Puerto Rico and residing at the Guaynabo State Home for Boys. Cruz contended, in a class action suit, that he was not receiving adequate rehabilitative treatment and therefore the defendants were depriving him of his rights secured by the due process clause as guaranteed by the Fifth and Fourteenth Amendments. During the discovery and filing of legal memoranda in this case, a motion to dismiss was filed by the defendant alleging, among other grounds, that Cruz had escaped from the Guaynabo Treatment Center and thus could not represent the juveniles residing at the Guaynabo Home for Boys. Thereafter, Cruz returned to the Guaynabo Home for Boys, escaped again a few days later, and returned again four days later. Cruz was then transferred to the Industrial School for Boys in Mayaguez. Thereafter, Cruz filed a motion for a temporary restraining order alleging that the Mayaguez Industrial School was a maximum security juvenile institution which housed hardened delinquents, and that he had been transferred thereto without a hearing, all in deprivation of his constitutional rights to due process and equal protection. The court granted the order pending the outcome of a hearing on that issue.

ISSUE

Does the transfer of a juvenile from a nonsecure facility to a secure facility without a judicial hearing violate the due process and equal protection provisions of the Constitution?

HOLDING

No. The juvenile did not have a liberty expectation under the law of Puerto Rico to remain in one juvenile institution, so the transfer without a judicial hearing did not violate due process or equal protection rights.

RATIONALE

The court contended that *In re Gault* 387 U.S. 1 (1967) was not applicable to this case because the issue was at the postadjudicatory stage. The determination must be whether a life, liberty, or property interest within the meaning of the due process clause is at stake.

CRUZ v. COLLAZO (cont.)

The court pointed to *Meachum v. Fano* 427 U.S. 215 (1976), in which the Supreme Court held that an individual's grievous loss as a result of a state action is not by itself enough to trigger the application of the due process clause. Thus, for the due process clause to apply in the present case, Cruz had show some kind of liberty entitlement not to be transferred to a maximum security juvenile institution. Important to note are the FACTS that the transfer did not change the classification of Cruz as a juvenile and that the transfer occurred within the system of juvenile institutions in Puerto Rico. In *Meachum v. Fano,* the Supreme Court rejected the notion that any change in the conditions of confinement having a substantial adverse impact on the prisoner involved was sufficient to invoke the protections of the due process clause. The Supreme Court further said that the Constitution, by its own force, does not require that a person be confined in any particular prison. This court drew a line between the present case and *Meachum.* Therefore, it did not find a liberty interest had been created so as to accord the plaintiff a cause of action. The law states that once a juvenile is committed to the custody of the Puerto Rico Secretary of Social Services he or she is to be placed in a facility deemed appropriate by the secretary. Consequently, the request for permanent injunction was denied.

CASE EXCERPT

"For the Due Process Clause to apply in the present case, plaintiff must show some kind of liberty entitlement not to be transferred to a maximum security juvenile institution. It should be borne in mind that such transfer entails no change of plaintiff's classification as a juvenile delinquent and that the transfer is one within the system of *juvenile* institutions in Puerto Rico. Given a valid adjudication of juvenile delinquency, plaintiff has been constitutionally deprived of his liberty to the extent that the State may confine him and to subject him to its juvenile institution system so long as the conditions of confinement do not otherwise violate the Constitution."

CASE SIGNIFICANCE

This case is important because it represented the continuing trend of the courts to apply adult criminal case law to juvenile matters. In this case, the court used the Supreme Court's ruling in *Meachum,* where it held that change in a prisoner's confinement status does not

have a substantial enough impact to invoke the Fifth Amendment guarantee to due process. Essentially, the Court contended this is not a "critical stage" in the process. In the present case, the juvenile was transferred from one juvenile facility to another absent a hearing. The court held that the juvenile was not guaranteed any such hearing. In addition, the court pointed out that the juvenile remained in the juvenile system in Puerto Rico and the transfer did not change the juvenile's status. Consequently, the transfer was made under the parens patriae philosophy, as the juvenile was untreatable at the less secure facility because of his frequent escapes.

C.J.W. BY AND THROUGH L.W. v. STATE

853 P.2d 4 (Kan. 1993)

FACTS

On two separate occasions C.J.W., a 12-year-old boy, was allegedly assaulted and sexually molested by a boy named Randy while both were being detained at Johnson County Juvenile Hall. Randy had been committed to the custody of the State of Kansas Department of Social and Rehabilitative Services seven years before the alleged incident in a different county. Social and Rehabilitative Services files revealed that various officials, including Randy's social worker, had knowledge of Randy's violent and aggressive behavior long before the alleged attacks on C.J.W. The record revealed a long history of Randy acting out violently and aggressively at various placements throughout his journey through the juvenile justice system. Prior to being placed in the juvenile detention center, he had been at a group home where he had assaulted another resident with a pool ball. Allegedly, his first attack on C.J.W. took place the day he was transferred to the juvenile detention center. The records also indicated that there was knowledge that Randy had sexually deviant tendencies. Upon his transfer to juvenile hall, Randy's social worker talked with officials there, but did not provide any records or information regarding his history. C.J.W. contended that the state, because of its knowledge of Randy, had a duty to protect him from such a juvenile. The state contended it had immunity from liability in this case because it did not have an obligation to release such information unless directly asked by the juvenile detention staff.

ISSUES

Did the state have an obligation to ensure the safety of a minor placed in its care by taking reasonable steps to convey known information regarding the history of an aggressive and sexually deviant juvenile with whom the minor was likely to come into contact? Is the state liable under state law for the injuries suffered by the minor due to its failure to convey known relevant information to the appropriate authorities?

HOLDING

Yes and yes. The state owed a duty to the 12-year-old juvenile who was sexually assaulted while in a juvenile detention facility by a 17-year-old fellow inmate, to warn the juvenile detention authorities of the 17-year-old inmate's propensity for violence and sexually deviant conduct and to take reasonable steps to protect the juvenile from such an inmate when such information was known by both the juvenile caseworker and the Social and Rehabilitation Services Department. Such negligence by the state can lead to liability under the State Tort Claims Act.

RATIONALE

The court relied on an earlier case, *Durflinger v. Artiles* 727 F.2d 888 (1984), in which negligence was said to exist where there is a duty owed by one person to another and a breach of that duty occurs. In addition, for recovery to be had for such negligence the plaintiff must show (1) a causal connection between the duty breached and the injury received; and (2) that he or she was damaged by the negligence. The court pointed out that in the absence of a special relationship there was no duty on a person to control the conduct of a third person to prevent harm to others. C.J.W. argued that because the state had custody of Randy for the seven years prior to the alleged incident and knew of his dangerous tendencies, the state had a special relationship with both him and Randy that created a duty on behalf of the state to control Randy and protect him. C.J.W. relied on the Restatement of Torts that states that the state has a responsibility to provide reasonable care or to control the conduct of a third person to prevent him or her from intentionally harming others. C.J.W. also pointed to the Supreme Court's decision in *Cansler v. State* 675 P.2d 57 (1984), which stated that prison officials owe a duty of ordinary or reasonable care to safeguard a prisoner in their custody or control from attack from other prisoners. This duty is not violated in the absence of a

determination that the danger was known or, in the exercise of ordinary care, should have been known by prison officials. The state only becomes liable in the event that damage proximity results from a failure to exercise reasonable care to prevent harm. The court in the present case applied the Restatement of Torts indicating that the state had not only a duty to warn detention officials of Randy's propensities, but also to take reasonable steps to protect C.J.W. from Randy. In resolving the issue of liability, the state relied upon a discretionary function exception, indicating that it was up to the caseworker's judgment whether to inform the detention facility about Randy's history. The court contended that because of the state's duty to control Randy, warning others about his dangerous propensities and protecting persons in the position of C.J.W. was imposed by law and was ministerial, not discretionary. Consequently, the state was not entitled to the protection afforded by the discretionary function protection.

CASE EXCERPT

"Children who are taken into custody should be protected from others in custody and the duty to children such as the plaintiff is more compelling than that due either of the plaintiffs in *Cansler* and *Washington*. We have no hesitancy in concluding that §§ 315, 319, and 320 of the Restatement (Second) of Torts apply to this case and that the State not only had a duty to warn the officials of Juvenile Hall of Randy's propensities to commit violence but also to take reasonable steps to protect the plaintiff from Randy. Because the State's duty to control Randy, to warn others about his dangerous propensities, and to protect persons in the position of the plaintiff is imposed by law and is ministerial, not discretionary, the State is not entitled to the protection afforded by the discretionary function exception. SRS cannot rely upon its manual to avoid liability for its acts regarding a duty imposed by law."

CASE SIGNIFICANCE

This case is important because it attached liability to the state's actions or lack thereof. The court drew from the parens patriae philosophy, which is the underlying principle of most juvenile law and provides that the state must act in the best interest of the children in its care. In this case, the court held that the state had a responsibility to protect the juvenile in its care from another. In addition, the negligence on the part of the

C.J.W. BY AND THROUGH L.W. v. STATE *(cont.)*
social worker to provide the information so that the juvenile detention staff could provide such protection is open for liability suit.

STATE EX REL. SOUTHER v. STUCKEY
867 S.W.2d 579 (Mo. App. 1993)

FACTS
A suit was filed alleging that Souther negligently performed her duties as the administrator of the Waverly Youth Center, a residential youth facility operated by the Division of Youth Services. The petition alleged a youth was allowed to escape. The youth then went to the petitioner's home, assaulted the female petitioner and burned her home. The petitioner alleged that there were at least six other escapes from the center and asserted that Souther breached her duty to immediately notify the local police upon discovery of an escape or runaway. Souther was also alleged to have carelessly, negligently, and deliberately failed to maintain adequate security at the facility and supervision of the residents in numerous respects, including but not limited to the following: She did not provide for an adequate number of staff to supervise the residents of the facility; she did not provide adequate security measures to prevent the residents from leaving the building without authorization; she did not provide for adequate physical barriers preventing escape of residents, such as locks on doors, bars on windows, and a perimeter fence of the area; and she did not make adequate provision to ensure that the staff were trained in security procedures. These acts were characterized as duties mandatory, ministerial, and nondiscretionary, and the petitioner asked the court to grant relief due to Souther's negligent and reckless acts. Souther claimed protection under the official immunity doctrine, which provides that a public official is not civilly liable to members of the public for negligence arising out of the performance of discretionary duties.

ISSUE
Was the administrator liable to private citizens for the actions of an escaped juvenile who was under state custody and care at the time of the escape?

HOLDING
No. A residential youth facility administrator's regulatory duty to report a runaway to police is a duty owed to the state, not to the victims. Therefore, the public duty doctrine barred the victims from suing the facility administrator for actions of a juvenile while on escape status.

RATIONALE
The official immunity doctrine provides that a public official is not civilly liable to members of the public for negligence arising out of the performance of discretionary duties. The general rule is that public officers acting within the scope of their authority are not liable for injuries arising from their discretionary acts or omission, but they may be held liable for torts committed when acting in ministerial capacities. The court relied on *Kanagawa v. State* 685 S.W.2d 831 (1985) and *Sherrill v. Wilson* 653 S.W.2d 661 (1983), where those courts freed administrators from civil liability for discretionary decisions. Therefore, Souther was given official immunity as well. In addition, the court contended that Souther was not negligent in carrying out her ministerial duties. The duties of the administrator are to report runaways to the police, not to the individual citizens.

CASE EXCERPT
"It is clear that the allegations against relator should be dismissed based upon official immunity. The public duty doctrine recognizes that the duties of public officers are normally owed only to the general public and that a breach of such a duty will not support a cause of action by an individual injured thereby. The plaintiffs have not demonstrated that the regulation serves the 'special, direct, and distinctive interests' of individual members of the public, and therefore does not create a duty owed to them, a breach of which provides the basis for a private cause of action."

CASE SIGNIFICANCE
This case is important because it demonstrated the court's willingness to protect public employees from suits based upon the actions of individuals under their care or supervision. Similar to many other states, Missouri has in its law an immunity doctrine that protects public officials from suits alleging they were negligent in their duties, which caused public harm. Although previous court decisions have determined public employees are responsible to the individuals who are under their care or supervision, the courts have not attached a liability to the public. The court, therefore, contended these employees are liable to the state and not the general public.

HORN BY PARKS v. MADISON COUNTY FISCAL COURT
22 F.3d 653 (6th Cir. 1994)

FACTS

Horn, age 17, pleaded guilty to a robbery charge in the Madison County District Court. He was committed to the Cabinet of Human Resources and released to the custody of his parents pending placement under the condition that he remain within arm's reach of his parents. Five days later, Horn's parents reported that he had left home and his whereabouts were unknown. A complaint was signed and a pick-up order issued by a judge. The following day Horn turned himself in to his caseworker and was taken to a detention center. The detention center was an adult jail, newly opened, and designated for use as an intermittent juvenile holding facility where juvenile offenders could be held under statutorily prescribed conditions for a period not to exceed 24 hours. Horn was processed into the facility with his caseworker present. Both she and the jail deputy later testified Horn appeared in a good mood and coherent. Horn was taken to his cell and routine checks were performed about every 15 minutes. Five minutes after a check, where Horn appeared to be okay, he was found hanging from the bunk in his cell with a bedsheet tied around his neck. He subsequently suffered from brain damage and paralysis confining him to a wheelchair. His family filed suit, holding the county was negligent in his care.

ISSUES

Did the actions of the county detention facility staff amount to deliberate indifference to the juvenile's medical needs? Are juvenile detainees as a group at such high risk for suicide as to constitute a special class requiring special consideration based strictly on their age?

HOLDING

No and no. The failure of jail officials to take more than ordinary precautions to protect juvenile defendants from suicide did not constitute deliberate indifference to Horn's medical needs. Actions by such employees were consistent with the policies in place within the detention facility. Even though the Juvenile Justice Act discourages the placement of juveniles in facilities primarily dedicated to adult inmate care, the actions of the staff in this case did not amount to negligence. This

is true even if juveniles as a class are determined to be prone to suicide.

RATIONALE

The court assumed that the appellant would have been able to establish that his temporary lodging in the Madison County Detention Center was technically in violation of the Juvenile Justice Act because an acceptable alternative placement was available. However, the court could not find anything in the record showing the center's nature contributed in any way to the appellant's suicide attempt or resulting injury. The record demonstrated that the appellant was scrupulously shielded from the deleterious influences associated with adult facilities. The court pointed to the statutory guidance for the holding procedures and the special care the intake worker and staff took to protect the juvenile from the perils of adult confinement. The appellant's theory that he would have been better cared for in a juvenile facility because the staff would have been better equipped to handle him was just that, theory. It was speculation and the court did not find support for it in the record. The court pointed out that in order to demonstrate deliberate indifference the appellant would have had to show the conduct for which liability attached to be more culpable than mere negligence. In addition, it would have had to demonstrate deliberateness tantamount to intent to punish. The court contended that was not the case here.

CASE EXCERPT

"The first question posed is whether the alleged violation of this plan requirement is a deprivation of a 'right, privilege or immunity.' This inquiry turns on whether the requirement was intended to benefit appellant Horn. If so, the provision creates a right enforceable under Section 1983 unless it reflects merely a congressional preference rather than a binding obligation, or unless it is so vague and amorphous as to be beyond the competence of the judiciary to enforce. The requirement that juveniles not be detained in adult facilities unless no acceptable alternative is available is unquestionably intended to benefit juveniles like appellant."

CASE SIGNIFICANCE

This case is important because it illustrated that some states still allowed for the jailing of juveniles in adult facilities. In this jurisdiction special measures were

HORN BY PARKS v. MADISON COUNTY FISCAL COURT
(cont.)

in place so as not to subject a juvenile to long-term confinement in an adult facility. Nevertheless, confinement in an adult facility was still allowed. In addition, the court determined that jail officials did not have to provide the juvenile with any special treatment. Although the court discouraged the placing of the juveniles in adult facilities, it did not overturn the state's ability to utilize such a facility, nor did it require special attention be given to those juveniles confined there. This was important because it contradicted the separation of juveniles and adults intended by the juvenile court.

TUNSTALL EX REL. TUNSTALL v. BERGESON

5 P.3d 691 (Wash. 2000)

FACTS

Inmates brought a class action suit against the state and those school districts where Department of Corrections facilities are located. The inmates' class was certified to include all the individuals who are now, or who will in the future be committed to the custody of the Washington Department of Corrections, who are allegedly denied access to basic or special education during that custody, and who are, during that custody, under the age of 21, or disabled and under the age of 22. The inmates alleged that the state's failure to provide them with basic and special education services violated Article IX of the Washington constitution, the Federal Individuals with Disabilities Education Act, the Rehabilitation Act of 1973, and constitutional due process and equal protection clauses in the Fourteenth Amendment.

ISSUE

Does Article IX require the state to provide basic and special education to persons up to age 21 or 22 who are incarcerated in adult Department of Corrections facilities, and if so, is the state meeting its obligation?

HOLDING

No. The state is constitutionally required to provide educational services to children incarcerated in Department of Corrections facilities only up to age 18.

RATIONALE

For the purpose of deciding the issue in this case, the court first had to define "children" for the purposes of Article IX. The court held children under Article IX includes individuals up to age 18, including those children incarcerated in adult department of corrections facilities. The court pointed to the draft age, age of consent to marriage, ability to vote, and the like in supporting their definition of children. The court then countered the state's argument that the inmates' criminal conduct deprived them of their right to education by pointing to the legislature's decision that all children have a right to education up until age 18. Further, the legislature has seen fit to provide an educational program to department of corrections inmates. The court then turned its attention to whether the children incarcerated in the department's facilities were receiving their education. Article IX requires the state to create and provide for a general and uniform system of public schools, but nothing mandates that the education must be identical for all children within the state's borders. The court refused to micromanage the education system and disagreed with the inmates. The court contended the state was providing ample educational opportunities to the incarcerated children. The court supported the rational basis test in upholding the legislature's decision to treat incarcerated children differently from nonincarcerated children. The rationale supporting this is laid out in *Tommy P. v. Board of Commissioners* 645 P.2d 697 (1982), which indicated that incarcerated juveniles may in fact need an alternative style of schooling. In sum, the court held that children, as defined in Article IX of the Washington constitution, included individuals up to age 18, including individuals incarcerated in Department of Corrections facilities.

CASE EXCERPT

"We hold that 'children' under article IX includes individuals up to age 18, including those children incarcerated in adult DOC facilities. Under current law, only individuals *under* age 18 are required to attend school. This statute supports the idea that individuals are treated like adults once they hit age 18, as *choice* is commonly recognized as a hallmark of adulthood...Finally, although not within the education context, individuals over age 18 are generally emancipated and are able to marry without parental consent, to execute a will, to vote, to enter into a legally binding contract, to make medical decisions about their own care and those of their issue, and to sue and be sued. These statutes further demonstrate that the common understanding of the definition of 'children' for most purposes in Washington, including education, includes individuals up to age 18."

CASE SIGNIFICANCE

This case is important because it afforded rights to juveniles who have been transferred to the adult criminal justice system. Juveniles who are incarcerated in juvenile facilities are typically provided education in keeping with the rehabilitative ideal of the juvenile justice system. However, those youth who are transferred to adult criminal court and convicted as adults are typically housed in adult correctional facilities which are more philosophically grounded in punishment and incapacitation. Consequently, they may not have the educational opportunities available in the juvenile system. Although the court held that juveniles are entitled to an education until they reach age 18, the court did not specify what type of education. Therefore, the state must merely provide youth in adult correctional facilities with a basic education.

DISCUSSION QUESTIONS

1. What have the courts said constitutes cruel and unusual punishment in reference to confinement?
2. Why do juveniles have a right to treatment?
3. What do government employees owe juveniles in their care?
4. What do government employees owe the public with regard to the juveniles under their supervision?
5. According to the courts, what rights are guaranteed to confined juveniles?
6. In order to transfer a juvenile from a nonsecure facility to a secure facility; must a judicial hearing first occur?
7. According to the courts, may a state be held liable for injuries suffered by a minor due to its failure to convey known relevant information to the appropriate authorities?
8. Are states constitutionally required to provide basic education to incarcerated juveniles?
9. According to the courts, what is the main purpose of confining juveniles?
10. What is the purpose of the public duty doctrine?

CHAPTER NINE

THE RELEASE DECISION

BENJAMIN STEINER, UNIVERSITY OF NEBRASKA – OMAHA
RIANE MILLER, UNIVERSITY OF SOUTH CAROLINA

REED v. DUTER, *416 F.2D 733 (7TH CIR. 1969)*

P.R. ET AL. v. STATE, *210 S.E.2D 839 (GA. APP. 1974)*

M.J.W. v. STATE, *210 S.E.2D 842 (GA. APP. 1974)*

STATE EX REL. J.R. v. MACQUEEN, *259 S.E.2D 420 (W. VA. 1979)*

IN THE MATTER OF RODRIGUEZ, *687 S.W.2D 421 (TEX. APP. 1985)*

WATTS v. HADDEN, *627 F.SUPP. 727 (D. COLO. 1986)*

IN THE INTEREST OF DAVIS, *546 A.2D 1149 (PA. SUPER. 1988)*

IN RE CURTIS T., *263 CAL.RPTR. 296 (CAL. CT. APP. 1989)*

J.K.A. v. STATE, *855 S.W.2D 58 (TEX. APP. 1993)*

IN THE MATTER OF LUCIO F.T., *888 P.2D 958 (N.M. APP. 1994)*

MATTER OF TAPLEY, *865 P.2D 12 (WASH. APP. 1994)*

J.R.W. v. STATE, *879 S.W.2D 254 (TEX. APP. 1994)*

IN THE INTEREST OF D.S. AND J.V., *MINOR CHILDREN, 652 SO.2D 892 (FLA. APP. 1995)*

IN RE KACY S., *80 CAL.RPTR.2D 432 (CAL. CT. APP. 1998)*

IN RE J.W., *787 N.E.2D 727 (ILL. S.C. 2003)*

INTRODUCTION

In the adult criminal system, probation is a conditional sentence that both punishes offenders and provides them with the opportunity to rehabilitate themselves in community-based programs. Parole is a conditional release that offers offenders the opportunity to finish their sentences in the community. In the juvenile justice system, a disposition of probation is fashioned to rehabilitate youths who have come to the attention of the court. Parole is seen as an opportunity for juveniles to transition and adjust back into their home environments. Given these two divergent philosophies, the juvenile court often individualizes a youthful offender's disposition of aftercare treatment under the guise of parens patriae.

It is common for the terms and conditions of probation to include measures of accountability that are designed to rehabilitate the juvenile, not just punish. Some juvenile probation and parole conditions are designed to protect the community; however, they are also ordered in an effort to provide structure and guidance to a young person's life. In addition, the juvenile court also imposes skill-building or competency development terms that are designed to treat juveniles or teach them to recognize the factors that led to the commission of a delinquent act. This balanced approach to sentencing is currently the model most juvenile courts employ when they disposition juvenile offenders.

However, this balanced approach was not always modus operandi in the juvenile justice system. In this country's early years, the state relied solely on families to deal with juvenile misbehavior. If juveniles committed acts serious enough to warrant formal intervention, they were often dealt with in the same forum as their adult counterparts. However, with the industrial revolution more people began working long hours and the once strong social control of the family broke down. This marked the growth of what was dubbed the "dangerous class," which was largely made up of street youth. Consequently the state, acting under parens patriae, began to rely on more formal measures of control when dealing with juvenile delinquents. The courts became involved and began to send wayward youth to reformatories and foster homes in an effort to teach them discipline and self-control. This course of action also coincided with the child-savers movement, led by wealthy, civic-minded citizens who tried to rescue unfortunate children by placing them in houses of refuge and reform schools. The undergirding theory of these movements was that youth would remain in these facilities until they conformed to value hard work and desired to become contributing members of society.

The ideology of the child savers and early reform movements paved the way for an autonomous juvenile court. Established in 1899 in Cook County, Illinois, the juvenile court was completely separate from the adult criminal court and was designed to deal in a paternalistic fashion with the juveniles who came to its attention. Delinquency was viewed as a problem that could be remedied and dispositions were fashioned in a way that would "cure" the underlying problem that led to the commission of the act. Most of these dispositions were community based, as the concept of probation had also recently been developed.

This rehabilitative style of justice continued up through the 1960s, when the civil liberties of adults and eventually juveniles became of concern. During this period, the Supreme Court heard several juvenile cases and afforded them many of the same rights guaranteed adults during the court process. This led to a formalization of the juvenile court and marked the beginning of the justice model, which replaced the medical model under which the juvenile court had previously operated. Under the justice model, which emerged in the late 1970s and early 1980s, the juvenile court became focused on accountability and "just deserts." The underlying philosophy of this approach was that by imposing punishment a juvenile would be deterred from future offending.

The justice model is still widely in use today. However, many states have begun to swing back toward rehabilitation, which has led to a balance between the two philosophies. Juveniles are now dispositioned in a manner that holds them accountable, but also provides them with the necessary skills to become contributing members of society. Again, as in other areas in juvenile justice, the courts have largely guided what can

and cannot be done with a juvenile who comes to the attention of the court.

Some of the provisions the courts have handed down that have guided the judiciary in their decisions to release juveniles are analogous to those in the adult criminal system. The courts have afforded juveniles due process protections by defining several stages of the process as "critical." The courts have also allowed the ordering of terms and conditions such as restitution, community service, curfews, and waivers of Fourth Amendment rights. However, in ordering these terms and conditions the courts have justified them under parens patriae, and not the best interests of society like the adult criminal system. In rationalizing their holdings, they illustrate the lesson that juveniles can learn by abiding by these terms and conditions, not how society will be satisfied or protected. These decisions reflect the trend in the juvenile justice system to become more like the adult criminal system, but still maintain the desire to act in the best interests of the child. In this chapter, we review some of the leading cases dealing with the decision to release.

REED v. DUTER

416 F.2d 733 (7th Cir. 1969)

FACTS

Reed, then 17 years of age and confined at the Wisconsin School for Girls, filed a petition for a writ of habeas corpus seeking to obtain her release from custody. The court found that the petition showed the state of Wisconsin did not provide a remedy to the appellant and that available state remedies were ineffective to protect her rights. An order was entered denying the petition on the ground that Reed had not exhausted her state remedies as required. Reed was found by the court to be a delinquent minor and committed to the custody of the Department of Social Services for confinement until she reached 21 years of age. Immediately prior to the hearing which led to her confinement, a voluntary public defender appeared to represent her. The case then proceeded to an immediate hearing to the delinquency finding, and her commitment to custody. Neither the court nor her counsel advised Reed that she had a right to appeal that decision. In addition, she was not advised of her right to the appointment of counsel for the purposes of pursuing an appeal. No appeal was taken. After expiration of the 40-day period of time for a direct

REED v. DUTER (cont.)

appeal, Reed first sought to invoke postcommitment procedures in the state courts for the review of constitutional questions related to the adjudication of her delinquency. She then filed an affidavit of indigency and a petition for the appointment of counsel to assist her in pursuing the postcommitment remedies available to her. The petition was denied because it had been filed in the wrong court, outside her county of residence. Reed subsequently filed an affidavit of indigency and her petition for appointment of counsel in her county of residence. Her petition was denied because the court indicated the petition had to be filed in the county where she was confined. Thereafter, Reed's present counsel filed a petition in the Supreme Court of Wisconsin. The petition was denied. Later that month, the Supreme Court of Wisconsin issued an order for each court to show cause for denial; that process was pending at the time of this filing.

ISSUE

Do juveniles have the same right of indigency appeal and appointment of counsel as adults under the Fourteenth Amendment equal protection clause?

HOLDING

Yes. The equal protection clause of the Fourteenth Amendment requires that juveniles be afforded the same rights and privileges as adults in the appointment of counsel for indigency appeals.

RATIONALE

The court contended that *In re Gault*, 387 U.S. 1 (1967) must be construed to incorporate all of the constitutional safeguards of the Fifth and Sixth Amendments to the Constitution which apply in criminal proceedings in juvenile court procedures. Included in those, the juvenile must not be denied the right to counsel, and he or she must be advised that counsel will be appointed, upon request, if he or she is indigent. Consequently, the court contended that Wisconsin could not deny Reed the right to an effective review of the proceedings that led to her commitment. In addition, she could not be held accountable for any consequences that might attach to the fact that the immediate avenue for review of direct appeal was lost because of her inaction, since it appeared that she was never advised that she had the right to appeal and the right to have counsel appointed for that purpose. Wisconsin does provide

preliminary judicial consideration of merit to claims of error by prisoners and does appoint counsel for indigent adult prisoners. In this case, Reed had not been able to obtain any consideration on the merits of her petition or other rights to counsel thereon, apparently because of concern by the courts with what public funds would be used to pay for counsel. Under *Gault*, there cannot be any permissible discrimination between the adult prisoner and the juvenile held in state custody.

CASE EXCERPT

"*Gault* must be construed as incorporating in juvenile court procedures, which may lead to deprivation of liberty, all of the constitutional safeguards of the Fifth and Sixth Amendments to the Constitution of the United States which apply, by operation of the Fourteenth Amendment, in criminal proceedings. Under *Gault*, there can be no constitutionally permissible discrimination between the adult prisoner and the juvenile defendant held in state custody."

CASE SIGNIFICANCE

This case is important because it extended several rights guaranteed to adult defendants in criminal proceedings to juvenile defendants in juvenile court proceedings. First, the court held that a juvenile has a right to know the rationale behind his or her commitment to a juvenile institution. The court's rationale for this decision was in view of the second right it extended to the juvenile defendant, the right to appeal the decision. The court contended that juveniles must know the factual basis for their commitment if they are to assist in their appeal. The court contended that juveniles shall be afforded the right to appeal any stage of the juvenile proceeding which may result in their loss of liberty, as the commitment surely does. Second, the court attached *Gault* to the appeal process by holding that the juvenile had a right to be represented by counsel in any stage of the process in which liberty is at stake, as in the appeal stage. In addition, the court contended that indigency is not a reason for denying counsel in this stage. The court indicated that most juveniles who have been committed do not have the means to hire effective counsel and therefore, the court must appoint such representation at the expense of the state. As in other areas of juvenile law, the court extended rights guaranteed adults in similar procedures to the juvenile court proceedings.

P.R. ET AL. v. STATE
210 S.E.2d 839 (Ga. App. 1974)

FACTS

Two brothers, then 16 and 13 years old, were ruled delinquent of theft after taking publications valued at 25 dollars from a self-service store. The principle witness in the case was a female clerk who testified that she saw the brothers and one other juvenile take the books and magazines out of the store by putting them under their shirts. Although she had not seen them put the books there, she indicated she did see bulges in their shirts that were not noticeable when they entered the store. She allowed them to leave because she was fearful of harm, and subsequently phoned the police. When the police caught the boys no merchandise was found on them. Both brothers denied the charges, but they were found guilty and sentenced to 12 months' probation. One condition of probation was that each pay seven dollars and fifty cents as restitution to the merchant where the goods were taken from. The juveniles appealed the condition.

ISSUE

Does the juvenile court have the power to order restitution as a condition of probation?

HOLDING

Yes. If a juvenile is found guilty of a crime that deprived another of property, the court can order the juvenile to pay restitution for the amount of the stolen item.

RATIONALE

The fundamental nature of the state of Georgia's Juvenile Code is to treat or rehabilitate juvenile offenders into secure law-abiding citizens. The Code allows for the court to place a child adjudicated delinquent on probation under the conditions and limitations the court prescribes. It is incumbent upon the juvenile court to make the child before it aware that he or she has committed a wrongful act and to teach him or her why that act is wrong and to restore him or her, if possible. The court contended that it is both therapeutic and rehabilitative to require the child to make such restitution as he or she is able to. Restitution is beneficial to both the child and the victim. The court indicated the difference between fines and restitution by observing that restitution is related directly to the offense and is therefore rehabilitative in nature, whereas a fine is simply punitive. The court did say that the state must show that the restitution is a fair amount and that the victim should not profit from the payment. However, it indicated that if the evidence suggested a defendant committed an offense that harmed another monetarily, said defendant could be ordered to compensate the victim for his or her loss.

CASE EXCERPT

"Both the power and necessity to require restitution as a condition for probation exist under our Juvenile Court Code. Appellants' contention would equate a fine with restitution. This would be erroneous because a fine is penal in nature with payment to the government and with no relationship to the offense. Whereas restitution is rehabilitative in nature, is related directly to the offense, and goes to the party who has been deprived of property. Restitution is indemnification rather than forfeiture."

CASE SIGNIFICANCE

This case is important because it displayed the juvenile court's rationale for ordering a juvenile to pay restitution. That rationale reflects the difference between the adult criminal court and the juvenile court. In the adult criminal court, the ordering of restitution is theoretically driven to secure retribution for the victim; however, as the court in the present case made clear, the juvenile court orders restitution for the rehabilitative effects it has on the juvenile. Although the court did point out the benefits for the victim when restitution is secured, much more emphasis was placed on the juvenile court's obligation to rehabilitate juveniles who come to its attention. Consequently, the court held that the juvenile court can order restitution if there is convincing evidence that a juvenile committed a crime.

M.J.W. v. STATE
210 S.E.2d 842 (Ga. App. 1974)

FACTS

M.J.W., a juvenile, was adjudicated of criminal trespass. In committing this offense, M.J.W. lit a match and threw it into a school restroom trash container causing it to burst into flames. The fire was put out and cost the school less than 25 dollars. M.J.W. disputed the adjudication, but the court of appeals affirmed the lower court's decision. M.J.W. was placed on probation for one year. He was required, as a condition of probation,

M.J.W. v. STATE *(cont.)*

to contribute 100 hours to the Parks and Recreation Department. M.J.W. then contested the order of community service hours.

ISSUE

Does the imposition that a juvenile contribute free labor to the Parks and Recreation Department amount to involuntary servitude in violation of his constitutional rights?

HOLDING

No. The juvenile court may impose community service if its intent is partially rehabilitative in nature.

RATIONALE

The premise behind Georgia's juvenile law is that juvenile offenders can be rehabilitated and transformed into productive citizens by a system specially designed to achieve those ends. The court pointed out that the imposition of community service is closer to the imposition of restitution than that of imposing fines. The work does not resemble a monetary penalty and it is consistent with the rehabilitative ideology of probation. Therefore, it is constructive rather than punitive. The juvenile court is allowed by statute to make such dispositions as are suited to act in the best interests of the child. Furthermore, the punishment should fit the crime. In this case, the crime was committed against a public school; therefore, it was appropriate to have the juvenile work to improve the city. This innovative approach seeks to avoid a trauma left on the victim or the community while aiming to give the offender a chance for a sense of satisfaction, an accomplishment that prison rarely offers.

CASE EXCERPT

"In *P.R. v. State of Ga.*, 133 Ga. App. 346, we made an exhaustive examination into this subject of probation conditions and concluded that a requirement of restitution was permissible because it was not in the nature of a fine. The reasoning in that case applies here in two respects. The first is that designation of work of a public purpose for destruction of public property is akin to restitution and does not resemble a monetary penalty. Secondly, useful services for the public good are in the pattern of probation, which is a specialized judicial tool and is helpful towards achieving the statute's pervading purpose of producing a good adult citizen."

CASE SIGNIFICANCE

The importance of this case lies in the court's justification for the decision to uphold the juvenile court's imposition. The court contended that the imposition of community service is rehabilitative in nature, which is consistent with the juvenile court's mission. In the adult criminal court, community service is imposed for punitive reasons first and rehabilitative motives second. The court also made reference to the restorative justice ideology without actually calling it such. In employing a restorative justice approach, the court alluded to the reparation of harm to the victim, in this case the city, by doing community service for the victim. Theoretically, this would repair the harm caused by the victim and restore the juvenile offender's standing within the community.

STATE EX REL. J.R. v. MACQUEEN
259 S.E.2d 420 (W. Va. 1979)

FACTS

J.R., a juvenile, was adjudicated as a delinquent for the charges of truancy and breaking and entering. He was placed in the Industrial School for Boys on or about April 15, 1978. In December of the same year, J.R. was placed on parole for a period of one year or until further order of the court. In January 1979, J.R. was charged by petition for the commission of robbery by violence. The petition was never filed with the court; however, the petitioner was taken into custody and placed in the Kanawha Home for Children in Dunbar. Two days later, J.R. was given notice of a proposed hearing on the alleged parole violations. The notice set forth the conditions of parole allegedly violated, the specific facts upon which the alleged violations were predicated, the fact that a probable cause hearing would be held, and that, if necessary, a parole revocation hearing would be scheduled. At the preliminary hearing, it was determined there was probable cause to believe a parole violation occurred and a revocation hearing was scheduled. At that hearing, J.R.'s counsel moved to dismiss the parole revocation proceeding contending that the court had no statutory authority to proceed against a juvenile on an alleged parole violation; that the state, by using West Virginia Code 49-5-14, as amended, in conjunction with the revocation procedure for adult parolees was depriving J.R. of due process of law; and that J.R.'s parole could not be revoked before he was convicted of a violation of state law upon a formal charge. Furthermore, J.R. contended that the standard of proof of such violation must be that of "proof beyond a reasonable doubt." The circuit court denied the motion but stayed the proceeding to permit J.R. to seek prohibition in this court.

ISSUE

Is a juvenile to be afforded the same rights as an adult in a parole revocation hearing? Is the standard of proof in a juvenile parole revocation that of proof beyond a reasonable doubt? In a juvenile parole revocation proceeding, is the conviction of formal charges a prerequisite to a parole revocation?

HOLDING

Yes, no, and no. A juvenile must be afforded all of the constitutional protections afforded an adult in parole revocation proceedings. A revocation could be accomplished upon finding of clear and convincing proof of substantial violation of conditions of parole. A conviction of formal charges is not a prerequisite to parole revocation.

RATIONALE

The court disagreed with J.R.'s contention that the West Virginia Code, as amended, deals solely with the modification of dispositional orders and does not encompass procedures for revocation of parole. The court contended that the order placing J.R. on parole was a dispositional order. The court pointed to the statute which provides, in part, that if a motion or request for review of disposition is based upon an alleged violation of a court order, the court may modify the dispositional order to a more restrictive alternative if it finds clear and convincing proof of substantial violation. The court contended that when the lower court placed the juvenile on parole it was the equivalent of "further disposition" as referred to in the statute. In regard to J.R.'s claim that the application of adult parole revocation procedure to the revocation of parole of a juvenile is constitutionally impermissible, the court also disagreed. Although the court acknowledged that neither the state supreme court nor the Supreme Court has ruled on this matter, the Supreme Court has held that juveniles are entitled to procedural protections previously denied them under the doctrine of parens patriae. The court relied on the Supreme Court's decisions in *Breed v. Jones*, 421 U.S. 519 (1975), *In re Winship*, 397 U.S. 358 (1970), *In re Gault*, 387 U.S. 1 (1967), and *Kent v. United States*, 383 U.S. 541 (1966) in making their

finding. The court then pointed to *Morrissey v. Brewer*, 408 U.S. 471 (1972), in which the Supreme Court held that a parolee's liberty, although indeterminate, is valuable and is within the protection of the Fourteenth Amendment. The Supreme Court also afforded the parolee certain due process rights such as the rights to notice, disclosure of evidence against him or her, to be heard and present his or her own evidence, to cross-examine witnesses against him or her, to a neutral and detached hearing body, and to a written statement by the fact finders. This court then pointed to a number of adult cases in which *Morrissey* was applied. In agreeing with the thrust of those cases, the court held that the nature of the juvenile parolee is no less valuable than that of an adult parolee. Consequently, the termination of liberty afforded by parole must be accomplished through some orderly process. The court contended that J.R. was, or was likely to be, afforded those rights in this case. With regard to J.R.'s final claim that the violation leading to revocation must be proven beyond a reasonable doubt, the court did not agree. The court pointed to the code, which requires a "clear and convincing" standard in determining guilt. In addition, the court again pointed to *Morrissey*, where the Supreme Court noted that a parole revocation is not a part of a criminal prosecution and that the full panoply of rights due a defendant in such proceeding need not be afforded in revocation of parole.

CASE EXCERPT

"It is of great moment, however, that a juvenile being subjected to parole revocation be afforded all of the constitutional protections afforded an adult. Parole revocation is not a criminal prosecution. It is a proceeding stemming from an alleged violation of the conditions imposed as a condition of release from confinement. The violation may be proved as noted herein and the revocation may be effected so long as the minimum requirements of due process are afforded. A conviction on a formal charge is not a prerequisite."

CASE SIGNIFICANCE

This case is important because it occurred soon after the Supreme Court decided *Morrissey*. In this case, the state court effectively applied the Supreme Court's ruling in *Morrissey* to a juvenile case. In doing so, the court moved the juvenile court away from the parens patriae philosophy and toward the more formal methods of the adult criminal court. This is consistent with a growing trend in many states to formalize

STATE EX REL. J.R. v. MACQUEEN (*cont.*)

their juvenile court proceedings. Essentially, the court determined that a juvenile is to be afforded many of the due process protections of an adjudication hearing that were supplied to juvenile matters by *Gault*. However, the court did not extend all of those rights when they held that the allegation of parole violation must only be proven to a clear and convincing standard. This is important in this case because the juvenile's parole was revoked for violating a condition that prohibited him from breaking any further laws while on parole. By allowing the court to find the allegation of violation true, the juvenile was essentially found guilty of a new crime by a standard below that of reasonable doubt, as the revocation proceeding would be admissible in the juvenile or criminal court proceeding for the new matter. Consequently, juvenile parolees must request a continuance, which may subject them to a longer period of preventative detention if they have been detained, if in fact they intend to challenge the new petition for which they were violated.

IN THE MATTER OF RODRIGUEZ

687 S.W.2d 421 (Tex. App. 1985)

FACTS

Rodriguez, a juvenile, was adjudicated delinquent for making bomb threats at a high school. He was placed on probation for 12 months. One condition of his probation was a curfew that required him to be home between 7:00 p.m. and 7:00 a.m. Sunday through Thursday, and 10:00 p.m. and 7:00 a.m. on Friday and Saturday. The order did not allow for exceptions unless authorized in writing in advance by his probation officer, or if he was with his relative or guardian. A petition was filed to revoke the probation. One of the grounds listed in support of the application to revoke was that Rodriguez had violated his curfew on a certain day. At the hearing, the trial court determined that he had violated his curfew and he was committed to the Texas Youth Commission. Rodriguez appealed.

ISSUE

Is an order of probation conditioning a child's curfew a reasonable one?

HOLDING

Yes. A probation condition that specifies a child's curfew is a reasonable one.

RATIONALE

Rodriguez contended that the only evidence that he violated curfew was hearsay testimony, which did not support modifying the disposition order. The testimony that convicted him was from a police officer who was relying on the dispatcher's log for the time. The court indicated this was sufficient evidence to support the allegation. As for the reasonableness of the curfew condition, the court contended that originally the condition was ordered because Rodriguez was deemed to be out of control. Therefore, the court was acting in an effort to rehabilitate the child and the condition was not unreasonable. The court pointed out the need to individualize dispositions based on the rehabilitative needs of juveniles.

CASE EXCERPT

"Even if we accept the premise that the State had to disprove the exceptions to the curfew condition, there is some evidence that Rodriguez did not have permission and was not with a relative or guardian. The probation officer recommended that Rodriguez be committed to the Texas Youth Commission for the curfew violation. A logical inference from that fact is that the probation officer did not authorize, in writing, the curfew violation. The basis of this court's decision in *In re D.E.P.* 512 S.W.2d 789 (Tex. App. 1974) was that these uncontrollable circumstances made the order of the court unreasonable, not that a curfew is an unreasonable condition. Given the facts in this case, the trial court's order conditioning the child's probation on his following the curfew was a reasonable order of the court."

CASE SIGNIFICANCE

This case is important because it showed the juvenile court's willingness to fashion terms the court determines are in the best interests of the child, thereby acting consistent with the parens patriae philosophy. There are two issues on which the juvenile appealed. First, the court upheld the hearsay testimony of a police officer. In upholding this testimony, the court used the same rules of evidence that are allowed in the adult criminal system, which allow hearsay evidence at probation revocation hearings. Second, the court upheld the constitutionality of the curfew condition by noting the juvenile court was attempting to fashion an individualized disposition that was in the best interests of that juvenile. The court pointed out that the child was out of control and the curfew condition was ordered to provide structure to the juvenile's routine. Consequently, in the same holding, the court made the juvenile court analogous to the adult criminal court by upholding the introduction of hearsay evidence, while maintaining the rehabilitative nature of the juvenile court by upholding the justification of the curfew condition.

WATTS v. HADDEN

627 F.Supp. 727 (D. Colo. 1986)

FACTS

This class action suit was filed on behalf of persons who had been committed for treatment under the Youth Corrections Act. The dispute concerned the manner in which the parole commission determined the conditional release date of a Youth Corrections Act inmate, and the respective roles of the United States Parole Commission and Federal Bureau of Prisons. Even though the Act had been repealed, the suit focused on offenders who remained incarcerated because of it. The appellants contended that as the number of commitments dropped, the Federal Bureau of Prisons and the United States Parole Commission focused less emphasis on those who remained in the system and their mandate as charged in the Youth Corrections Act, such that youthful offenders were not receiving appropriate classification for the purpose of determining their treatment needs, those treatment needs were not being addressed, progress reports were not being developed and reported to the Parole Commission, and the Parole Commission was not assuming joint responsibility for the appropriate treatment of youthful offenders committed under the Youth Corrections Act.

ISSUE

Are controlling agencies responsible for continuing treatment of an offender population sentenced under specialized acts that have since been repealed?

HOLDING

Yes. The Federal Bureau of Prisons and the United States Parole Commission are jointly responsible for determining the appropriate treatment required for inmates sentenced under the Youth Rehabilitation Act. This responsibility does not decrease as the affected population dwindles, and stays until no Youth Corrections Act offenders remain in the system.

RATIONALE

The court contended that the fact that the Act was repealed had no effect on the inmates who were incarcerated under it. Those inmates were still treated as if it were in effect. In this case, the Parole Commission continued to focus on offense severity to guide its decision. However, the Youth Corrections Act called for a difference in time for inmates no matter the offense. The Act focused more on the individual needs of offenders and how much progress they had made in their treatment. The court relied on *Dorszynski v. United States*, 418 U.S. 424 (1974), in which the Supreme Court said the execution of the sentence must fit the person, not the crime for which he was sentenced. In the present case, the authorities were resistant to that holding. Consequently, the court contended that a mechanism should be developed to review inmates' program plans and indicate an earliest possible release date. A second mandate of the court was that the director must develop a periodic reporting on the inmate's progress in treatment, with written reports to the parole commission no less frequently than at six-month intervals. In addition, the director must put in place a process whereby a recommendation for conditional release would be made to the Parole Commission. In order to make these reports and recommendations meaningful the Parole Commission must meet with each inmate within 90 days of the receipt of the interim reports and within 60 days of receipt of a release recommendation. Although the court contended the use of contract providers might be more appropriate as this population continued to dwindle, it would have to be determined if that would best meet inmates' treatment needs. This was only addressed to remind the authorities that there are alternatives that can be used when treating the Youth Corrections Act inmates under the new circumstances resulting from the change in the law.

CASE EXCERPT

"There is a joint responsibility for both the Bureau of Prisons and the Parole Commission to act together to determine the appropriate treatment required for an individual inmate, and to determine the time when he has responded to that treatment sufficiently to warrant release after consideration of the other two criteria in section 4206(a)...It seems apparent that the Act contemplates participation by the Parole Commission in the treatment program design for each inmate. There would be no other purpose for the statutory requirements that it receive the classification report with

WATTS v. HADDEN (cont.)

recommendations and that it conduct an early parole interview."

CASE SIGNIFICANCE

This case is important because the court held that juveniles committed to a facility under a repealed law are still governed by the procedures of that law, even though they are mostly housed with individuals committed under a new law. Consequently, many facilities and states had to implement measures to accommodate individuals sentenced under the prior juvenile codes. During the time period surrounding this case, many states were rewriting or changing sections of their juvenile codes to become consistent with "get tough" legislation being passed nationally. At the same time, violent juvenile crime was on the rise and legislation was passed in many states to better handle violent youthful offenders. Consequently, this court's decision had implications for more than the group of offenders on whose behalf it was acting.

IN THE INTEREST OF DAVIS

546 A.2d 1149 (Pa. Super. 1988)

FACTS

Davis, a juvenile, had been adjudicated delinquent on May 6, 1985, on a charge of simple assault. At the dispositional hearing, he was placed on probation with the condition that he attend school with no absences, lateness, or suspensions. On August 28, 1985, Davis's probation officer filed a motion to review the order of probation, with a request that Davis be committed to Glenn Mills Diagnostic Center because there were "problems in the home and Davis appears to be in need of an extensive diagnostic study." At the revocation hearing, the probation officer testified to Davis's father advising him that Davis had pulled a knife on him. After overruling Davis's attorney's objection to the hearsay testimony, the court revoked probation. Davis appealed, and argued that his right to confrontation under the state and federal constitutions were violated when the trial court based its decision to revoke probation solely on the hearsay testimony of the probation officer.

ISSUES

Is hearsay testimony admissible in a juvenile probation revocation hearing? Does a juvenile have the right to confront his or her accuser in a juvenile probation revocation hearing?

HOLDING

No and yes. Admitting hearsay testimony in the proceeding violated the juvenile's state and federal confrontation rights. Juveniles have the same substantial interest in retaining their liberty as adults. Due process considerations entailing the right to confront and cross-examine an accuser must extend to juvenile probation revocation hearings.

RATIONALE

The court indicated that the Juvenile Act provides that extrajudicial statements, which would be inadmissible in a criminal proceeding, shall not be used against a juvenile in an adjudicatory proceeding. However, in dispositional hearings the statute provides that "all evidence helpful in determining the questions presented, including oral and written reports, may be received by the court and relied upon to the extent of its probative value even though not otherwise competent in the hearing on the petition." With respect to revocation hearings, the Act is silent. The court held that thereafter a juvenile's probation could not be revoked solely on the basis of extrajudicial statements made by an accuser whom the juvenile had not been permitted to confront. In support of this holding, the court first pointed to *In re Gault* 387 U.S. 1 (1967), in which the Supreme Court extended most of the due process protections guaranteed adults to juvenile matters. In *Gault*, one of the rights extended to juveniles was the right to confront their accusers. Consequently, the court contended an adjudication based solely on hearsay evidence should be reversed. The court also pointed to *Morrissey v. Brewer* 408 U.S. 471 (1972), where the Supreme Court held that an adult parolee had a substantial interest in retaining his or her liberty until it had been determined he or she had violated conditions of his or her parole and that, therefore, parole could not be revoked absent due process. In this case, the Supreme Court formulated a two-step procedure. The first step is a factual inquiry to determine if probable cause exists, and the second step is a fact-finding hearing to determine if parole was violated. In both of these proceedings there exist constitutional rights to confront accusers. These rights were extended to an adult probationer in *Gagnon v. Scarpelli*, 411 U.S. 778 (1973). The court then relied on state court case law that has determined a juvenile has the same substantial interest in retaining his liberty as an adult. In addition, the court contended society's interests in a juvenile probationer are no different than its interest in an adult probationer or parolee. Consequently, the court concluded that in view of a juvenile's substantial liberty interests that exist in a probation revocation proceeding, due process considerations entailing the right to confront and cross-examine an accuser must extend to juveniles in these proceedings.

CASE EXCERPT

"A juvenile has the same substantial interest in retaining his liberty as an adult. Similarly, society's interests in a juvenile probationer are no different than its interests in an adult probationer or parolee. In view of the substantial liberty interests which exist in not having probation revoked on the basis of unverified facts or erroneous information, we conclude that due process considerations entailing the right to confront and cross-examine an accuser must extend to probation revocation proceedings for a juvenile."

CASE SIGNIFICANCE

This case is important because it is representative of what occurred in many states after the Supreme Court decided *Morrissey* and *Gagnon*. In this case, the state court effectively applied the Supreme Court's ruling in *Morrissey* and *Gagnon* to a juvenile case. In doing so, the court moved the juvenile court away from the parens patriae philosophy it formerly operated under and more toward the formal methods of the adult criminal court. This is consistent with a growing trend in many states to formalize juvenile court proceedings. Essentially, the court determined that a juvenile is to be afforded many of the due process protections of an adjudication hearing which were supplied to juvenile matters by *Gault,* in this case, specifically the right to confront his accuser.

IN RE CURTIS T.

263 Cal. Rptr. 296 (Cal. Ct. App. 1989)

FACTS

A petition was filed alleging Curtis had unlawfully possessed cocaine. He was placed on home supervision pursuant to an agreement signed by Curtis and his mother. Several days later an officer assigned to the home supervision detail called Curtis's home and asked to speak with him. His mother answered and told her Curtis was not at home, a violation of the terms of Curtis's home supervision agreement. The officer indicated she would come by the following morning and pick up Curtis and take him to juvenile hall for violating home supervision. The following day two probation officers accompanied by two police officers went to the home. Curtis's mother invited the officers into the home. The mother indicated Curtis was in his room sleeping. There was discrepancy in the testimony as to whether the officers gave the mother a choice about whether they should accompany her to get Curtis. Once in the bedroom one of the police officers noticed an inordinate amount of stereo equipment. The officer testified he believed it to be stolen. The officer noticed three of the items had obliterated serial numbers. He called in the fourth item, which had not been reported stolen. It was later determined the equipment was stolen. Curtis challenged the seizure, stating that the officers did not have a right to search his bedroom.

ISSUE

Does the access condition of a home supervision agreement authorize police officers entry into a minor's bedroom in order to take the minor into custody following violation of a condition of home supervision release?

HOLDING

Yes. The access condition of a home supervision agreement allows officers access to the bedroom of a minor if they are there to arrest him for a violation of the agreement.

RATIONALE

Home supervision is an alternative to detention, and a minor on home supervision is in effect in detention. He or she signs a contract with his parent to abide by certain rules while in his or her home. Any violations of that contract can result in his or her being detained and subject to a detention hearing before the court. Therefore, the court contended that such minors were subject to the same legal protections as minors in secure detention. However, the court did point out the problem that the contract only allowed for access to the minor. The court applied the *People v. Bravo*, (1987) 43 Cal. 3d 600 case, in which the Supreme Court stated that a search condition must be interpreted on the basis of what a reasonable person would understand from the language of the condition itself, not on the

IN RE CURTIS T. (*cont.*)

basis of the appellant's understanding, or under a strict test in which a presumption against waiver is applied. Therefore, the court concluded a reasonable person would understand the language of the access condition to permit the entry into Curtis's bedroom.

CASE EXCERPT

"The purpose of the access condition is to ensure the minor complies with his written promises. Since the home supervision agreement contemplates the minor will be at home (unless he is at another permitted location such as a school or place of employment), the probation officer in charge of the home supervision must necessarily have access to the minor in his home. Reasonably, this access would extend to the place in the home normally occupied by the minor, i.e., his bedroom."

CASE SIGNIFICANCE

This case is important for a couple of reasons. First, the court ruled on the home confinement issue. In recent years, the use of home confinement and electronic monitoring has become more prevalent as an alternative to preventative detention. However, the placement of juveniles into home confinement programs is conditional, as they are still in custody in the eyes of the court. Consequently, they can be detained without judicial review for violating a condition of their home confinement agreement. The court contended that since the juvenile was still in lawful custody, he was subject to the same conditions as he would be in an institution. One of those conditions is a relinquishing of the Fourth Amendment protections from search and seizure. Therefore, the seizure of the items in the juvenile's bedroom did not offend his Fourth Amendment rights. However, the juvenile also challenged the seizure on the basis that the home and room in which the items were found were not his, but his parents'. The court applied the reasonableness test to this challenge. The court held that a reasonable person would be led to believe a juvenile's room, although not his by ownership, would contain only his belongings. Consequently, the cost of having a juvenile with a search condition on his agreement of supervision residing in an individual's home would be a loss of the expectation of privacy in the areas the juvenile frequents. This holding is important because it would likely be applicable to a search condition of probation as well.

J.K.A. v. STATE

855 S.W.2d 58 (Tex. App. 1993)

FACTS

A juvenile court found that J.K.A. had engaged in delinquent conduct. The court committed him to the Texas Youth Commission but suspended the commitment. The court placed him in the custody of his mother under the supervision of the juvenile probation department and rules of probation for one year. A few months later, J.K.A. was caught with a gun at school. The state filed a petition to modify disposition alleging violation of a rule of probation and requesting the court to enter further custody orders. A hearing was held. The fourth rule of J.K.A's probation order specified that J.K.A. not violate any law of the state. J.K.A. signed a stipulation of evidence admitting that he violated that rule by committing the weapons offense. The trial court modified the prior disposition by revoking J.K.A.'s probation and committing him to the Youth Commission. J.K.A appealed, challenging the wording of the court's orders to clarify that the court did not adjudicate J.K.A. guilty of new felonious delinquent conduct for the weapons offense, but instead violated an order of the court, or rule of probation.

ISSUES

In modifying the disposition proceeding, did the court find the juvenile delinquent of a new felony charge or did the court merely revoke based on a violation of a condition of probation? If the juvenile was found delinquent on a new felony charge, was full due process afforded the juvenile?

HOLDING

The court's order modifying the disposition and revoking probation was based on the court's finding that the juvenile had violated a reasonable and lawful order of the court. The juvenile was not found delinquent based on the felony charge of possession of a weapon, even though the weapon offense was the reason for seeking incarceration of the juvenile probationer. Therefore, the court was not required to conduct a full due process adjudication hearing to find that the juvenile had violated a rule of probation.

RATIONALE

The court contended that the description of the weapons offense in the recital portion of the judgment modifying disposition did not equate to the entering of a judgment adjudicating J.K.A. guilty of felonious conduct. In addition, the court found that the judgment revoking probation related back to the previous adjudication and not the new offense. Further, the wording was that of revoking probation and not that of a new offense. The court contended that since the hearing only involved a modification of the disposition order, due process was not guaranteed. Had the state attempted to adjudicate J.K.A. of a new offense, he would have been guaranteed all the normal due process rights. However, since this was in effect a dispositional hearing, those rights did not apply. In essence, J.K.A. only violated a court order and therefore reduced due process safeguards were adequate.

CASE EXCERPT

"If the State wants an adjudication of felonious delinquent conduct with its serious classification implications, it must afford an opportunity for a full 54.03 adjudication hearing. On the other hand, if the State merely wishes to modify a disposition by obtaining a finding that the youth violated a reasonable and lawful order of the court, then a 54.05 hearing to modify disposition is all that is required."

CASE SIGNIFICANCE

This case is important because it demonstrated the reduced due process protections afforded to juveniles in probation revocation hearings versus adjudication hearings. The Supreme Court had already afforded juveniles most of the due process protections of the Constitution with their decision in *In re Gault* 387 U.S. 1 (1967). However, as this case made clear, those standards and protections do not apply to a revocation hearing. In this case, the juvenile signed a stipulation that he had violated a rule of his probation order and the court subsequently modified its original judgment and committed the juvenile to the Youth Commission. The juvenile challenged, stating the rule for which he was violated was that of breaking a law and therefore he should be afforded the due process protections of an adjudicatory hearing. However, the court pointed out that the state did not charge the juvenile with a new delinquency offense, although they could have, but instead merely revoked the juvenile's probation and modified his disposition. In addition, the juvenile signed a stipulation admitting the violation. Consequently, the protections afforded a juvenile in an adjudicatory hearing do not apply.

IN THE MATTER OF LUCIO F.T.

888 P.2d 958 (N.M. App. 1994)

FACTS

Lucio F.T., while still a juvenile, was charged with the commission of three criminal offenses. The court dismissed two of the charges and Lucio F.T. admitted to the third. He was placed on probation for a period of two years. Less than 24 hours after being placed on probation, Lucio F.T. was arrested on four new charges. At this time he was 18 years old and was charged in criminal court. On the same day, the children's court attorney filed a petition to revoke Lucio F.T.'s juvenile probation based on his offenses as an adult. Lucio F.T. appeared in criminal court, pled guilty to all four new offenses, and was fined. Thereafter, he was transferred to the juvenile detention center and subsequently filed a motion to dismiss the petition to revoke based on the admitted allegations. The motion was denied and he was committed to the Children, Youth and Families Department.

ISSUE

Did the use of adult charges as the basis for revoking a concurrent juvenile probation sentence violate the constitutional prohibition against double jeopardy?

HOLDING

No. A proceeding in juvenile court to revoke prior juvenile probation due to adult offenses for which the appellant has been convicted in criminal court does not amount to new or separate punishment and therefore does not constitute double jeopardy.

RATIONALE

Double jeopardy protects defendants from more than one criminal prosecution for the same criminal offense. A probation revocation proceeding is not a new criminal trial to impose new punishment, but instead is a hearing to determine whether, during the probationary period, the defendant has conformed to or violated the course of conduct outlined in the probation order. The probationer's punishment is imposed when he or she is originally sentenced, not when his or her probation is revoked. The court pointed to numerous federal cases that allow for revocation of probation based on new offenses. In addition, the state courts have considered any revocation

IN THE MATTER OF LUCIO F.T. *(cont.)*

proceeding to merely be addressing whether the individual is still a candidate for the probation disposition. In this case, the defendant argued that proceedings were different in juvenile courts because the sentencing options are more expansive. The court contended that the distinctions do not alter the material differences between a revocation proceeding and a trial for new charges. The court again pointed to the fact that the punishment had already been imposed and the court merely had the option of changing the original disposition.

CASE EXCERPT

"A revocation hearing is simply an exercise of the trial court's supervision over a defendant during probation and the consequence of revocation is execution of a penalty previously imposed. When a child is placed on probation in New Mexico, all of the possible dispositions that are not imposed are withheld, but only conditionally. The child must obey his probation conditions, and, if the child violates them, any of the previously withheld dispositions may be imposed…when a child's probation is revoked, the children's court is merely enforcing its previous sentence and is not imposing a new and separate sentence. By express legislative provision, the children's court retains jurisdiction to extend the period of probation or to revoke an individual's probation during the period of such probation, even though the person has reached his eighteenth birthday."

CASE SIGNIFICANCE

This case is important because it illustrated that the probation sentence is merely a disposition that can be modified if its conditions are violated at any time. In this case, the juvenile's probation was violated after he committed and was convicted of several offenses as an adult. The juvenile challenged, claiming the double jeopardy protection guaranteed him through the Fifth Amendment, which the Supreme Court applied to juvenile matters in *Breed v. Jones* 421 U.S. 519 (1975). However, the court pointed out that a probation violation is not an adjudication or conviction, but merely a modification of a disposition. Consequently, jeopardy does not apply. In so holding, the court allowed the state to revoke probation if a juvenile commits any new offense, whether adult or juvenile.

MATTER OF TAPLEY

865 P.2d 12 (Wash. App. 1994)

FACTS

Tapley was committed as a juvenile. Under the standard sentencing range, the juvenile court committed Tapley for 206 to 258 weeks. Tapley was subsequently placed at Green Hill School, which is a serious offender juvenile corrections facility operated by the Department of Social and Health Services. Tapley began his commitment on May 22, 1991. Under the terms of his sentence, Tapley's earliest release date was May 1, 1995, and his latest was August 6, 1995. Upon entry to the Green Hill School, Tapley was assigned a release date based on the Treatment Behavior Contract (TBC) method. Under this method, the juvenile and a counselor meet and sign a contract, establishing individual treatment and behavior expectations. The initial release date is automatically set as the latest, but the juvenile may work off days toward the earliest release date by complying with TBC expectations. The staff then conducts periodic reviews in which they assess whether the expectations are being met. If so, then a specified number of credit days may be awarded. Tapley was handled in this manner upon coming into the facility. He subsequently filed a personal restraint petition challenging the release policy.

ISSUE

Does an institutional release policy utilizing a progressive behavior contract system violate a juvenile's due process and equal protection rights?

HOLDING

No. Release policies of this nature do not deprive juveniles of their right to due process as long as administrative regulations and policies do not create an expectation that a juvenile's release date will be the maximum amount of time possible. The procedural difference used by juvenile facilities regarding the manner in which juvenile minimum release dates are calculated do not violate the equal protection clause.

RATIONALE

The court contended that Washington law requires only that the department set a release date within the standard range prior to the expiration of 60 percent of the minimum term. Green Hill's method was well within the 60 percent deadline. The court indicated that setting a maximum release date for each juvenile entering the facility without further consideration would violate Washington law. However, the Green Hill policy used the latest date merely as a starting date. In addition, the staff regularly evaluated each case to determine an appropriate release date. Consequently, the policy allowed for the type of discretion the legislature intended. In addressing the due process challenge of the release date, the court found to the contrary. Initially, the release dates were set prior to the expiration of 60 percent of the minimum term. Second, there was a review prior to the release date being set beyond the minimum term. Further, Tapley met with a counselor and had the contract explained to him in full. Nothing in the law states that a juvenile has a right to a formal process to discuss his or her release date. In addition, each juvenile has the opportunity to work down his or her release date if he or she so desires. The court contended the law merely mandates that juveniles be informed of their release date and why it was set. As for the equal protection claim of the juvenile, the court found that the Green Hill manner, although different from procedures used in other facilities, was still consistent with the idea that a juvenile must earn an early release date. Consequently, the juvenile's claims were rejected.

CASE EXCERPT

"The Green Hill release policy is consistent with the two primary principles underlying the Juvenile Justice Act of 1977: rehabilitation and retribution. Contrary to petitioners' characterization of Green Hill's release policy, the TBC method is not simply an automatic mass offender processing approach. Rather, the TBC method is a complex program in which each juvenile is not only held accountable for his or her conduct during commitment, but where each juvenile is also empowered to participate in the designation of those individual behavior expectations to which he or she will be held."

CASE SIGNIFICANCE

This case is significant because it demonstrated the individualized manner in which juvenile release dates are determined in juvenile correctional facilities. Many states commit a juvenile to the Department of Youth Corrections for a period not to exceed a certain age; however, a juvenile can typically be released far ahead of that age if he or she demonstrates good behavior and completes his or her individual treatment plan. In this case, the juvenile was sentenced in a state that uses a presumptive sentencing scheme, thereby specifying a minimum and maximum period of time the juvenile can serve. The facility in this case sets the juvenile's release date at the maximum period, but explains to each juvenile that he or she can reduce his or her time by showing good behavior and accomplishing certain goals. This is consistent with the parens patriae philosophy, as the facility attempts to get juveniles to participate in the treatment program because it will be in their best interest. The court determined that a juvenile does not have any due process rights to determine how long he or she will serve in custody for a given offense. That decision is statutorily left up to the facility to which he or she is committed, provided the facility adheres to the minimum and maximum sentence the law prescribes. The court believed the manner in which this facility allows juveniles to attain a lesser sentence is consistent with the legislative intent in the statute. In this design, the juvenile must earn an early release by demonstrating good behavior.

J.R.W. v. STATE

879 S.W.2d 254 (Tex. App. 1994)

FACTS

J.R.W. was adjudicated by a juvenile court for attempted capital murder, aggravated kidnapping, and unauthorized use of a motor vehicle. The jury recommended and the trial court imposed a 30-year determinate sentence in the Texas Youth Commission. After serving 22 months of the term, the trial court held a release hearing. At the hearing, the Texas Youth Commission administrator, state psychologist, and appellant's volunteer mentors recommended that the trial court release appellant to the SECOR program. Texas law allows for three options when a hearing of this nature is held: release from custody, remand to the Texas Youth Commission without a determinate sentence, or transfer to the Texas Department of Criminal Justice upon a juvenile's 18th birthday. In this case, the trial court ordered J.R.W.'s transfer to the Texas Department of Criminal Justice when he reached 18 years of age. No findings of fact or conclusions of law were made.

ISSUE

Did the court exceed its authority in deciding to continue custody of a juvenile delinquent in prison upon his turning 18?

J.R.W. v. STATE (cont.)

HOLDING

No. Trial courts in juvenile proceedings have broad power and discretion. The decision to transfer the delinquent juvenile to adult prison on his 18th birthday, as authorized by state law, was supported by the evidence presented. The court did not abuse its discretion by not following the recommendations of the staff. The responsibility for proper placement of the juvenile was with the court.

RATIONALE

The statute uses the word "may" because it is permissive rather than mandatory. Juvenile proceedings allow for much discretion in their dispositional options because they attempt to focus on individual treatment of juvenile offenders. Therefore, the court reviewed the decision made under an abuse of discretion standard. The court contended an abuse of discretion does not exist if the trial court bases its decision on conflicting evidence and some evidence supports the court's decision. In this case, the court had heard testimony from the victims and police supporting the transfer. The court also recognized that J.R.W. had some difficulties at the Texas Youth Commission. Although there was testimony supporting J.R.W. remaining in the Youth Commission, conflicting evidence did not support a decision one way or another. Therefore, the court upheld the lower court's decision by finding it was within their discretionary power to make this decision based on some evidence supporting said decision.

CASE EXCERPT

"A statute that uses the word 'may' is permissive rather than mandatory unless there is something in the statute to show a legislative intent that 'may' is mandatory. A permissive statute gives the trial court discretion to decide under the framework of the statute...The record shows the trial court...followed the guiding statute in deciding the issue. Appellant also complains the trial court breached its duty to rehabilitate appellant. Under section 54.11, the trial court has no duty to rehabilitate the appellant. The trial court determines only whether to transfer appellant to TDCJ, release him under supervision, discharge him, or recommit him to TYC. The trial court did not abuse its discretion or breach a duty to rehabilitate appellant."

CASE SIGNIFICANCE

This case is important because it demonstrated the juvenile court's latitude in its discretion when imposing a disposition. In this case, the juvenile was sentenced under a state law that allowed him to be effectively waived to adult criminal court but sentenced to a juvenile facility until his 18th birthday, at which time the court would review the case and determine if it should modify its disposition and release the juvenile, order him back to the Youth Commission, or move him to an adult prison. Many states are implementing or already have a similar sentencing scheme in an attempt to rehabilitate youthful offenders while removing them from the harshness of adult facilities until they are in fact adults. In this case, the court upheld the lower court's decision to remand the juvenile to the adult prison even though there was conflicting testimony as to what the appropriate disposition should be. Consequently, the lower court did not abuse its discretion when it acted in the manner in which it did.

IN THE INTEREST OF D.S. AND J.V., MINOR CHILDREN

652 So.2d 892 (Fla. App. 1995)

FACTS

Two juveniles were found guilty of simple battery in circuit court and were subsequently placed on supervised probation. One of the conditions of their probation was to not associate with gang members. The juveniles appealed their convictions on the grounds that the probation condition violated the First Amendment.

ISSUE

Are restrictions of freedom of association of a juvenile constitutional?

HOLDING

Yes. The condition that juvenile delinquents not associate with gang members was proper. However, sanctions for violating such a condition could be enforced only if it could be proved that the juveniles knew that the individuals with whom they were associating were gang members.

RATIONALE

The court upheld this condition of probation because it would be correct to argue it would be in the best interest of the child not to associate with gang members. However, the court clarified this provision in the effect that, just as any violation of probation must include the element of intent, there would have to be a showing that the juveniles knew the individuals were gang members when they allegedly associated with them.

CASE EXCERPT

"We further affirm the trial court's imposition of a condition of community control that appellant D.S. 'not associate with gang members.' However, we clarify this provision to the effect that, just as any violation of probation must include the element of intent, there would have to be a showing that D.S. *knew* the individuals were gang members before he could be found guilty of *knowingly* violating such a provision."

CASE SIGNIFICANCE

This case is important for a couple of reasons. First, it demonstrated the court's willingness to uphold association clauses of probation. In adult criminal court, it is common for the supervision agreement to order an offender not to associate with persons on probation or parole. However, in juvenile court, association clauses can be extended beyond those on probation or parole to friends who are deemed inappropriate by the probation officer, the juvenile's parent, or the court. In this case, the juvenile court ordered the juveniles not to associate with any individuals in gangs. This has become common as gang violence and crime have escalated. Therefore, in remaining consistent with parens patriae and acting in the best interests of the child, the court ordered the "juvenile not association with gang members" clause to be constitutional. However, the court did point out that for a juvenile court to revoke a juvenile's probation for the "no association" condition it must prove intent. Consequently, the state would have to show that the juvenile knew the person with whom he or she was associating was a gang member and that the juvenile knowingly associated with him or her. While this may seem like a heavy burden to carry, it is important to remember that hearsay testimony is allowed at revocation hearings. Consequently, if a probation officer testifies that he or she advised the juvenile not to associate with an individual because he or she is in a gang and the juvenile continued to associate with that individual, the state will have met its burden.

IN RE KACY S.

80 Cal.Rptr.2d 432 (Cal. Ct. App. 1998)

FACTS

Kacy S. admitted he was within the provisions of Welfare and Institutions Code Section 602 in that, in

a public place, he used offensive words which were inherently likely to provoke an immediate, violent reaction. Kacy S. was placed on probation. One of the conditions of his probation was that he submit to urine testing to determine the presence of alcohol and illegal drugs in his system. Kacy S. appealed, contending that imposition of the urine testing was improper.

ISSUE

Is the urine test of a juvenile for the purpose of detecting alcohol or illegal drugs constitutional?

HOLDING

Yes. It is reasonable and constitutional to require a juvenile to submit to a urine test for the purpose of detecting illegal drugs or alcohol as a condition of his or her probation.

RATIONALE

California law allows for urine testing to be a condition of a juvenile's probation. Within the wording of the law, the word "may" is used implying that the court or judge has the discretion to order said condition. The minor contended that since his social history or offense did not indicate any history of substance abuse, the condition was unsupported. This court indicated that may be true; however, the law does not require that the court make a finding to support why it ordered a particular condition of a juvenile's probation. In *People v. Lent* 15 Cal. 3d 481 (1975) the court determined a condition of probation will not be held invalid unless it has no relationship to the crime for which the offender was convicted, relates to conduct that is not in itself criminal, and requires or forbids conduct that is not reasonably related to future criminality. The urine testing condition was designed to detect the presence of a substance whose use by minors is unlawful. Therefore, the testing relates to conduct that is itself criminal. Further, the legislature has found that alcohol and drug abuse are precursors of serious criminality. Therefore, the testing is also reasonably related to future criminality. As for the defendant's Fourth Amendment claim, the court contended a probationer's expectation of privacy is diminished by his or her status as a probationer. In addition, a minor staying off drugs is directly related to his or her rehabilitation, which is the underlying principle of probation.

CASE EXCERPT

"A probationer's expectations of privacy are diminished by his probation status and are subordinated

IN RE KACY S. *(cont.)*

to governmental activities which reasonably limit the right of privacy. The testing condition is a reasonable intrusion upon a probationer's expectations of privacy. The juvenile court's goals are to protect the public and rehabilitate the minor. Section 729.3 serves both goals. It protects the public by establishing procedures to deter or prevent use of alcohol and unlawful drugs by minors. It advances the rehabilitation of young offenders by seeking to detect alcohol or drug use as a precursor of criminal activity in order to facilitate intervention at the earliest time. Although urine testing constitutes an intrusion on privacy, the effect of the intrusion is outweighed by the government's legitimate interest in closely monitoring the rehabilitation of minors who are granted probation and returned to the custody of their parents."

CASE SIGNIFICANCE

This case is important for a couple of reasons. First, the court allowed the juvenile court to impose a condition that has no factual support for its imposition. In doing this, the court relied on a previous case, *Lent,* in which the court held that a court may impose a condition of probation if it prevents the individual from committing conduct which is in itself criminal or requires or forbids conduct which is reasonably related to future criminality. The court contended that substance use is illegal for any juvenile and has been shown to contribute to future delinquency. Therefore, the juvenile's abstinence from drugs was rehabilitative in nature. Consequently, the urine testing condition was a valid one. Second, the court turned its attention to the defendant's Fourth Amendment claim. As has typically been the case in the adult system, the court ruled that a probationer has a reduced expectation of privacy. Therefore, the requirement of a juvenile to produce a sample of his urine for testing was constitutional.

IN RE J.W.
787 N.E.2d 747 (Ill. S.C. 2003)

FACTS

J.W., a 12-year-old boy, was adjudicated delinquent following his admission to two counts of aggravated criminal sexual assault, and was sentenced to a term of five years' probation. Among the conditions of his probation, J.W. was ordered to register as a sex offender. In addition, J.W. was prohibited from residing in or

going to the Village of South Elgin, Illinois, the community where J.W. lived and where the aggravated criminal sexual assaults took place. J.W. appealed two of the conditions of his probation. He contended that (1) requiring a 12-year-old child to register as a sex offender was unconstitutional; and (2) prohibiting him from residing in or visiting South Elgin as a condition of probation was overly broad and void.

ISSUES

Did the trial court's order requiring a juvenile to register as a sex offender for the rest of his natural life violate substantive due process, proscription against double jeopardy, and constitute cruel and unusual punishment in violation of the Eighth Amendment of the Constitution? Is the trial court's condition that a juvenile not reside in or enter an entire town (South Elgin) during the term of his probation too broad and consequently violate his constitutional rights?

HOLDING

No and yes. An act requiring a juvenile sexual offender to register as a sexual offender for the rest of his life is constitutional. A condition that a juvenile not reside in or enter an entire town during the term of his probation is too broad, and thus violates his constitutional rights.

RATIONALE

With regard to J.W.'s challenge to the registration requirement, the court determined that J.W. fell within the state's definition of a juvenile sex offender because he was adjudicated as such. The court also found that J.W. fell within the state's definition of a sexual predator. Sexual predators, juvenile or adult, are required to register as a sexual offender for their entire life. Regarding J.W.'s claim that the order requiring him to register for life violated substantive due process, the court applied the rational basis test. Pursuant to this test, a statute should be upheld if it bears a reasonable relationship to a public interest to be served, and the means adopted are a reasonable method of accomplishing the desired objective. The court advised that the statute served the public interest by aiding law enforcement in the protection of children by providing law enforcement with ready access to information on known child sexual offenders. Further, the public interest to be served does not change if the sexual offender is 12 years old. The court reminded that, although one purpose of the Juvenile Court Act is to rehabilitate juveniles, the legislature also intended for the Act to protect citizens from juvenile crime and to hold juveniles accountable for their acts. With regard to J.W.'s claim that the requirement that he register as a sexual offender for life constituted cruel and unusual punishment in violation of the Eighth Amendment, the court also disagreed. The Court pointed out that J.W.'s interpretation of the registration act as permitting unfettered access to the information that he was a sexual offender was incorrect. Instead, the court observed that the information is restricted to law enforcement and only those individuals whose safety might be compromised for some reason related to the particular juvenile sex offender, such as school officials. Since J.W.'s claim that the registration act violated the proscription against double jeopardy was based on the claim that the registration requirement constituted cruel and unusual punishment, the court rejected that claim as well. Finally, with regard to the probation condition restricting J.W. from entering an entire town, the court found the condition reasonable because it was directly related to the offense. However, the court also found the condition overly broad because it did not allow for an exception to the condition, such as obtaining permission from probation officials.

CASE EXCERPT

"J.W.'s argument that requiring him to register as a sex offender violates the proscription against double jeopardy is based on his claim that the registration requirement constitutes cruel and unusual punishment. Because we hold that the registration requirement does not constitute punishment, J.W.'s double jeopardy argument likewise must fail."

CASE SIGNIFICANCE

This case is important because it is one of a growing number of cases in which courts have upheld the constitutionality of laws requiring juvenile sex offenders to register as sexual offenders. In this case, the court went so far as to allow a lifetime registration requirement be imposed on a juvenile who committed a sex offense when he was 12 years old. The court specifically acknowledged the shift in purpose of the Juvenile Court Act from one of solely rehabilitation, to also include protection of the public and holding juveniles accountable. The court further acknowledged that juvenile sexual offenders present a unique problem. Thus, the case is illustrative of a shift in the juvenile justices system, at least with regard to juvenile sexual offenders. The court went on to state that a condition of probation that banned a juvenile from an entire town was reasonable, yet the court said that the condition was unconstitutional because it was too vague. However, the court explicitly stated they would have upheld the condition if it would have provided a provision for the juvenile to enter the area for legitimate purposes. Thus, the decision opened the door for courts to impose such conditions in the future.

DISCUSSION QUESTIONS

1. What probation conditions have the courts allowed juveniles to be subject to?
2. What justification have the courts given for the conditions they have imposed?
3. What rights do juveniles have in revocation hearings?
4. What rules govern a home supervision agreement?
5. Why is a revocation of parole or probation for a new offense not considered double jeopardy?
6. What have the courts said regarding release policies?
7. Why are association clauses legal and why are they rarely enforced?
8. What have the courts said regarding the ability of a state to require a juvenile to register as a sex offender?
9. According to the courts, do indigent juveniles have a right to be represented by counsel during any stage of the juvenile court process?
10. What have the courts said regarding transferring a juvenile to adult prison on their 18th birthday?

GLOSSARY

Accessory   Someone who intentionally helps another person commit a felony by giving advice before the crime or helping to conceal evidence or the perpetrator after it has been committed. An accessory is usually not physically present during the crime.

Accomplice   Someone who helps another person commit a crime. Unlike an accessory, an accomplice is usually present when the crime is committed. An accomplice is guilty of the same offense and usually receives the same sentence as the principal.

Acquittal   A decision by a judge or jury that the defendant in a criminal case is not guilty of a crime. An acquittal is not a finding of innocence; it is simply a conclusion that the prosecution has not proved its case beyond a reasonable doubt.

Actus reus   Latin: "a guilty act." The *actus reus* is the act which, in combination with a mental state such as intent or recklessness, constitutes a crime.

Adjudication   The process of rendering a judicial decision as to whether the facts alleged in a petition or other pleading are true. An adjudicatory hearing is that court proceeding in which it is determined whether the allegations of a petition are supported by legally admissible evidence; also called an evidentiary hearing.

Ad litem   See **guardian ad litem.**

Admission   (1) An out-of-court statement offered into evidence as an exception to the hearsay rule.

(2) One side's statement that certain facts are true in response to a request from the other side during discovery.

Allegation   A statement by a party in a pleading describing what that party's position is and what that party intends to prove.

Appeal   A written request to a higher court to modify or reverse the judgment of a trial court or intermediate-level appellate court. Normally, an appellate court accepts as true all the facts that the trial judge or jury found to be true, and decides only whether the judge made mistakes in understanding and applying the law. If the appellate court decides that a mistake was made that changed the outcome, it will direct the lower court to conduct a new trial, but often the mistakes are deemed "harmless" and the judgment is left alone. Some mistakes are corrected by the appellate court—such as a miscalculation of monetary damages—without sending the case back to the trial court. An appeal begins when the loser at trial—or in an intermediate-level appellate court—files a notice of appeal, which must be done within strict time limits (often 30 days from the date of judgment).

Appellant   A party to a lawsuit who appeals a losing decision to a higher court in an effort to have it modified or reversed.

Appellee   A party to a lawsuit who wins in trial court—or sometimes on a first appeal—only to have the other party (the appellant) file for an appeal. An appellee files a written brief and often makes an oral argument before the appellate court, asking that the lower court's judgment be upheld. In some courts, an appellee is called a respondent.

Arraignment   The court appearance in which a defendant enters a plea.

Assault   When a person is put in fear of harm. Actual physical contact is not necessary; threatening gestures that would alarm any reasonable person can constitute an assault.

Bail   Money paid to the court, usually at arraignment or shortly thereafter, to ensure that an arrested person who is released from jail will appear at all required court appearances. The amount of bail is determined by the local bail schedule, which is based on the seriousness of the offense. The judge can increase the bail if the prosecutor convinces him or her that the defendant is likely to flee (for example, if the defendant has failed to show up in court in the past), or he or she can decrease it if the defense attorney shows that the defendant is unlikely to run (for example, the defendant has strong ties to the community by way of a steady job and a family).

Battery   A crime consisting of physical contact that is intended to harm. Unintentional harmful contact is not battery, no matter how careless the behavior or how severe the injury.

Burden of proof   The requirement of convincing the jury or judge that one's version of the facts is true. In a civil trial, it means that the plaintiff must convince the judge or jury "by a preponderance of the evidence" that the plaintiff's version is true—that is, more than 50 percent of the believable evidence is in the plaintiff's favor. In a criminal case, because a person's liberty is at stake, the government has a harder job, and must convince the judge or jury that the defendant is guilty beyond a reasonable doubt.

Burglary   The crime of breaking into and entering a building with the intention to commit a felony. The breaking and entering need not be by force, and the felony need not be theft.

Certification   The process of transferring a minor's case from juvenile court to adult court for trial.

Certiorari   A writ issued by an appellate court accepting a lower court's decision for review.

Circuit court   The name of the principal trial court in many states. In the federal system, appellate courts are organized into 13 circuits.

Class action   A lawsuit in which a large number of people with similar legal claims join together in a group (the "class") to sue an entity, usually a company or organization.

Competency   In the law of evidence, a witness's ability to observe, recall, and recount events under oath.

Complaint   Papers filed with the court clerk by a plaintiff to initiate a lawsuit by setting out facts and legal claims, usually called causes of action. In some states and in some types of legal actions, such as divorce, complaints are called petitions and the person filing is called the petitioner.

Continuance   The postponement of a hearing, trial, or other scheduled court proceeding, at the request of one or both parties, or by the judge without consulting them.

Corpus delicti   Latin: "the body of the crime." Used to describe physical evidence, such as the corpse of a murder victim or the charred frame of a torched building.

Cross-examination   At trial, the opportunity to question any witness who testifies on direct examination, including one's opponent.

Custody   The legal authority to make decisions affecting a child's interests (legal custody) and the responsibility of taking care of the child (physical custody).

Defendant   The person against whom a lawsuit is filed. In certain states, and in certain types of lawsuits, the defendant is called the respondent.

Delinquency   The commission of an illegal act by a juvenile. Increasingly used to refer to those acts which would be crimes if committed by an adult, but state laws vary in their definitions.

De novo Latin: "from the beginning."

Detention The temporary confinement of a minor by a public officer pursuant to law.

Detention hearing A judicial hearing, usually held after the filing of a petition, to determine the interim custody of a minor pending an adjudication of a petition.

Direct file When the prosecutor begins a case against a juvenile in adult criminal court.

Disposition The order of a juvenile court determining what is to be done with a minor already adjudged to be within the court's jurisdiction. Analogous to the sentencing in a criminal case.

District court In federal court and in some states, the name of the main trial court. A suit filed in federal court will normally be heard in federal district court. States may also group their appellate courts into districts.

Diversion Procedures for handling relatively minor juvenile problems informally, without referral to the juvenile court.

Evidence The many types of information presented to a judge or jury designed to convince them of the truth or falsity of key facts. Evidence typically includes testimony of witnesses, documents, photographs, items of damaged property, government records, videos, and laboratory reports. Rules that are as strict as they are quirky and technical govern what types of evidence can be properly admitted as part of a trial.

Family court A separate court, or more likely a separate division of the regular state trial court, that considers only cases involving divorce (dissolution of marriage), child custody and support, guardianship, adoption, and other cases having to do with family-related issues, including the issuance of restraining orders in domestic violence cases.

Felony A serious crime (contrasted with misdemeanors and infractions, which are less serious crimes), usually punishable by a prison term of more than one year or, in some cases, by death.

Fruit of the poisonous tree Evidence obtained by police as a result of violating the Fourth Amendment.

Guardian ad litem (GAL) A person, not necessarily a lawyer, who is appointed by a court to represent and protect the interests of a child or an incapacitated adult during a lawsuit. For example, a guardian ad litem may be appointed to represent the interests of a child whose parents are locked in a contentious battle for custody, or to protect a child's interests in a lawsuit where there are allegations of child abuse. The GAL may conduct interviews and investigations, make reports to the court, and participate in court hearings or mediation sessions. Sometimes called court-appointed special advocates (CASAs).

Habeas corpus Latin: "you have the body." A prisoner files a petition for writ of habeas corpus in order to challenge the authority of the prison or jail warden to hold him or her. If the judge orders a hearing after reading the writ, the prisoner can argue that his or her confinement is illegal. These writs are frequently filed by convicted prisoners who challenge their convictions on the grounds that trial attorneys failed to prepare the defense and were incompetent. Prisoners sentenced to death may also file habeas petitions challenging the constitutionality of the state death penalty law. Habeas writs are different from and do not replace appeals, which are arguments for reversal of a conviction based on claims that the judge conducted the trial improperly. Often, convicted prisoners file both.

Hearing In the trial court context, a legal proceeding (other than a full-scale trial) held before a judge. During a hearing, evidence and arguments are presented in an effort to resolve a disputed factual or legal issue. Hearings typically, but by no means always, occur prior to trial when a party asks the judge to decide a specific issue—often on an interim basis—such as whether a temporary restraining order or preliminary injunction should be issued, or temporary child custody or child support awarded. In the administrative or agency law context, a hearing is usually a proceeding before an administrative hearing officer or judge representing an agency that has the power to regulate a particular field or oversee a governmental benefit program.

Information   A filing by a prosecutor; substitutes for an indictment.

Injunction   A flexible, discretionary process of preventive and remedial justice, exercised by courts that have equity powers. Typically, an injunction is issued to restrain a person from committing a specific act.

In loco parentis   Latin: "in the place of the parent." Refers to actions of a custodian, guardian, or other person acting in the parent's place and stead.

In re   Latin: "in the case of." Used in some juvenile matters.

Interlocutory   Incident to a suit still pending. An order or decree made during the progress of a case which does not amount to a final decision is interlocutory.

Jurisdiction   The authority of a court to hear and decide a case. To make a legally valid decision in a case, a court must have both "subject-matter jurisdiction" (power to hear the type of case in question, which is granted by the state legislatures and Congress) and "personal jurisdiction" (power to make a decision affecting the parties involved in the lawsuit, which a court gets as a result of the parties' actions).

Mens rea   Latin: "guilty mind." The mental component of criminal liability. To be guilty of most crimes, a defendant must have committed the criminal act (the *actus reus*) in a certain mental state (the mens rea).

Miranda warnings   Warnings that the police must give to a suspect before conducting an interrogation in order for the suspect's answers to be used as evidence at trial. The Miranda warnings require that the suspect be told that he or she has the right to remain silent, the right to have an attorney present when being questioned, and the right to a court-appointed attorney if a private attorney is unaffordable, and that any statements made by the suspect can be used against him or her in court. Giving the Miranda warning is also known as "reading a suspect his [or her] rights."

Misdemeanor   A crime, less serious than a felony, punishable by no more than one year in jail.

Motion   During a lawsuit, a request to the judge for a decision—called an order or ruling—to resolve procedural or other issues that come up during litigation.

Nolo contendere   Latin: "I will not contest it." A plea of no contest that admits guilt in a criminal case, limited by the condition that the finding cannot be used against the defendant in any subsequent civil cases.

Order to show cause   An order from a judge that directs a party to come to court and convince the judge why he or she shouldn't grant an action proposed by the other side or by the judge on his or her own (*sua sponte*).

Ordinance   A law adopted by a town or city council, county board of supervisors, or other municipal governing board. Typically, local governments issue ordinances establishing zoning and parking rules and regulating noise, garbage removal, and the operation of parks and other areas that affect people who live or do business within a locality's borders.

Parens patriae   Latin   "the father of his country." From English law, the legal doctrine under which the crown assumed the protection of certain minors, orphans, and other persons in need of protection. Though not wholly accurate, the phrase is sometimes used to express the benevolent, rehabilitative philosophy of the juvenile court.

Petition   A formal written request made to a court asking for an order or ruling on a particular matter.

Petitioner   A person who initiates a lawsuit; a synonym for plaintiff, used almost universally in some states and in others specifically for certain types of lawsuits, most commonly divorce and other family law cases.

PINS   Person in need of supervision; a juvenile status offender who is involved in noncriminal misbehavior.

Plaintiff   A person, corporation, or other legal entity that initiates a lawsuit. In certain states and for some types of lawsuits, the term petitioner is used instead of plaintiff.

Plea The defendant's formal answer to criminal charges. Typically defendants enter one of the following pleas guilty, not guilty, or nolo contendere. A plea is usually entered when charges are formally brought (at arraignment).

Plea bargain A negotiation between the defense and prosecution (and sometimes the judge) that settles a criminal case. The defendant typically pleads guilty to a lesser crime (or fewer charges) than originally charged in exchange for a guaranteed sentence that is shorter than what the defendant might face if convicted at trial. The prosecution is certain of a conviction and a known sentence; the defendant avoids the risk of a higher sentence; and the judge can move on to other cases.

Respondent A term used instead of defendant or appellee in some states—especially for divorce and other family law cases—to identify the party who is sued and must respond to the petitioner's complaint.

Social report A report prepared by a probation officer or social caseworker for the judge's consideration at a dispositional hearing. Such reports review a minor's behavior and family history and often contain information that would be inadmissible in most judicial proceedings.

Status offense Noncriminal misbehavior that would not be criminal if committed by an adult, but is when committed by a juvenile.

Statute A written law passed by Congress or a state legislature and signed into law by the president or a state governor. (In fairly rare circumstances, a legislative act can become law without the approval of the head of the executive branch of government.) Statutes are often gathered into compilations called "codes," large sets of books that can be found in many public and all law libraries, or sometimes on the Internet.

Subpoena (subpena) A subpoena is a court order issued at the request of a party requiring a witness to appear in court.

Summons A paper prepared by the plaintiff and issued by a court that informs the defendant that he or she has been sued. The summons requires that the defendant file a response with the court—or in many small claims courts, simply appear in person on an appointed day—within a given time period or risk losing the case under the terms of a default judgment.

Superior court The main county trial court in many states, mostly in the West.

Supreme Court America's highest court, which has the final power to decide cases involving the interpretation of the US Constitution, certain legal areas set forth in the Constitution (called "federal questions"), and federal laws. It also makes final decisions in certain lawsuits between parties in different states. The US Supreme Court has nine justices—one of whom is Chief Justice—who are appointed for life by the president and must be confirmed by the US Senate. Most states also have a supreme court, which is the final arbiter of the state's constitution and state laws. However, in several states the highest state court uses a different name, most notably New York and Maryland, where it is called the Court of Appeals, and Massachusetts, where it it is called the Supreme Judicial Court.

Title 42 U.S.C., Section 1983 A tort action or civil suit provided for in the United States Code. Commonly referred to as "1983 actions," these suits are typically brought by citizens against police officers or other government authorities acting under "the color of authority" who violate a person's civil rights.

Transfer The sending of a case from juvenile court to adult court for trial.

Venue The proper court to hear a case, often based on the convenience of the defendant. Because state courts have jurisdiction to hear cases from a wide geographical area, additional rules, called rules of venue, have been developed to ensure that the defendant is not needlessly inconvenienced. Practically, venue rules mean that a defendant can't usually be sued far from where he or she lives or does business, unless key events happened at that location. Venue for a criminal case is normally the judicial district where the crime was committed.

Waiver (1) The understanding and voluntary relinquishment of a known right, such as the right to counsel or the right to remain silent during police interrogation. (2) The juvenile court's relinquishment of its jurisdiction over a minor, allowing transfer of the case to adult court for trial.

Ward   A minor who is under the jurisdiction of the juvenile court for a delinquent act, status offense, or an allegation or finding of abuse, neglect, or dependency.

Writ of certiorari   An order of a superior court requesting that that the record of an inferior court be brought forward for review or inspection. This is a typical avenue for cases to travel to the United States Supreme Court.

Writ of habeas corpus   Habeas corpus, sometimes referred to as "the Great Writ," is a legal device used to request that a judicial body review the reasons for a person's capture and confinement, or the conditions of his or her confinement.

INDEX